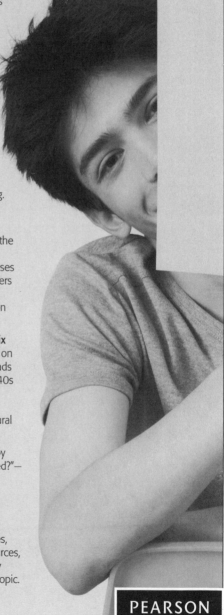

Why Do You Need This New Edition?

If you're wondering why you should buy this fourth edition of *Writing and Reading Across the Curriculum: Brief Edition,* here are 6 good reasons!

❶ **More than 20 new readings** span the disciplines and help stimulate your writing by offering new, engaging perspectives on all themes found in **Part II: An Anthology of Readings**.

❷ **A new Chapter 5, "The Changing Landscape of Work in the Twenty-first Century"** challenges you to rethink the dynamic role of work in contemporary society and examines how the workplace of today is distinctly different from that of our parents' and grandparents' generations. Drawing on such disciplines as economics, management consulting, sociology, labor statistics, history, and education, the chapter provides a wide variety of perspectives to stimulate your thinking and writing.

❸ **"Green Power" moves to the forefront in an all-new Chapter 6.** Cutting-edge coverage offers numerous opportunities to think and write about the hot topics of climate crisis and renewable energy. Scientific research, reportage, and individual analyses presented by scientists, environmentalists, members of government, and journalists at the heart of the debate will help you develop your own position on global warming and energy independence.

❹ **An updated Chapter 9, "New and Improved: Six Decades of Advertising,"** features a new section on TV commercials, in addition to 22 full-page print ads from popular American magazines of the mid-1940s through today. This wealth of carefully selected advertisements and commercials will prompt you to analyze and comment upon our changing cultural and consumerist values.

❺ **Chapter 1, "Summary,"** presents a **new article** by economist Alan Blinder—"Will Your Job Be Exported?"— as the basis for a **fresh example summary.**

❻ **Chapter 3, "Synthesis,"** features a **new model synthesis focusing on the debate over student privacy rights and campus safety** in the wake of the 2007 Virginia Tech shooting. Employing articles, editorials, investigative reports, and the law as sources, the argument synthesis demonstrates how to fully support a well-developed position on a complex topic.

PEARSON

Writing and Reading Across the Curriculum

BRIEF EDITION

FOURTH EDITION

Laurence Behrens
University of California Santa Barbara

Leonard J. Rosen
Bentley University

Longman
Boston   Columbus   Indianapolis   New York   San Francisco
Upper Saddle River   Amsterdam   Cape Town   Dubai   London   Madrid
Milan   Munich   Paris   Montréal   Toronto   Delhi   Mexico City   São Paulo
Sydney   Hong Kong   Seoul   Singapore   Taipei   Tokyo

Executive Editor: Suzanne Phelps Chambers
Director of Development: Mary Ellen Curley
Associate Development Editor: Erin Reilly
Senior Marketing Manager: Sandra McGuire
Senior Supplements Editor: Donna Campion
Production Manager: Savoula Amanatidis
Project Coordination, Interior Design, and Electronic
    Page Makeup: Integra Software Services, Inc.
Cover Design Manager: Wendy Ann Fredericks
Photo Researcher: Rona Tuccillo
Senior Manufacturing Buyer: Roy L. Pickering, Jr.
Printer and Binder: R. R. Donnelley and Sons Company–Crawfordsville
Cover Printer: R. R. Donnelley and Sons Company–Crawfordsville

For permission to use copyrighted material, grateful acknowledgment is made to the copyright holders on pp. 425–427, which are hereby made part of this copyright page.

Library of Congress Cataloging-in-Publication Data

Behrens, Laurence.
Writing and reading across the curriculum, brief edition / Laurence Behrens,
    Leonard J. Rosen.—Brief ed.
    p. cm.
Includes index.
ISBN 978-0-205-00069-2
1. College readers.   2. Interdisciplinary approach in education—Problems, exercises, etc.
3. English language—Rhetoric—Problems, exercises, etc.   4. Academic writing—
Problems, exercises, etc.   I. Rosen, Leonard J.   II. Title.
PE1417.B3965 2010
808'.0427—dc22

                                                                    2010034968

1 2 3 4 5 6 7 8 9 10—DOC—14 13 12 11

Longman
is an imprint of

www.pearsonhighered.com

ISBN-13: 978-0-205-00069-2
ISBN-10:   0-205-00069-X

To: Keiko and Charlotte

Detailed Contents

Part II

An Anthology of Readings   131

ECONOMICS
Chapter 5 The Changing Landscape of Work
in the Twenty-first Century   133

ENVIRONMENT/PUBLIC POLICY
Chapter 6 Green Power   185

SOCIOLOGY
Chapter 7 Marriage and Family in America   249

BIOLOGY

Chapter 8 To Sleep   310

Preface

Writing and Reading Across the Curriculum: Brief Edition was created for those who find the standard edition appealing and useful but who also find its length impractical. The present text offers five of the most popular anthology chapters, somewhat abridged, from the longer edition. The rhetoric section preceding the anthology of readings has been abbreviated to cover those writing types for which Writing and Reading Across the Curriculum (WRAC) is best known: the summary, the critique, the synthesis, and the analysis. The Brief Edition does not include the longer text's chapters on introductions, conclusions, and theses. Many instructors, however, already supplement their course reader with a handbook that provides ample coverage of these topics, as well as coverage of research and documentation.

STRUCTURE

Like the longer text, Writing and Reading Across the Curriculum: Brief Edition is divided into two parts. The first part introduces the strategies of summary, critique, synthesis, and analysis. We take students step by step through the process of writing papers based on source material, explaining and demonstrating how summaries, critiques, syntheses, and analyses can be generated from the kinds of readings students will encounter later in the book—and throughout their academic careers. The second part of the text consists of a series of five subject chapters drawn from both academic and professional disciplines. Each subject is not only interesting in its own right, but is also representative of the kinds of topics typically studied during the course of an undergraduate education. We also believe that students and teachers will discover connections among the thematic chapters of this edition that further enhance opportunities for writing, discussion, and inquiry.

CONTINUED FOCUS ON ARGUMENTATION

Part I of Writing and Reading Across the Curriculum: Brief Edition is designed to prepare students for college-level assignments across the disciplines. The fourth edition continues the previous edition's strengthened emphasis on the writing process and on argument, in particular. In treating argument, we emphasize the following:

- **The Elements of Argument: Claim, Support, Assumption.** This section adapts the Toulmin approach to argument to the kinds of readings that students will encounter in Part II of the text.

- **Developing and Organizing the Support for Your Arguments.** This section helps students to mine source materials for facts, expert opinions, and examples that will support their arguments.
- **Annotated Student Argument Paper.** A sample student paper highlights and discusses argumentative strategies that a student writer uses in drafting and developing a paper.

PART I: NEW APPARATUS, TOPICS, READINGS, AND STUDENT PAPERS

Chapter 1: Summary

Students are taken through the process of writing a summary of economist Alan S. Blinder's "Will Your Job Be Exported?" (a selection new to this edition). We demonstrate how to annotate a source and divide it into sections, how to develop a thesis, and how to write and smoothly join section summaries.

Chapter 3: Synthesis

Chapter 3 provides a new argument synthesis focusing on the debate over student privacy rights and campus safety that was generated by the Virginia Tech shootings in April 2007. The synthesis builds on several articles and editorials on the subject, the report of the panel that investigated the shootings, and the applicable federal laws on student privacy.

Chapter 4: Analysis

The chapter now includes a new section, "When *Your* Perspective Guides the Analysis," highlighting an alternative, more personal approach to analysis than the type that is based on the use of formal principles and definitions and that continues to underlie the greater part of this chapter.

PART II: NEW THEMATIC CHAPTERS

As in earlier editions, Part II of *Writing and Reading Across the Curriculum* provides students with opportunities to practice the skills of summary, synthesis, critique, and analysis that they have learned in Part I. We have prepared two new chapters for the fourth edition of *WRAC* Brief.

Chapter 5: The Changing Landscape of Work in the Twenty–first Century

"The Changing Landscape of Work in the Twenty-first Century," new to this edition, offers students a wealth of information and informed opinion on how the workplace they are about to enter already differs markedly from the workplaces their parents and grandparents have known. Emphasizing the promise and perils of the new economy, the chapter draws from a number of disciplines: economics, management consulting, sociology, labor studies, history, and education. Among the numerous questions posed by the readings: How has the nature of work changed? What role has technology played in its change? Which jobs of the future look to be secure and insecure? Are careers (as the term was once understood) still possible in an economy in which workers can expect to change jobs, and skill sets, multiple times?

We open with definitions of *work* and related terms. Subsequent readings divide into two broad sections: The first distinguishes work of the present and future from work of the past; the second explores expected changes in specific professions. To supplement the coverage of particular professions in this chapter, we point students to an extraordinarily rich Web site maintained by the Bureau of Labor Statistics, a site that provides information on virtually every job category. Ultimately, the chapter invites students to explore through writing the ways in which their choices now can position them strategically for the workplace they will soon enter.

Chapter 6: Green Power

A growing body of evidence points to a global climate crisis caused by massive levels of carbon dioxide and other greenhouse gases continuously spewed into the atmosphere by the burning of coal and oil. Reducing our dependence on these fossil fuels involves developing renewable sources of clean energy that can power our cars, our homes, our businesses, and our public buildings. In this new chapter, students will consider the views of scientists, environmentalists, members of a government task force, and reporters about the nature of the problem and about ways of addressing it.

In the first section of the chapter, students will discover how scientists measure climate change; they will review the enormous challenge of significantly reducing our carbon footprint; and they will consider how government and business can work together to reduce the nation's dependence on oil. In the second part of the chapter, the focus shifts to some of the most promising—though often controversial—sources of renewable energy: nuclear, solar, and wind. An article considers whether electric cars are likely to replace gasoline-powered vehicles in the near future. All told, the selections in this chapter will provide students with an occasion to write and an opportunity to contribute to the public debate about climate change and renewable energy. Students will increase their understanding of the energy-related problems we face and also expand their awareness of available options for moving into an era of green power.

PART II: REVISED THEMATIC CHAPTERS

Three anthology chapters are carried over from the third edition; many of the reading selections for each, however, are new to this edition.

Chapter 7: Marriage and Family in America

Definitions of marriage and family, husband and wife, mother and father are changing before our eyes. A once-stable (or so we thought) institution seems under attack—an unusually fertile context in which to offer a chapter on "Marriage and Family in America." The chapter opens with a historical perspective by Stephanie Coontz. Other selections, such as those by Terry Martin Hekker, Hope Edelman, and Eric Bartels, offer personal, often charged accounts of marriage from the inside. Students will follow the debate over gay marriage; they will also examine the ongoing controversies concerning working mothers versus stay-at-home mothers (often referred to as "the Mommy Wars") and the so-called "stalled revolution"—the feminist complaint that, in an age of working women, men have not shouldered their share of household work. We've selected readings that will challenge student assumptions and produce writing informed not only by the provocative and sometimes emotionally raw views of chapter authors but also by their own personal experiences. For each of our students has direct experience with marriage and family—some positive, some not—and each, we believe, can bring the authority of that experience to bear in mature, college-level writing.

Chapter 8: To Sleep

Sleep is the most common and, until recently, one of the least understood of human behaviors. Annually, tens of millions of dollars fund basic research on sleep, but experts do not yet know precisely *why* we sleep. This chapter gathers the work of biologists, neurologists, psychologists, and journalists who specialize in science writing to investigate an activity that accounts for one-third of every person's life. Students will read an overview of sleep and an introduction to the physiology of sleep before moving on to the principal focus of the chapter: the sleep of adolescents—particularly of college-age adolescents. Various researchers report on the state of adolescent sleep (generally insufficient) and the causes and consequences of, and potential solutions to, adolescent sleep debt. Quite aside from providing an insight into the science of sleep, this chapter serves a practical function: to educate college students on the mechanics and dangers of sleep debt. Even for those not intending a career in the sciences, learning what happens cognitively and physically when we deprive ourselves of sleep should make for fascinating reading—and create ample opportunities to practice college-level writing.

Chapter 9: New and Improved: Six Decades of Advertising

The centerpiece of this chapter is a set of two portfolios of memorable advertising: 22 full-page print ads and 18 TV commercials. The print ads, which have appeared in popular American magazines since the mid-1940s, promote cigarettes, liquor and beer, automobiles, food, and beauty and cleaning products. This edition also features a new section on TV commercials, referring students to historical and current gems of the genre viewable on YouTube. Like genetic markers, print advertisements and TV commercials are key indicators of our consumerism, our changing cultural values, and our less variable human psychology. Students will find this material both entertaining and well-suited for practicing and honing their analysis skills.

RESOURCES FOR TEACHERS AND STUDENTS

- The *Instructor's Manual* for the fourth edition of *Writing and Reading Across the Curriculum: Brief Edition* (ISBN: **0-205-02779-2**) provides sample syllabi and course calendars, chapter summaries, classroom ideas for writing assignments, introductions to each set of readings, and answers to review questions. Materials for each subject chapter in the anthology include a listing of videolinks—materials students can access online (usually through YouTube) that complement the chapter readings. Included as well are tips on how to incorporate MyCompLab into the course material.

- PEARSON
  mycomplab The Web site *MyCompLab* integrates the market-leading instruction, multimedia tutorials, and exercises for writing, grammar, and research that users have come to identify with the program, along with a new online composing space and new assessment tools. The result is a revolutionary application that offers a seamless and flexible teaching and learning environment built specifically for writers. Created by faculty and students across the country, the new MyCompLab provides help for writers in the context of their writing, with instructor and peer commenting functionality, proven tutorials and exercises for writing, grammar and research, an e-portfolio, an assignment-builder, a bibliography tool, tutoring services, and a gradebook and course management organization created specifically for writing classes. Visit www.mycomplab.com for information.

ACKNOWLEDGMENTS

We have benefited over the years from the suggestions and insights of many teachers—and students—across the country. We would especially like to thank these reviewers of the fourth edition: Angela Adams, Loyola University Chicago; Fabián Álvarez, Western Kentucky University; Laurel Bollinger, University of Alabama in Huntsville; David Elias, Eastern Kentucky University; Wanda Fries, Somerset Community College; Kerrie

Kawasaki-Hull, Ohlone College; Kathy Mendt, Front Range Community College, Larimer Campus; RoseAnn Morgan, Middlesex County College; Alison Reynolds, University of Florida; Deborah L. Ruth, Owensboro Community & Technical College; and Mary R. Seel, Broome Community College.

We would also like to thank the following reviewers for their help in the preparation of past editions: James Allen, College of DuPage; Chris Anson, North Carolina State University; Phillip Arrington, Eastern Michigan University; Anne Bailey, Southeastern Louisiana University; Carolyn Baker, San Antonio College; Bob Brannan, Johnson County Community College; Joy Bashore, Central Virginia Community College; Nancy Blattner, Southeast Missouri State University; Mary Bly, University of California, Davis; Paul Buczkowski, Eastern Michigan University; Jennifer Bullis, Whatcom Community College; Paige Byam, Northern Kentucky University; Susan Callendar, Sinclair Community College; Anne Carr, Southeast Community College; Jeff Carroll, University of Hawaii; Joseph Rocky Colavito, Northwestern State University; Michael Colonneses, Methodist College; James A. Cornette, Christopher Newport University; Timothy Corrigan, Temple University; Kathryn J. Dawson, Ball State University; Cathy Powers Dice, University of Memphis; Kathleen Dooley, Tidewater Community College; Judith Eastman, Orange Coast College; David Elias, Eastern Kentucky University; Susan Boyd English, Kirkwood Community College; Kathy Evertz, University of Wyoming; Kathy Ford, Lake Land College; University of Wyoming; Bill Gholson, Southern Oregon University; Karen Gordon, Elgin Community College; Deborah Gutschera, College of DuPage; Lila M. Harper, Central Washington University; M. Todd Harper, University of Louisville; Kip Harvigsen, Ricks College; Michael Hogan, Southeast Missouri State University; Sandra M. Jensen, Lane Community College; Anita Johnson, Whatcom Community College; Mark Jones, University of Florida; Daven M. Kari, Vanguard University; Jane Kaufman, University of Akron; Rodney Keller, Ricks College; Walt Klarner, Johnson County Community College; Jeffery Klausman, Whatcom Community College; Alison Kuehner, Ohlone College; William B. Lalicker, West Chester University; Dawn Leonard, Charleston Southern University; Lindsay Lewan, Arapahoe Community College; Clifford L. Lewis, University of Massachusetts Lowell; Signee Lynch, Whatcom Community College; Jolie Martin; San Francisco State University; Krista L. May, Texas A&M University; Stella Nesanovich, McNeese State University; Kathy Mendt, Front Range Community College–Larimer Campus; RoseAnn Morgan, Middlesex County College; David Moton, Bakersfield College; Roark Mulligan, Christopher Newport University; Joan Mullin, University of Toledo; Susie Paul, Auburn University at Montgomery; Thomas Pfau, Bellevue Community College; Aaron Race, Southern Illinois University–Carbondale; Nancy Redmond, Long Beach City College; Deborah Reese, University of Texas at Arlington; Priscilla Riggle, Bowling Green State University; Jeanette Riley, University of New Mexico; Robert Rongner, Whatcom Community College; Sarah C. Ross,

Southeastern Louisiana University; Amy Rybak, Bowling Green State University; Raul Sanchez, University of Utah; Rebecca Shapiro, Westminster College; Mary Sheldon, Washburn University; Horacio Sierra, University of Florida; Philip Sipiora, University of Southern Florida; Joyce Smoot, Virginia Tech; Bonnie A. Spears, Chaffey College; Bonnie Startt, Tidewater Community College; R. E. Stratton, University of Alaska–Fairbanks; Katherine M. Thomas, Southeast Community College; Victor Villanueva, Washington State University; Deron Walker, California Baptist University; Jackie Wheeler, Arizona State University; Pat Stephens Williams, Southern Illinois University at Carbondale; and Kristin Woolever, Northeastern University.

We gratefully acknowledge the work of Michael Behrens, who made significant contributions to the "Synthesis" and the "Marriage and Family in America" chapters.

A special thanks to Suzanne Phelps Chambers, Erin Reilly, Karyn Morrison, and Martha Beyerlein for helping shepherd the manuscript through the editorial and production process. And our continued gratitude to Joe Opiela, longtime friend, supporter, and publisher.

LAURENCE BEHRENS
LEONARD J. ROSEN

Your sociology professor asks you to write a paper on attitudes toward the homeless population of an urban area near your campus. You are expected to consult books, articles, Web sites, and other online sources on the subject, and you are also encouraged to conduct surveys and interviews.

Your professor is making a number of assumptions about your capabilities. Among them:

- that you can research and assess the value of relevant sources;
- that you can comprehend college-level material, both print and electronic;
- that you can use theories and principles learned from one set of sources as tools to investigate other sources (or events, people, places, or things);
- that you can synthesize separate but related sources;
- that you can intelligently respond to such material.

In fact, these same assumptions underlie practically all college writing assignments. Your professors will expect you to demonstrate that you can read and understand not only textbooks but also critical articles and books, primary sources, Internet sources, online academic databases, CD-ROMs, and other material related to a particular subject of study. For example: For a paper on the progress of the Human Genome Project, you would probably look to articles and Internet sources for the most recent information. Using an online database, you would find articles on the subject in such print journals as *Nature, Journal of the American Medical Association,* and *Bioscience,* as well as leading newspapers and magazines. A Web search engine might lead you to a useful site called "A New Gene Map of the Human Genome" (http://www.ncbi.nlm.nih.gov/genemap99/) and the site of the "Human Genome Sequencing Department" at the Lawrence Berkeley National Laboratory (http://www-hgc.lbl.gov/). You would be expected to assess the relevance of such sources to your topic and to draw from them the information and ideas you need. It's even possible that the final product of your research and reading may not be a conventional paper at all, but rather a Web site you create that explains the science behind the Human Genome Project, explores a particular controversy about the project, or describes the future benefits geneticists hope to derive from the project.

You might, for a different class, be assigned a research paper on the films of director Martin Scorsese. To get started, you might consult your film studies textbook, biographical sources on Scorsese, and anthologies of criticism. Instructor and peer feedback on a first draft might lead you to articles in both popular magazines (such as *Time*) and scholarly journals (such as *Literature/Film Quarterly*), a CD-ROM database (such as *Film Index International*), and relevant Web sites (such as the "Internet Movie Database," http://us.imdb.com).

These two example assignments are very different, of course, but the skills you need to work with them are the same. You must be able to research relevant sources. You must be able to read and comprehend these sources. You must be able to perceive the relationships among several pieces of source material. And you must be able to apply your own critical judgments to these various materials.

Writing and Reading Across the Curriculum: Brief Edition provides you with the opportunity to practice the essential college-level skills we have just outlined and the forms of writing associated with them, namely:

- the *summary*
- the *critique*
- the *synthesis*
- the *analysis*

Each chapter of Part II of this text represents a subject from a particular area of the academic curriculum: sociology, economics, biology, public policy, business, and advertising. These chapters, dealing with such topics as "Marriage and Family in America" and "Green Power," illustrate the types of material you will study in your other courses.

Questions following the readings will allow you to practice typical college writing assignments. Review Questions help you recall key points of content. Discussion and Writing Suggestions ask you for personal, sometimes imaginative, responses to the readings. Synthesis Activities allow you to practice assignments of the type that are covered in detail in Part I of this book. For instance, you may be asked to *summarize* the problems created by carbon-based energy sources like oil or coal or compare and contrast the practicality of non-carbon-based energy alternatives, such as nuclear and solar power. Finally, Research Activities ask you to go beyond the readings in this text in order to conduct your own independent research on these subjects.

In this book, you'll find articles and essays written by physicians, sociologists, psychologists, lawyers, political scientists, journalists, and specialists from other fields. Our aim is that you become familiar with the various subjects and styles of academic writing and that you come to appreciate the interrelatedness of knowledge. Human activity and human behavior are classified into separate subjects only for convenience. The novel you read in your literature course may be able to shed some light on an assigned article for your economics course—and vice versa.

We hope, therefore, that your writing course will serve as a kind of bridge to your other courses and that as a result of this work you will become more skillful at perceiving relationships among diverse topics. Because it involves such critical and widely applicable skills, your writing course may well turn out to be one of the most valuable—and one of the most interesting—of your academic career.

LAURENCE BEHRENS
LEONARD J. ROSEN

Part I

How to Write Summaries, Critiques, Syntheses, and Analyses

Chapter 1

Summary

WHAT IS A SUMMARY?

The best way to demonstrate that you understand the information and the ideas in any piece of writing is to compose an accurate and clearly written summary of that piece. By a *summary* we mean a *brief restatement, in your own words, of the content of a passage* (a group of paragraphs, a chapter, an article, a book). This restatement should focus on the *central idea* of the passage. The briefest of summaries (one or two sentences) will do no more than this. A longer, more complete summary will indicate, in condensed form, the main points in the passage that support or explain the central idea. It will reflect the order in which these points are presented and the emphasis given to them. It may even include some important examples from the passage. But it will not include minor details. It will not repeat points simply for the purpose of emphasis. And it will not contain any of your own opinions or conclusions. A good summary, therefore, has three central qualities: *brevity, completeness,* and *objectivity.*

CAN A SUMMARY BE OBJECTIVE?

Objectivity could be difficult to achieve in a summary. By definition, writing a summary requires you to select some aspects of the original and leave out others. Because deciding what to select and what to leave out calls for your personal judgment, your summary really is a work of interpretation. And, certainly, your interpretation of a passage may differ from another person's.

One factor affecting the nature and quality of your interpretation is your *prior knowledge* of the subject. For example, if you're attempting to summarize an anthropological article and you're a novice in that field, then your summary of the article will likely differ from that of your professor, who has spent twenty years studying this particular area and whose judgment about what is more or less significant is undoubtedly more reliable than your own. By the same token, your personal or professional *frame of reference* may also affect your interpretation. A union representative and a management representative attempting to summarize the latest management offer would probably come up with two very different accounts. Still, we believe that in most cases it's possible to produce a reasonably objective summary of a passage if you make a conscious, good-faith effort to be unbiased and to prevent your own feelings on the subject from coloring your account of the author's text.

USING THE SUMMARY

In some quarters, the summary has a bad reputation—and with reason. Summaries are often provided by writers as substitutes for analyses. As students, many of us have summarized books that we were supposed to *review critically*. All the same, the summary does have a place in respectable college work. First, writing a summary is an excellent way to understand

WHERE DO WE FIND WRITTEN SUMMARIES?

Here are just a few of the types of writing that involve summary:

Academic Writing

- **Critique papers** summarize material in order to critique it.
- **Synthesis papers** summarize to show relationships between sources.
- **Analysis papers** summarize theoretical perspectives before applying them.
- **Research papers** require summary for note-taking and reporting research.
- **Literature reviews** are overviews of work presented in brief summaries.
- **Argument papers** summarize evidence and opposing arguments.
- **Essay exams** demonstrate understanding of course materials through summary.

Workplace Writing

- **Policy briefs** condense complex public policy.
- **Business plans** summarize costs, relevant environmental impacts, and other important matters.
- **Memos, letters, and reports** summarize procedures, meetings, product assessments, expenditures, and more.
- **Medical charts** record patient data in summarized form.
- **Legal briefs** summarize relevant facts and arguments of cases.

what you read. This in itself is an important goal of academic study. If you don't understand your source material, chances are you won't be able to refer to it usefully in a paper. Summaries help you understand what you read because they force you to put the text into your own words. Practice with writing summaries also develops your general writing habits, because a good summary, like any other piece of good writing, is clear, coherent, and accurate.

Second, summaries are useful to your readers. Let's say you're writing a paper about the McCarthy era in the United States, and in part of that paper you want to discuss Arthur Miller's *The Crucible* as a dramatic treatment of the subject. A summary of the plot would be helpful to a reader who hasn't seen or read—or who doesn't remember—the play. Or perhaps you're writing a paper about the politics of recent American military interventions. If your reader isn't likely to be familiar with American actions in Kosovo and Afghanistan, it would be a good idea to summarize these events at some early point in the paper. In many cases (an exam, for instance), you can use a summary to demonstrate your knowledge of what your professor already knows; when writing a paper, you can use a summary to inform your professor about some relatively unfamiliar source.

Third, summaries are required frequently in college-level writing. For example, on a psychology midterm, you may be asked to explain Carl Jung's theory of the collective unconscious and to show how it differs from Sigmund Freud's theory of the personal unconscious. You may have read about Jung's theory in your textbook or in a supplementary article, or your instructor may have outlined it in her lecture. You can best demonstrate your understanding of it by summarizing it. Then you'll proceed to contrast it with Freud's theory—which, of course, you must also summarize.

THE READING PROCESS

It may seem to you that being able to tell (or retell) in summary form exactly what a passage says is a skill that ought to be taken for granted in anyone who can read at high school level. Unfortunately, this is not so: For all kinds of reasons, people don't always read carefully. In fact, it's probably safe to say that usually they don't. Either they read so inattentively that they skip over words, phrases, or even whole sentences, or, if they do see the words in front of them, they see them without registering their significance.

When a reader fails to pick up the meaning and implications of a sentence or two, usually there's no real harm done. (An exception: You could lose credit on an exam or paper because you failed to read or to realize the significance of a crucial direction by your instructor.) But over longer stretches—the paragraph, the section, the article, or the chapter—inattentive or haphazard reading interferes with your goals as a reader: to perceive the shape of the argument, to grasp the central idea, to determine the main points that compose it, to relate the parts of the whole, and to note key examples. This kind of reading takes a lot more energy and determination than casual reading.

CRITICAL READING FOR SUMMARY

- *Examine the context.* Note the credentials, occupation, and publications of the author. Identify the source in which the piece originally appeared. This information helps illuminate the author's perspective on the topic he or she is addressing.
- *Note the title and subtitle.* Some titles are straightforward; the meanings of others become clearer as you read. In either case, titles typically identify the topic being addressed and often reveal the author's attitude toward that topic.
- *Identify the main point.* Whether a piece of writing contains a thesis statement in the first few paragraphs or builds its main point without stating it up front, look at the entire piece to arrive at an understanding of the overall point being made.
- *Identify the subordinate points.* Notice the smaller subpoints that make up the main point, and make sure you understand how they relate to the main point. If a particular subpoint doesn't clearly relate to the main point you've identified, you may need to modify your understanding of the main point.
- *Break the reading into sections.* Notice which paragraphs make up a piece's introduction, body, and conclusion. Break up the body paragraphs into sections that address the writer's various subpoints.
- *Distinguish among points, examples, and counterarguments.* Critical reading requires careful attention to what a writer is *doing* as well as what he or she is *saying.* When a writer quotes someone else, or relays an example of something, ask yourself why this is being done. What point is the example supporting? Is another source being quoted as support for a point or as a counterargument that the writer sets out to address?
- *Watch for transitions within and between paragraphs.* To follow the logic of a piece of writing, as well as to distinguish among points, examples, and counterarguments, pay attention to the transitional words and phrases writers use. Transitions function like road signs, preparing the reader for what's next.
- *Read actively and recursively.* Don't treat reading as a passive, linear progression through a text. Instead, read as though you are engaged in a dialogue with the writer: Ask questions of the text as you read, make notes in the margin, underline key ideas in pencil, and put question or exclamation marks next to passages that confuse or excite you. Go back to earlier points once you finish a reading, stop during your reading to recap what's come so far, and move back and forth through a text.

But in the long run it's an energy-saving method because it enables you to retain the content of the material and to draw upon that content in your own responses. In other words, it allows you to develop an accurate and coherent written discussion that goes beyond summary.

HOW TO WRITE SUMMARIES

Every article you read will present its own challenge as you work to summarize it. As you'll discover, saying in a few words what has taken someone else a great many can be difficult. But like any other skill, the ability to summarize improves with practice. Here are a few pointers to get you started. They represent possible stages, or steps, in the process of writing a summary. These pointers are not meant to be ironclad rules; rather, they are designed to encourage habits of thinking that will allow you to vary your technique as the situation demands.

GUIDELINES FOR WRITING SUMMARIES

- *Read the passage carefully.* Determine its structure. Identify the author's purpose in writing. (This will help you distinguish between more important and less important information.) Make a note in the margin when you get confused or when you think something is important; highlight or underline points sparingly, if at all.
- *Reread.* This time divide the passage into sections or stages of thought. The author's use of paragraphing will often be a useful guide. *Label*, on the passage itself, each section or stage of thought. *Underline* key ideas and terms. Write notes in the margin.
- *Write one-sentence summaries,* on a separate sheet of paper, of each stage of thought.
- *Write a thesis—a one- or two-sentence summary of the entire passage.* The thesis should express the central idea of the passage, as you have determined it from the preceding steps. You may find it useful to follow the approach of most newspaper stories—naming the *what, who, why, where, when,* and *how* of the matter. For persuasive passages, summarize in a sentence the author's conclusion. For descriptive passages, indicate the subject of the description and its key feature(s). Note: In some cases, *a suitable thesis statement may already be in the original passage.* If so, you may want to quote it directly in your summary.
- *Write the first draft of your summary* by (1) combining the thesis with your list of one-sentence summaries or (2) combining the thesis with one-sentence summaries *plus* significant details from the passage. In either case, eliminate repetition and less important information. Disregard minor details or generalize them (e.g., Bill Clinton and George W. Bush might be generalized as "recent presidents"). Use as few words as possible to convey the main ideas.
- *Check your summary against the original passage* and make whatever adjustments are necessary for accuracy and completeness.
- *Revise your summary,* inserting transitional words and phrases where necessary to ensure coherence. Check for style. *Avoid a series of short, choppy sentences.* Combine sentences for a smooth, logical flow of ideas. Check for grammatical correctness, punctuation, and spelling.

DEMONSTRATION: SUMMARY

To demonstrate these points at work, let's go through the process of summarizing a passage of expository material—that is, writing that is meant to inform and/or persuade. Read the following selection carefully. Try to identify its parts and understand how they work together to create an overall statement.

WILL YOUR JOB BE EXPORTED?

Alan S. Blinder

Alan S. Blinder is the Gordon S. Rentschler Memorial Professor of Economics at Princeton University. He has served as vice chairman of the Federal Reserve Board and was a member of President Clinton's original Council of Economic Advisers.

The great conservative political philosopher Edmund Burke, who probably would not have been a reader of *The American Prospect*, once observed, "You can never plan the future by the past."* But when it comes to preparing the American workforce for the jobs of the future, we may be doing just that.

For about a quarter-century, demand for labor appears to have shifted toward the college-educated and away from high school graduates and dropouts. This shift, most economists believe, is the primary (though not the sole) reason for rising income inequality, and there is no end in sight. Economists refer to this phenomenon by an antiseptic name: skill-biased technical progress. In plain English, it means that the labor market has turned ferociously against the low skilled and the uneducated.

In a progressive society, such a worrisome social phenomenon might elicit some strong policy responses, such as more compensatory education, stepped-up efforts at retraining, reinforcement (rather than shredding) of the social safety net, and so on. You don't fight the market's valuation of skills; you try to mitigate its more deleterious effects. We did a bit of this in the United States in the 1990s, by raising the minimum wage and expanding the Earned Income Tax Credit.† Combined with tight labor markets, these measures improved things for the average worker. But in this decade, little or no mitigation has been attempted. Social Darwinism has come roaring back.‡

---

*Edmund Burke (1729–1797) was a conservative British statesman, philosopher, and author. *The American Prospect*, in which "Will Your Job Be Exported?" first appeared in the November 2006 issue, describes itself as "an authoritative magazine of liberal ideas."
†The Earned Income Tax Credit, an anti-poverty measure enacted by Congress in 1975 and revised in the 1980s and 1990s, provides a credit against federal income taxes for any filer who claims a dependent child.
‡Social Darwinism, a largely discredited philosophy dating from the Victorian era and espoused by Herbert Spencer, asserts that Charles Darwin's observations on natural selection apply to human societies. Social Darwinists argue that the poor are less fit to survive than the wealthy and should, through a natural process of adaptation, be allowed to die out.

With one big exception: We have expended considerable efforts to keep more young people in school longer (e.g., reducing high-school dropouts and sending more kids to college) and to improve the quality of schooling (e.g., via charter schools and No Child Left Behind*). Success in these domains may have been modest, but not for lack of trying. You don't have to remind Americans that education is important; the need for educational reform is etched into the public consciousness. Indeed, many people view education as the silver bullet. On hearing the question "How do we best prepare the American workforce of the future?" many Americans react reflexively with: "Get more kids to study science and math, and send more of them to college."

Which brings me to the future. As I argued in a recent article in *Foreign Affairs* magazine, the greatest problem for the next generation of American workers may not be lack of education, but rather "offshoring"—the movement of jobs overseas, especially to countries with much lower wages, such as India and China. Manufacturing jobs have been migrating overseas for decades. But the new wave of offshoring, of *service* jobs, is something different.

Traditionally, we think of service jobs as being largely immune to foreign competition. After all, you can't get your hair cut by a barber or your broken arm set by a doctor in a distant land. But stunning advances in communication technology, plus the emergence of a vast new labor pool in Asia and Eastern Europe, are changing that picture radically, subjecting millions of presumed-safe domestic service jobs to foreign competition. And it is not necessary actually to move jobs to low-wage countries in order to restrain wage increases; the mere threat of offshoring can put a damper on wages.

Service-sector offshoring is a minor phenomenon so far, Lou Dobbs notwithstanding; probably well under 1 percent of U.S. service jobs have been outsourced.[†] But I believe that service-sector offshoring will eventually exceed manufacturing-sector offshoring by a hefty margin—for three main reasons. The first is simple arithmetic: There are vastly more service jobs than manufacturing jobs in the United States (and in other rich countries). Second, the technological advances that have made service-sector offshoring possible will continue and accelerate, so the range of services that can be moved offshore will increase ineluctably. Third, the number of (e.g., Indian and Chinese) workers capable of performing service jobs offshore seems certain to grow, perhaps exponentially.

I do not mean to paint a bleak picture here. Ever since Adam Smith and David Ricardo, economists have explained and extolled the gains in living

---

*Charter schools are public schools with specialized missions to operate outside of regulations that some feel restrict creativity and performance in traditional school settings. The No Child Left Behind Act of 2001 (NCLB) mandates standards-based education for all schools receiving federal funding. Both the charter schools movement and NCLB can be understood as efforts to improve public education.
[†]Lou Dobbs, a conservative columnist and political commentator for CNN, is well known for his anti-immigration views.

standards that derive from international trade.* Those arguments are just as valid for trade in services as for trade in goods. There really *are* net gains to the United States from expanding service-sector trade with India, China, and the rest. The offshoring problem is not about the adverse nature of what economists call the economy's eventual equilibrium. Rather, it is about the so-called transition—the ride from here to there. That ride, which could take a generation or more, may be bumpy. And during the long adjustment period, many U.S. wages could face downward pressure.

Thus far, only American manufacturing workers and a few low-end service workers (e.g., call-center operators) have been competing, at least potentially, with millions of people in faraway lands eager to work for what seems a pittance by U.S. standards. But offshoring is no longer limited to low-end service jobs. Computer code can be written overseas and e-mailed back to the United States. So can your tax return and lots of legal work, provided you do not insist on face-to-face contact with the accountant or lawyer. In writing and editing this article, I communicated with the editors and staff of *The American Prospect* only by telephone and e-mail. Why couldn't they (or I, for that matter) have been in India? The possibilities are, if not endless, at least vast.

10   What distinguishes the jobs that cannot be offshored from the ones that can? The crucial distinction is not—and this is the central point of this essay—the required levels of skill and education. These attributes have been critical to labor-market success in the past, but may be less so in the future. Instead, the new critical distinction may be that some services either require personal delivery (e.g., driving a taxi and brain surgery) or are seriously degraded when delivered electronically (e.g., college teaching—at least, I hope!), while other jobs (e.g., call centers and keyboard data entry) are not. Call the first category personal services and the second category impersonal services. With this terminology, I have three main points to make about preparing our workforce for the brave, new world of the future.

First, we need to think about, plan, and redesign our educational system with the crucial distinction between personal service jobs and impersonal service jobs in mind. Many of the impersonal service jobs will migrate offshore, but the personal service jobs will stay here.

Second, the line that divides personal services from impersonal services will move in only one direction over time, as technological progress makes it possible to deliver an ever-increasing array of services electronically.

Third, the novel distinction between personal and impersonal jobs is quite different from, and appears essentially unrelated to, the traditional distinction between jobs that do and do not require high levels of education.

---

*Adam Smith (1723–1790), Scottish author of *An Inquiry into the Nature and Causes of the Wealth of Nations* (1776), established the foundations of modern economics. David Ricardo (1772–1823) was a British businessman, statesman, and economist who founded the classical school of economics and is best known for his studies of monetary policy.

For example, it is easy to offshore working in a call center, typing transcripts, writing computer code, and reading X-rays. The first two require little education; the last two require quite a lot. On the other hand, it is either impossible or very difficult to offshore janitorial services, fast-food restaurant service, college teaching, and open-heart surgery. Again, the first two occupations require little or no education, while the last two require a great deal. There seems to be little or no correlation between educational requirements (the old concern) and how "offshorable" jobs are (the new one).

If so, the implications could be startling. A generation from now, civil engineers (who must be physically present) may be in greater demand in the United States than computer engineers (who don't). Similarly, there might be more divorce lawyers (not offshorable) than tax lawyers (partly offshorable). More imaginatively, electricians might earn more than computer programmers. I am not predicting any of this; lots of things influence relative demands and supplies for different types of labor. But it all seems within the realm of the possible as technology continues to enhance the offshorability of even highly skilled occupations. What does seem highly likely is that the relative demand for labor in the United States will shift away from impersonal services and toward personal services, and this shift will look quite different from the familiar story of skill-biased technical progress. So Burke's warning is worth heeding.

I am *not* suggesting that education will become a handicap in the job market of the future. On the contrary, to the extent that education raises productivity and that better-educated workers are more adaptable and/or more creative, a wage premium for higher education should remain. Thus, it still makes sense to send more of America's youth to college. But, over the next generation, the kind of education our young people receive may prove to be more important than how much education they receive. In that sense, a college degree may lose its exalted "silver bullet" status.

Looking back over the past 25 years, "stay in school longer" was excellent advice for success in the labor market. But looking forward over the next 25 years, more subtle occupational advice may be needed. "Prepare yourself for a high-end personal service occupation that is not offshorable" is a more nuanced message than "stay in school." But it may prove to be more useful. And many non-offshorable jobs—such as carpenters, electricians, and plumbers—do not require college education.

The hard question is how to make this more subtle advice concrete and actionable. The children entering America's educational system today, at age 5, will emerge into a very different labor market when they leave it. Given gestation periods of 13 to 17 years and more, educators and policymakers need to be thinking now about the kinds of training and skills that will best prepare these children for their future working lives. Specifically, it is essential to educate America's youth for the jobs that will actually be available in America 20 to 30 years from now, not for the jobs that will have moved offshore.

Some of the personal service jobs that will remain in the United States will be very high-end (doctors), others will be less glamorous though well paid (plumbers), and some will be "dead end" (janitor). We need to think long and hard about the types of skills that best prepare people to deliver high-end personal services, and how to teach those skills in our elementary and high schools. I am not an education specialist, but it strikes me that, for example, the central thrust of No Child Left Behind is pushing the nation in exactly the wrong direction. I am all for accountability. But the nation's school system will not build the creative, flexible, people-oriented work-force we will need in the future by drilling kids incessantly with rote preparation for standardized tests in the vain hope that they will perform as well as memory chips.

20   Starting in the elementary schools, we need to develop our young-sters' imaginations and people skills as well as their "reading, writing, and 'rithmetic." Remember that kindergarten grade for "works and plays well with others"? It may become increasingly important in a world of personally delivered services. Such training probably needs to be contin-ued and made more sophisticated in the secondary schools, where, for example, good communications skills need to be developed.

More vocational education is probably also in order. After all, nurses, carpenters, and plumbers are already scarce, and we'll likely need more of them in the future. Much vocational training now takes place in commu-nity colleges; and they, too, need to adapt their curricula to the job market of the future.

While it is probably still true that we should send more kids to college and increase the number who study science, math, and engineering, we need to focus on training more college students for the high-end jobs that are unlikely to move offshore, and on developing a creative workforce that will keep America incubating and developing new processes, new prod-ucts, and entirely new industries. Offshoring is, after all, mostly about fol-lowing and copying. America needs to lead and innovate instead, just as we have in the past.

Educational reform is not the whole story, of course. I suggested at the outset, for example, that we needed to repair our tattered social safety net and turn it into a retraining trampoline that bounces displaced workers back into productive employment. But many low-end personal service jobs cannot be turned into more attractive jobs simply by more training—think about janitors, fast-food workers, and nurse's aides, for example. Running a tight labor market would help such workers, as would a higher minimum wage, an expanded Earned Income Tax Credit, universal health insurance, and the like.

Moving up the skill ladder, employment is concentrated in the pub-lic or quasi-public sector in a number of service occupations. Teachers and health-care workers are two prominent examples. In such cases, government policy can influence wages and working conditions directly by upgrading the structure and pay of such jobs—developing more professional early-childhood teachers and fewer casual daycare workers for example—as long as the taxpayer is willing to foot the bill. Similarly, some service jobs such as registered nurses are in short supply mainly because we are not training enough qualified personnel. Here, too, public policy can help by widening the pipeline to allow more workers through. So there are a variety of policy levers that might do some good—if we are willing to pull them.

But all that said, education is still the right place to start. Indeed, it is much more than that because the educational system affects the entire population and because no other institution is nearly as important when it comes to preparing our youth for the world of work. As the first industrial revolution took hold, America radically transformed (and democratized) its educational system to meet the new demands of an industrial society. We may need to do something like that again. There is a great deal at stake here. If we get this one wrong, the next generation will pay dearly. But if we get it (close to) right, the gains from trade promise coming generations a prosperous future.

The somewhat inchoate challenge posed here—preparing more young Americans for personal service jobs—brings to mind one of my favorite Churchill quotations: "You can always count on Americans to do the right thing—after they've tried everything else." It is time to start trying.

Read, Reread, Highlight

Let's consider our recommended pointers for writing a summary.

As you reread the passage, note in the margins of the essay important points, shifts in thought, and questions you may have. Consider the essay's significance as a whole and its stages of thought. What does it say? How is it organized? How does each part of the passage fit into the whole? What do all these points add up to?

Here is how several paragraphs from the middle of Blinder's article might look after you have marked the main ideas by highlighting and by marginal notations.

fshored rvice jobs l eclipse + manu- cturing s—3 asons

Service-sector offshoring is a minor phenomenon so far, Lou Dobbs notwithstanding; probably well under 1 percent of U.S. service jobs have been outsourced. But I believe that service-sector offshoring will eventually exceed manufacturing-sector offshoring by a hefty margin—for three main reasons. The first is simple arithmetic: There are vastly more service jobs than manufacturing jobs in the United States (and in other rich countries). Second, the technological advances that have made service-sector offshoring possible will continue and accelerate, so the range of services that can be moved offshore will increase ineluctably. Third, the number of (e.g., Indian and Chinese) workers capable of performing service jobs off-shore seems certain to grow, perhaps exponentially.

Long-term economy will be ok. Short to middle term will be "bumpy"

I do not mean to paint a bleak picture here. Ever since Adam Smith and David Ricardo, economists have explained and extolled the gains in living standards that derive from international trade. Those arguments are just as valid for trade in services as for trade in goods. There really *are* net gains to the United States from expanding service-sector trade with India, China, and the rest. The offshoring problem is not about the adverse nature of what economists call the economy's eventual equilibrium. Rather, it is about the so-called transition—the ride from here to there. That ride, which could take a generation or more, may be bumpy. And during the long adjustment period, many U.S. wages could face downward pressure.

Thus far, only American manufacturing workers and a few low-end service workers (e.g., call-center operators) have been competing, at least potentially, with millions of people in far-away lands eager to work for what seems a pittance by U.S. standards. But offshoring is no longer limited to low-end service jobs. Computer code can be written overseas and e-mailed back to the United States. So can your tax return and lots of legal work, provided you do not insist on face-to-face contact with the accountant or lawyer. In writing and editing this article, I communicated with the editors and staff of *The American Prospect* only by telephone and e-mail. Why couldn't they (or I, for that matter) have been in India? The possibilities are, if not endless, at least vast.

High-end jobs to be lost

B's main point: Key distinction: Personal service jobs stay; impersonal jobs go 3 points re: prep of future workforce

What distinguishes the jobs that cannot be offshored from the ones that can? The crucial distinction is not—and this is the central point of this essay—the required levels of skill and education. These attributes have been critical to labor-market success in the past, but may be less so in the future. Instead, the new critical distinction may be that some services either require personal delivery (e.g., driving a taxi and brain surgery) or are seriously degraded when delivered electronically (e.g., college teaching—at least, I hope!), while other jobs (e.g., call centers and keyboard data entry) are not. Call the first category personal services and the second category impersonal services. With this terminology, I have three main points to make about preparing our workforce for the brave, new world of the future.

First, we need to think about, plan, and redesign our educational system with the crucial distinction between personal service jobs and impersonal service jobs in mind. Many of the impersonal service jobs will migrate offshore, but the personal service jobs will stay here.

Movement:
impersonal
→ personal
Level of ed.
note related
to future job
security

Second, the line that divides personal services from impersonal services will move in only one direction over time, as technological progress makes it possible to deliver an ever-increasing array of services electronically.

Third, the novel distinction between personal and impersonal jobs is quite different from, and appears essentially unrelated to, the traditional distinction between jobs that do and do not require high levels of education.

Divide into Stages of Thought

When a selection doesn't contain sections with topic headings, as is the case with "Will Your Job Be Exported?" how do you determine where one stage of thought ends and the next one begins? Assuming that what you have read is coherent and unified, this should not be difficult. (When a selection is unified, all of its parts pertain to the main subject; when a selection is coherent, the parts follow one another in logical order.) Look particularly for transitional sentences at the beginning of paragraphs. Such sentences generally work in one or both of two ways: (1) they summarize what has come before; (2) they set the stage for what is to follow.

Look at the sentences that open paragraphs 5 and 10: "Which brings me to the future" and "What distinguishes the jobs that cannot be offshored from the ones that can?" In both cases Blinder makes a clear announcement. Grammatically speaking, "Which brings me to the future" is a fragment, not a sentence. Experienced writers will use fragments on occasion to good effect, as in this case. The fragment clearly has the sense of a complete thought: the pronoun "which" refers readers to the content of the preceding paragraphs, asking readers to summarize that content and then, with the predicate "brings me to the future," to move forward into the next part of the article. Similarly, the question "What distinguishes the jobs that cannot be offshored from the ones that can?" implicitly asks readers to recall an important distinction just made (the definitions of offshorable and non-offshorable jobs) and then clearly moves readers forward to new, related content. As you can see, the openings of paragraphs 5 and 10 announce new sections in the article.

Each section of an article generally takes several paragraphs to develop. Between paragraphs, and almost certainly between sections of an article, you will usually find transitions that help you understand what you have just read and what you are about to read. For articles that have no subheadings, try writing your own section headings in the margins as you take notes. Blinder's article can be divided into five sections.

Section 1: *Recent past: education of workers important*—For twenty-five years, the labor market has rewarded workers with higher levels of education (paragraphs 1–4).

Section 2: *Future: ed level won't always matter—workers in service sector will lose jobs offshore*—Once thought immune to outsourcing, even highly trained service workers will lose jobs to overseas competition (paragraphs 5–9).

Section 3: *Which service jobs at highest risk?*—Personal service workers are safe; impersonal service workers, both highly educated and not, will see jobs offshored (paragraphs 10–15).

Section 4: *Educating the future workforce*—Emphasizing the kind, not amount, of education will help to prepare workers for jobs of the future (paragraphs 16–22).

Section 5: *Needed policy reforms*—Government can improve conditions for low-end service workers and expand opportunities for higher-end service workers; start with education (paragraphs 23–26).

Write a Brief Summary of Each Stage of Thought

The purpose of this step is to wean you from the language of the original passage, so that you are not tied to it when writing the summary. Here are brief summaries, one for each stage of thought in "Will Your Job Be Exported?"

Section 1: Recent past: education of workers important (paragraphs 1–4).

> For the past twenty-five years, the greater a worker's skill or level of education, the better and more stable the job.

Section 2: Future: ed level won't always matter—workers in service sector will lose jobs offshore (paragraphs 5–9).

> Advances in technology have brought to the service sector the same pressures that forced so many manufacturing jobs offshore to China and India. The rate of offshoring in the service sector will accelerate and "eventually exceed" job losses in manufacturing, says Blinder, and jobs requiring both relatively little education (like call-center staffing) and extensive education (like software development) will be lost to workers overseas.

Section 3: Which service jobs at highest risk? (paragraphs 10–15).

> While "personal services" workers (like barbers and surgeons) will be relatively safe from offshoring because their work requires close physical proximity to customers, "impersonal services" workers (like call-center operators and radiologists), regardless of their skill or education, will be at risk because their work can be completed remotely without loss of quality and then delivered via phone or computer. Blinder believes that "the relative demand for labor in the United States will [probably] shift away from impersonal services and toward personal services."

Section 4: Educating the future workforce (paragraphs 16–22).

> Blinder advises young people to plan for "a high-end personal
> service occupation that is not offshorable." He also urges educators
> to prepare the future workforce by anticipating the needs of a
> personal services economy and redesigning classroom instruction
> and vocational training accordingly.

Section 5: Needed policy reforms (paragraphs 23–26).

> Blinder urges the government to develop policies that will improve
> wages and conditions for low-wage personal service workers (like
> janitors); to encourage more low-wage workers (like daycare providers)
> to retrain and take on better jobs; and to increase opportunities for
> professional and vocational training in high-demand areas (like
> nursing and carpentry).

Write a Thesis: A Brief Summary of the Entire Passage

The thesis is the most general statement of a summary (or any other type of
academic writing). It is the statement that announces the paper's subject and
the claim that you or—in the case of a summary—another author will be
making about that subject. Every paragraph of a paper illuminates the thesis
by providing supporting detail or explanation. The relationship of these
paragraphs to the thesis is analogous to the relationship of the sentences
within a paragraph to the topic sentence. Both the thesis and the topic sentences are general statements (the thesis being the more general) that are
followed by systematically arranged details.

To ensure clarity for the reader, *the first sentence of your summary should
begin with the author's thesis, regardless of where it appears in the article itself.* An
author may locate her thesis at the beginning of her work, in which case the
thesis operates as a general principle from which details of the presentation
follow. This is called a *deductive* organization: thesis first, supporting details
second. Alternatively, an author may locate his thesis at the end of the work,
in which case the author begins with specific details and builds toward a
more general conclusion, or thesis. This is called an *inductive* organization.
And, as you might expect, an author might locate the thesis anywhere
between beginning and end, at whatever point it seems best positioned.*

---

*Blinder positions his thesis midway through his five-section article. He opens the selection
by discussing the role of education in the labor market during the past twenty-five years
(Section 1, pars. 1–4). He continues by summarizing an earlier article on the ways in which
service jobs are following manufacturing jobs offshore (Section 2, pars. 5–9). He then presents
a two-sentence thesis in answer to the question that opens paragraph 10: "What distinguishes
the jobs that cannot be offshored from the ones that can?" The remainder of the article either
develops this thesis (Section 3, pars. 10–15) or follows its implications for education (Section 4,
pars. 16–22) and public policy (Section 5, pars. 23–26).

A thesis consists of a subject and an assertion about that subject. How can we go about fashioning an adequate thesis for a summary of Blinder's article? Probably no two versions of Blinder's thesis statement would be worded identically, but it is fair to say that any reasonable thesis will indicate that Blinder's subject is the future loss to offshoring of American jobs in the service sector—that part of the economy that delivers services to consumers, from low end (e.g., janitorial services) to high end (e.g., neurosurgery). How does Blinder view the situation? How secure will service jobs be if Blinder's distinction between personal and impersonal services is valid? Looking back over our section summaries, we find that Blinder insists on three points: (1) that education and skill matter less than they once did in determining job quality and security; (2) that the distinction between personal and impersonal services will increasingly determine which jobs remain and which are offshored; and (3) that the distinction between personal and impersonal has implications for both the future of education and public policy.

Does Blinder make a statement anywhere in this passage that pulls all this together? Examine paragraph 10 and you will find his thesis—two sentences that answer his question about which jobs will and will not be sent offshore: "The crucial distinction is not—and this is the central point of this essay—the required levels of skill and education.... Instead, the new critical distinction may be that some services either require personal delivery (e.g., driving a taxi and brain surgery) or are seriously degraded when delivered electronically (e.g., college teaching—at least, I hope!), while other jobs (e.g., call centers and keyboard data entry) are not."

You may have learned that a thesis statement must be expressed in a single sentence. We would offer a slight rewording of this generally sound advice and say that a thesis statement must be *expressible* in a single sentence. For reasons of emphasis or style, a writer might choose to distribute a thesis across two or more sentences. Certainly, the sense of Blinder's thesis can take the form of a single statement: "The critical distinction is X, not Y." For reasons largely of emphasis, he divides his thesis into two sentences—in fact, separating these sentences with another sentence that explains the first part of the thesis: "These attributes [that is, skill and education] have been critical to labor-market success in the past, but may be less so in the future."

Here is a one-sentence version of Blinder's two-sentence thesis:

> The quality and security of future jobs in America's service sector will be determined by how "offshorable" those jobs are.

Notice that the statement anticipates a summary of the *entire* article: both the discussion leading up to Blinder's thesis and his discussion after. To clarify for our readers the fact that this idea is Blinder's and not ours, we might qualify the thesis as follows:

> In "Will Your Job Be Exported?" economist Alan S. Blinder argues that the quality and security of future jobs in America's service sector will be determined by how "offshorable" those jobs are.

The first sentence of a summary is crucially important, for it orients readers by letting them know what to expect in the coming paragraphs. In the example above, the first sentence refers directly to an article, its author, and the thesis for the upcoming summary. The author and title reference could also be indicated in the summary's title (if this were a free-standing summary), in which case their mention could be dropped from the thesis statement. And lest you become frustrated too quickly with how much effort it takes to come up with this crucial sentence, keep in mind that writing an acceptable thesis for a summary takes time. In this case, it took three drafts, roughly ten minutes, to compose a thesis and another few minutes of fine-tuning after a draft of the entire summary was completed. The thesis needed revision because the first draft was vague; the second draft was improved but too specific on a secondary point; the third draft was more complete but too general on a key point:

Draft 1: We must begin now to train young people for high-quality personal service jobs.

Vague. The question of why we should begin training isn't clear, nor is the phrase "high-quality personal service jobs." Define this term or make it more general.

Draft 2: Alan S. Blinder argues that, unlike in the past, the quality and security of future American jobs will not be determined by skill level or education but rather by how "offshorable" those jobs are.

Better, but the reference to "skill level or education" is secondary to Blinder's main point about offshorable jobs.

Draft 3: In "Will Your Job Be Exported?" economist Alan S. Blinder argues that the quality and security of future jobs will be determined by how "offshorable" those jobs are.

Close—but not "all" jobs. Blinder specifies which types of jobs are "offshorable."

Final Draft: In "Will Your Job Be Exported?" economist Alan S. Blinder argues that the quality and security of future jobs in America's service sector will be determined by how "offshorable" those jobs are.

Write the First Draft of the Summary

Let's consider two possible summaries of Blinder's article: (1) a short summary, combining a thesis with brief section summaries, and (2) a longer summary, combining thesis, brief section summaries, and some carefully chosen details. Again, keep in mind that you are reading final versions; each of the following summaries is the result of at least two full drafts. Highlighting indicates transitions added to smooth the flow of the summary.

Summary 1: Combine Thesis Sentence with Brief Section Summaries

In "Will Your Job Be Exported?" economist Alan S. Blinder argues that the quality and security of future jobs in America's service sector will be determined by how "offshorable" those jobs are. For the past twenty-five years, the greater a worker's skill or level of education, the better and more stable the job. No longer. Advances in technology have brought to the service sector the same pressures that forced so many manufacturing jobs offshore to China and India. The rate of offshoring in the service sector will accelerate, and jobs requiring both relatively little education (like call-center staffing) and extensive education (like software development) will increasingly be lost to workers overseas.

These losses will "eventually exceed" losses in manufacturing, but not all services jobs are equally at risk. While "personal services" workers (like barbers and surgeons) will be relatively safe from offshoring because their work requires close physical proximity to customers, "impersonal services" workers (like call-center operators and radiologists), regardless of their skill or education, will be at risk because their work can be completed remotely without loss of quality and then delivered via phone or computer. "[T]he relative demand for labor in the United States will [probably] shift away from impersonal services and toward personal services."

Blinder recommends three courses of action: He advises young people to plan for "a high-end personal service occupation that is not offshorable." He urges educators to prepare the future workforce by anticipating the needs of a personal services economy and redesigning classroom instruction and vocational training accordingly. Finally, he urges the government to adopt policies that will improve existing personal services jobs by increasing wages for low-wage workers; retraining workers to take on better jobs; and increasing opportunities in high-demand, well-paid areas like nursing and carpentry. Ultimately, Blinder wants America to prepare a new generation to "lead and innovate" in an economy that will continue exporting jobs that require "following and copying."

The Strategy of the Shorter Summary   This short summary consists essentially of a restatement of Blinder's thesis plus the section summaries, modified or expanded a little for stylistic purposes. You'll recall that Blinder locates his thesis midway through the article, in paragraph 10. But note that this model summary *begins* with a restatement of his thesis. Notice also the relative weight given to the section summaries within the model. Blinder's main point, his "critical distinction" between personal and impersonal services jobs, is summarized in paragraph 2 of the model. The other paragraphs combine summaries of relatively less important (that is, supporting or explanatory) material. Paragraph 1 combines summaries of the article's Sections 1 and 2; paragraph 3 combines summaries of Sections 4 and 5.

Between the thesis and the section summaries, notice the insertion of three (highlighted) transitions. The first—a fragment (*No longer*)—bridges the first paragraph's summaries of Sections 1 and 2 of Blinder's article. The second transition links a point Blinder makes in his Section 2 (*Losses in the service sector will "eventually exceed" losses in manufacturing*) with an introduction to the key point he will make in Section 3 (*Not all service jobs are equally at risk*). The third transition (*Blinder recommends three courses of action*) bridges the summary of Blinder's Section 3 to summaries of Sections 4 and 5. Each transition, then, links sections of the whole: each casts the reader back to recall points just made; each casts the reader forward by announcing related points about to be made. Our model ends with a summary of Blinder's motivation for writing, the sense of which is implied by the section summaries but nowhere made explicit.

Summary 2: Combine Thesis Sentence, Section Summaries, and Carefully Chosen Details

The thesis and brief section summaries could also be used as the outline for a more detailed summary. However, most of the details in the passage won't be necessary in a summary. It isn't necessary even in a longer summary of this passage to discuss all of Blinder's examples of jobs that are more or less likely to be sent offshore. It would be appropriate, though, to mention one example of such a job; to review his reasons for thinking "that service-sector offshoring will eventually exceed manufacturing-sector offshoring by a hefty margin"; and to expand on his point that a college education in itself will no longer ensure job security.

None of these details appeared in the first summary, but in a longer summary, a few carefully selected details might be desirable for clarity. How do you decide which details to include? First, working with Blinder's point that one's job type (personal services vs. impersonal services) will matter more for future job quality and security than did the once highly regarded "silver bullet" of education, you may want to cite some of the most persuasive evidence supporting this idea. For example, you could explore why some highly paid physicians, like radiologists, might find themselves competing for jobs with lower-paid physicians overseas. Further, your expanded summary might reflect the relative weight Blinder gives to education (seven paragraphs, the longest of the article's five sections).

You won't always know which details to include and which to exclude. Developing good judgment in comprehending and summarizing texts is largely a matter of reading skill and prior knowledge (see p. 3). Consider the analogy of the seasoned mechanic who can pinpoint an engine problem by simply listening to a characteristic sound that to a less-experienced person is just noise. Or consider the chess player who can plot three separate winning strategies from a board position that to a novice looks like a hopeless jumble. In the same way, the more practiced a reader you are, the more knowledgeable you become about the subject and the better able you will be to make critical distinctions between elements of greater and lesser importance. In the meantime, read as carefully as you can and use your own best judgment as to how to present your material.

Here's one version of a completed summary with carefully chosen details. Note that we have highlighted phrases and sentences added to the original, briefer summary.

In "Will Your Job Be Exported?" economist Alan S. Blinder argues that the quality and security of future jobs in America's service sector will be determined by how "offshorable" those jobs are. For the past twenty-five years, the greater a worker's skill or level of education, the better and more stable the job. Americans have long regarded education as the "silver bullet" that could propel motivated people to better jobs and a better life. No longer. Advances in technology have brought to the service sector the same pressures that forced so many manufacturing jobs offshore to China and India. The rate of offshoring in the service sector will accelerate, says Blinder, and jobs requiring both relatively little education (like call- center staffing) and extensive education (like software development) will increasingly be lost to workers overseas.

Blinder expects that job losses in the service sector will "eventually exceed" losses in manufacturing, for three reasons. Developed countries have more service jobs than manufacturing jobs; as technology speeds communications, more service jobs will be offshorable; and the numbers of qualified offshore workers is increasing. Service jobs lost to foreign competition may cause a "bumpy" period as the global economy sorts out what work gets done where, by whom. In time, as the global economy finds its "eventual equilibrium," offshoring will benefit the United States; but the consequences in the meantime may be painful for many.

That pain will not be shared equally by all service workers, however. While "personal service" workers (like barbers and surgeons) will be relatively safe from offshoring because their work requires close physical proximity to customers, "impersonal service" workers (like audio transcribers and radiologists), regardless of their skill or education, will be at risk because their work can be completed remotely without loss of quality and then delivered via phone or computer. In the coming decades, says Blinder, "the relative demand for labor in the United States will [probably] shift away from impersonal services and toward personal services." This shift will be influenced by the desire to keep good jobs in the United States while exporting jobs that require "following and copying." Highly trained computer coders will face the same pressures of outsourcing as relatively untrained call-center attendants. A tax attorney whose work requires no face-to-face interaction with clients may see her work migrate overseas while a divorce attorney, who must interact with clients on a case-by-case basis, may face no such competition. Same educations, different outcomes: what determines their fates in a global economy is the nature of their work (that is, personal vs. impersonal), not their level of education.

Based on this analysis, Blinder recommends three courses of action: First, he advises young people to plan for "a high-end personal service occupation that is not offshorable." Many good jobs, like carpentry and plumbing, will not require a college degree. Next, Blinder urges educators to prepare the future workforce by anticipating the needs of a personal services economy and redesigning classroom instruction and vocational training accordingly. These efforts should begin in elementary school and develop imagination and interpersonal skills rather than capacities for rote memorization. Finally, Blinder urges the government to develop policies that will improve wages and conditions for low-wage personal services workers (like janitors); to encourage more low-wage workers (like daycare providers) to retrain and take on better service jobs; and to increase opportunities for professional and vocational training for workers in high-demand services areas (like nurses and electricians). Ultimately, Blinder wants America to prepare a new generation of workers who will "lead and innovate . . . just as we have in the past."

The Strategy of the Longer Summary   Compared to the first, briefer summary, this effort (seventy percent longer than the first) includes Blinder's reasons for suggesting that job losses in the services sector will exceed losses in manufacturing. It emphasizes Blinder's point that job type (personal vs. impersonal services), not a worker's education level, will ensure job security. It includes Blinder's point that offshoring in the service sector is part of a larger global economy seeking "equilibrium." And it offers more on Blinder's thoughts concerning the education of future workers.

The final two of our suggested steps for writing summaries are (1) to check your summary against the original passage, making sure that you have included all the important ideas, and (2) to revise so that the summary reads smoothly and coherently. The structure of this summary generally reflects the structure of the original article—with one significant departure, as noted earlier. Blinder uses a modified inductive approach, stating his thesis midway through the article. The summary, however, states the thesis immediately and then proceeds deductively to develop that thesis.

HOW LONG SHOULD A SUMMARY BE?

The length of a summary depends both on the length of the original passage and on the use to which the summary will be put. If you are summarizing an entire article, a good rule of thumb is that your summary should be no longer than one-fourth the length of the original passage. Of course, if you were summarizing an entire chapter or even an entire book, it would have to be much shorter than that. The longer summary above is one-quarter the length of Alan Blinder's original. Although it shouldn't be very much longer, you have seen (p. 20) that it could be quite a bit shorter.

The length as well as the content of the summary also depends on the *purpose* to which it will be put. Let's suppose you decided to use Blinder's piece in a paper that dealt with the loss of manufacturing jobs in the United States and the rise of the service economy. In this case, in an effort to explain the complexities of the service economy to your readers, you might summarize *only* Blinder's core distinction between jobs in personal services and impersonal services, likely mentioning that jobs in the latter category are at risk of offshoring. If, instead, you were writing a paper in which you argued that the forces of globalization will eventually collapse the world's economies into a single, global economy, you would likely give less attention to Blinder's distinction between personal and impersonal services. More to the point might be his observation that highly skilled, highly educated workers in the United States are now finding themselves competing with qualified, lower-wage workers in China and India. Thus, depending on your purpose, you would summarize either selected portions of a source or an entire source. We will see this process more fully demonstrated in the upcoming chapter on synthesis.

Exercise 1.1

Individual and Collaborative Summary Practice

Turn to Chapter 8 and read Lawrence Epstein's article "Improving Sleep" (pp. 316–322). Follow the steps for writing summaries outlined above—read, underline, and divide into stages of thought. Write a one- or two-sentence summary of each stage of thought in Epstein's article. Then gather in groups of three or four classmates and compare your summary sentences. Discuss the differences in your sentences, and come to some consensus about the divisions in Epstein's stages of thought—and the ways in which to best sum them up.

As a group, write a one- or two-sentence thesis statement summing up the entire passage. You could go even further, and, using your individual summary sentences—or the versions of them your group revised—put together a brief summary of Epstein's essay. Model your work on the brief summary of Blinder's article, on p. 20.

AVOIDING PLAGIARISM

Plagiarism is generally defined as the attempt to pass off the work of another as one's own. Whether born out of calculation or desperation, plagiarism is the least tolerated offense in the academic world. The fact that most plagiarism is unintentional—arising from an ignorance of the conventions rather than deceitfulness—makes no difference to many professors.

The ease of cutting and pasting whole blocks of text from Web sources into one's own paper makes it tempting for some to take the easy way out and avoid doing their own research and writing. But, apart from the serious ethical issues involved, the same technology that makes such acts possible also makes it possible for instructors to detect them. Software marketed to instructors allows them to conduct Web searches, using suspicious phrases as keywords. The results often provide irrefutable evidence of plagiarism.

Of course, plagiarism is not confined to students. Recent years have seen a number of high-profile cases—some of them reaching the front pages of newspapers—of well-known scholars who were shown to have copied passages from sources into their own book manuscripts, without proper attribution. In some cases, the scholars maintained that these appropriations were simply a matter of carelessness, that in the press and volume of work they had lost track of which words were theirs and which were the words of their sources. But such excuses sounded hollow: These careless acts inevitably embarrassed the scholars professionally, tarnished their otherwise fine work and reputations, and disappointed their many admirers.

You can avoid plagiarism and charges of plagiarism by following the basic rules provided on p. 26.

The following is a passage from an article by Richard Rovere on Senator Joseph P. McCarthy, along with several student versions of the ideas represented.

> McCarthy never seemed to believe in himself or in anything he had said. He knew that Communists were not in charge of American foreign policy. He knew that they weren't running the United States Army. He knew that he had spent five years looking for Communists in the government and that—although some must certainly have been there, since Communists had turned up in practically every other major government in the world—he hadn't come up with even one.*

One student version of this passage reads:

> McCarthy never believed in himself or in anything he had said. He knew that Communists were not in charge of American foreign policy and weren't running the United States Army. He knew that he had spent five years looking for Communists in the government, and although there must certainly have been some there, since Communists were in practically every other major government in the world, he hadn't come up with even one.

Clearly, this is intentional plagiarism. The student has copied the original passage almost word for word.

Here is another version of the same passage:

> McCarthy knew that Communists were not running foreign policy or the Army. He also knew that, although there must have been some Communists in the government, he hadn't found a single one, even though he had spent five years looking.

This student has attempted to put the ideas into her own words, but both the wording and the sentence structure are so heavily dependent on the original passage that even if it *were* cited, most professors would consider it plagiarism.

---

*Richard Rovere, "The Most Gifted and Successful Demagogue This Country Has Ever Known," *New York Times Magazine*, 30 Apr. 1967.

In the following version, the student has sufficiently changed the wording and sentence structure, and she uses a *signal phrase* (a phrase used to introduce a quotation or paraphrase, signaling to the reader that the words to follow come from someone else) to properly credit the information to Rovere, so that there is no question of plagiarism:

> According to Richard Rovere, McCarthy was fully aware that Communists were running neither the government nor the Army. He also knew that he hadn't found a single Communist in government, even after a lengthy search (192).

And although this is not a matter of plagiarism, as noted above, it's essential to quote accurately. You are not permitted to change any part of a quotation or to omit any part of it without using brackets or ellipses.

RULES FOR AVOIDING PLAGIARISM

- Cite *all* quoted material and *all* summarized and paraphrased material, unless the information is common knowledge (e.g., the Civil War was fought from 1861 to 1865).
- Make sure that both the *wording* and the *sentence structure* of your summaries and paraphrases are substantially your own.

2

Critical Reading and Critique

CRITICAL READING

When writing papers in college, you are often called on to respond critically to source materials. Critical reading requires the abilities to both summarize and evaluate a presentation. As you have seen in Chapter 1, a *summary* is a brief restatement in your own words of the content of a passage. An *evaluation*, however, is a more ambitious undertaking. In your college work, you read to gain and *use* new information; but because sources are not equally valid or equally useful, you must learn to distinguish critically among them by evaluating them.

There is no ready-made formula for determining validity. Critical reading and its written equivalent—the *critique*—require discernment, sensitivity, imagination, knowledge of the subject, and, above all, willingness to become involved in what you read. These skills are developed only through repeated practice. You must begin somewhere, though, and we recommend that you start by posing two broad questions about passages, articles, and books that you read: (1) To what extent does the author succeed in his or her purpose? (2) To what extent do you agree with the author?

Question 1: To What Extent Does the Author Succeed in His or Her Purpose?

All critical reading *begins with an accurate summary.* Thus, before attempting an evaluation, you must be able to locate an author's thesis and identify the selection's content and structure. You must understand the author's *purpose.* Authors write to inform, to persuade, and to entertain. A given piece may be primarily *informative* (a summary of the research on cloning), primarily *persuasive* (an argument on why the government must do something to alleviate homelessness), or primarily *entertaining* (a play about the frustrations of young lovers). Or it may be all three (as in John Steinbeck's novel *The Grapes of Wrath,* about migrant workers during the Great Depression). Sometimes authors are not fully conscious of their purpose. Sometimes their purpose changes as they write. Also, multiple purposes can overlap: An essay may need to inform the reader about an issue in order to make a persuasive point. But if the finished piece is coherent, it will have a primary reason for having been written, and it should be apparent that the author is attempting primarily to inform, persuade, or entertain a particular audience. To identify this primary reason—this purpose—is your first job as a critical reader. Your next job is to determine how successful the author has been.

As a critical reader, you bring various criteria, or standards of judgment, to bear when you read pieces intended to inform, persuade, or entertain.

Writing to Inform

A piece intended to inform will provide definitions, describe or report on a process, recount a story, give historical background, and/or provide facts and figures. An informational piece responds to questions such as:

What (or who) is _____?

How does _____ work?

What is the controversy or problem about?

WHERE DO WE FIND WRITTEN CRITIQUES?

Here are just a few of the types of writing that involve critique:

Academic Writing

- **Research papers** critique sources in order to establish their usefulness.
- **Position papers** stake out a position by critiquing other positions.
- **Book reviews** combine summary with critique.
- **Essay exams** demonstrate understanding of course material by critiquing it.

Workplace Writing

- **Legal briefs and legal arguments** critique previous arguments made by opposing counsel.
- **Business plans and proposals** critique other less cost-effective, efficient, or reasonable approaches.
- **Policy briefs** communicate failings of policies and legislation through critique.

What happened?

How and why did it happen?

What were the results?

What are the arguments for and against _____?

To the extent that an author answers these and related questions and the answers are a matter of verifiable record (you could check for accuracy if you had the time and inclination), the selection is intended to inform. Having determined this, you can organize your response by considering three other criteria: accuracy, significance, and fair interpretation of information.

Evaluating Informative Writing

Accuracy of Information   If you are going to use any of the information presented, you must be satisfied that it is trustworthy. One of your responsibilities as a critical reader, then, is to find out if it is accurate. This means you should check facts against other sources. Government publications are often good resources for verifying facts about political legislation, population data, crime statistics, and the like. You can also search key terms in library databases and on the Web. Since material on the Web is essentially self-published, however, you must be especially vigilant in assessing its legitimacy. A wealth of useful information is now available on the Internet—but there is also a tremendous amount of misinformation, distorted "facts," and unsupported opinion.

Significance of Information   One useful question that you can put to a reading is "So what?" In the case of selections that attempt to inform, you may reasonably wonder whether the information makes a difference. What can the reader gain from this information? How is knowledge advanced by the publication of this material? Is the information of importance to you or to others in a particular audience? Why or why not?

Fair Interpretation of Information   At times you will read reports, the sole purpose of which is to relate raw data or information. In these cases, you will build your response on Question 1, introduced on page 27: To what extent does the author succeed in his or her purpose? More frequently, once an author has presented information, he or she will attempt to evaluate or interpret it—which is only reasonable, since information that has not been evaluated or interpreted is of little use. One of your tasks as a critical reader is to make a distinction between the author's presentation of facts and figures and his or her attempts to evaluate them. Watch for shifts from straightforward descriptions of factual information ("20 percent of the population") to assertions about what this information means ("a *mere* 20 percent of the population"), what its implications are, and so on. Pay attention to whether the logic with which the author connects interpretation with facts is sound. You may find that the information is valuable but the interpretation is not. Perhaps the author's conclusions are not justified. Could you offer a contrary explanation for the same facts? Does more information need to be gathered before firm conclusions can be drawn? Why?

Writing to Persuade

Writing is frequently intended to persuade—that is, to influence the reader's thinking. To make a persuasive case, the writer must begin with an assertion that is arguable, some statement about which reasonable people could disagree. Such an assertion, when it serves as the essential organizing principle of the article or book, is called a *thesis*. Here are two examples:

> Because they do not speak English, many children in this affluent land are being denied their fundamental right to equal educational opportunity.

> Bilingual education, which has been stridently promoted by a small group of activists with their own agenda, is detrimental to the very students it is supposed to serve.

Thesis statements such as these—and the subsequent assertions used to help support them—represent conclusions that authors have drawn as a result of researching and thinking about an issue. You go through the same process yourself when you write persuasive papers or critiques. And just as you are entitled to evaluate critically the assertions of authors you read, so your professors—and other students—are entitled to evaluate *your* assertions, whether they be written arguments or comments made in class discussion.

Keep in mind that writers organize arguments by arranging evidence to support one conclusion and oppose (or dismiss) another. You can assess the validity of an argument and its conclusion by determining whether the author has (1) clearly defined key terms, (2) used information fairly, and (3) argued logically and not fallaciously (see pp. 34–38).

Exercise 2.1

Informative and Persuasive Thesis Statements

With a partner from your class, identify at least one informative and one persuasive thesis statement from two passages of your own choosing. Photocopy these passages, and highlight the statements you have selected.

As an alternative, and also working with a partner, write one informative and one persuasive thesis statement for *three* of the topics listed at the end of this exercise. For example, for the topic of prayer in schools, your informative thesis statement could read:

> Both advocates and opponents of school prayer frame their position as a matter of freedom.

Your persuasive thesis statement might be worded:

> As long as schools don't dictate what kinds of prayers students should say, then school prayer should be allowed and even encouraged.

Don't worry about taking a position that you agree with or feel you could support; this exercise doesn't require that you write an essay. The topics:

school prayer

gun control

stem cell research

grammar instruction in English class

violent lyrics in music

teaching computer skills in primary schools

curfews in college dormitories

course registration procedures

Evaluating Persuasive Writing

Read the argument that follows on the nation's troubled "star" system for producing elite athletes and dancers. We will illustrate our discussion on defining terms, using information fairly, and arguing logically by referring to Joan Ryan's argument. The model critique that follows these illustrations will be based on this same argument.

WE ARE NOT CREATED EQUAL IN EVERY WAY

Joan Ryan

In an opinion piece for the San Francisco Chronicle *(December 12, 2000), columnist and reporter Joan Ryan takes a stand on whether the San Francisco Ballet School did or did not discriminate against 8-year-old Fredrika Keefer when it declined to admit her on the grounds that she had the wrong body type to be a successful ballerina. Keefer's mother subsequently sued the ballet school for discrimination, claiming that the rejection had caused her daughter confusion and humiliation. Ryan examines the question of setting admissions standards and also the problems some parents create by pushing their young children to meet these standards.*

Fredrika Keefer is an 8-year-old girl who likes to dance, just like her mother and grandmother before her. She relishes playing the lead role of Clara in the Pacific Dance Theater's "Petite Nutcracker." So perhaps she is not as shy as many fourth-graders. But I wonder how she feels about her body being a topic of public discussion.

Fredrika and her mother filed suit because, as her mother puts it, she "did not have the right body type to be accepted" by the San Francisco Ballet School. "My daughter is very sophisticated, so she understands why we're doing this," Krissy Keefer said. "And the other kids think she's a celebrity."

There is no question Keefer raises a powerful point in her complaint. The values placed on an unnaturally thin body for female performers drives some dancers to potentially fatal eating disorders. But that isn't exactly the issue here. This is: Does the San Francisco Ballet School have the right to give preference to leaner body types in selecting 300 students from this year's 1,400 applicants?

Yes, for the same reason UC Berkeley can reject students based on mental prowess and a fashion modeling school can reject students based on comeliness. Every institution has standards that weed out those who are less likely to succeed. I know this flies in the face of American ideals. But the reality is that all men and women are not created equal.

5   Like it or not, the ethereal, elongated body that can float on air is part of the look and feel of classical ballet. You and I might think ballet would be just as pleasing with larger bodies. But most of those who practice the art disagree, which is their right. This doesn't mean that women with different body types cannot become professional dancers. They just have to find a different type of dance—jazz, tap, modern—just as athletes have to find sports that fit certain body types. A tall, blocky man, for example, could not be a jockey but he could play baseball.

Having written extensively about the damaging pressures on young female gymnasts and figure skaters, I understand Keefer's concerns about body type. But for me, the more disturbing issue in this story isn't about weight but age.

The San Francisco Ballet School is very clear and open about the fact it is strictly a training ground for professional dancers. "We are not a recreation department," said a ballet spokeswoman.

In other words, children at age 8 are already training for adult careers. By age 12 or 13, the children are training so much that they either begin homeschooling or attend a school that accommodates the training schedule. The child has thrown all her eggs into this one little basket at an age when most kids can barely decide what to wear to school in the morning. And the child knows the parents are paying lots of money for this great opportunity.

The ballet school usually has a psychologist to counsel the students, but at the moment there is not one on staff. And the parents are given no training by the school on the pitfalls their daughters might encounter as they climb the ballet ladder: weight issues, physical ailments, social isolation, psychological pressure.

10   Just as in elite gymnastics and figure skating, these children are in the netherland of the law. They are neither hobbyists nor professionals. There is no safety net for them, no arm of government that makes sure that the adults in their lives watch out for their best interests.

Keefer said she would drop her lawsuit if the school accepted her daughter. The San Francisco Ballet School offers the best training in the Bay Area, she said. Fredrika, however, has said she is quite happy dancing where she is. Still, the mother gets to decide what's best for her daughter's dancing career. The child is clearly too young to make such a decision. Yet, in the skewed logic of elite athletics and dancing, she is not too young to pay the price for it.

Exercise 2.2

Critical Reading Practice

Look back at the Critical Reading for Summary box on p. 6 of Chapter 1. Use each of the guidelines listed there to examine the essay by Joan Ryan. Note in the margins of the selection, or on a separate sheet of paper, the essay's main point, subpoints, and use of examples.

Persuasive Strategies

Clearly Defined Terms   The validity of an argument depends to some degree on how carefully an author has defined key terms. Take the assertion, for example, that American society must be grounded in "family values." Just what do people who use this phrase mean by it? The validity of their argument depends on whether they and their readers agree on a definition of "family values"—as well as what it means to be "grounded in" family values. If an author writes that in the recent past "America's elites accepted as a matter of course that a free society can sustain itself only through virtue and temperance in the people,"* readers need to know what exactly the author means by "elites" and by "virtue and temperance" before they can assess the validity of the argument. In such cases, the success of the argument—its ability to persuade—hinges on the definition of a term. So, in responding to an argument, be sure you (and the author) are clear on what exactly is being argued. Unless you are, no informed response is possible.

Ryan uses several terms important for understanding her argument. The primary one is the "body type" that the San Francisco Ballet School uses as an application standard. Ryan defines this type (paragraph 5) as the "elongated body that can float on air." Leaving other terms undefined, she writes that the ballet school's use of body type as a standard "flies in the face of American ideals" (paragraph 4). Exactly *which* ideals she leaves for the reader to define: They might include fair play, equality of access, or the belief that decisions ought to be based on talent, not appearance. The reader cannot be sure. When she reports that a spokeswoman for the school stated that "We are not a recreation department," Ryan assumes the reader will understand the reference. The mission of a recreation department is to give *all* participants equal access. In a youth recreation league, children of all abilities would get to play in a baseball game. In a league for elite athletes, in which winning was a priority, coaches would permit only the most talented children to play.

When writing a paper, you will need to decide, like Ryan, which terms to define and which you can assume the reader will define in the same way you do. As the writer of a critique, you should identify and discuss any undefined or ambiguous term that might give rise to confusion.

---

*Charles Murray, "The Coming White Underclass," *Wall Street Journal*, October 20, 1993.

Fair Use of Information   Information is used as evidence in support of arguments. When you encounter such evidence, ask yourself two questions: (1) "Is the information accurate and up to date?" At least a portion of an argument becomes invalid when the information used to support it is inaccurate or out of date. (2) "Has the author cited *representative* information?" The evidence used in an argument must be presented in a spirit of fair play. An author is less than ethical when he presents only evidence favoring his own views even though he is well aware that contrary evidence exists. For instance, it would be dishonest to argue that an economic recession is imminent and to cite only indicators of economic downturn while ignoring and failing to cite contrary (positive) evidence.

As you have seen, "We Are Not Created Equal in Every Way" is not an information-heavy essay. The success of the piece turns on the author's use of logic, not facts and figures. In this case, the reader has every reason to trust that Ryan has presented the facts accurately: An 8-year-old girl has been denied admission to a prestigious ballet school. The mother of the girl has sued the school.

Logical Argumentation: Avoiding Logical Fallacies

At some point, you will need to respond to the logic of the argument itself. To be convincing, an argument should be governed by principles of *logic*—clear and orderly thinking. This does *not* mean that an argument should not be biased. A biased argument—that is, an argument weighted toward one point of view and against others, which is in fact the nature of argument—may be valid as long as it is logically sound.

Let's examine several types of faulty thinking and logical fallacies you will need to watch for.

Emotionally Loaded Terms   Writers sometimes attempt to sway readers by using emotionally charged words. Words with positive connotations (e.g., "family values") are intended to sway readers to the author's point of view; words with negative connotations (e.g., "paying the price") try to sway readers away from an opposing point of view. The fact that an author uses emotionally loaded terms does not necessarily invalidate an argument. Emotional appeals are perfectly legitimate and time-honored modes of persuasion. But in academic writing, which is grounded in logical argumentation, they should not be the *only* means of persuasion. You should be sensitive to *how* emotionally loaded terms are being used. In particular, are they being used deceptively or to hide the essential facts?

Ryan appeals to our desire to protect children in "We Are Not Created Equal in Every Way." She writes of "disturbing issue[s]," lack of a "safety net" for young people on the star track to elite performance, and an absence of adults "watch[ing] out for [the children's] best interests." Ryan understands that no reader wants to see a child abused; and while she does not use the word *abuse* in her essay, she implies that parents who push young children too hard to succeed commit abuse. That implication is enough to engage the sympathies of the reader. As someone evaluating the essay, you should be alert to this appeal to your emotions and then judge whether or not the appeal is fair and convincing. Above all, you should not let an emotional appeal blind you to shortcomings of logic, ambiguously defined terms, or a misuse of facts.

Ad Hominem **Argument**   In an *ad hominem* argument, the writer rejects opposing views by attacking the person who holds them. By calling opponents names, an author avoids the issue. Consider this excerpt from a political speech:

> I could more easily accept my opponent's plan to increase revenues by collecting on delinquent tax bills if he had paid more than a hundred dollars in state taxes in each of the past three years. But the fact is, he's a millionaire with a millionaire's tax shelters. This man hasn't paid a wooden nickel for the state services he and his family depend on. So I ask you: Is *he* the one to be talking about taxes to *us?*

It could well be that the opponent has paid virtually no state taxes for three years; but this fact has nothing to do with, and is used as a ploy to divert attention from, the merits of a specific proposal for increasing revenues. The proposal is lost in the attack against the man himself, an attack that violates principles of logic. Writers (and speakers) should make their points by citing evidence in support of their views and by challenging contrary evidence.

Does Ryan attack Fredrika Keefer's mother in this essay? You be the judge. Here are lines referring directly or indirectly to Krissy Keefer. Is Ryan criticizing the mother, directly or indirectly? Cite specific words and phrases to support your conclusion.

> Fredrika and her mother filed suit because, as her mother puts it, she "did not have the right body type to be accepted" by the San Francisco Ballet School. "My daughter is very sophisticated, so she understands why we're doing this," Krissy Keefer said. "And the other kids think she's a celebrity."
>
> There is no question Keefer raises a powerful point in her complaint.
>
> Keefer said she would drop her lawsuit if the school accepted her daughter. The San Francisco Ballet School offers the best training in the Bay Area, she said. Fredrika, however, has said she is quite happy dancing where she is. Still, the mother gets to decide what's best for her daughter's dancing career. The child is clearly too young to make such a decision. Yet, in the skewed logic of elite athletics and dancing, she is not too young to pay the price for it.

Faulty Cause and Effect   The fact that one event precedes another in time does not mean that the first event has caused the second. An example: Fish begin dying by the thousands in a lake near your hometown. An environmental

TONE

Tone refers to the overall emotional effect produced by a writer's choice of language. Writers might use especially emphatic words to create a tone: A film reviewer might refer to a "magnificent performance," or a columnist might criticize "sleazeball politics."

These are extreme examples of tone; but tone can be more subtle, particularly if the writer makes a special effort *not* to inject emotion into the writing. As we indicated in the section on emotionally loaded terms, the fact that a writer's tone is highly emotional does not necessarily mean that the writer's argument is invalid. Conversely, a neutral tone does not ensure an argument's validity.

Many instructors discourage student writing that projects a highly emotional tone, considering it inappropriate for academic or preprofessional work. (One sure sign of emotion: the exclamation mark, which should be used sparingly.)

group immediately cites chemical dumping by several manufacturing plants as the cause. But other causes are possible: A disease might have affected the fish, the growth of algae might have contributed to the deaths, or acid rain might be a factor. The origins of an event are usually complex and are not always traceable to a single cause. So you must carefully examine cause-and-effect reasoning when you find a writer using it. In Latin, this fallacy is known as *post hoc, ergo propter hoc* ("after this, therefore because of this").

The debate over the San Francisco Ballet School's refusal to admit Fredrika Keefer involves a question of cause and effect. Fredrika Keefer's rejection by the ballet school was caused by the school's insistence that its students have an "ethereal, elongated body." If the school changes that standard, the outcome could change: Fredrika Keefer might be admitted.

Ryan also uses cause-and-effect logic in her essay to suggest that Fredrika Keefer's mother, and by extension all parent managers, can cause their children harm by pushing them too hard in their training. At the end of the essay, Ryan writes that Fredrika is too young "to decide what's best for her...dancing career" but that "she is not too young to pay the price for" the decisions her mother makes to promote that career. The "price" Fredrika pays will be "caused" by her mother's (poor) decisions.

Either/Or Reasoning   Either/or reasoning also results from an unwillingness to recognize complexity. If in analyzing a problem an author artificially restricts the range of possible solutions by offering only two courses of action, and then rejects the one that he opposes, he cannot logically argue that the remaining course of action, which he favors, is therefore the only one that makes sense. Usually, several other options (at least) are possible. For whatever reason, the author has chosen to overlook them. As an example, suppose you are reading a selection on genetic engineering in which the author builds an argument on the basis of the following:

> Research in gene splicing is at a crossroads: Either scientists will be carefully monitored by civil authorities and their efforts limited to acceptable applications, such as disease control; or, lacking regulatory guidelines, scientists will set their own ethical standards and begin programs in embryonic manipulation that, however well intended, exceed the proper limits of human knowledge.

Certainly other possibilities for genetic engineering exist beyond the two mentioned here. But the author limits debate by establishing an either/or choice. Such a limitation is artificial and does not allow for complexity. As a critical reader, you need to be on the alert for either/or reasoning.

Hasty Generalization   Writers are guilty of hasty generalization when they draw their conclusions from too little evidence or from unrepresentative evidence. To argue that scientists should not proceed with the human genome project because a recent editorial urged that the project be abandoned is to make a hasty generalization. That lone editorial may be unrepresentative of the views of most individuals—both scientists and laypeople—who have studied and written about the matter. To argue that one should never obey authority because Stanley Milgram's Yale University experiments in the 1960s showed the dangers of obedience is to ignore the fact that Milgram's experiments were concerned primarily with obedience to *immoral* authority. Thus, the experimental situation was unrepresentative of most routine demands for obedience—for example, to obey a parental rule or to comply with a summons for jury duty—and a conclusion about the malevolence of all authority would be a hasty generalization.

False Analogy   Comparing one person, event, or issue to another may be illuminating, but it can also be confusing or misleading. Differences between the two may be more significant than their similarities, and conclusions drawn from one may not necessarily apply to the other. A writer who argues that it is reasonable to quarantine people with AIDS because quarantine has been effective in preventing the spread of smallpox is assuming an analogy between AIDS and smallpox that is not valid (because of the differences in transmission between the two diseases).

Ryan compares the San Francisco Ballet School's setting an admissions standard to both a university's and a modeling school's setting standards. Are the analogies apt? Certainly one can draw a parallel between the standards used by the ballet school and those of a modeling school: Both emphasize a candidate's appearance, among other qualities. Are the admissions standards of a university based on appearance? In principle, no. At least that's not a criterion any college admissions office would post on its Web site. A critical reader might therefore want to object that one of Ryan's analogies is faulty.

Ryan attempts to advance her argument by making another comparison:

> [The rejection of a candidate because she does not have a body suited to classical ballet] doesn't mean that women with different body types cannot become professional dancers. They just have to find a different type of dance—jazz, tap, modern—just as athletes have to find sports that fit certain body types. A tall, blocky man, for example, could not be a jockey but he could play baseball.

The words "just as" signal an attempt to advance the argument by making an analogy. What do you think? Is the analogy sufficiently similar to Fredrika Keefer's situation to persuade you?

Begging the Question   To beg the question is to assume as proven fact the very thesis being argued. To assert, for example, that America is not in decline because it is as strong and prosperous as ever does not prove anything: It merely repeats the claim in different words. This fallacy is also known as *circular reasoning.*

When Ryan writes that "There is no safety net for [children placed into elite training programs], no arm of government that makes sure that the adults in their lives watch out for their best interests," she assumes that there should be such a safety net. But, as you will read in the model critique, this is a point that must be argued, not assumed. Is such intervention wise? Under what circumstances would authorities intervene in a family? Would authorities have the legal standing to get involved if there were no clear evidence of physical abuse? Ryan is not necessarily wrong in desiring "safety nets" for young, elite athletes and dancers, but she assumes a point that she should be arguing.

Non Sequitur   *Non sequitur* is Latin for "it does not follow"; the term is used to describe a conclusion that does not logically follow from a premise. "Because minorities have made such great strides in the past few decades," a writer may argue, "we no longer need affirmative action programs." Aside from the fact that the premise itself is arguable (*have* minorities made such great strides?), it does not follow that because minorities *may* have made great strides, there is no further need for affirmative action programs.

Oversimplification   Be alert for writers who offer easy solutions to complicated problems. "America's economy will be strong again if we all 'buy American,'"

Exercise 2.3

Understanding Logical Fallacies

Make a list of the nine logical fallacies discussed in the preceding section. Briefly define each one in your own words. Then, in a group of three or four classmates, review your definitions and the examples we've provided for each logical fallacy. Collaborate with your group to find or invent examples for each of the fallacies. Compare your examples with those generated by the other groups in your class.

a politician may argue. But the problems of America's economy are complex and cannot be solved by a slogan or a simple change in buying habits. Likewise, a writer who argues that we should ban genetic engineering assumes that simple solutions ("just say no") will be sufficient to deal with the complex moral dilemmas raised by this new technology.

Writing to Entertain

Authors write not only to inform and persuade but also to entertain. One response to entertainment is a hearty laugh, but it is possible to entertain without encouraging laughter: A good book or play or poem may prompt you to reflect, grow wistful, become elated, or get angry. Laughter is only one of many possible reactions. Like a response to an informative piece or an argument, your response to an essay, poem, story, play, novel, or film should be precisely stated and carefully developed. Ask yourself some of the following questions (you won't have space to explore all of them, but try to consider the most important): Did I care for the portrayal of a certain character? Did that character (or a group of characters united by occupation, age, ethnicity, etc.) seem overly sentimental, for example, or heroic? Did his adversaries seem too villainous or stupid? Were the situations believable? Was the action interesting or merely formulaic? Was the theme developed subtly or powerfully, or did the work come across as preachy or shrill? Did the action at the end of the work follow plausibly from what had come before? Was the language fresh and incisive or stale and predictable? Explain as specifically as possible what elements of the work seemed effective or ineffective and why. Offer an overall assessment, elaborating on your views.

Question 2: To What Extent Do You Agree with the Author?

When formulating a critical response to a source, try to distinguish your evaluation of the author's purpose and success at achieving that purpose from your own agreement or disagreement with the author's views. The distinction allows you to respond to a piece of writing on its merits. As an unbiased, evenhanded critic, you evaluate an author's clarity of presentation, use of evidence, and adherence to principles of logic. To what extent has the author succeeded in achieving his or her purpose? Still withholding judgment, offer your assessment and give the author (in effect) a grade. Significantly, your assessment of the presentation may not coincide with your views of the author's conclusions: You may agree with an author entirely but feel that the presentation is superficial; you may find the author's logic and use of evidence to be rock solid but at the same time you may resist certain conclusions. A critical evaluation works well when it is conducted in two parts. After evaluating the author's purpose and design for achieving that purpose, respond to the author's main assertions. In doing so, you'll want to identify points of agreement and disagreement and also evaluate assumptions.

Identify Points of Agreement and Disagreement

Be precise in identifying where you agree and disagree with an author. You should state as clearly as possible what *you* believe, and an effective way of doing this is to define your position in relation to that presented in the piece. Whether you agree enthusiastically, agree with reservations, or disagree, you can organize your reactions in two parts: (1) summarize the author's position, and (2) state your own position and elaborate on your reasons for holding it. The elaboration, in effect, becomes an argument itself, and this is true regardless of the position you take. An opinion is effective when you support it by supplying evidence from your reading (which should be properly cited), your observation, or your personal experience. Without such evidence, opinions cannot be authoritative. "I thought the article on inflation was lousy." Or: "It was terrific." Why? "I just thought so, that's all." This opinion is worthless because the criticism is imprecise: The critic has taken neither the time to read the article carefully nor the time to explore his or her own reactions carefully.

Exercise 2.4

Exploring Your Viewpoints—in Three Paragraphs

Go to a Web site that presents short persuasive essays on current social issues, such as reason.com, drudgereport.com, or Speakout.com. Or go to an Internet search engine and type in a social issue together with the word "articles," "editorials," or "opinion," and see what you find. Locate a selection on a topic of interest that takes a clear, argumentative position. Print out the selection on which you choose to focus. Write one paragraph summarizing the author's key argument. Write two paragraphs articulating your agreement or disagreement with the author. (Devote each paragraph to a *single* point of agreement or disagreement.) Be sure to explain why you think or feel the way you do and, wherever possible, cite relevant evidence—from your reading, experience, or observation.

Explore the Reasons for Agreement and Disagreement: Evaluate Assumptions

One way of elaborating your reactions to a reading is to explore the underlying *reasons* for agreement and disagreement. Your reactions are based largely on assumptions that you hold and how those assumptions compare with the author's. An *assumption* is a fundamental statement about the world and its operations that you take to be true. A writer's assumptions may be explicitly stated; but just as often, assumptions are implicit and you can only infer them.

Assumptions provide the foundation on which entire presentations are built. When you find an author's assumptions invalid—that is, not supported by factual evidence—or if you disagree with value-based assumptions underlying an author's position, you may well disagree with the conclusions that follow from these assumptions. Alternatively, if you find that your own assumptions are contradicted by actual experience, you may be forced to conclude that your premises were mistaken.

An interesting example of an assumption fatally colliding with reality was revealed during a recent congressional investigation into the financial meltdown of late 2008 precipitated by the collapse of the home mortgage market—itself precipitated, many believed, by an insufficiently regulated banking and financial system run amuck. During his testimony before the House Oversight Committee in October of that year, former Federal Reserve chairman Alan Greenspan was grilled by committee chairman Henry Waxman (D-CA) about his "ideology"—essentially an assumption or set of assumptions raised to the level of a governing principle.

Greenspan responded, "I do have an ideology. My judgment is that free, competitive markets are by far the unrivaled way to organize economies. We have tried regulation; none meaningfully worked." Greenspan defined an ideology as "a conceptual framework [for] the way people deal with reality. Everyone has one. You have to. To exist, you need an ideology." And he pointed out that the assumptions on which he and the Federal Reserve operated were supported by "the best banking lawyers in the business . . . and an outside counsel of expert professionals to advise on regulatory matters."

Greenspan then admitted that, in light of the economic disaster engulfing the nation, he had found a "flaw" in his ideology. The testimony continues:

Chairman Waxman: You found a flaw?

Mr. Greenspan: I found a flaw in the model that I perceived is the critical functioning structure that defines how the world works, so to speak.

Chairman Waxman: In other words, you found that your view of the world, your ideology, was not right, it was not working.

Mr. Greenspan: Precisely. That's precisely the reason I was shocked, because I had been going for 40 years or more with very considerable evidence that it was working exceptionally well.*

The lesson? All the research, expertise, and logical argumentation in the world will fail if the premise (assumption, ideology) on which it is based turns out to be "flawed."

How do you determine the validity of assumptions once you have identified them? In the absence of more scientific criteria, you may determine validity by how well the author's assumptions stack up against your own experience, observations, reading, and values. A caution, however: The overall value of an article or book may depend only to a small

---

United States. Cong. House Committee on Oversight and Government Reform. *The Financial Crisis and the Role of Federal Regulators.* 110th Cong., 2nd sess. Washington: GPO, 2008.

degree on the validity of the author's assumptions. For instance, a sociologist may do a fine job of gathering statistical data on the incidence
of crime in urban areas along the eastern seaboard. The sociologist might
also be a Marxist, and you may disagree with the subsequent analysis
of the data. Yet you may still find the data extremely valuable for your
own work.

Readers will want to examine two assumptions at the heart of Ryan's
essay on Fredrika Keefer and the San Francisco Ballet School's refusal to
admit her. First, Ryan assumes that setting a standard for admission based
on a candidate's appearance is equivalent to setting a standard based on a
candidate's "mental prowess," the admissions standard (presumably) used
by universities. An appearance-based standard, Ryan writes, will "weed
out those who are less likely to succeed" in professional ballet. The writer
of the critique that follows agrees with Ryan's assumption. But you may
not. You may assume, by contrast, that standards based on appearance are
arbitrary while those based on intellectual ability rest on documented talent
(SAT scores or high school transcripts, for instance). Ryan makes a second
assumption: that there are appropriate and inappropriate ways to raise children. She does not state the ways explicitly, but that does not keep her from
using them to judge Krissy Keefer harshly. You may disagree with her and
find a reason to cheer Krissy Keefer's defense of her daughter's rights.
That's your decision. What you must do as a critical reader is recognize
assumptions whether they are stated or not. You should spell them out and
then accept or reject them. Ultimately, your agreement or disagreement
with an author will rest on your agreement or disagreement with the
author's assumptions.

CRITIQUE

In Chapter 1 we focused on summary—the condensed presentation of ideas
from another source. Summary is key to much of academic writing because
it relies so heavily on the works of others for the support of claims. It's not
going too far to say that summarizing is the critical thinking skill from
which a majority of academic writing builds. However, most academic
thinking and writing do not stop at summary; usually we use summary to
restate our understanding of things we see or read. Then we put that summary to use. In academic writing, one typical use of summary is as a prelude
to critique.

A *critique* is a *formalized, critical reading of a passage*. It is also a personal
response, but writing a critique is considerably more rigorous than saying
that a movie is "great," or a book is "fascinating," or "I didn't like it." These
are all responses, and, as such, they're a valid, even essential, part of your
understanding of what you see and read. But such responses don't illuminate the subject—even for you—if you haven't explained how you arrive
at your conclusions.

GUIDELINES FOR WRITING CRITIQUES

- *Introduce.* Introduce both the passage under analysis and the author. State the author's main argument and the point(s) you intend to make about it.

  Provide background material to help your readers understand the relevance or appeal of the passage. This background material might include one or more of the following: an explanation of why the subject is of current interest; a reference to a possible controversy surrounding the subject of the passage or the passage itself; biographical information about the author; an account of the circumstances under which the passage was written; a reference to the intended audience of the passage.

- *Summarize.* Summarize the author's main points, making sure to state the author's purpose for writing.

- *Assess the presentation.* Evaluate the validity of the author's presentation, as distinct from your points of agreement or disagreement. Comment on the author's success in achieving his or her purpose by reviewing three or four specific points. You might base your review on one or more of the following criteria:

  Is the information accurate?

  Is the information significant?

  Has the author defined terms clearly?

  Has the author used and interpreted information fairly?

  Has the author argued logically?

- *Respond to the presentation.* Now it is your turn to respond to the author's views. With which views do you agree? With which do you disagree? Discuss your reasons for agreement and disagreement, when possible tying these reasons to assumptions—both the author's and your own. Where necessary, draw on outside sources to support your ideas.

- *Conclude.* State your conclusions about the overall validity of the piece—your assessment of the author's success at achieving his or her aims and your reactions to the author's views. Remind the reader of the weaknesses and strengths of the passage.

Your task in writing a critique is to turn your critical reading of a passage into a systematic evaluation in order to deepen your reader's (and your own) understanding of that passage. Among other things, you're interested in determining what an author says, how well the points are made, what assumptions underlie the argument, what issues are overlooked, and what implications can be drawn from such an analysis. Critiques, positive or negative, should include a fair and accurate summary of the passage; they may draw on and cite information and ideas from other sources (your reading or your personal experience and observations); and they should also include a statement of your own assumptions. It is important to remember that you bring to bear an entire set of assumptions about the world. Stated or not, these assumptions underlie every evaluative comment you make; you therefore have an obligation, both to the reader and to yourself, to clarify your standards by making your assumptions explicit. Not only do your readers stand to gain by your forthrightness, but so do you. In the process of writing a critical assessment, you are forced to examine your own knowledge, beliefs, and assumptions. Ultimately, the critique is a way of learning about yourself—yet another example of the ways in which writing is useful as a tool for critical thinking.

How to Write Critiques

You may find it useful to organize a critique into five sections: introduction, summary, assessment of the presentation (on its own terms), your response to the presentation, and conclusion.

The box on p. 43 offers guidelines for writing critiques. They do not constitute a rigid formula. Thousands of authors write critiques that do not follow the structure outlined here. Until you are more confident and practiced in writing critiques, however, we suggest you follow these guidelines. They are meant not to restrict you but rather to provide a workable sequence for writing critiques.

DEMONSTRATION: CRITIQUE

The critique that follows is based on Joan Ryan's op-ed piece "We Are Not Created Equal in Every Way" (pp. 31–32), which we have already begun to examine. In this formal critique, you will see that it is possible to agree with an author's main point, at least provisionally, yet disagree with other elements of the argument. Critiquing a different selection, you could just as easily accept the author's facts and figures but reject the conclusion he draws from them. As long as you carefully articulate the author's assumptions and your own, explaining in some detail your agreement and disagreement, the critique is yours to take in whatever direction you see fit.

Let's summarize the preceding sections by returning to the core questions that guide critical reading. You will see how, when applied to Joan Ryan's argument, they help to set up a critique.

To What Extent Does the Author Succeed in His or Her Purpose?

To answer this question, you will need to know the author's purpose. Joan Ryan's "We Are Not Created Equal in Every Way" is an argument—actually, *two* related arguments. She wants readers to accept her view that (1) a school of performing arts has the right to set admissions standards according to criteria it believes will ensure the professional success of its graduates, and (2) parents may damage their children by pushing them too hard to meet the standards set by these schools.

By supporting a ballet school's right to set admission standards based on appearance, Ryan supports the star system that produces our elite athletes and performers. At the same time, she disapproves of parents who risk their children's safety and welfare by pushing them through this system. Ryan both defends the system and attacks it. Her ambivalence on the issue keeps the argument from succeeding fully.

To What Extent Do You Agree with the Author? Evaluate Assumptions

Ryan's views on the debate surrounding Fredrika Keefer's rejection by the San Francisco School of Ballet rest on the assumption that the school has the right to set its own admissions standards—even if we find those standards harsh. All private institutions, she claims, have that right. The writer of the critique that follows agrees with Ryan, although we have seen how it is possible to disagree.

Ryan's second argument concerns the wisdom of subjecting an 8-year-old to the rigors of professional training. Ryan disapproves. The writer of the critique, while sympathetic to Ryan's concerns, states that as a practical and even as a legal matter it would be nearly impossible to prevent parents such as Krissy Keefer from doing exactly as they please in the name of helping their children. In our culture, parents have the right (short of outright abuse) to raise children however they see fit.

Finally, the writer of the critique notes a certain ambivalence in Ryan's essay: her support of the ballet school's admission standards on the one hand and her distaste for parent managers like Krissy Keefer on the other. The writer does not find evidence of a weak argument in Ryan's mixed message but rather a sign of confusion in the broader culture: We love our young stars, but we condemn parents for pushing children to the breaking point in the name of stardom.

The selections you are likely to critique will be those, like Ryan's, that argue a specific position. Indeed, every argument you read is an invitation to agree or disagree. It remains only for you to speak up and justify your position.

MODEL CRITIQUE

Eric Ralston

Professor Reilly

Writing 2

11 January 2008

A Critique of "We Are Not Created Equal

in Every Way" by Joan Ryan

(1)   Most freshmen know how it feels to apply to a school and be rejected. Each year, college admissions offices mail thousands of thin letters that begin: "Thank you for your application. The competition this year was unusually strong. . . ." We know that we will not get into every college on our list or pass every test or win the starring role after every audition, but we believe that we deserve the chance to try. And we can tolerate rejection if we know that we compete on a level playing field. But when that field seems to arbitrarily favor some candidates over others, we take offense. At least that's when an ambitious mother took offense, bringing to court a suit that claimed her eight-year-old daughter, Fredrika Keefer, was denied admission to the prestigious San Francisco Ballet School because she had the wrong "body type" (A29).

(2)   In an opinion piece for the *San Francisco Chronicle* (12 December 2000), Joan Ryan asks: "Does [a ballet school] have the right to give preference to leaner body types?" Her answer is a firm yes. Ryan argues that institutions have the right to set whatever standards they want to ensure that those they admit meet the physical or intellectual requirements for professional success. But she also believes that some parents push their children too hard to meet those standards. Ryan offers a questionable approach to protecting children from the possible abuses of such parents. Overall, however, she raises timely issues in discussing the star system that produces our world-class athletes and performers. The sometimes conflicting concerns she expresses reflect contradictions and tensions in our larger culture.

(3)   The issue Ryan discusses is a particularly sensitive one because the child's mother charged the ballet school with discrimination. As a society

Ralston 2

we have made great strides over the past few decades in combating some
of the more blatant forms of discrimination—racial, ethnic, and sexual.
But is it possible, is it desirable, to eliminate *all* efforts to distinguish one
person from another? When is a standard that permits some (but not all)
people entry to an institution discriminatory and when is it a necessary
part of doing business? Ryan believes that schools discriminate all the
time, and rightly so when candidates for admission fail to meet the stated
criteria for academic or professional success. That UC Berkeley does not
accept every applicant is *discriminating,* not discriminatory. Ryan
recognizes the difference.

She maintains, correctly, that the San Francisco Ballet School, like
any other private institution, has the right to set standards by which it
will accept or reject applicants. Rejection is a part of life, she writes,
expressing the view that gives her essay its title: "We Are Not Created
Equal in Every Way." And because we are not created equal, not everyone
will be admitted to his or her number one school or get a turn on stage.
That's the inevitable consequence of setting standards: Some people
will meet them and gain admission, others won't. Ryan quotes the
spokesperson who explained that the San Francisco Ballet School is
"'not a recreation department'" (A29). In other words, a professional
ballet school, like a university, is within its rights to reject applicants
with body types unsuited to its view of success in professional ballet.
The standard may be cruel and to some even arbitrary, but it is
understandable. To put the matter bluntly, candidates with unsuitable
body types, however talented or otherwise attractive, are less likely to
succeed in professional ballet than those with "classical" proportions.
Female dancers, for example, must regularly be lifted and carried, as if
effortlessly, by their male counterparts—a feat that is difficult enough
even with "leaner body types." Ryan points out that candidates without
the ideal body type for ballet are not barred from professional dance:
"[t]hey just have to find a different type of dance . . . just as athletes
have to find sports that fit certain body types" (A29).

④

Ralston 3

⑤   The San Francisco Ballet School is *not* saying that people of a certain skin color or religious belief are not welcome. That *would* be discriminatory and wrong. But the standard concerning body type cuts across *all* people, rich or poor, black or white, Protestant or Jew, male or female. Such a broad standard could be termed an equal opportunity standard: If it can be used to distinguish among all people equally, it is discriminating, not discriminatory.

⑥   Ryan's parallel concern in this essay is the damage done to children by parents who push them at an early age to meet the high standards set by professional training programs. Children placed onto such star tracks attend special schools (or receive home schooling) in order to accommodate intense training schedules that sometimes lead to physical or psychological injuries. In healthy families, we might expect parents to protect children from such dangers. But parents who manage what they view as their children's "careers" may be too single-minded to realize that their actions may place Johnny and Susie at risk.

⑦   Ryan disapproves of a star track system that puts children into professional training at a young age. In pursuing a career in dance, for instance, a young "child has thrown all her eggs into this one little basket at an age when most kids can barely decide what to wear to school in the morning" (A29). The law makes no provision for protecting such elite performers in training, writes Ryan: "There is no safety net for them, no arm of government that makes sure that the adults in their lives watch out for their best interests" (A29).

⑧   Like the rest of us, Ryan assumes there are appropriate and less appropriate ways to raise children. While she does not explicitly share her preferred approach, she uses language effectively (both her own and her subjects') to suggest what does not work: pushing an otherwise "quite happy" eight-year-old who "relishes" dancing into professional ballet school. Ryan is subtle enough not to attack Krissy Keefer directly, instead letting the mother undermine herself with a comment few could take seriously: "My daughter is very sophisticated, so she understands why we're [bringing a lawsuit]." No eight-year-old could fully understand the motivations behind a lawsuit, and the statement suggests a mother pursuing her own—not her daughter's—agenda. Ryan suggests that Krissy Keefer has succumbed to "the skewed logic of elite athletics and dancing" that has damaged too many young people. When Ryan points out that "no arm of government" looks out for children like Frederika, she implies the need for a Department of Youth Services to supervise parent managers. This is not a good idea.

There is no sure way to tell when a parent's managing of a child's dance or athletic schedule is abusive or constructive. Intense dedication is necessary for would-be elite athletes and performers to succeed, and such dedication often begins in childhood. Since young children are not equipped to organize their lives in pursuit of a single goal, parents step in to help. That's what the parents of Tiger Woods did on recognizing his talents:

> [H]is father . . . [started] him very early. . . . [Tiger] was
> on the Mike Douglas show hitting golf balls when he was
> three years old. I mean, this is a prodigy type thing. This
> is like Mozart writing his first symphony when he was six,
> that sort of thing, and he did show unique ability right
> from the beginning. And his life has been channeled into
> being a pro. His father has devoted his life to bringing
> him to this point. His father hasn't worked full-time
> since 1988. That's what it's been all about. (Feinstein)

Ryan would point out, correctly, that for every Tiger Woods or Michelle Kwan there are many child-athletes and performing artists who fall short of their goals. They may later regret the single-minded focus that robbed them of their childhood, but there is no way to know before committing a child to years of dedicated practice whether he or she will become the next Tiger or an embittered also-ran. We simply do not have the wisdom to intervene in a parent manager's training program for her child. And Joan Ryan is not going to find an "arm of government" to intervene in the child rearing of Fredrika Keefer, however much she may "pay the price for" (A29) her mother's enthusiasm.

The tension in Ryan's essay over high standards and the intense preparation to meet them mirrors a tension in the larger culture. On the one hand, Ryan argues persuasively that elite institutions like the San Francisco Ballet School have the right to set standards for admission. At such institutions, high standards give us high levels of achievement— dancers, for instance, who "can float on air" (A29). We cheer brilliant performers like Tiger Woods and Michelle Kwan who started on their roads to success while still children. The star system produces stars. On the other hand, Ryan condemns parents who buy into the star system by pushing their children into professional training programs that demand a single-minded focus. We are horrified to learn that Macaulay Culkin of the *Home Alone* movies never really had a childhood (Peterson). Of course Culkin and others like him didn't have childhoods: They were too busy practicing their lines or their jumps and spins. If Ryan defends high standards in one breath and criticizes parents in the next for pushing children to achieve these standards, she is only reflecting a confusion in the larger culture: We love our stars, but we cannot have our stars without a star system that demands total (and often damaging) dedication from our youngest and most vulnerable citizens. That parents can be the agent of this damage is especially troubling.

12   Joan Ryan is right to focus on the parents of would-be stars, and she is right to remind us that young children pressured to perform at the highest levels can suffer physically and psychologically. Perhaps it was better for Fredrika Keefer the child (as opposed to Fredrika Keefer the future professional dancer) that she was not admitted to the San Francisco School of Ballet. For Keefer's sake and that of other child performers, we should pay attention to the dangers of the star system and support these children when we can. But without clear evidence of legally actionable neglect or abuse, we cannot interfere with parent managers, however much we may disagree with their decisions. We may be legitimately concerned, as is Ryan, that such a parent is driving her child to become not the next Tiger Woods but the next admission to a psychiatric ward. In a free society, for better or for worse, parents have the right to guide (or misguide) the lives of their children. All the rest of us can do is watch—and hope for the best.

Ralston 6

Works Cited

Feinstein, John. "Year of the Tiger." Interview by Jim Lehrer. *Online News Hour.* PBS, 14 Apr. 1997. Web. 8 Jan. 2008.

Peterson, Paul. Interview by Gary James. *ClassicBands.com.* Classic Bands, 12 Feb. 2000. Web. 8 Jan. 2008. <http://www.classicbands.com/paulPetersonInterview.html>.

Ryan, Joan. "We Are Not Created Equal in Every Way." *San Francisco Chronicle* 12 Dec. 2000: A29. Print.

Exercise 2.5

Informal Critique of the Model Critique

Before reading our analysis of this model critique, write your own informal response to the critique. What are its strengths and weaknesses? To what extent does the critique follow the general Guidelines for Writing Critiques that we outlined on p. 43? To the extent it varies from the guidelines, speculate on why. Jot down ideas for a critique that takes a different approach to Ryan's essay.

CRITICAL READING FOR CRITIQUE

- *Use the tips from Critical Reading for Summary on p. 6.* Remember to examine the context; note the title and subtitle; identify the main point; identify the subpoints; break the reading into sections; distinguish between points, examples, and counterarguments; watch for transitions within and between paragraphs; and read actively.
- *Establish the writer's primary purpose in writing.* Is the piece meant primarily to inform, persuade, or entertain?
- *Evaluate informative writing. Use these criteria (among others):*
    Accuracy of information
    Significance of information
    Fair interpretation of information
- *Evaluate persuasive writing. Use these criteria (among others):*
    Clear definition of terms
    Fair use and interpretation of information
    Logical reasoning

(continued)

- *Evaluate writing that entertains. Use these criteria (among others):*
  Interesting characters
  Believable action, plot, and situations
  Communication of theme
  Use of language
- *Decide whether you agree or disagree with the writer's ideas, position, or message.* Once you have determined the extent to which an author has achieved his or her purpose, clarify your position in relation to the writer's.

The Strategy of the Critique

- Paragraph 1 of the model critique introduces the issue to be reviewed. It provides brief background information and sets a general context that explains why the topic of fair (and unfair) competition is important.

- Paragraph 2 introduces the author and the essay and summarizes the author's main claims. The paragraph ends (see the final three sentences) with the writer's overall assessment of the essay.

- Paragraph 3 sets a specific context for evaluating Ryan's first claim concerning admissions standards. The writer summarizes Ryan's position by making a distinction between the terms *discriminating* and *discriminatory*.

- Paragraph 4 evaluates Ryan's first claim, that the ballet school has the right to set admission standards. The writer supports Ryan's position.

- Paragraph 5 continues the evaluation of Ryan's first claim. Again, the writer of the critique supports Ryan, returning to the distinction between *discriminating* and *discriminatory*.

- Paragraphs 6–7 summarize Ryan's second claim, that parents can damage their children by pushing them too hard through professional training programs at too early an age.

- Paragraphs 8–10 evaluate Ryan's second claim. In paragraph 8 the writer states that Ryan makes a mistake in implying that a government agency should safeguard the interests of children like Fredrika Keefer. Paragraphs 9–10 present the logic for disagreeing with Ryan on this point.

- Paragraph 11 evaluates the essay as a whole. Ryan defends the right of schools in the star system to set high standards but objects when parents push young children into this system. This "tension" in the essay reflects a confusion in the larger culture.

- Paragraph 12 concludes the critique. The writer offers qualified support of Ryan's position, agreeing that children caught in the star system can suffer. The writer also states that there is not much we can do about the problem except watch and hope for the best.

Chapter 3

Synthesis

WHAT IS A SYNTHESIS?

A *synthesis* is a written discussion that draws on two or more sources. It follows that your ability to write syntheses depends on your ability to infer relationships among sources—essays, articles, fiction, and also nonwritten sources such as lectures, interviews, visual media, and observations. This process is nothing new for you because you infer relationships all the time—say, between something you've read in the newspaper and something you've seen for yourself, or between the teaching styles of your favorite and least favorite instructors. In fact, if you've written research papers, you've already written syntheses. In a *synthesis*, you make explicit the relationships that you have inferred among separate sources.

The skills you've already learned and practiced in the previous chapters will be vital in writing syntheses. Before you're in a position to draw relationships between two or more sources, you must understand what those sources say; you must be able to *summarize* those sources. Readers will frequently benefit from at least partial summaries of sources in your synthesis essays. At the same time, you must go beyond summary to make judgments— judgments based on your *critical reading* of your sources: what conclusions you've drawn about the quality and validity of these sources, whether you agree or disagree with the points made in your sources, and why you agree or disagree.

In a synthesis, you go beyond the critique of individual sources to determine the relationships among them. Is the information in source B, for example, an extended illustration of the generalizations in source A? Would it be useful to compare and contrast source C with source B? Having read and considered sources A, B, and C, can you infer something else—in other words, D (not a source but your own idea)?

Because a synthesis is based on two or more sources, you will need to be selective when choosing information from each. It would be neither possible nor desirable, for instance, to discuss in a ten-page paper on the American Civil War every point that the authors of two books make about their subject. What you as a writer must do is select from each source the ideas and information that best allow you to achieve your purpose.

PURPOSE

Your purpose in reading source materials and then drawing on them to write your own material is often reflected in the wording of an assignment. For instance, consider the following assignments on the Civil War:

> *American History:* Evaluate the author's treatment of the origins of the Civil War.

> *Economics:* Argue the following proposition, in light of your readings: "The Civil War was fought not for reasons of moral principle but for reasons of economic necessity."

WHERE DO WE FIND WRITTEN SYNTHESES?

Here are just a few of the types of writing that involve synthesis:

Academic Writing

- **Analysis papers** synthesize and apply several related theoretical approaches.
- **Research papers** synthesize multiple sources.
- **Argument papers** synthesize different points into a coherent claim or position.
- **Essay exams** demonstrate understanding of course material through comparing and contrasting theories, viewpoints, or approaches in a particular field.

Workplace Writing

- **Newspaper and magazine articles** synthesize primary and secondary sources.
- **Position papers and policy briefs** compare and contrast solutions for solving problems.
- **Business plans** synthesize ideas and proposals into one coherent plan.
- **Memos and letters** synthesize multiple ideas, events, and proposals into concise form.
- **Web sites** synthesize information from various sources to present it in Web pages and related links.

Government: Prepare a report on the effects of the Civil War on Southern politics at the state level between 1870 and 1917.

Mass Communications: Discuss how the use of photography during the Civil War may have affected the perceptions of the war by Northerners living in industrial cities.

Literature: Select two Southern writers of the twentieth century whose work you believe was influenced by the divisive effects of the Civil War. Discuss the ways this influence is apparent in a novel or a group of short stories written by each author. The works should not be *about* the Civil War.

Applied Technology: Compare and contrast the technology of warfare available in the 1860s with the technology available a century earlier.

Each of these assignments creates a particular purpose for writing. Having located sources relevant to your topic, you would select for possible use in a paper only the parts of those sources that helped you in fulfilling this purpose. And how you used those parts—how you related them to other material from other sources—would also depend on your purpose. For instance, if you were working on the government assignment, you might draw on the same source as a student working on the literature assignment by referring to Robert Penn Warren's novel *All the King's Men*, about Louisiana politics in the early part of the twentieth century. But because the purposes of the two assignments are different, you and the other student would make different uses of this source. The parts or aspects of the novel that you find worthy of detailed analysis might be mentioned only in passing—or not at all—by the other student.

USING YOUR SOURCES

Your purpose determines not only what parts of your sources you will use but also how you will relate them to one another. Because the very essence of synthesis is the combining of information and ideas, you must have some basis on which to combine them. *Some relationships among the material in your sources must make them worth synthesizing.* It follows that the better able you are to discover such relationships, the better able you will be to use your sources in writing syntheses. Notice that the mass communications assignment requires you to draw a *cause-and-effect* relationship between photographs of the war and Northerners' perceptions of the war. The applied technology assignment requires you to *compare and contrast* state-of-the-art weapons technology in the eighteenth and nineteenth centuries. The economics assignment requires you to *argue* a proposition. In each case, *your purpose will determine how you relate your source materials to one another.*

Consider some other examples. You may be asked on an exam question or in the instructions for a paper to *describe* two or three approaches to prison reform during the past decade. You may be asked to *compare and contrast* one country's approach to imprisonment with another's. You may be asked to *develop an argument* of your own on this subject, based on your reading. Sometimes (when you are not given a specific assignment) you determine your own purpose: You are interested in exploring a particular subject; you are interested in making a case for one approach or another. In any event, your purpose shapes your essay. Your purpose determines which sources you research, which ones you use, which parts of them you use, at which points in your paper you use them, and in what manner you relate them to one another.

TYPES OF SYNTHESES: EXPLANATORY AND ARGUMENT

In this chapter, we categorize syntheses into two main types: *explanatory* and *argument*. The easiest way to recognize the difference between the two types may be to consider the difference between a news article and an editorial on the same subject. For the most part, we'd say that the main purpose of the news article is to convey *information,* and the main purpose of the editorial is to convey *opinion* or *interpretation*. Of course, this distinction is much too simplified: News articles often convey opinion or bias, sometimes subtly, sometimes openly, and editorials often convey unbiased information along with opinion. But as a practical matter we can generally agree on the distinction between a news article that primarily conveys information and an editorial that primarily conveys opinion. You should be able to observe this distinction in the selections shown here as explanation and argument.

Explanation: News Article from the New York Times

PRIVATE GETS 3 YEARS FOR IRAQ PRISON ABUSE

By David S. Cloud
September 28, 2005

Pfc. Lynndie R. England, a 22-year-old clerk in the Army who was photographed with naked Iraqi detainees at Abu Ghraib prison, was sentenced on Tuesday to three years in prison and a dishonorable discharge for her role in the scandal.

After the sentence was announced, Private England hung her head and cried briefly before hugging her mother, one of the few signs of emotion she showed in the six-day trial.

She had been found guilty on Monday of one count of conspiracy to maltreat prisoners, four counts of maltreatment and one count of committing an indecent act.

She made no comment on Tuesday as she was led out of the courthouse in handcuffs and leg shackles.

Earlier in the day, though, she took the stand and apologized for abusing the prisoners, saying her conduct was influenced by Specialist Charles A. Graner Jr., her boyfriend at the time.

She said she was "embarrassed" when photographs showing her posing next to naked detainees became public in 2004.

"I was used by Private Graner," she said. "I didn't realize it at the time."

Specialist Graner was reduced in rank after he was convicted in January as ringleader of the abuse.

Often groping for words and staring downward, Private England directed her apology to the detainees and to any American troops and their families who might have been injured or killed as a result of the insurgency in Iraq gaining strength.

Prosecutors argued on Tuesday that the anti-American feeling generated in Arab and Muslim countries by the Abu Ghraib scandal justified sentencing Private England to four to six years in prison and dishonorably discharging her from the Army. The charges the jury found her guilty of on Monday carried a maximum penalty of nine years....

Argument: Editorial from the Boston Globe

MILITARY ABUSE

September 28, 2005

The court-martial conviction Monday of reservist Lynndie England for her role in the abuse of Iraqi prisoners at Abu Ghraib should fool no one that the Pentagon is taking seriously the mistreatment of Iraqis, especially after the release last Friday of a report on torture by members of the 82d Airborne Division stationed near Fallujah....

If the [new] allegations are found credible, they further demolish the contention by officials that the abuse first reported at Abu Ghraib in 2004 was an isolated case of a few bad apples. Pentagon brass also tried to explain away the activities of England's unit as the actions of relatively untrained reservists. It is less easy to dismiss as a fluke such abuse when it occurs at the hands of the 82d Airborne, a thoroughly trained and highly decorated division.

The new charges, along with other accusations of abuse that have emerged since Abu Ghraib, including 28 suspicious detainee deaths, provide strong evidence that both reservist and active duty troops throughout Iraq were confused about their responsibility to treat detainees as prisoners of war under the terms of the Geneva Conventions....Congress should have long since created a special commission, as proposed in a bill by Senator Carl Levin of Michigan, to investigate the issue of prisoner abuse....

A truly independent inquiry, along the lines of the one done by the 9/11 commission, could trace accountability for prisoner abuse through statements and policies by ranking civilian and military officials in the Bush administration. Accountability for the shame of prisoner torture and abuse should not stop with Lynndie England and her cohort.

We'll say, for the sake of convenience, that the news article provides an *explanation* of England's sentence and that the editorial provides an *argument* for investigating responsibility *beyond* England.

As a further example of the distinction between explanation and argument, read the following paragraph:

> Researchers now use recombinant DNA technology to analyze genetic changes. With this technology, they cut and splice DNA from different species, then insert the modified molecules into bacteria or other types of cells that engage in rapid replication and cell division. The cells copy the foreign DNA right along with their own. In short order, huge populations produce useful quantities of recombinant DNA molecules. The new technology also is the basis of genetic engineering, by which genes are isolated, modified, and inserted back into the same organism or into a different one.*

Now read this paragraph:

> Many in the life sciences field would have us believe that the new gene splicing technologies are irrepressible and irreversible and that any attempt to oppose their introduction is both futile and retrogressive. They never stop to even consider the possibility that the new genetic science might be used in a wholly different manner than is currently being proposed. The fact is, the corporate agenda is only one of two potential paths into the Biotech Century. It is possible that the growing number of anti-eugenic activists around the world might be able to ignite a global debate around alternative uses of the new science— approaches that are less invasive, more sustainable and humane and that conserve and protect the genetic rights of future generations.†

Both of these passages deal with the topic of biotechnology, but the two take quite different approaches. The first passage comes from a biology textbook, while the second appears in a magazine article. As we might expect from a textbook on the broad subject of biology, the first passage is explanatory and informative; it defines and explains some of the key concepts of biotechnology without taking a position or providing commentary about

---

*Cecie Starr and Ralph Taggart, "Recombinant DNA and Genetic Engineering," *Biology: The Unity and Diversity of Life* (New York: Wadsworth, 1998).
†Jeremy Rifkin, "The Ultimate Therapy: Commercial Eugenics on the Eve of the Biotech Century," *Tikkun* May–June 1998: 35.

the implications of the technology. Magazine articles often present information in the same ways; however, many magazine articles take specific positions, as we see in the second passage. This passage is argumentative or persuasive: Its primary purpose is to convey a point of view regarding the topic of biotechnology.

While each of these excerpts presents a clear instance of writing that is either explanatory or argumentative, it is important to note that both the textbook chapter and the magazine article contain elements of both explanation and argument. The textbook writers, while they refrain from taking a particular position, do note the controversies surrounding biotechnology and genetic engineering. They might even subtly reveal a certain bias in favor of one side of the issue, through their word choice and tone, and perhaps through devoting more space and attention to one point of view. Explanatory and argumentative writing are not mutually exclusive. The overlap of explanation and argument is also found in the magazine article: In order to make his case against genetic engineering, the writer has to explain certain elements of the issue. Yet even while these categories overlap to a certain extent, the second passage clearly has argument as its primary purpose, and the first passage is primarily explanatory.

In Chapter 2 we noted that the primary purpose in a piece of writing may be informative, persuasive, or entertaining (or some combination of the three). Some scholars of writing argue that all writing is essentially persuasive, and even without entering into that complex argument, we've just seen how the varying purposes in writing do overlap. In order to persuade others of a particular position, we typically must inform them about it; conversely, a primarily informative piece of writing must also work to persuade the reader that its claims are truthful. Both informative and persuasive writing often include entertaining elements, and writing intended primarily to entertain also typically contains information and persuasion. For practical purposes, however, it is possible—and useful—to identify the *primary* purpose in a piece of writing as informative/explanatory, persuasive/argumentative, or entertaining. Entertainment as a primary purpose is the one least often practiced in purely academic writing—perhaps to your disappointment!—but information and persuasion are ubiquitous. So, while recognizing the overlap that will occur between these categories, we distinguish in this chapter between two types of synthesis writing: explanatory (or informative) and argument (or persuasive). Just as distinguishing the primary purpose in a piece of writing helps you to critically read and evaluate it, distinguishing the primary purpose in your own writing will help you to make the appropriate choices regarding your approach.

HOW TO WRITE SYNTHESES

Although writing syntheses can't be reduced to a lockstep method, it should help you to follow the guidelines listed in the box below.

GUIDELINES FOR WRITING SYNTHESES

- *Consider your purpose in writing.* What are you trying to accomplish in your paper? How will this purpose shape the way you approach your sources?
- *Select and carefully read your sources,* according to your purpose. Then reread the passages, mentally summarizing each. Identify those aspects or parts of your sources that will help you fulfill your purpose. When rereading, *label* or *underline* the sources for main ideas, key terms, and any details you want to use in the synthesis.
- *Take notes on your reading.* In addition to labeling or underlining key points in the readings, you might write brief one- or two-sentence summaries of each source. This will help you in formulating your thesis statement and in choosing and organizing your sources later.
- *Formulate a thesis.* Your thesis is the main idea that you want to present in your synthesis. It should be expressed as a complete sentence. You might do some predrafting about the ideas discussed in the readings in order to help you work out a thesis. If you've written one-sentence summaries of the readings, looking them over will help you to brainstorm connections between readings and to devise a thesis.

  When you write your synthesis drafts, you will need to consider where your thesis fits in your paper. Sometimes the thesis is the first sentence, but more often it is *the final sentence of the first paragraph.* If you are writing an *inductively arranged* synthesis (see pp. 78–79), the thesis sentence may not appear until the final paragraphs.
- *Decide how you will use your source material.* How will the information and the ideas in the passages help you fulfill your purpose?
- *Develop an organizational plan,* according to your thesis. How will you arrange your material? It is not necessary to prepare a formal outline. But you should have some plan that will indicate the order in which you will present your material and that will indicate the relationships among your sources.
- *Draft the topic sentences for the main sections.* This is an optional step, but you may find it a helpful transition from organizational plan to first draft.
- *Write the first draft* of your synthesis, following your organizational plan. Be flexible with your plan, however. Frequently, you will use an outline to get started. As you write, you may discover new ideas and make room for them by adjusting the outline. When this happens, reread your work frequently, making sure that your thesis still accounts for what follows and that what follows still logically supports your thesis.

(continued)

- *Document your sources.* You must do this by crediting sources within the body of the synthesis—citing the author's last name and the page number from which the point was taken—and then providing full citation information in a list of "Works Cited" at the end. Don't open yourself to charges of plagiarism! (See pp. 24–26.)
- *Revise your synthesis,* inserting transitional words and phrases where necessary. Make sure that the synthesis reads smoothly, logically, and clearly from beginning to end. Check for grammatical correctness, punctuation, and spelling.

Note: The writing of syntheses is a recursive process, and you should accept a certain amount of backtracking and reformulating as inevitable. For instance, in developing an organizational plan (step 6 of the procedure), you may discover a gap in your presentation that will send you scrambling for another source—back to step 2. You may find that formulating a thesis and making inferences among sources occur simultaneously; indeed, inferences are often made before a thesis is formulated. Our recommendations for writing syntheses will give you a structure that will get you started. But be flexible in your approach; expect discontinuity and, if possible, be assured that through backtracking and reformulating you will produce a coherent, well-crafted paper.

THE ARGUMENT SYNTHESIS

It's likely that most of the papers you'll be writing in the next few years will be focused on developing support for particular positions or claims, so we'll consider the argument synthesis first and in more detail. An argument synthesis is *persuasive* in purpose. An example: *Welfare reform has largely succeeded* (or *failed*). Writers working with the same source material might conceive of and support other, opposite theses. So the thesis for an argument synthesis is a claim about which reasonable people could disagree. It is a claim with which—given the right arguments—your audience might be persuaded to agree. The strategy of your argument synthesis is therefore to find and use convincing *support* for your *claim*.

The Elements of Argument: Claim, Support, and Assumption

One way of looking at an argument is to see it as an interplay of three essential elements: claim, support, and assumption. A *claim* is a proposition or conclusion that you are trying to prove. You prove this claim by using *support* in the form of fact or expert opinion. Linking your supporting evidence to your claim is your *assumption* about the subject. This assumption, also called a *warrant,* is—as we've discussed in Chapter 2—an underlying belief or principle about some aspect of the world and how it operates. By nature, assumptions (which are often unstated) tend to be more general than either claims or supporting evidence.

Here are the essential elements of an argument advocating parental restriction of television viewing for high school children:

Claim

> High school students should be restricted to no more than two hours of TV viewing per day.

Support

> An important new study and the testimony of educational specialists reveal that students who watch more than two hours of TV a night have, on average, lower grades than those who watch less TV.

Assumption

> Excessive TV viewing adversely affects academic performance.

For another example, here's an argumentative claim on the topic of what some call computer-mediated communication (CMC):

> CMC threatens to undermine human intimacy, connection, and ultimately community.

Here are the other elements of this argument:

Support

> - While the Internet presents us with increased opportunities to meet people, these meetings are limited by geographical distance.
> - People are spending increasing amounts of time in cyberspace: In 1998, the average Internet user spent over four hours per week online, a figure that has nearly doubled recently.
> - College health officials report that excessive Internet use threatens many college students' academic and psychological well-being.
> - New kinds of relationships fostered on the Internet often pose challenges to pre-existing relationships.

Assumptions

> - The communication skills used and the connections formed during Internet contact fundamentally differ from those used and formed during face-to-face contact.
> - "Real" connection and a sense of community are sustained by face-to-face contact, not by Internet interactions.

For the most part, arguments should be constructed logically so that assumptions link evidence (supporting facts and expert opinions) to claims. As we'll see, however, logic is only one component of effective arguments.

Practicing Claim, Support, and Assumption

Devise two sets of claims, support, and assumptions. First, in response to the example above on computer-mediated communication and relationships, write a one-sentence claim addressing the positive impact (or potentially positive impact) of CMC on relationships—whether you personally agree with the claim or not. Then list the supporting statements on which such a claim might rest and the assumptions that underlie them. Second, write a claim that states your own position on any debatable topic you choose. Again, devise statements of support and relevant assumptions.

The Limits of Argument

Here we must acknowledge a potentially troubling but undeniable reality: Arguments are not won on the basis of logic and evidence alone. In the real world, arguments don't operate like academic debates. If the purpose of argument is to get people to change their minds or to agree that the writer's or speaker's position on a particular topic is the best available, then the person making the argument must be aware that factors other than evidence and good reasoning come into play when readers or listeners are considering the matter.

These factors involve deep-seated cultural, religious, ethnic, racial, and gender identities, moral predilections, and the effects of personal experiences (either pleasant or unpleasant) that are generally impervious to the weight of reasoning, however well-framed. Try—using the best available arguments—to convince someone who is pro-life to agree with the pro-choice position (or vice versa). Try to persuade someone who opposes capital punishment to believe that state-endorsed executions are necessary for deterrence (or for any other reason). Marshal your evidence and logic to convince someone whose family members have had run-ins with the law that police efforts are directed at protecting the law-abiding. On such emotionally loaded topics, it is extremely difficult, if not impossible, to get people to change their minds because they are so personally invested in their beliefs. (See the discussion of *assumptions* in Chapter 2, pp. 40–42.) It is not just a matter of their forming or choosing an opinion on a particular topic; it is a matter of an opinion's emerging naturally from an often long-established component of the person's psyche. Someone who believes that all life is sacred is not likely to be swayed by an argument that abortion or stem-cell research that involves the destruction of a fetus is acceptable. As Susan Jacoby, author of *The Age of American Unreason*, notes, "Whether watching television news, consulting political blogs, or (more rarely) reading books, Americans today have become a people in search of validation for opinions that they already hold."*

The tenacity with which people hold on to longtime beliefs does not mean, however, that they cannot change their minds or that subjects like abortion, capital punishment, gun control, and gay marriage should be off-limits to reasoned debate. It means only that you should be aware of the limits of argument. The world is not populated by Mr. and Ms. Spocks of *Star Trek* fame, whose brains function by reason alone. Even those who claim to be open-minded on a given topic are often captive to deeply held beliefs and, so, deceive themselves concerning their willingness to respond rationally to arguments. As one letter writer to the *New York Times Book Review* observed, "[P]eople often fail to identify their own biases because of a compelling human desire to believe they are fair-minded and decent."†

The most fruitful topics for argument in a freshman composition setting, therefore, tend to be those on which most people are persuadable, either because they know relatively little about the topic or because deep-rooted cultural, religious, or moral beliefs are not involved. At least initially in your career as a writer of academic papers, it's probably best to avoid "hot button" topics that are the focus of broader cultural debates, and to focus instead on topics in which emotion plays less of a part. Most people are not heavily invested in plug-in hybrid or hydrogen-powered vehicles, so an argument on behalf of the more promising technology for the coming decades will not be complicated by deep-seated beliefs. Similarly, most people don't know enough about the mechanics of sleep to have strong opinions on how to deal with sleep deprivation. Your arguments on such topics, therefore, will provide opportunities both to inform your readers or listeners and to convince them that your arguments, if well reasoned and supported by sound evidence, are at least plausible if not entirely convincing.

DEMONSTRATION: DEVELOPING AN ARGUMENT SYNTHESIS—BALANCING PRIVACY AND SAFETY IN THE WAKE OF VIRGINIA TECH

To demonstrate how to plan and draft an argument synthesis, let's suppose you are taking a course on Law and Society or Political Science or (from the Philosophy Department) Theories of Justice, and you find yourself considering the competing claims of privacy and public safety. The tension between

*Susan Jacoby, "Talking to Ourselves: Americans Are Increasingly Close-Minded and Unwilling to Listen to Opposing Views," *Los Angeles Times* 20 Apr. 2008: M10.
†Susan Abendroth, letter in *New York Times Book Review* 30 Mar. 2008: 12.

these two highly prized values burst anew into public consciousness in 2007 after a mentally disturbed student at the Virginia Polytechnic Institute shot to death 32 fellow students and faculty members and injured 17 more. Unfortunately, this incident was only the latest in a long history of mass killings at American schools.* It was later revealed that the shooter had a documented history of mental instability, but because of privacy rules this information was not made available to university officials. Many people demanded to know why this information was not shared with campus police or other officials so that Virginia Tech could take measures to protect members of the university community. Didn't the safety of those who were injured and killed outweigh the privacy of the shooter? At what point, if any, *does* the right to privacy outweigh the right to safety? What *should* the university have done before the killing started? Should federal and state laws on privacy be changed or even abandoned in the wake of this and other similar incidents?

Suppose, in preparing to write a paper on balancing privacy and safety, you located (among others) the following sources:

- *Mass Shootings at Virginia Tech, April 16, 2007: Report of the Review Panel Presented to Governor Kaine, Commonwealth of Virginia*, August 2007 (a report)
- "Laws Limit Schools Even After Alarms" (a newspaper article)
- "Perilous Privacy at Virginia Tech" (an editorial)
- "Colleges Are Watching Troubled Students" (a newspaper article)
- "Virginia Tech Massacre Has Altered Campus Mental Health Systems" (a newspaper article)
- *The Family Educational Rights and Privacy Act (FERPA)*, sec. 1232g (a federal statute)

Read these sources (which follow) carefully, noting the kinds of information and ideas you could draw on to develop an *argument synthesis*. Some of these passages are excerpts only; in preparing your paper, you would draw on the entire articles, reports, and book chapters from which these passages were taken. And you would draw on more sources than these in your search for supporting materials (as the writer of the model synthesis has done; see pp. 82–89). But these six sources provide a good introduction to the subject. Our discussion of how these passages can form the basis of an argument synthesis resumes on p. 77.

---

*In 1966 a student at the University of Texas at Austin, shooting from the campus clock tower, killed 14 people and wounded 31. In 2006 a man shot and killed five girls at an Amish school in Lancaster, Pennsylvania.

MASS SHOOTINGS AT VIRGINIA TECH, APRIL 16, 2007

Report of the Review Panel
Presented to Governor Kaine, Commonwealth of Virginia,
August 2007

The following passage leads off the official report of the Virginia Tech shootings by the panel appointed by Virginia Governor Tim Kaine to investigate the incident. The mission of the panel was "to provide an independent, thorough, and objective incident review of this tragic event, including a review of educational laws, policies and institutions, the public safety and health care procedures and responses, and the mental health delivery system." Panel members included the chair, Colonel Gerald Massenghill, former Virginia State Police superintendent; Tom Ridge, former director of Homeland Security and former governor of Pennsylvania; Gordon Davies; Dr. Roger L. Depue; Dr. Aradhana A. "Bela" Sood; Judge Diane Strickland; and Carol L. Ellis. The panel Web site may be found at <http://www.vtreviewpanel.org/panel_info/>.

Summary of Key Findings

On April 16, 2007, Seung Hui Cho, an angry and disturbed student, shot to death 32 students and faculty of Virginia Tech, wounded 17 more, and then killed himself.

The incident horrified not only Virginians, but people across the United States and throughout the world.

Tim Kaine, Governor of the Commonwealth of Virginia, immediately appointed a panel to review the events leading up to this tragedy; the handling of the incidents by public safety officials, emergency services providers, and the university; and the services subsequently provided to families, survivors, caregivers, and the community.

The Virginia Tech Review Panel reviewed several separate but related issues in assessing events leading to the mass shootings and their aftermath:

- The life and mental health history of Seung Hui Cho, from early childhood until the weeks before April 16.
- Federal and state laws concerning the privacy of health and education records.
- Cho's purchase of guns and related gun control issues.
- The double homicide at West Ambler Johnston (WAJ) residence hall and the mass shootings at Norris Hall, including the responses of Virginia Tech leadership and the actions of law enforcement officers and emergency responders.
- Emergency medical care immediately following the shootings, both onsite at Virginia Tech and in cooperating hospitals.
- The work of the Office of the Chief Medical Examiner of Virginia.
- The services provided for surviving victims of the shootings and others injured, the families and loved ones of those killed and injured, members of the university community, and caregivers.

The panel conducted over 200 interviews and reviewed thousands of pages of records, and reports the following major findings:

1. Cho exhibited signs of mental health problems during his childhood. His middle and high schools responded well to these signs and, with his parents' involvement, provided services to address his issues. He also received private psychiatric treatment and counseling for selective mutism and depression.

   In 1999, after the Columbine shootings, Cho's middle school teachers observed suicidal and homicidal ideations in his writings and recommended psychiatric counseling, which he received. It was at this point that he received medication for a short time. Although Cho's parents were aware that he was troubled at this time, they state they did not specifically know that he thought about homicide shortly after the 1999 Columbine school shootings.

2. During Cho's junior year at Virginia Tech, numerous incidents occurred that were clear warnings of mental instability. Although various individuals and departments within the university knew about each of these incidents, the university did not intervene effectively. No one knew all the information and no one connected all the dots.

3. University officials in the office of Judicial Affairs, Cook Counseling Center, campus police, the Dean of Students, and others explained their failures to communicate with one another or with Cho's parents by noting their belief that such communications are prohibited by the federal laws governing the privacy of health and education records. In reality, federal laws and their state counterparts afford ample leeway to share information in potentially dangerous situations.

4. The Cook Counseling Center and the university's Care Team failed to provide needed support and services to Cho during a period in late 2005 and early 2006. The system failed for lack of resources, incorrect interpretation of privacy laws, and passivity. Records of Cho's minimal treatment at Virginia Tech's Cook Counseling Center are missing.

5. Virginia's mental health laws are flawed and services for mental health users are inadequate. Lack of sufficient resources results in gaps in the mental health system including short term crisis stabilization and comprehensive outpatient services. The involuntary commitment process is challenged by unrealistic time constraints, lack of critical psychiatric data and collateral information, and barriers (perceived or real) to open communications among key professionals.

6. There is widespread confusion about what federal and state privacy laws allow. Also, the federal laws governing records of health care provided in educational settings are not entirely compatible with those governing other health records.

7. Cho purchased two guns in violation of federal law. The fact that in 2005 Cho had been judged to be a danger to himself and ordered to

outpatient treatment made him ineligible to purchase a gun under federal law.

8. Virginia is one of only 22 states that report any information about mental health to a federal database used to conduct background checks on would-be gun purchasers. But Virginia law did not clearly require that persons such as Cho—who had been ordered into out-patient treatment but not committed to an institution—be reported to the database. Governor Kaine's executive order to report all persons involuntarily committed for outpatient treatment has temporarily addressed this ambiguity in state law. But a change is needed in the Code of Virginia as well.

9. Some Virginia colleges and universities are uncertain about what they are permitted to do regarding the possession of firearms on campus.

• • •

As reflected in the body of the report, the panel has made more than 70 recommendations directed to colleges, universities, mental health providers, law enforcement officials, emergency service providers, lawmakers, and other public officials in Virginia and elsewhere.

LAWS LIMIT SCHOOLS EVEN AFTER ALARMS*

Jeff Gammage and Stacey Burling

This article first appeared in the *Philadelphia Inquirer* on April 19, 2007, just three days after the Virginia Tech shootings. *Inquirer* staff writer Paul Nussbaum contributed to the article.

If Cho Seung-Hui had been a warning light, he would have been blinking bright red.

Two female students complained to campus police that he was stalking them. His poetry was so twisted that his writing professor said she would quit if he weren't removed from her room. Some students found him so menacing that they refused to attend class with him.

Yet Virginia Tech, like other colleges trying to help emotionally troubled students, had little power to force Cho off campus and into treatment.

"We can't even pick up the phone and call their family. They're adults. You have to respect their privacy," said Brenda Ingram-Wallace, director of counseling and chair of the psychology department at Albright College in Reading.

5   In the aftermath of the deadliest shooting in U.S. history, counselors, police authorities, and mental-health professionals say privacy laws

Philadelphia Inquirer 19 Apr. 2007: A01.

prevent colleges from taking strong action regarding students who might be dangerous.

Many at Tech saw Cho as a threat—and shared those fears with authorities. In 2005, after the second stalking complaint, the school obtained a temporary detention order that resulted in Cho undergoing a psychiatric evaluation. But the 23-year-old remained enrolled at the university until the moment he shot himself to death.

Federal laws such as the 1974 Family Educational Rights and Privacy Act (FERPA) and the 1996 Health Insurance Portability and Accountability Act (HIPAA) protect students' right to privacy by banning disclosure of any mental-health problems—even to family members—without a signed waiver.

Patient-therapist confidentiality is crucial, privacy advocates say. Students may shy from treatment for fear of exposure.

FERPA does allow colleges to release information without permission in cases of "health and safety emergencies." But the criteria are so vague, and the potential liability so severe, that administrators say they hesitate to act in any but the most dire circumstances.

"The law tends to be protective of individual autonomy rather than getting in there and forcing people to get treatment," said Anthony Rostain, associate professor of psychiatry at the University of Pennsylvania School of Medicine.

Lots of students write violent stories, he noted. How do you distinguish between a future Cho Seung-Hui and a future Quentin Tarantino?*

"This kind of problem happens all the time across college campuses," Rostain said.

The law puts colleges in a tough position, said Dana Fleming, a lawyer with the college and university practice group at Nelson, Kinder, Mousseau & Saturley in Manchester, N.H. Schools may face legal trouble if they try to keep ill students out, if they try to send them home, or if they let them stay.

"No matter which decision they make," she said, "they can find liability on the other end."

Colleges can't screen students for mental illnesses during the admissions process because that violates the Americans With Disabilities Act. As a result, schools know which students will need tutoring or want to play soccer, but have no idea who is likely to need mental-health care, Fleming said.

Virginia Tech and most other universities cannot summarily suspend a student. Formal disciplinary charges must be filed and hearings held. Students who initiate a complaint often end up dropping the matter.

Nor can schools expect courts to hospitalize a student involuntarily without solid evidence that he poses a danger to himself or others.

---

*Director, screenwriter, and producer of frequently violent films such as *Reservoir Dogs* (1992), *Pulp Fiction* (1994), and *Kill Bill* (vol. 1, 2003; vol. 2, 2004).

That has left many colleges trying to find creative ways to identify and help troubled students.

At Albright College, administrators recently updated a program where anyone concerned about a student's behavior—a work supervisor, a professor or another student—can fill out a "student alert form."

20   Perhaps friends notice a student has become withdrawn or has stopped showing up for class. If multiple forms arrive concerning the same person, counseling director Ingram-Wallace said, the counseling center investigates by contacting housing officials or by reaching the student via phone or e-mail.

But the choice to speak with a psychological counselor stays with the student. The center can't send a therapist to knock on the student's door, she said.

"On the surface, it sounds like a caring thing to do," she said, but "if they haven't been dangerous to themselves or others, there's no reason to mandate them into any kind of services."

Among students who have been referred to the counseling center, "the responses are mixed," she said. "Some people felt imposed upon."

At St. Lawrence University in Canton, N.Y., every student who visits the health center—even for a head cold—is screened for depression and signs of other mental illness. The effort follows a national study that showed depression rising among college students.

25   If a screening shows someone needs help from the health center, "we literally walk them over there," said Patricia Ellis, director of counseling services.

More than a year before Monday's massacre of 32 students and staff members, Cho was twice accused of stalking female students and taken to a mental-health facility amid fears he was suicidal, police said yesterday.

After the first incident, in November 2005, police referred him to the university disciplinary system. Ed Spencer, Tech's assistant vice president of student affairs, said he could not comment on any proceedings against the gunman because federal law protects students' medical privacy even after death.

The university obtained the detention order after the second stalking complaint, in December 2005. "His insight and judgment are normal," an examiner at the psychiatric hospital concluded.

Yet poet Nikki Giovanni, one of his professors, told CNN that students were so unnerved by Cho's behavior, which included taking cell-phone photos of them in class, that most stopped attending the course. She insisted that he be removed.

30   Lucinda Roy, a codirector of the creative writing program, tutored Cho after that, and tried to get him into counseling. He always refused. Roy sent samples of Cho's writing, with its images of people attacking each other with chain saws, to the campus police, student-affairs office, and other agencies.

PERILOUS PRIVACY AT VIRGINIA TECH

This editorial appeared in the *Christian Science Monitor* on September 4, 2007.

Colleges didn't need last week's report on the Virginia Tech shootings to address a key finding: a faster alert during the crisis may have saved lives. Many colleges have already set blast-notice plans. But here's what needs careful study: the report's conclusions about privacy.

Privacy is a huge issue on campuses. Colleges and universities are dealing with young people who have just become legal adults, but who may still require supervision and even intervention.

That was the case with Seung-Hui Cho, the student who killed 32 people and then himself on April 16. According to the report, which was commissioned by Virginia Gov. Timothy Kaine, this troubled student's behavior raised serious questions about his mental stability while he was at VT, yet no one contacted his parents, and communication about his case broke down among school, law-enforcement, and mental-health officials.

A big reason? A "widespread perception" that privacy laws make it difficult to respond to troubled students, according to the report. But this is "only partly correct."

Lack of understanding about federal and state laws is a major obstacle to helping such students, according to the report. The legal complexity, as well as concerns about liability, can easily push teachers, administrators, police, and mental-health workers into a "default" position of withholding information, the report found.

There's no evidence that VT officials consciously decided not to inform Mr. Cho's parents. But the university's lawyer told the panel investigating Cho's case that privacy laws prevent sharing information such as that relating to Cho.

That's simply not true. The report listed several steps that could quite legally have been taken:

The Virginia Tech police, for instance, could have shared with Cho's parents that he was temporarily detained, pending a hearing to commit him involuntarily to a mental-health institution, because that information was public.

And teachers and administrators could have called Cho's parents to notify them of his difficulties, because only student records—not personal observations or conversations—are shielded by the federal privacy law that covers most secondary schools.

Notifying Cho's parents was intuitively the right course. Indeed, his middle school contacted his parents to get him help, and they cooperated. His high school also made special arrangements. He improved.

The report points out that the main federal privacy laws that apply to a college student's health and campus records recognize exceptions for information sharing in emergencies that affect public health and safety.

Privacy is a bedrock of American law and values. In a mental-health case, it gives a patient the security to express innermost thoughts, and protects that person from discrimination. But the federal law, at least, does recognize a balance between privacy and public safety, even when colleges can't, or won't.

The report is to be commended for pointing out this disconnect, and for calling for greater clarification of privacy laws and school policies.

Perhaps now, common sense can match up with legal obligations so both privacy and public safety can be served.

COLLEGES ARE WATCHING TROUBLED STUDENTS

Jeffrey McMurray

During the year following the Virginia Tech shootings, many colleges and universities took a hard look at their policies on student privacy and their procedures for monitoring and sharing information about troubled students. This article, by the Associated Press, was first published on March 28, 2008. AP writer Sue Lindsay contributed to this report.

On the agenda: A student who got into a shouting match with a faculty member. Another who harassed a female classmate. Someone found sleeping in a car. And a student who posted a threat against a professor on Facebook.

In a practice adopted at one college after another since the massacre at Virginia Tech, a University of Kentucky committee of deans, administrators, campus police and mental health officials has begun meeting regularly to discuss a watch list of troubled students and decide whether they need professional help or should be sent packing.

These "threat assessment groups" are aimed at heading off the kind of bloodshed seen at Virginia Tech a year ago and at Northern Illinois University last month.

"You've got to be way ahead of the game, so to speak, expect what may be coming. If you're able to identify behaviors early on and get these people assistance, it avoids disruptions in the classrooms and potential violence," said Maj. Joe Monroe, interim police chief at Kentucky.

5   The Kentucky panel, called Students of Concern, held its first meeting last week and will convene at least twice a month to talk about students whose strange or disturbing behavior has come to their attention.

Such committees represent a change in thinking among U.S. college officials, who for a long time were reluctant to share information about students' mental health for fear of violating privacy laws.

"If a student is a danger to himself or others, all the privacy concerns go out the window," said Patricia Terrell, vice president of student affairs, who created the panel.

Terrell shared details of the four discussed cases with The Associated Press on the condition that all names and other identifying information be left out.

Among other things, the panel can order a student into counseling or bar him or her from entering a particular building or talking to a certain person. It can also order a judicial hearing that can lead to suspension or expulsion if the student's offense was a violation of the law or school policy.

Although the four cases discussed last week were the ones administrators deemed as needing the most urgent attention, a database listing 26 other student cases has been created, providing fodder for future meetings.

Students are encouraged during their freshman orientation to report suspicious behavior to the dean of students, and university employees all the way down to janitors and cafeteria workers are instructed to tell their supervisors if they see anything.

Virtually every corner of campus is represented in the group's closed-door meetings, including dorm life, academics, counseling, mental health and police.

"If you look back at the Virginia Tech situation, the aftermath, there were several people who knew that student had problems, but because of privacy and different issues, they didn't talk to others about it," said Lee Todd, UK president.

High schools have been doing this sort of thing for years because of shootings, but only since Virginia Tech, when a disturbed student gunman killed 32 people and committed suicide, have colleges begun to follow suit, said Mike Dorn, executive director of Safe Havens International, a leading campus safety firm.

"They didn't think it was a real threat to them," Dorn said.

Virginia Tech has added a threat assessment team since the massacre there. Boston University, the University of Utah, the University of Illinois–Chicago and numerous others also have such groups, said Gwendolyn Dungy, executive director of the National Association of Student Personnel Administrators.

Bryan Cloyd, a Virginia Tech accounting professor whose daughter Austin was killed in the rampage, welcomed the stepped-up efforts to monitor troubled students but stressed he doesn't want to turn every college campus into a "police state."

"We can't afford to overreact," Cloyd said, but "we also can't afford to underreact."...

VIRGINIA TECH MASSACRE HAS ALTERED CAMPUS MENTAL HEALTH SYSTEMS

This article, prepared by the Associated Press, is representative of numerous reports of how college administrators across the nation responded to the Virginia Tech killings. Many schools reviewed their existing policies on student privacy and communication and instituted new procedures. The article appeared in the *Los Angeles Times* on April 14, 2008.

The rampage carried out nearly a year ago by a Virginia Tech student who slipped through the mental health system has changed how American colleges reach out to troubled students.

Administrators are pushing students harder to get help, looking more aggressively for signs of trouble and urging faculty to speak up when they have concerns. Counselors say the changes are sending even more students their way, which is both welcome and a challenge, given that many still lack the resources to handle their growing workloads.

Behind those changes, colleges have edged away in the last year from decades-old practices that made student privacy paramount. Now, they are more likely to err on the side of sharing information—with the police, for instance, and parents—if there is any possible threat to community safety. But even some who say the changes are appropriate worry it could discourage students from seeking treatment.

Concerns also linger that the response to shooters like Seung-hui Cho at Virginia Tech and Steven Kazmierczak, who killed five others at Northern Illinois University, has focused excessively on boosting the capacity of campus police to respond to rare events. Such reforms may be worthwhile, but they don't address how to prevent such a tragedy in the first place.

5   It was last April 16, just after 7 a.m., that Cho killed two students in a Virginia Tech dormitory, the start of a shooting spree that continued in a classroom building and eventually claimed 33 lives, including his own.

Cho's behavior and writing had alarmed professors and administrators, as well as the campus police, and he had been put through a commitment hearing where he was found to be potentially dangerous. But when an off-campus psychiatrist sent him back to the school for outpatient treatment, there was no follow-up to ensure that he got it.

People who work every day in the campus mental health field—counselors, lawyers, advocates and students at colleges around the country—say they have seen three major types of change since the Cho shootings:

Faculty are speaking up more about students who worry them. That's accelerating a trend of more demand for mental health services that was already under way before the Virginia Tech shootings.

Professors "have a really heightened level of fear and concern from the behavior that goes on around them," said Ben Locke, assistant director of the counseling center at Penn State University.

10   David Wallace, director of counseling at the University of Central Florida, said teachers are paying closer attention to violent material in writing assignments—warning bells that had worried Cho's professors.

"Now people are wondering, 'Is this something that could be more ominous?'" he said. "Are we talking about the Stephen Kings of the future or about somebody who's seriously thinking about doing something harmful?"

The downside is officials may be hypersensitive to any eccentricity. Says Susan Davis, an attorney who works in student affairs at the University of

Virginia: "There's no question there's some hysteria and there's some things we don't need to see."

Changes are being made to privacy policies. In Virginia, a measure signed into law Wednesday by Gov. Tim Kaine requires colleges to bring parents into the loop when dependent students may be a danger to themselves or others.

Even before Virginia Tech, Cornell University had begun treating students as dependents of their parents unless told otherwise—an aggressive legal strategy that gives the school more leeway to contact parents with concerns without students' permission.

In Washington, meanwhile, federal officials are trying to clarify privacy guidelines so faculty won't hesitate to report potential threats.

"Nobody's throwing privacy out the window, but we are coming out of an era when individual rights were paramount on college campuses," said Brett Sokolow, who advises colleges on risk management. "What colleges are struggling with now is a better balance of those individual rights and community protections."...

THE FAMILY EDUCATIONAL RIGHTS AND PRIVACY ACT

United States Code
Title 20. Education
Chapter 31. General Provisions Concerning Education
§ 1232g. Family Educational and Privacy Rights

Following are excerpts from the *Family Educational Rights and Privacy Act (FERPA)*, the federal law enacted in 1974 that governs restrictions on the release of student educational records. FERPA provides for the withholding of federal funds to educational institutions that violate its provisions, and it is the federal guarantor of the privacy rights of post-secondary students.

(1)(A) No funds shall be made available under any applicable program to any educational agency or institution which has a policy of denying, or which effectively prevents, the parents of students who are or have been in attendance at a school of such agency or at such institution, as the case may be, the right to inspect and review the education records of their children. If any material or document in the education record of a student includes information on more than one student, the parents of one of such students shall have the right to inspect and review only such part of such material or document as relates to such student or to be informed of the specific information contained in such part of such material. Each educational agency or institution shall establish appropriate procedures for the granting of a request by parents for access to the education records of their children within a reasonable period of time, but in no case more than forty-five days after the request has been made....

(C) The first sentence of subparagraph (A) shall not operate to make available to students in institutions of postsecondary education the following materials:

(i) financial records of the parents of the student or any information contained therein;

(ii) confidential letters and statements of recommendation, which were placed in the education records prior to January 1, 1975, if such letters or statements are not used for purposes other than those for which they were specifically intended;

(iii) if the student has signed a waiver of the student's right of access under this subsection in accordance with subparagraph (D), confidential recommendations—

(I) respecting admission to any educational agency or institution,

(II) respecting an application for employment, and

(III) respecting the receipt of an honor or honorary recognition.

....

(B) The term "education records" does not include—

(i) records of instructional, supervisory, and administrative personnel and educational personnel ancillary thereto which are in the sole possession of the maker thereof and which are not accessible or revealed to any other person except a substitute;

(ii) records maintained by a law enforcement unit of the educational agency or institution that were created by that law enforcement unit for the purpose of law enforcement;

(iii) in the case of persons who are employed by an educational agency or institution but who are not in attendance at such agency or institution, records made and maintained in the normal course of business which relate exclusively to such person in that person's capacity as an employee and are not available for use for any other purpose; or

(iv) records on a student who is eighteen years of age or older, or is attending an institution of postsecondary education, which are made or maintained by a physician, psychiatrist, psychologist, or other recognized professional or paraprofessional acting in his professional or paraprofessional capacity, or assisting in that capacity, and which are made, maintained, or used only in connection with the provision of treatment to the student, and are not available to anyone other than persons providing such treatment, except that such records can be personally reviewed by a physician or other appropriate professional of the student's choice....

(h) Certain disciplinary action information allowable. Nothing in this section shall prohibit an educational agency or institution from—

(1) including appropriate information in the education record of any student concerning disciplinary action taken against such student for

conduct that posed a significant risk to the safety or well-being of that student, other students, or other members of the school community; or

(2) disclosing such information to teachers and school officials, including teachers and school officials in other schools, who have legitimate educational interests in the behavior of the student.

Exercise 3.2

Critical Reading for Synthesis

Having read the selections relating to privacy and safety, pp. 66–77, write a one-sentence summary of each. On the same page, list two or three topics that you think are common to several of the selections. Beneath each topic, list the authors who have something to say and briefly note what they have to say. Finally, for each topic, jot down what *you* have to say. Now regard your effort: With each topic you have created a discussion point suitable for inclusion in a paper. (Of course, until you determine the claim of such a paper, you won't know to what end you would put the discussion.) Write a paragraph or two in which you introduce the topic and then conduct a brief conversation among the interested parties (including yourself).

Consider Your Purpose

Your specific purpose in writing an argument synthesis is crucial. What exactly you want to do will affect your claim and how you organize the evidence. Your purpose may be clear to you before you begin research, or it may not emerge until after you have completed your research. Of course, the sooner your purpose is clear to you, the fewer wasted motions you will make. On the other hand, the more you approach research as an exploratory process, the likelier that your conclusions will emerge from the sources themselves rather than from preconceived ideas. Each new writing project will have its rhythm in this regard. Be flexible in your approach: Through some combination of preconceived structures and invigorating discoveries, you will find your way to the source materials that will yield a promising paper.

Let's say that while reading these six (and additional) sources on the debate about campus safety and student privacy you shared the outrage of many who blamed the university (and the federal privacy laws on which it relied) for not using the available information in a way that might have spared the lives of those who died. Perhaps you also blamed the legislators who wrote the privacy laws for being more concerned about the confidentiality of the mental health records of the individual person than with the safety of the larger college population. Perhaps, you concluded, society has gone too far in valuing privacy more than it appears to value safety.

On the other hand, in your own role as a student, perhaps you share the high value placed on the privacy of sensitive information about yourself.

After all, one of the functions of higher education is to foster students' independence as they make the transition from adolescence to adulthood. You can understand that many students like yourself might not want parents or others to know details about academic records or disciplinary measures, much less information about therapy sought and undertaken at school. Historically, in the decades since the university officially stood *in loco parentis*—in place of parents—students have struggled hard to win the same civil liberties and rights (including the right to privacy) of their elders.

Further, you may wonder whether federal privacy laws do in fact forbid the sharing of information about potentially dangerous students when the health and safety of others are at stake. A little research may begin to confirm your doubts about whether Virginia Tech officials were as helpless as they claim they were.

Your purpose in writing, then, emerges from these kinds of responses to the source materials you find.

Making a Claim: Formulate a Thesis

As we indicated in the introduction to this chapter, one useful way of approaching an argument is to see it as making a *claim*. A claim is a proposition, a conclusion that you have made, that you are trying to prove or demonstrate. If your purpose is to argue that we should work to ensure campus safety without enacting restrictive laws that overturn the hard-won privacy rights of students, then that claim (generally expressed in one-sentence form as a *thesis*) is at the heart of your argument. You will draw support from your sources as you argue logically for your claim.

Not every piece of information in a source is useful for supporting a claim. You must read with care and select the opinions, facts, and statistics that best advance your position. You may even find yourself drawing support from sources that make claims entirely different from your own. For example, in researching the subject of student privacy and campus safety, you may come across editorials arguing that in the wake of the Virginia Tech shootings student privacy rights should be greatly restricted. Perhaps you will find information in these sources to help support your own contrary arguments.

You might use one source as part of a *counterargument*—an argument opposing your own—so you can demonstrate its weaknesses and, in the process, strengthen your own claim. On the other hand, the author of one of your sources may be so convincing in supporting a claim that you will adopt it yourself, either partially or entirely. The point is that *the argument is in your hands*. You must devise it yourself and use your sources in ways that will support the claim you present in your thesis.

You may not want to divulge your thesis until the end of the paper, thereby drawing the reader along toward your conclusion, allowing that thesis to flow naturally out of the argument and the evidence on which it is based. If you do this, you are working *inductively*. Or you may wish to be more direct and (after an introduction) *begin* with your thesis, following the thesis statement with evidence and reasoning to support it. If you do this, you are working *deductively*. In academic papers, deductive arguments are far more common than inductive ones.

Based on your reactions to reading sources—and perhaps also on your own inclinations as a student—you may find yourself essentially in sympathy with the approach to privacy taken by one of the schools covered in your sources, M.I.T. At the same time, you may feel that M.I.T.'s position does not demonstrate sufficient concern for campus safety and that Cornell's position, on the other hand, restricts student privacy too much. Perhaps most important, you conclude that we don't need to change the law because, if correctly interpreted, the law already incorporates a good balance between privacy and safety. After a few tries, you develop this thesis:

> In responding to the Virginia Tech killings, we should resist rolling back federal rules protecting student privacy; for as long as college officials effectively respond to signs of trouble, these rules already provide a workable balance between privacy and public safety.

Decide How You Will Use Your Source Material

Your claim commits you to (1) arguing that student privacy should remain protected and (2) demonstrating that federal law already strikes a balance between privacy and public safety. The sources (some provided here, some located elsewhere) offer information and ideas—evidence—that will allow you to support your claim. The excerpt from the official report on the Virginia Tech shootings reveals a finding that school officials failed to correctly interpret federal privacy rules and failed to "intervene effectively." The article "Virginia Tech Massacre Has Altered Campus Mental Health Systems" outlines some of the ways that campuses around the country have instituted policy changes regarding troubled students and privacy in the wake of Virginia Tech. And the excerpt from the Family Educational Rights and Privacy Act (FERPA), the federal law, reveals that restrictions on revealing students' confidential information have a crucial exception for "the safety or well-being of ... students, or other members of the school community." (These and several other sources not included in this chapter will be cited in the model argument paper.)

Develop an Organizational Plan

Having established your overall purpose and your claim, having developed a thesis (which may change as you write and revise the paper), and having decided how to draw upon your source materials, how do you logically organize your paper? In many cases, a well-written thesis will suggest an organization. Thus, the first part of your paper will deal with the debate over rolling back student privacy. The second part will argue that as long as educational institutions behave proactively—that is, as long as they actively seek to help troubled students and foster campus safety—existing federal rules already preserve a balance between privacy and safety. Sorting through your material and categorizing it by topic and subtopic, you might compose the following outline:

I. Introduction. Recap Va. Tech shooting. College officials, citing privacy rules, did not act on available info about shooter with history of mental problems.

II. Federal rules on privacy. Subsequent debate over balance between privacy and campus safety. Pendulum now moving back toward safety. *Thesis.*

III. Developments in student privacy in recent decades.
   A. Doctrine of *in loco parentis* defines college-student relationship.
   B. Movement away from *in loco parentis* begins in 1960s, in context not only of student rights but also broader civil rights struggles of the period.
   C. FERPA, enacted 1974, establishes new federal rules protecting student privacy.

IV. Arguments *against* student privacy.
   A. In wake of Virginia Tech, many blame FERPA protections and college officials, believing privacy rights have been taken too far, putting campus community at risk.
   B. Cornell rolls back some FERPA privacy rights.

V. Arguments *for* student privacy.
   A. M.I.T. strongly defends right to privacy.
   B. Problem is not federal law but incorrect interpretation of federal law. FERPA provides health and safety exceptions. Virginia Tech officials erred in citing FERPA for not sharing info about shooter earlier.
   C. Univ. of Kentucky offers good balance between competing claims of privacy and safety.
      1. watch lists of troubled students
      2. threat assessment groups
      3. open communication among university officials

VI. Conclusion.
   A. Virginia Tech incident was tragic but should not cause us to over-turn hard-won privacy rights.
   B. We should support a more proactive approach to student mental health problems and improve communication between departments.

Formulate an Argument Strategy

The argument that emerges through this outline will build not only on evidence drawn from sources but also on the writer's assumptions. Consider the bare-bones logic of the argument:

Laws protecting student privacy serve a good purpose. (*assumption*)

If properly interpreted and implemented, federal law as currently written is sufficient both to protect student privacy and to ensure campus safety. (*support*)

We should not change federal law to overturn or restrict student privacy rights. (*claim*)

The crucial point about which reasonable people will disagree is the *assumption* that laws protecting student privacy serve a good purpose. Those who wish to restrict the information made available to parents are likely to agree with this assumption. Those who favor a policy that allows college officials to inform parents of problems without their children's permission are likely to disagree.

Writers can accept or partially accept an opposing assumption by making a *concession*, in the process establishing themselves as reasonable and willing to compromise (see p. 97). David Harrison does exactly this in the model synthesis that follows when he summarizes the policies of the University of Kentucky. By raising objections to his own position and conceding some validity to them, he blunts the effectiveness of *counterarguments*. Thus, Harrison concedes the absolute requirement for campus safety, but he argues that this requirement can be satisfied as long as campus officials correctly interpret existing federal law and implement proactive procedures aimed at dealing more effectively with troubled students.

The *claim* of the argument about privacy vs. safety is primarily a claim about *policy*, about actions that should (or should not) be taken. An argument can also concern a claim about *facts* (Does X exist? How can we define X? Does X lead to Y?), a claim about *value* (What is X worth?), or a claim about *cause and effect* (Why did X happen?). The present argument rests to some degree on a dispute about cause and effect. No one disputes that the primary cause of this tragedy was that a disturbed student was not stopped before he killed people. But many have disputed the secondary cause: Did the massacre happen, in part, because federal law prevented officials from sharing crucial information about the disturbed student? Or did it happen, in part, because university officials failed to interpret correctly what they could and could not do under the law? As you read the following paper, observe how these opposing views are woven into the argument.

Draft and Revise Your Synthesis

The final draft of an argument synthesis, based on the outline above, follows. Thesis, transitions, and topic sentences are highlighted; Modern Language

Association (MLA) documentation style is used throughout (except in the citing of federal law).

A cautionary note: When writing syntheses, it is all too easy to become careless in properly crediting your sources. Before drafting your paper, always review the section on Avoiding Plagiarism (pp. 24–26).

MODEL SYNTHESIS

David Harrison

Professor Shanker

Law and Society I

14 February 2009

Balancing Privacy and Safety in the Wake of Virginia Tech

①   On April 16, 2007, Seung Hui Cho, a mentally ill student at Virginia Polytechnic Institute, shot to death 32 fellow students and faculty members, and injured 17 others, before killing himself. It was the worst mass shooting in U.S. history, and the fact that it took place on a college campus lent a special horror to the event. In the days after the tragedy, several facts about Seung Hui Cho came to light. According to the official Virginia State Panel report on the killings, Cho had exhibited signs of mental disturbance, including "suicidal and homicidal ideations" dating back to high school. And during Cho's junior year at Virginia Tech, numerous incidents occurred that provided clear warnings of Cho's mental instability and violent impulses (Virginia Tech Review 1). University administrators, faculty, and officials were aware of these incidents but failed to intervene to prevent the impending tragedy.

②   In the search for answers, attention quickly focused on federal rules governing student privacy that Virginia Tech officials said prevented them from communicating effectively with each other or with Cho's parents regarding his troubles. These rules, the officials argued, prohibit the sharing of information concerning students' mental health with parents or other students. The publicity about such restrictions revived an ongoing debate over university policies that balance student privacy against campus safety. In the wake of the Virginia Tech tragedy, the pendulum

seems to have swung in favor of safety. In April 2008, Virginia Governor
Tim Kaine signed into law a measure requiring colleges to alert parents
when dependent students may be a danger to themselves or to others
("Virginia Tech Massacre" 1). Peter Lake, an educator at Stetson University
College of Law, predicted that in the wake of Virginia Tech, "people will go
in a direction of safety over privacy" (qtd. in Bernstein, "Mother").

The shootings at Virginia Tech demonstrate, in the most horrifying   ③
way, the need for secure college campuses. Nevertheless, privacy remains
a crucial right to most Americans—including college students, many of
whom for the first time are exercising their prerogatives as adults. Many
students who pose no threat to anyone will, and should, object
strenuously to university administrators peering into and making
judgments about their private lives. Some might be unwilling to seek
professional therapy if they know that the records of their counseling
sessions might be released to their parents or to other students.
In responding to the Virginia Tech killings, we should resist rolling back
federal rules protecting student privacy; for as long as college officials
effectively respond to signs of trouble, these rules already provide a
workable balance between privacy and public safety.

In these days of *Facebook* and reality TV, the notion of privacy   ④
rights, particularly for young people, may seem quaint. In fact, recently
a top lawyer for the search engine *Google* claimed that, in the Internet
age, young people just don't care about privacy the way they once did
(Cohen A17). Whatever the changing views of privacy in a wired world,
the issue of student privacy rights is a serious legal matter that must
be seen in the context of the student-college relationship, which has
its historical roots in the doctrine of *in loco parentis*, Latin for "in the
place of the parents." Generally, this doctrine is understood to mean
that the college stands in place as the student's parent or guardian.
The college therefore has "a duty to protect the safety, morals, and
welfare of their students, just as parents are expected to protect their
children" (Pollet).

⑤   Writing of life at the University of Michigan before the 1960s, one historian observes that *"in loco parentis* comprised an elaborate structure of written rules and quiet understandings enforced in the trenches by housemothers [who] governed much of the what, where, when, and whom of students' lives, especially women: what to wear to dinner, what time to be home, where, when, and for how long they might receive visitors" (Tobin).

⑥   During the 1960s court decisions began to chip away at the doctrine of *in loco parentis.* These rulings illustrate that the students' rights movement during that era was an integral part of a broader contemporary social movement for civil rights and liberties. In *Dixon v. Alabama State Board of Education,* Alabama State College invoked *in loco parentis* to defend its decision to expel six African-American students without due process for participating in a lunchroom counter sit-in. Eventually, a federal appeals court rejected the school's claim to unrestrained power, ruling that students' constitutional rights did not end once they stepped onto campus (Weigel).

⑦   Students were not just fighting for the right to hold hands in dorm rooms; they were also asserting their rights as the vanguard of a social revolution. As Stetson law professor Robert Bickel notes: "The fall of *in loco parentis* in the 1960s correlated exactly with the rise of student economic power and the rise of student civil rights" (qtd. in Weigel).

⑧   The students' rights movement received a further boost with the Family Educational Rights and Privacy Act (FERPA), signed into law by President Ford in 1974. FERPA barred schools from releasing educational records—including mental health records—without the student's permission. The Act provides some important exceptions: educational records *can* be released in the case of health and safety emergencies or if the student is declared a dependent on his or her parents' tax returns (*Federal*).

⑨   In the wake of Virginia Tech, however, many observers pointed the finger of blame at federal restrictions on sharing available mental

Harrison 4

health information. Also held responsible were the school's officials, who admitted knowing of Cho's mental instability but claimed that FERPA prevented them from doing anything about it. The State of Virginia official report on the killings notes as follows:

> University officials...explained their failures to communi-
> cate with one another or with Cho's parents by noting
> their belief that such communications are prohibited by
> the federal laws governing the privacy of health and
> education records. (Virginia Tech Review 2)

Observers were quick to declare the system broken. "Laws Limit Schools Even after Alarms," trumpeted a headline in the *Philadelphia Inquirer* (Gammage and Burling). Commentators attacked federal privacy law, charging that the pendulum had swung too far away from campus safety. Judging from this letter to the editor of the *Wall Street Journal*, many agreed wholeheartedly: "Parents have a right to know if their child has a serious problem, and they need to know the progress of their child's schoolwork, especially if they are paying the cost of the education. Anything less than this is criminal" (Guerriero).

⑩

As part of this public clamor, some schools have enacted policies that effectively curtail student privacy in favor of campus safety. For example: after Virginia Tech, Cornell University began assuming that students were dependents of their parents. Exploiting what the *Wall Street Journal* termed a "rarely used legal exception" in FERPA allows Cornell to provide parents with confidential information without students' permission (Bernstein, "Bucking" A9).

⑪

Conversely, the Massachusetts Institute of Technology lies at the opposite end of the spectrum from Cornell in its staunch defense of student privacy. M.I.T. has stuck to its position even in the wake of Virginia Tech, recently demanding that the mother of a missing "M.I.T. student obtain a subpoena in order to access his dorm room and e-mail records. That student was later found dead, an apparent suicide (Bernstein, "Mother"). Even in the face of lawsuits,

⑫

M.I.T. remains committed to its stance. Its Chancellor explained the school's position this way:

> Privacy is important.... Different students will do different things they absolutely don't want their parents to know about.... Students expect this kind of safe place where they can address their difficulties, try out lifestyles, and be independent of their parents. (qtd. in Bernstein, "Mother")

⑬ One can easily understand how parents would be outraged by the M.I.T. position. No parent would willingly let his or her child enter an environment where that child's safety cannot be assured. Just as the first priority for any government is to protect its citizens, the first priority of an educational institution must be to keep its students safe. But does this responsibility justify rolling back student privacy rights or returning to a more traditional interpretation of *in loco parentis* in the relationship between a university and its students? No, for the simple reason that the choice is a false one.

⑭ As long as federal privacy laws are properly interpreted and implemented, they do nothing to endanger campus safety. The problem at Virginia Tech was not the federal government's policy; it was the university's own practices based on a faulty interpretation of that policy. The breakdown began with the failure of Virginia Tech officials to understand federal privacy laws. Interpreted correctly, these laws would *not* have prohibited officials from notifying appropriate authorities of Cho's problems. The Virginia Tech Review Panel report was very clear on this point: "[F]ederal laws and their state counterparts afford ample leeway to share information in potentially dangerous situations" (2). FERPA does, in fact, provide for a "health and safety emergencies" exception; educational records *can* be released without the student's consent "in connection with an emergency, [to] appropriate persons if the knowledge of such information is necessary to protect the health or safety of the student or other person..." (232g (b) (1) (g-h)). But Virginia Tech administrators did not invoke this important exception to FERPA's privacy rules.

Harrison 6

An editorial in the *Christian Science Monitor* suggested several other ⑮
steps that the university could legally have taken, including informing
Cho's parents that he had been briefly committed to a mental health
facility, a fact that was public information. The editorial concluded,
scornfully, that "federal law, at least, does recognize a balance between
privacy and public safety, even when colleges can't, or won't" ("Perilous").

To be fair, such confusion about FERPA's contingencies appears ⑯
widespread among college officials. For this reason, the U.S. Department
of Education's revised privacy regulations, announced in March 2008 and
intended to "clarify" when schools may release student records, are
welcome and necessary. But simply reassuring anxious university officials
that they won't lose federal funds for revealing confidential student
records won't be enough to ensure campus safety. We need far more
effective intervention for troubled students than the kind provided by
Virginia Tech, which the Virginia Tech Review Panel blasted for its "lack
of resources" and "passivity" (2).

Schools like the University of Kentucky offer a positive example of ⑰
such intervention, demonstrating that colleges can adopt a robust
approach to student mental health without infringing on privacy rights.
At Kentucky, "threat assessment groups" meet regularly to discuss a
"watch list" of troubled students and decide what to do about them
(McMurray). These committees emphasize proactiveness and
communication—elements that were sorely missing at Virginia Tech.
The approach represents a prudent middle ground between the extreme
positions of M.I.T. and Cornell.

Schools such as Kentucky carry out their policies with a firm eye ⑱
toward student privacy rights. For example, the University of Kentucky's
director of counseling attends the threat assessment group's meetings but
draws a clear line at what information she can share—for instance,
whether or not a student has been undergoing counseling. Instead, the
group looks for other potential red flags, such as a sharp drop-off in
grades or difficulty functioning in the campus environment (McMurray).

This open communication between university officials will presumably also help with delicate judgments—whether, for example, a student's violent story written for a creative writing class is an indication of mental instability or simply an early work by the next Stephen King ("Virginia Tech Massacre" 1).

⑲   What happened at Virginia Tech was a tragedy. Few of us can appreciate the grief of the parents of the shooting victims at Virginia Tech, parents who trusted that their children would be safe and who were devastated when that faith was betrayed. To these parents, the words of the MIT chancellor quoted earlier—platitudes about students "try[ing] out lifestyles" or "address[ing] their difficulties"—must sound hollow. But we must guard against allowing a few isolated incidents, however tragic, to restrict the rights of millions of students, the vast majority of whom graduate college safely and without incident. Schools must not use Virginia Tech as a pretext to bring back the bad old days of resident assistants snooping on the private lives of students and infringing on their privacy. That step is the first down a slippery slope of dictating morality. Both the federal courts and Congress have rejected that approach and for good reason have established the importance of privacy rights on campus. These rights must be preserved.

⑳   The Virginia Tech shooting does not demonstrate a failure of current policy, but rather a breakdown in the enforcement of policy. In its wake, universities have undertaken important modifications to their procedures. We should support changes that involve a more proactive approach to student mental health and improvements in communication between departments, such as those at the University of Kentucky. Such measures will not only bring confidential help to the troubled students who need it, they will also improve the safety of the larger college community. At the same time, these measures will preserve hard-won privacy rights on campus.

Harrison 8

Works Cited

Bernstein, Elizabeth. "Bucking Privacy Concerns, Cornell Acts as
    Watchdog." *Wall Street Journal* 27 Dec. 2007: A1+.
    LexisNexis. Web. 10 Feb. 2009.

---. "A Mother Takes On MIT." *Wall Street Journal* 20 Sept. 2007: A1.
    LexisNexis. Web. 10 Feb. 2009.

Cohen, Adam. "One Friend Facebook Hasn't Made Yet: Privacy Rights."
    New York Times 18 Feb. 2008: A1+. *Academic Search Complete*.
    Web. 9 Feb. 2009.

Federal Educational Rights and Privacy Act (FERPA). 20 U.S.C. §1232g
    (b) (1) (g–h) (2006). Print.

Gammage, Jeff, and Stacy Burling. "Laws Limit Schools Even after
    Alarms." *Philadelphia Inquirer* 19 Apr. 2007: A1. *Academic Search
    Complete*. Web. 10 Feb. 2009.

Guerriero, Dom. Letter. *Wall Street Journal* 7 Jan. 2008. *LexisNexis*.
    Web. 11 Feb. 2009.

McMurray, Jeffrey. "Colleges Are Watching Troubled Students." *AP
    Online*. Associated Press, 28 Mar. 2008. Web. 11 Feb. 2009.

"Perilous Privacy at Virginia Tech." Editorial. *Christian Science Monitor*
    4 Sept. 2007: 8. *Academic Search Complete*. Web. 10 Feb. 2009.

Pollet, Susan J. "Is 'In Loco Parentis' at the College Level a Dead
    Doctrine?" *New York Law Journal* 288 (2002): 4. Print.

Tobin, James. "The Day 'In Loco Parentis' Died." *Michigan Today*. U of
    Michigan, Nov. 2007. Web. 10 Feb. 2009.

"Virginia Tech Massacre Has Altered Campus Mental Health Systems." *Los
    Angeles Times* 14 Apr. 2008: A1+. *LexisNexis*. Web. 8 Feb. 2009.

Virginia Tech Review Panel. *Mass Shootings at Virginia Tech, April 16, 2007:
    Report of the Virginia Tech Review Panel Presented to Timothy M. Kaine,
    Governor, Commonwealth of Virginia.* Arlington, VA: n.p., 2007. Print.

Weigel, David. "Welcome to the Fun-Free University: The Return of *In
    Loco Parentis* Is Killing Student Freedom." *Reasononline*. Reason
    Magazine, Oct. 2004. Web. 7 Feb. 2009.

The Strategy of the Argument Synthesis

In his argument synthesis, Harrison attempts to support a *claim*—one that favors laws protecting student privacy while at the same time helping to ensure campus safety—by offering *support* in the form of facts (what campuses such as the University of Kentucky are doing, what Virginia Tech officials did and failed to do) and opinions (testimony of persons on both sides of the issue). However, because Harrison's claim rests on an *assumption* about the value of student privacy laws, its effectiveness depends partially on the extent to which we, as readers, agree with this assumption. (See our discussion of assumptions in Chapter 2, pp. 40–42.) An assumption (sometimes called a warrant) is a generalization or principle about how the world works or should work—a fundamental statement of belief about facts or values. In this case, the underlying assumption is that college students, as emerging adults, and as citizens with civil rights, are entitled to keep their educational records private. Harrison makes this assumption explicit. Though you are under no obligation to do so, stating assumptions explicitly will clarify your arguments to readers.

Assumptions are often deeply rooted in people's psyches, sometimes derived from lifelong experiences and observations and not easily changed, even by the most logical of arguments. People who lost loved ones in incidents such as Virginia Tech, or people who believe that the right to safety of the larger campus community outweighs the right of individual student privacy, are not likely to accept the assumption underlying this paper, nor are they likely to accept the support provided by Harrison. But readers with no firm opinion might well be persuaded and could come to agree with him that existing federal law protecting student privacy is sufficient to protect campus safety, provided that campus officials act responsibly.

A discussion of the model argument's paragraphs, along with the argument strategy for each, follows. Note that the paper devotes one paragraph to developing each section of the outline on p. 80. Note also that Harrison avoids plagiarism by the careful attribution and quotation of sources.

- **Paragraph 1:** Harrison summarizes the key events of the Virginia Tech killings and establishes that Cho's mental instability was previously known to university officials.

  Argument strategy: Opening with the bare facts of the massacre, Harrison proceeds to lay the basis for the reaction against privacy rules that will be described in the paragraphs to follow. To some extent, Harrison encourages the reader to share the outrage by many in the general public that university officials failed to act to prevent the killings before they started.

- **Paragraph 2:** Harrison now explains the federal rules governing student privacy and discusses the public backlash against such rules and the new law signed by the governor of Virginia restricting privacy at colleges within the state.

Argument strategy: This paragraph highlights the debate over student privacy—and in particular the sometimes conflicting demands of student privacy and campus safety that will be central to the rest of the paper. Harrison cites both fact (the new Virginia law) and opinion (the quotation by Peter Lake) to develop this paragraph.

- **Paragraph 3:** Harrison further clarifies the two sides of the apparent conflict between privacy and safety, maintaining that both represent important social values but concluding with a thesis that argues for not restricting privacy.

   Argument strategy: For the first time, Harrison reveals his own position on the issue. He starts the paragraph by conceding the need for secure campuses but begins to make the case for privacy (for example, without privacy rules students might be reluctant to enter therapy). In his thesis he emphasizes that the demands of both privacy and safety can be satisfied because existing federal rules incorporate the necessary balance.

- **Paragraphs 4–7:** These paragraphs constitute the next section of the paper (see outline, p. 80), covering the developments in student privacy over the past few decades. Paragraphs 4 and 5 treat the doctrine of *in loco parentis*; paragraph 6 discusses how court decisions like *Dixon v. Alabama State Board of Education* began to erode this doctrine.

   Argument strategy: This section of the paper establishes the situation that existed on college campuses before the 1960s—and presumably would exist again were privacy laws to be rolled back. By linking the erosion of the *in loco parentis* doctrine to the civil rights struggle, Harrison attempts to bestow upon pre-1960s college students (especially women), who were "parented" by college administrators, something of the ethos of African–Americans fighting for full citizenship during the civil rights era. Essentially, Harrison is making an analogy between the two groups—one that readers may or may not accept.

- **Paragraph 8:** This paragraph on FERPA constitutes the final part of the section of the paper dealing with the evolution of student privacy since before the 1960s. Harrison explains what FERPA is and introduces an exception to its privacy rules that will be more fully developed later in the paper.

   Argument strategy: FERPA is the federal law central to the debate over the balance between privacy and safety, so Harrison introduces it here as the culmination of a series of developments that weakened *in loco parentis* and guaranteed a certain level of student privacy. But since Harrison in his thesis argues that federal law on student privacy already establishes a balance between privacy and safety, he ends the paragraph by referring to the "health and safety" exception, an exception that will become important later in his argument.

- **Paragraphs 9–11:** These paragraphs constitute the section of the paper that covers the arguments **against** student privacy. Paragraph 9 treats public reaction against both FERPA and Virginia Tech officials who were accused of being more concerned with privacy than with safety. Paragraph 10 cites anti-privacy sentiments expressed in newspapers. Paragraph 11 explains how, in the wake of Virginia Tech, schools like Cornell have enacted new policies restricting student privacy.

Argument strategy: Harrison sufficiently respects the sentiments of those whose position he opposes to deal at some length with the counterarguments to his thesis. He quotes the official report on the mass shootings to establish that Virginia Tech officials believed that they were acting according to the law. He quotes the writer of an angry letter about parents' right to know without attempting to rebut its arguments. In outlining the newly restrictive Cornell policies on privacy, Harrison also establishes what he considers an extreme reaction to the massacres: essentially gutting student privacy rules. He is therefore setting up one position on the debate, which will later be contrasted with other positions—those of M.I.T. and the University of Kentucky.

- **Paragraphs 12–16:** These paragraphs constitute the section of the paper devoted to arguments **for** student privacy. Paragraphs 12 and 13 discuss the M.I.T. position on privacy, as expressed by its chancellor. Paragraph 14 refocuses on FERPA and quotes language to demonstrate that existing federal law provides a health and safety exception to the enforcement of privacy rules. Paragraph 15 quotes an editorial supporting this interpretation of FERPA. Paragraph 16 concedes the existence of confusion about federal rules and makes the transition to an argument about the need for more effective action by campus officials to prevent tragedies like this one.

  Argument strategy: Because these paragraphs express Harrison's position, as embedded in his thesis, this is the longest segment of the discussion. Paragraphs 12 and 13 discuss the M.I.T. position on student privacy, which (given that school's failure to accommodate even prudent demands for safety) Harrison believes is too extreme. Notice the transition at the end of paragraph 13: Conceding that colleges have a responsibility to keep students safe, Harrison poses a question: Does the goal of keeping students safe justify the rolling back of privacy rights? In a pivotal sentence, he responds, "No, for the simple reason that the choice is a false one." Paragraph 14 develops this response and presents the heart of Harrison's argument. Recalling the health and safety exception introduced in paragraph 8, Harrison now explains *why* the choice is false: He quotes the exact language of FERPA to establish that the problem at Virginia Tech was not due to federal law that prevented campus officials from protecting students but rather to campus officials who *misunderstood* the law. Paragraph 15 amplifies Harrison's argument with a reference to an editorial in the *Christian Science Monitor*. Paragraph 16 marks a transition, within this section, to a position (developed in paragraphs 17 and 18) that Harrison believes represents a sensible stance in the debate over campus safety and student privacy. Harrison bolsters his case by citing here, as elsewhere in the paper, the official report on the Virginia Tech killings. The report, prepared by an expert panel that devoted months to investigating the incident, carries considerable weight as evidence in this argument.

- **Paragraphs 17–18:** These paragraphs continue the arguments in favor of Harrison's position. They focus on new policies in practice at the University of Kentucky that offer a "prudent middle ground" in the debate.

    Argument strategy: Having discussed schools such as Cornell and M.I.T. where the reaction to the Virginia Tech killings was inadequate or unsatisfactory, Harrison now outlines a set of policies and procedures in place at the University of Kentucky since April 2007. Following the transition at the end of paragraph 16 on the need for more effective intervention on the part of campus officials, Harrison explains how Kentucky established a promising form of such intervention: watch lists of troubled students, threat assessment groups, and more open communication among university officials. Thus, Harrison positions what is happening at the University of Kentucky—as opposed to rollbacks of federal rules—as the most effective way of preventing future killings like those at Virginia Tech. Kentucky therefore becomes a crucial example for Harrison of how to strike a good balance between the demands of student privacy and campus safety.

- **Paragraphs 19–20:** In his conclusion, Harrison reiterates points made in the body of the paper. In paragraph 19, he agrees that what happened at Virginia Tech was a tragedy but maintains that an isolated incident should not become an excuse for rolling back student privacy rights and bringing back "the bad old days" when campus officials took an active, and intrusive, interest in students' private lives. In paragraph 20, Harrison reiterates the position stated in his thesis: that the problem at Virginia Tech was not a restrictive federal policy that handcuffed administrators but a breakdown in enforcement. He concludes on a hopeful note that new policies established since Virginia Tech will both protect student privacy and improve campus safety.

    Argument strategy: The last two paragraphs provide Harrison with a final opportunity for driving home his points. These two paragraphs to some degree parallel the structure of the thesis itself. In paragraph 19, Harrison makes a final appeal against rolling back student privacy rights. This appeal parallels the first clause of the thesis ("In responding to the Virginia Tech killings, we should resist rolling back federal rules protecting student privacy"). In paragraph 20, Harrison focuses not on federal law itself but rather on the kind of measures adopted by schools like the University of Kentucky that go beyond mere compliance with federal law—and thereby demonstrate the validity of part two of Harrison's thesis ("As long as college officials effectively respond to signs of trouble, these rules already provide a workable balance between privacy and public safety"). Harrison thus ends a paper on a grim subject with a note that provides some measure of optimism and that attempts to reconcile proponents on both sides of this emotional debate.

Another approach to an argument synthesis based on the same and additional sources could argue (along with some of the sources quoted in the model paper) that safety as a social value should never be outweighed by the right to privacy. Such a position could draw support from other practices in contemporary society—searches at airports, for example—illustrating that most people are willing to give up a certain measure of privacy, as well as convenience, in the interest of the safety of the community. Even if such an argument were not to call for a rollback of federal privacy rules, it could recommend modifying the language of the law to make doubly clear that safety trumps privacy. Some have even argued that safety would be improved if students and teachers were permitted to bring guns to campus and were thereby able to defend themselves and others in the event of being confronted by a deranged gunman. In the wake of Virginia Tech and other recent mass killings (such as the shooting deaths of five Amish children at their schoolhouse in 2006), it is difficult to conceive of support for an extreme claim that the rights of the individual are paramount and that privacy should always trump safety. A more reasonable argument might be made, working in counterpoint to the pro-privacy position of the M.I.T. chancellor, specifying more precisely the criteria that would constitute (in the language of FERPA) "significant risk to the safety or well-being" of the campus community. Having met the clearly defined threshold of a grave risk, university officials could then breach student privacy in the interest of the greater good.

Whatever your approach to a subject, in first *critically examining* the various sources and then *synthesizing* them to support a position about which you feel strongly, you are engaging in the kind of critical thinking that is essential to success in a good deal of academic and professional work.

DEVELOPING AND ORGANIZING THE SUPPORT FOR YOUR ARGUMENTS

Experienced writers seem to have an intuitive sense of how to develop and present supporting evidence for their claims; this sense is developed through much hard work and practice. Less experienced writers wonder what to say first and, having decided on that, wonder what to say next. There is no single method of presentation. But the techniques of even the most experienced writers often boil down to a few tried and tested arrangements.

As we've seen in the model synthesis in this chapter, the key to devising effective arguments is to find and use those kinds of support that most persuasively strengthen your claim. Some writers categorize support into two broad types: *evidence* and *motivational appeals*. Evidence, in the form of facts, statistics, and expert testimony, helps make the appeal to reason. Motivational appeals—appeals grounded in emotion and upon the authority of the speaker—are employed to get people to change their minds, to agree with the writer or speaker, or to decide upon a plan of activity.

Following are the most common strategies for using and organizing support for your claims.

Summarize, Paraphrase, and Quote Supporting Evidence

In most of the papers and reports you will write in college and in the professional world, evidence and motivational appeals derive from your summarizing, paraphrasing, and quoting of material in sources that either have been provided to you or that you have independently researched. For example, in paragraph 9 of the model argument synthesis, Harrison uses a long quotation from the Virginia Tech Review Panel report to make the point that college officials believed they were prohibited by federal privacy law from communicating with one another about disturbed students like Cho. You will find another long quotation later in the synthesis and a number of brief quotations woven into sentences throughout. In addition, you will find summaries and paraphrases. In each case, Harrison is careful to cite a source.

Provide Various Types of Evidence and Motivational Appeals

Keep in mind that you can use appeals to both reason and emotion. The appeal to reason is based on evidence that consists of a combination of *facts* and *expert testimony*. The sources by Tobin and Weigel, for example, offer facts about the evolution over the past few decades of the *in loco parentis* doctrine. Bernstein and McMurray interview college adminstrators at Cornell, M.I.T., and the University of Kentucky who explain the changing policies at those institutions. The model synthesis makes an appeal to emotion by engaging the reader's self-interest: If campuses are to be made more secure from the acts of mentally disturbed persons, then college officials should take a proactive approach to monitoring and intervention.

Use Climactic Order

Climactic order is the arrangement of examples or evidence in order of anticipated impact on the reader, least to greatest. Organize by climactic order when you plan to offer a number of categories or elements of support for your claim. Recognize that some elements will be more important—and likely more persuasive—than others. The basic principle here is that you should *save the most important evidence for the end* because whatever you say last is what readers are likely to remember best. A secondary principle is that whatever you say first is what they are *next* most likely to remember. Therefore, when you have several reasons to offer in support of your claim, an effective argument strategy is to present the second most important, then one or more additional reasons, and finally the most important reason. Paragraphs 7–11 of the model synthesis do exactly this.

Use Logical or Conventional Order

Using logical or conventional order involves using as a template a pre-established pattern or plan for arguing your case.

- One common pattern is describing or arguing a *problem/solution*. Using this pattern, you begin with an introduction in which you typically define the problem, perhaps explain its origins, then offer one or more solutions, and then conclude.

- Another common pattern presents *two sides of a controversy*. Using this pattern, you introduce the controversy and (in an argument synthesis) your own point of view or claim, and then you explain the other side's arguments, providing reasons why your point of view should prevail.

- A third common pattern is *comparison and contrast*. This pattern is so important that we will discuss it separately in the next section.

The order in which you present elements of an argument is sometimes dictated by the conventions of the discipline in which you are writing. For example, lab reports and experiments in the sciences and social sciences often follow this pattern: *Opening* or *Introduction, Methods and Materials* (of the experiment or study), *Results, Discussion*. Legal arguments often follow the so-called IRAC format: *Issue, Rule, Application, Conclusion*.

Present and Respond to Counterarguments

When developing arguments on a controversial topic, you can effectively use *counterargument* to help support your claims. When you use counterargument, you present an argument *against* your claim and then show that this argument is weak or flawed. The advantage of this technique is that you demonstrate that you are aware of the other side of the argument and that you are prepared to answer it.

Here is how a counterargument is typically developed:

   I. Introduction and claim

  II. Main opposing argument

 III. Refutation of opposing argument

  IV. Main positive argument

Use Concession

Concession is a variation of counterargument. As in counterargument, you present an opposing viewpoint, but instead of dismissing that position you *concede* that it has some validity and even some appeal, although your own position is the more reasonable one. This concession bolsters your standing as a fair-minded person who is not blind to the virtues of the other side. In the model synthesis, Harrison acknowledges the grief and sense of betrayal of the parents of the students who were killed. He concedes that parents have a right to expect that "the first priority of an educational institution must be to keep students safe." But he insists that this goal of achieving campus safety can be accomplished without rolling back hard-won privacy rights.

Here is an outline for a typical concession argument:

    I. Introduction and claim

   II. Important opposing argument

  III. Concession that this argument has some validity

  IV. Positive argument(s)

Sometimes, when you are developing a counterargument or concession argument, you may become convinced of the validity of the opposing point of view and change your own views. Don't be afraid of this happening. Writing is a tool for learning. To change your mind because of new evidence is a sign of flexibility and maturity, and your writing can only be the better for it.

DEVELOPING AND ORGANIZING SUPPORT FOR YOUR ARGUMENTS

- *Summarize, paraphrase, and quote supporting evidence.* Draw on the facts, ideas, and language in your sources.
- *Provide various types of evidence and motivational appeal.*
- *Use climactic order.* Save the most important evidence in support of your argument for the *end*, where it will have the most impact. Use the next most important evidence *first*.
- *Use logical or conventional order.* Use a form of organization appropriate to the topic, such as problem/solution; sides of a controversy; comparison/contrast; or a form of organization appropriate to the academic or professional discipline, such as a report of an experiment or a business plan.
- *Present and respond to counterarguments.* Anticipate and evaluate arguments against your position.
- *Use concession.* Concede that one or more arguments against your position have some validity; re-assert, nonetheless, that your argument is the stronger one.

Avoid Common Fallacies in Developing and Using Support

In Chapter 2, in the section on critical reading, we considered criteria that, as a reader, you may use for evaluating informative and persuasive writing (see pp. 29–30, 33–39). We discussed how you can assess the accuracy, the significance, and the author's interpretation of the information presented. We also considered the importance in good argument of clearly defined key terms and the pitfalls of emotionally loaded language. Finally, we saw how to recognize such logical fallacies as either/or reasoning, faulty cause-and-effect reasoning, hasty generalization, and false analogy. As a writer, no less than as a critical reader, you need to be aware of these common problems and to avoid them.

Be aware, also, of your responsibility to cite source materials appropriately. When you quote a source, double- and triple-check that you have done so accurately. When you summarize or paraphrase, take care to use your own language and sentence structures (though you can, of course, also quote within these forms). When you refer to someone else's idea—even if you are not quoting, summarizing, or paraphrasing—give the source credit. By being ethical about the use of sources, you uphold the highest standards of the academic community.

THE COMPARISON-AND-CONTRAST SYNTHESIS

A particularly important type of argument synthesis is built on patterns of comparison and contrast. Techniques of comparison and contrast enable you to examine two subjects (or sources) in terms of one another. When you compare, you consider *similarities*. When you contrast, you consider *differences*. By comparing and contrasting, you perform a multifaceted analysis that often suggests subtleties that otherwise might not have come to your (or your reader's) attention.

To organize a comparison-and-contrast argument, you must carefully read sources in order to discover *significant criteria for analysis*. A *criterion* is a specific point to which both of your authors refer and about which they may agree or disagree. (For example, in a comparative report on compact cars, criteria for *comparison and contrast* might be road handling, fuel economy and comfort of ride.) The best criteria are those that allow you not only to account for obvious similarities and differences—those concerning the main aspects of your sources or subjects—but also to plumb deeper, exploring subtle yet significant comparisons and contrasts among details or subcomponents, which you can then relate to your overall thesis.

Note that comparison and contrast is frequently not an end in itself but serves some larger purpose. Thus, a comparison-and-contrast synthesis may be a component of a paper that is essentially a critique, an explanatory synthesis, an argument synthesis, or an analysis.

Organizing Comparison-and-Contrast Syntheses

Two basic approaches to organizing a comparison-and-contrast synthesis are organization by *source* and organization by *criteria*.

Organizing by Source or Subject

You can organize a comparative synthesis by first summarizing each of your sources or subjects and then discussing the significant similarities and differences between them. Having read the summaries and become familiar with the distinguishing features of each source, your readers will most likely be able to appreciate the more obvious similarities and differences. In the discussion, your task is to consider both the obvious and the subtle comparisons and contrasts, focusing on the most significant—that is, on those that most clearly support your thesis.

Organization by source or subject works best with passages that can be briefly summarized. If the summary of your source or subject becomes too long, your readers might have forgotten the points you made in the first summary when they are reading the second. A comparison-and-contrast synthesis organized by source or subject might proceed like this:

I. Introduce the paper; lead to thesis.

II. Summarize source/subject A by discussing its significant features.

III. Summarize source/subject B by discussing its significant features.

IV. Discuss in a paragraph (or two) the significant points of comparison and contrast between sources or subjects A and B. Alternatively, begin the comparison-contrast in Section III as you introduce source/subject B.

V. Conclude with a paragraph in which you summarize your points and, perhaps, raise and respond to pertinent questions.

Organizing by Criteria

Instead of summarizing entire sources one at a time with the intention of comparing them later, you could discuss two sources simultaneously, examining the views of each author point by point (criterion by criterion), comparing and contrasting these views in the process. The criterion approach is best used when you have a number of points to discuss or when passages or subjects are long and/or complex. A comparison-and-contrast synthesis organized by criteria might look like this:

I. Introduce the paper; lead to thesis.

II. Criterion 1

A. Discuss what author #1 says about this point. Or present situation #1 in light of this point.

B. Discuss what author #2 says about this point, comparing and contrasting #2's treatment of the point with #1's. Or present situation #2 in light of this point and explain its differences from situation #1.

III. Criterion 2

    A. Discuss what author #1 says about this point. Or present situation #1 in light of this point.

    B. Discuss what author #2 says about this point, comparing and contrasting #2's treatment of the point with #1's. Or present situation #2 in light of this point and explain its differences from situation #1.

And so on, proceeding criterion by criterion until you have completed your discussion. Be sure to arrange criteria with a clear method; knowing how the discussion of one criterion leads to the next will ensure smooth transitions throughout your paper. End by summarizing your key points and perhaps raising and responding to pertinent questions.

However you organize your comparison-and-contrast synthesis, keep in mind that comparing and contrasting are not ends in themselves. Your discussion should point to a conclusion, an answer to the question "So what—why bother to compare and contrast in the first place?" If your discussion is part of a larger synthesis, point to and support the larger claim. If you write a stand-alone comparison-and-contrast synthesis, though, you must by the final paragraph answer the "Why bother?" question. The model comparison-and-contrast synthesis that follows does exactly this.

Exercise 3.3 C

Comparing and Contrasting

Review the model argument synthesis (pp. 82–89) for elements of comparison and contrast—specifically those paragraphs concerning how Cornell University, M.I.T., and the University of Kentucky balance student privacy with the parental right to know about the health and welfare of their children.

1. From these paragraphs in the model paper, extract raw information concerning the positions of the three schools on the issue of student privacy and then craft your own brief comparison and contrast synthesis. Identify criteria for comparison and contrast, and discuss the positions of each school in relation to these criteria. *Note:* For this exercise, do not concern yourself with parenthetical citation (that is, with identifying your source materials).

2. Write a paragraph or two that traces the development of comparison and contrast throughout the model paper. Having discussed the *how* and *where* of this development, discuss the *why*. Answer this question: Why has the writer used comparison and contrast? (Hint: it is not an end in itself.) To what use is it put?

A Case for Comparison and Contrast: World War I and World War II

Let's see how the principles of comparison and contrast can be applied to a response to a final examination question in a course on modern history. Imagine that having attended classes involving lecture and discussion, and having read excerpts from John Keegan's *The First World War* and Tony Judt's *Postwar: A History of Europe Since 1945*, you were presented with this examination question:

> Based on your reading to date, compare and contrast the two world wars in light of any four or five criteria you think significant. Once you have called careful attention to both similarities and differences, conclude with an observation. What have you learned? What can your comparative analysis teach us?

Comparison and Contrast Organized by Criteria

Here is a plan for a response, essentially a comparison-and-contrast synthesis, organized by *criteria* and beginning with the thesis—and the *claim*.

> *Thesis*: In terms of the impact on cities and civilian populations, the military aspects of the two wars in Europe, and their aftermaths, the differences between World War I and World War II considerably outweigh the similarities.

    I. Introduction. World Wars I and II were the most devastating conflicts in history. *Thesis*

    II. Summary of main similarities: causes, countries involved, battlegrounds, global scope.

    III. First major difference: physical impact of war.
        A. WWI was fought mainly in rural battlegrounds.
        B. In WWII, cities were destroyed.

    IV. Second major difference: effect on civilians.
        A. WWI fighting primarily involved soldiers.
        B. WWII involved not only military but also massive noncombatant casualties: civilian populations were displaced, forced into slave labor, and exterminated.

    V. Third major difference: combat operations.
        A. World War I, in its long middle phase, was characterized by trench warfare.
        B. During the middle phase of World War II, there was no major military action in Nazi-occupied Western Europe.

    VI. Fourth major difference: aftermath.
        A. Harsh war terms imposed on defeated Germany contributed significantly to the rise of Hitler and World War II.
        B. Victorious allies helped rebuild West Germany after World War II but allowed Soviets to take over Eastern Europe.

    VII. Conclusion. Since the end of World War II, wars have been far smaller in scope and destructiveness, and warfare has expanded to involve stateless combatants committed to acts of terror.

The following model exam response, a comparison-and-contrast synthesis organized by criteria, is written according to the preceding plan. (Thesis and topic sentences are highlighted.)

MODEL COMPARISON-AND-CONTRAST SYNTHESIS

①   World War I (1914–18) and World War II (1939–45) were the most catastrophic and destructive conflicts in human history. For those who believed in the steady but inevitable progress of civilization, it was impossible to imagine that two wars in the first half of the twentieth century could reach levels of barbarity and horror that would outstrip those of any previous era. Historians estimate that more than 22 million people, soldiers and civilians, died in World War I; they estimate that between 40 and 50 million died in World War II. In many ways, these two conflicts were similar: they were fought on many of the same European and Russian battlegrounds, with more or less the same countries on opposing sides. Even many of the same people were involved: Winston Churchill and Adolf Hitler figured in both wars. And the main outcome in each case was the same: total defeat for Germany. However, in terms of the impact on cities and civilian populations, the military aspects of the two wars in Europe, and their aftermaths, the differences between World Wars I and II considerably outweigh the similarities.

②   The similarities are clear enough. In fact, many historians regard World War II as a continuation—after an intermission of about twenty years—of World War I. One of the main causes of each war was Germany's dissatisfaction and frustration with what it perceived as its diminished place in the world. Hitler launched World War II partly out of revenge for Germany's humiliating defeat in World War I. In each conflict Germany and its allies (the Central Powers in WWI, the Axis in WWII) went to war against France, Great Britain, Russia (the Soviet Union in WWII), and eventually, the United States. Though neither conflict included literally the entire world, the participation of countries not only in Europe but also in the Middle East, the Far East, and the Western hemisphere made both conflicts global in scope. And as indicated earlier, the number of casualties in each war was unprecedented in history, partly because modern technology had enabled the creation of deadlier weapons—including tanks, heavy artillery, and aircraft—than had ever been used in warfare.

Despite these similarities, the differences between the two world wars are considerably more significant. One of the most noticeable differences was the physical impact of each war in Europe and in Russia—the western and eastern fronts. The physical destruction of World War I was confined largely to the battlefield. The combat took place almost entirely in the rural areas of Europe and Russia. No major cities were destroyed in the first war; cathedrals, museums, government buildings, urban houses, and apartments were left untouched. During the second war, in contrast, almost no city or town of any size emerged unscathed. Rotterdam, Warsaw, London, Minsk, and—when the Allies began their counterattack—almost every major city in Germany and Japan, including Berlin and Tokyo, were flattened. Of course, the physical devastation of the cities created millions of refugees, a phenomenon never experienced in World War I.

The fact that World War II was fought in the cities as well as on the battlefields meant that the second war had a much greater impact on civilians than did the first war. With few exceptions, the civilians in Europe during WWI were not driven from their homes, forced into slave labor, starved, tortured, or systematically exterminated. But all of these crimes happened routinely during WWII. The Nazi occupation of Europe meant that the civilian populations of France, Belgium, Norway, the Netherlands, and other conquered lands, along with the industries, railroads, and farms of these countries, were put into the service of the Third Reich. Millions of people from conquered Europe—those who were not sent directly to the death camps—were forcibly transported to Germany and put to work in support of the war effort.

During both wars, the Germans were fighting on two fronts—the western front in Europe and the eastern front in Russia. But while both wars were characterized by intense military activity during their initial and final phases, the middle and longest phases—at least in

Europe—differed considerably. The middle phase of the First World War was characterized by trench warfare, a relatively static form of military activity in which fronts seldom moved, or moved only a few hundred yards at a time, even after major battles. By contrast, in the years between the German conquest of most of Europe by early 1941 and the Allied invasion of Normandy in mid-1944, there was no major fighting in Nazi-occupied Western Europe. (The land battles then shifted to North Africa and the Soviet Union.)

⑥   And of course, the two world wars differed in their aftermaths. The most significant consequence of World War I was that the humiliating and costly war reparations imposed on the defeated Germany by the terms of the 1919 Treaty of Versailles made possible the rise of Hitler and thus led directly to World War II. In contrast, after the end of the Second World War in 1945, the Allies helped rebuild West Germany (the portion of a divided Germany that it controlled), transformed the new country into a democracy, and helped make it one of the most thriving economies of the world. But perhaps the most significant difference in the aftermath of each war involved Russia. That country, in a considerably weakened state, pulled out of World War I a year before hostilities ended so that it could consolidate its 1917 Revolution. Russia then withdrew into itself and took no significant part in European affairs until the Nazi invasion of the Soviet Union in 1941. In contrast, it was the Red Army in World War II that was most responsible for the crushing defeat of Germany. In recognition of its efforts and of its enormous sacrifices, the Allies allowed the Soviet Union to take control of the countries of Eastern Europe after the war, leading to fifty years of totalitarian rule—and the Cold War.

⑦   While the two world wars that devastated much of Europe were similar in that, at least according to some historians, they were the same war interrupted by two decades, and similar in that combatants killed more efficiently than armies throughout history ever had, the differences between the wars were significant. In terms of the physical impact of the fighting, the impact on civilians, the action on the battlefield at mid-war, and the aftermaths, World Wars I and II differed in ways that matter to us decades later. Recently, the wars in Iraq, Afghanistan, and Bosnia have involved an alliance of nations pitted against single nations; but we have not seen, since the two world wars, grand alliances moving vast armies across continents. The destruction implied by such action is almost unthinkable today. Warfare is changing, and "stateless" combatants like Hamas and Al Qaeda wreak destruction of their own. But we may never see, one hopes, the devastation that follows when multiple nations on opposing sides of a conflict throw millions of soldiers—and civilians—into harm's way.

The Strategy of the Comparison-and-Contrast Synthesis

The general strategy of this argument is an organization by *criteria*. The writer argues that, although the two world wars exhibited some similarities, the differences between the two conflicts were more significant. Note that the writer's thesis doesn't merely establish these significant differences; it enumerates them in a way that anticipates both the content and the structure of the response to follow.

In argument terms, the *claim* the writer makes is the conclusion that the two global conflicts were significantly different, if superficially similar. The *assumption* is that careful attention to the impact of the wars upon cities and civilian populations and to the consequences of the Allied victories is the key to understanding the differences between them. The *support* comes in the form of historical facts regarding the levels of casualties, the scope of destruction, the theaters of conflict, the events following the conclusions of the wars, and so on.

- **Paragraph 1:** The writer begins by commenting on the unprecedented level of destruction of World Wars I and II and concludes with the thesis summarizing the key similarities and differences.
- **Paragraph 2:** The writer summarizes the key similarities in the two wars: the wars' causes, their combatants, their global scope, the level of destructiveness made possible by modern weaponry.
- **Paragraph 3:** The writer discusses the first of the key differences: the fact that the battlegrounds of World War I were largely rural, but in World War II cities were targeted and destroyed.
- **Paragraph 4:** The writer discusses the second of the key differences: the impact on civilians. In World War I, civilians were generally spared from the direct effects of combat; in World War II, civilians were targeted by the Nazis for systematic displacement and destruction.

- **Paragraph 5:** The writer discusses the third key difference: Combat operations during the middle phase of World War I were characterized by static trench warfare. During World War II, in contrast, there were no major combat operations in Nazi-occupied Western Europe during the middle phase of the conflict.
- **Paragraph 6:** The writer focuses on the fourth key difference: the aftermath of the two wars. After World War I, the victors imposed harsh conditions on a defeated Germany, leading to the rise of Hitler and the Second World War. After World War II, the Allies helped Germany rebuild and thrive. However, the Soviet victory in 1945 led to its postwar domination of Eastern Europe.
- **Paragraph 7:** In the conclusion, the writer sums up the key similarities and differences just covered and makes additional comments about the course of more recent wars since World War II. In this way, the writer responds to the questions posed at the end of the assignment: "What have you learned? What can your comparative analysis teach us?"

THE EXPLANATORY SYNTHESIS

Many of the papers you write in college will be more or less explanatory in nature. An explanation helps readers understand a topic. Writers explain when they divide a subject into its component parts and present them to the reader in a clear and orderly fashion. Explanations may entail descriptions that re-create in words some object, place, emotion, event, sequence of events, or state of affairs. As a student reporter, you may need to explain an event—to relate when, where, and how it took place. In a science lab, you would observe the conditions and results of an experiment and record them for review by others. In a political science course, you might review research on a particular subject—say, the complexities underlying the debate over gay marriage—and then present the results of your research to your professor and the members of your class.

Your job in writing an explanatory paper—or in writing the explanatory portion of an argumentative paper—is not to argue a particular point but rather *to present the facts in a reasonably objective manner.* Of course, explanatory papers, like other academic papers, should be based on a thesis. But the purpose of a thesis in an explanatory paper is less to advance a particular opinion than to focus the various facts contained in the paper.

Practice Explanatory Synthesis

Write an explanatory synthesis on student privacy rights and campus safety using the sources presented earlier in this chapter (pages 66–77), the sources referred to in the sample paper (pages 82–89) but not included in this chapter, and any other sources you might find on the topic. Use the following guidelines:

- **Consider your purpose.** Your purpose in this paper is to present the relevant facts about student privacy rights and campus safety in a reasonably objective manner. You yourself should not take a position on either side of the debate. Your responsibility, rather, is to report objectively on the opposing sides of the debate (as represented in your sources) as well as on the essential facts about the state of student privacy rights and campus safety today.

- **Select and carefully read your sources.** Draw upon the same sources that the writer of the argument synthesis used. You may use some or all of these sources; feel free to enhance your discussion by discovering additional sources through research.

- **Formulate a thesis.** Design your thesis primarily to *inform* rather than to *persuade.* Example: "In the wake of the violence at Virginia Tech, college administrators, parents, and students struggled to find a balance between student privacy rights and campus safety."

- **Decide how you will use your source material.** Locate facts and ideas from the readings that will help you to support your thesis.

- **Develop an organizational plan.** Devise an outline that will enable you to present your material effectively. A thesis will often imply an organizational plan. For example, the sample thesis above commits you to (1) recounting the violence at Virginia Tech, (2) explaining the current state of student privacy and campus safety, (3) exploring how these rights sometimes conflict with each other, and (4) describing public opinion and the various proposals for addressing the situation. This order might offer the most logical structure for your discussion, but during the composing process, you might decide on a different order— which may require you to modify your original thesis.

- **Draft clear, organizing statements for the main sections.** Expand each major point of your outline into a statement that distills the main idea(s) of the paragraph(s) it will organize. Give every paragraph within a section a clear topic sentence.

- **Write and revise your synthesis; document your sources.** See the model argument paper on student privacy rights and campus safety for an example synthesis with carefully documented sources.

SUMMARY OF SYNTHESIS TYPES

In this chapter we've considered three main types of synthesis: the *argument synthesis*, the *comparison-and-contrast synthesis*, and the *explanatory synthesis*. Although for ease of comprehension we've placed them in separate categories, these types are not mutually exclusive. Both explanatory syntheses and argument syntheses often involve elements of one another, and comparison-and-contrast syntheses can fall into either of the other two categories. Which approach you choose will depend on your *purpose* and the method that you decide is best suited to achieve this purpose.

If your main purpose is to help your audience understand a particular subject, and in particular to help them understand the essential elements or significance of this subject, then you will be composing an explanatory synthesis. If your main purpose, on the other hand, is to persuade your audience to agree with your viewpoint on a subject, or to change their minds, or to decide on a particular course of action, then you will be composing an argument synthesis. If one effective technique of making your case is to establish similarities or differences between your subject and another one, then you will compose a comparison-and-contrast synthesis—which may well be just *part* of a larger synthesis.

In planning and drafting these syntheses, you can draw on a variety of strategies: supporting your claims by summarizing, paraphrasing, and quoting from your sources and by choosing from among strategies such as climactic or conventional order, counterargument, and concession the approach that will best help you to achieve your purpose.

We turn, now, to analysis, which is another important strategy for academic thinking and writing. Chapter 4, "Analysis," will introduce you to a strategy that, like synthesis, draws upon all the strategies you've been practicing as you move through *Writing and Reading Across the Curriculum: Brief Edition.*

Chapter 4

Analysis

WHAT IS AN ANALYSIS?

An *analysis* is an argument in which you study the parts of something to understand how it works, what it means, or why it might be significant. The writer of an analysis uses an analytical tool: a *principle* or *definition* on the basis of which an object, an event, or a behavior can be divided into parts and examined. Here are excerpts from two analyses of the movie version of L. Frank Baum's *The Wizard of Oz:*

> At the dawn of adolescence, the very time she should start to distance herself from Aunt Em and Uncle Henry, the surrogate parents who raised her on their Kansas farm, Dorothy Gale experiences a hurtful reawakening of her fear that these loved ones will be rudely ripped from her, especially her Aunt (Em—M for Mother!).*

> [*The Wizard of Oz*] was originally written as a political allegory about grass-roots protest. It may seem harder to believe than Emerald City, but the Tin Woodsman is the industrial worker, the Scarecrow [is] the struggling farmer, and the Wizard is the president, who is powerful only as long as he succeeds in deceiving the people.†

As these paragraphs suggest, what you discover through an analysis depends entirely on the principle or definition you use to make your insights. Is *The Wizard of Oz* the story of a girl's psychological development, or is it a story about politics? The answer is *both*. In the first example, the psychiatrist Harvey Greenberg applies the principles of his profession and, not surprisingly, sees *The Wizard of Oz* in psychological terms. In the

---

*Harvey Greenberg, *The Movies on Your Mind* (New York: Dutton, 1975).
†Peter Dreier, "The Politics of Oz," *San Francisco Chronicle*, 24 Sept. 1989.

second example, a newspaper reporter applies the political theories of Karl Marx and, again not surprisingly, discovers a story about politics.

Different as they are, these analyses share an important quality: Each is the result of a specific principle or definition used as a tool to divide an object into parts in order to see what it means and how it works. The writer's choice of analytical tool simultaneously creates and limits the possibilities for analysis. Thus, working with the principles of Freud, Harvey Greenberg sees *The Wizard of Oz* in psychological, not political, terms; working with the theories of Karl Marx, Peter Dreier understands the movie in terms of the economic relationships among characters. It's as if the writer of an analysis who adopts one analytical tool puts on a pair of glasses and sees an object in a specific way. Another writer, using a different tool (and a different pair of glasses), sees the object differently.

WHERE DO WE FIND WRITTEN ANALYSES?

Here are just a few of the types of writing that involve analysis:

Academic Writing

- **Experimental and lab reports** analyze the meaning or implications of the study results in the Discussion section.
- **Research papers** analyze information in sources or apply theories to material being reported.
- **Process analyses** break down the steps or stages involved in completing a process.
- **Literary analyses** examine characterization, plot, imagery, or other elements in works of literature.
- **Essay exams** demonstrate understanding of course material by analyzing data using course concepts.

Workplace Writing

- **Grant proposals** analyze the issues you seek funding for in order to address them.
- **Reviews of the arts** employ dramatic or literary analysis to assess artistic works.
- **Business plans** break down and analyze capital outlays, expenditures, profits, materials, and the like.
- **Medical charts** record analytical thinking and writing in relation to patient symptoms and possible options.
- **Legal briefs** break down and analyze facts of cases and elements of legal precedents and apply legal rulings and precedents to new situations.
- **Case studies** describe and analyze the particulars of a specific medical, social service, advertising, or business case.

You might protest: Are there as many analyses of *The Wizard of Oz* as there are people to read the book or to see the movie? Yes, or at least as many analyses as there are analytical tools. This does not mean that all analyses are equally valid or useful. Each writer must convince the reader. In creating an essay of analysis, the writer must organize a series of related insights, using the analytical tool to examine first one part and then another of the object being studied. To read Harvey Greenberg's essay on *The Wizard of Oz* is to find paragraph after paragraph of related insights—first about Aunt Em, then the Wicked Witch, then Toto, and then the Wizard. All these insights point to Greenberg's single conclusion: that "Dorothy's 'trip' is a marvelous metaphor for the psychological journey every adolescent must make." Without Greenberg's analysis, we would probably not have thought about the movie as a psychological journey. This is precisely the power of an analysis: its ability to reveal objects or events in ways we would not otherwise have considered.

The writer's challenge is to convince readers that (1) the analytical tool being applied is legitimate and well matched to the object being studied, and (2) the analytical tool is being used systematically to divide the object into parts and to make a coherent, meaningful statement about these parts and the object as a whole.

When *Your* Perspective Guides the Analysis

In some cases a writer's analysis of a phenomenon or a work of art may not result from anything as structured as a principle or a definition. It may follow from the writer's cultural or personal outlook, perspective, or interests. Imagine reading a story or observing the lines of a new building and being asked to analyze it—not based on someone else's definition or principle, but on your own. Analyses in this case continue to probe the parts of things to understand how they work and what they mean. And they continue to be carefully structured, examining one part of a phenomenon at a time. The essential purpose of the analysis, to *reveal*, remains unchanged. This goal distinguishes the analysis from the critique, whose main purpose is to *evaluate* and *assess validity*.

Consider this passage from an op-ed article by Terri Martin Hekker, "The Satisfactions of Housewifery and Motherhood in an Age of 'Do Your Own Thing,'" which appeared in the *New York Times* in 1977:

> I come from a long line of women…who never knew they were unfulfilled. I can't testify that they were happy, but they *were* cheerful. And if they lacked "meaningful relationships," they cherished relations who meant something. They took pride in a clean, comfortable home and satisfaction in serving a good meal because no one had explained to them that the only work worth doing is that for which you get paid.
>
> They enjoyed rearing their children because no one ever told them that little children belonged in church basements and their mothers

belonged somewhere else. They lived, very frugally, on their husbands' paychecks because they didn't realize that it's more important
to have a bigger house and a second car than it is to rear your own
children. And they were so incredibly ignorant that they died never
suspecting they'd been failures.

That won't hold true for me. I don't yet perceive myself as a failure,
but it's not for want of being told I am.

The other day, years of condescension prompted me to fib in order
to test a theory. At a party where most of the guests were business
associates of my husband, a Ms. Putdown asked me who I was. I told
her I was Jack Hekker's wife. That had a galvanizing effect on her.
She took my hand and asked if that was all I thought of myself—just
someone's wife? I wasn't going to let her in on the five children but
when she persisted I mentioned them but told her that they weren't
mine, that they belonged to my dead sister. And then I basked in the
glow of her warm approval.

It's an absolute truth that whereas you are considered ignorant to
stay home to rear *your* children, it is quite heroic to do so for someone
else's children. Being a housekeeper is acceptable (even to the Social
Security office) as long as it's not *your* house you're keeping. And
treating a husband with attentive devotion is altogether correct as
long as he's not *your* husband.

Sometimes I feel like Alice in Wonderland. But lately, mostly, I feel
like an endangered species.

Hekker's view of the importance of what she calls "housewifery"—the
role of the traditional American wife and mother—derives from her own
personal standards and ideals, which themselves derive from a cultural
perspective that she admits is no longer in fashion in the late 1970s. This
cultural and personal perspective places great value on such aspects of
marriage and motherhood as having "a clean, comfortable home," the satisfaction of "serving a good meal," and the enjoyment of rearing "your own
children," and it places less value on "having a big house and a second car."
She refuses to consider herself a failure (as she believes others do) because
she takes pride in identifying herself as her husband's wife. Hekker's analysis of her own situation, in contrast to the situation of the more "liberated"
working wife, throws a revealing light on the cultural conflicts of that period
regarding marriage.

Almost thirty years after she wrote this op-ed article, Hekker's perspective had dramatically shifted. Her shattering experiences in the wake of her
unexpected divorce had changed her view—and, as a result, her analysis—
of the status, value, and prospects of the traditional wife:

Like most loyal wives of our generation, we'd contemplated eventual
widowhood but never thought we'd end up divorced. And "divorced"
doesn't begin to describe the pain of this process. "Canceled" is more
like it.... If I had it to do over again, I'd still marry the man I married and
have my children: they are my treasure and a powerful support system

for me and for one another. But I would have used the years after my youngest started school to further my education. I could have amassed two doctorates using the time and energy I gave myself to charitable and community causes and been better able to support myself.

Hekker's new analysis of the role of the traditional wife (published in the *New York Times* in 2006) derives from her changed perspective, based on her own experience and the similar experiences of a number of her divorced friends. Notice, again, that the analysis is meant to *reveal*. (The complete versions of these two op-eds by Terri Martin Hekker appear in Chapter 7, "Marriage and Family in America," pp. 274–279.)

If you find yourself writing an analysis guided by your own insights, not by someone else's, then you owe your reader a clear explanation of your guiding principles and the definitions by which you will probe the subject under study. Continue using the Guidelines for Writing Analyses (see p. 124), modifying this advice as you think fit to accommodate your own personal outlook, perspective, or interests. Above all, remember to structure your analysis with care. Proceed systematically and emerge with a clear statement about what the subject means, how it works, or why it might be significant.

DEMONSTRATION: ANALYSIS

Two examples of analyses follow. The first was written by a professional writer; the second was written by a student in response to an assignment in his sociology class. Each analysis illustrates the two defining features of analysis just discussed: a statement of an analytical principle or definition, and the use of that principle or definition in closely examining an object, behavior, or event. As you read, try to identify these features. An exercise with questions for discussion follows each example.

THE PLUG-IN DRUG

Marie Winn

This analysis of television viewing as an addictive behavior appeared originally in Marie Winn's book *The Plug-In Drug: Television, Computers, and Family Life* (2002). A writer and media critic, Winn has been interested in the effects of television on both individuals and the larger culture. In this passage, she carefully defines the term *addiction* and then applies it systematically to the behavior under study.

The word "addiction" is often used loosely and wryly in conversation. People will refer to themselves as "mystery-book addicts" or "cookie addicts." E. B. White wrote of his annual surge of interest in gardening: "We are hooked and are making an attempt to kick the habit." Yet nobody really believes that reading mysteries or ordering seeds by catalogue is serious enough to be compared with addictions to heroin or alcohol. In these cases the word "addiction" is used jokingly to denote a tendency to overindulge in some pleasurable activity.

People often refer to being "hooked on TV." Does this, too, fall into the lighthearted category of cookie eating and other pleasures that people pursue with unusual intensity? Or is there a kind of television viewing that falls into the more serious category of destructive addiction?

Not unlike drugs or alcohol, the television experience allows the participant to blot out the real world and enter into a pleasurable and passive mental state. To be sure, other experiences, notably reading, also provide a temporary respite from reality. But it's much easier to stop reading and return to reality than to stop watching television. The entry into another world offered by reading includes an easily accessible return ticket. The entry via television does not. In this way television viewing, for those vulnerable to addiction, is more like drinking or taking drugs—once you start it's hard to stop.

Just as alcoholics are only vaguely aware of their addiction, feeling that they control their drinking more than they really do ("I can cut it out any time I want—I just like to have three or four drinks before dinner"), many people overestimate their control over television watching. Even as they put off other activities to spend hour after hour watching television, they feel they could easily resume living in a different, less passive style. But somehow or other while the television set is present in their homes, it just stays on. With television's easy gratifications available, those other activities seem to take too much effort.

5   A heavy viewer (a college English instructor) observes:

> I find television almost irresistible. When the set is on, I cannot ignore it. I can't turn it off. I feel sapped, will-less, enervated. As I reach out to turn off the set, the strength goes out of my arms. So I sit there for hours and hours.

Self-confessed television addicts often feel they "ought" to do other things—but the fact that they don't read and don't plant their garden or sew or crochet or play games or have conversations means that those activities are no longer as desirable as television viewing. In a way, the lives of heavy viewers are as unbalanced by their television "habit" as drug addicts' or alcoholics' lives. They are living in a holding pattern, as it were, passing up the activities that lead to growth or development or a sense of accomplishment. This is one reason people talk about their television viewing so ruefully, so apologetically. They are aware that it is an unproductive experience, that by any human measure almost any other endeavor is more worthwhile.

It is the adverse effect of television viewing on the lives of so many people that makes it feel like a serious addiction. The television habit distorts the sense of time. It renders other experiences vague and curiously unreal while taking on a greater reality for itself. It weakens relationships by reducing and sometimes eliminating normal opportunities for talking, for communicating.

And yet television does not satisfy, else why would the viewer continue to watch hour after hour, day after day? "The measure of health," wrote the psychiatrist Lawrence Kubie, "is flexibility...and especially the freedom to cease when sated." But heavy television viewers can never be sated with their television experiences. These do not provide the true nourishment that satiation requires, and thus they find that they cannot stop watching.

Exercise 4.1

Reading Critically: Winn

In an analysis, an author first presents the analytical principle in full and then systematically applies parts of the principle to the object or phenomenon under study. In her brief analysis of television viewing, Marie Winn pursues an alternative, though equally effective, strategy by *distributing* parts of her analytical principle across the essay. Locate where Winn defines key elements of addiction. Locate where she uses each element as an analytical lens to examine television viewing as a form of addiction.

What function does paragraph 4 play in the analysis?

In the first two paragraphs, how does Winn create a funnel-like effect that draws readers into the heart of her analysis?

Recall a few television programs that genuinely moved you, educated you, humored you, or stirred you to worthwhile reflection or action. To what extent does Winn's analysis describe your positive experiences as a television viewer? (Consider how Winn might argue that, from within an addicted state, a person may feel "humored, moved, or educated" but is in fact—from a sober outsider's point of view—deluded.) If Winn's analysis of television viewing as an addiction does *not* account for your experience, does it follow that her analysis is flawed? Explain.

Edward Peselman wrote the following paper as a first-semester sophomore in response to this assignment from his English professor:

> Read Chapter 3, "The Paradoxes of Power," in Randall Collins's *Sociological Insight: An Introduction to Non-Obvious Sociology* (2nd ed., 1992). Use any of Collins's observations to examine the sociology of power in a group with which you are familiar. Write for readers much like yourself: freshmen or sophomores who have taken one course in sociology. Your object in this paper is to use Collins as a way of learning something "nonobvious" about a group to which you belong or have belonged.
>
> Note: This paper is formatted in MLA style.

MODEL ANALYSIS

Edward Peselman

Professor Sladko

Everyday Life Reconsidered

Murray State University

23 March 2010

The Coming Apart of a Dorm Society

(1) During my first year of college, I lived in a dormitory, like most freshmen on campus. We inhabitants of the dorm came from different cultural and economic backgrounds. Not surprisingly, we brought with us many of the traits found in people outside of college. Like many on the outside, we in the dorm sought personal power at the expense of others. The gaining and maintaining of power can be an ugly business, and I saw people hurt and in turn hurt others all for the sake of securing a place in the dorm's prized social order. Not until one of us challenged that order did I realize how fragile it was.

(2) Randall Collins, a sociologist at the University of California, Riverside, defines the exercise of power as the attempt "to make something happen in society" (61). A society can be understood as something as large and complex as "American society"; something more sharply defined, such as a corporate or organizational society; or something smaller still—a dorm society like my own, consisting of six 18-year-old men who lived at one end of a dormitory floor in an all-male dorm.

(3) In my freshman year, my society was a tiny but distinctive social group in which people exercised power. I lived with two roommates, Dozer and Reggie. Dozer was an emotionally unstable, excitable individual who vented his energy through anger. His insecurity and moodiness contributed to his difficulty in making friends. Reggie was a friendly, happy-go-lucky sort who seldom displayed emotions other than contentedness. He was shy when encountering new people, but when placed in a socially comfortable situation he would talk for hours.

(4) Eric and Marc lived across the hall from us and therefore spent a considerable amount of time in our room. Eric could be cynical and was

often blunt: He seldom hesitated when sharing his frank and sometimes unflattering opinions. He commanded a grudging respect in the dorm. Marc could be very moody and, sometimes, was violent. His temper and stubborn streak made him particularly susceptible to conflict. The final member of our miniature society was Benjamin, cheerful yet insecure. Benjamin had certain characteristics which many considered effeminate, and he was often teased about his sexuality—which in turn made him insecure. He was naturally friendly but, because of the abuse he took, he largely kept to himself. He would join us occasionally for a pizza or late-night television.

Together, we formed an independent social structure. Going out to parties together, playing cards, watching television, playing ball: These were the activities through which we got to know each other and through which we established the basic pecking order of our community. Much like a colony of baboons, we established a hierarchy based on power relationships. According to Collins, what a powerful person wishes to happen must be achieved by controlling others. Collins's observation can help to define who had how much power in our social group. In the dorm, Marc and Eric clearly had the most power. Everyone feared them and agreed to do pretty much what they wanted. Through violent words or threats of violence, they got their way. I was next in line: I wouldn't dare to manipulate Marc or Eric, but the others I could manage through occasional quips. Reggie, then Dozer, and finally Benjamin.

Up and down the pecking order, we exercised control through macho taunts and challenges. Collins writes that "individuals who manage to be powerful and get their own way must do so by going along with the laws of social organization, not by contradicting them" (61). Until mid-year, our dorm motto could have read: "You win through rudeness and intimidation." Eric gained power with his frequent and brutal assessments of everyone's behavior. Marc gained power with his temper—which, when lost, made everyone run for cover. Those who were not rude and intimidating drifted to the bottom of our social world. Reggie was quiet and unemotional, which

Peselman 3

allowed us to take advantage of him because we knew he would back down if pressed in an argument. Yet Reggie understood that on a "power scale" he stood above Dozer and often shared in the group's tactics to get Dozer's food (his parents were forever sending him care packages). Dozer, in turn, seldom missed opportunities to take swipes at Benjamin, with references to his sexuality. From the very first week of school, Benjamin could never—and never wanted to—compete against Eric's bluntness or Marc's temper. Still, Benjamin hung out with us. He lived in our corner of the dorm, and he wanted to be friendly. But everyone, including Benjamin, understood that he occupied the lowest spot in the order.

⑦ That is, until he left mid-year. According to Collins, "any social arrangement works because people avoid questioning it most of the time" (74). The inverse of this principle is as follows: When a social arrangement is questioned, that arrangement can fall apart. The more fragile the arrangement (the flimsier the values on which it is based), the more quickly it will crumble. For the entire first semester, no one questioned our rude, macho rules, and because of them we pigeon-holed Benjamin as a wimp. In our dorm society, gentle men had no power. To say the least, ours was not a compassionate community. From a distance of one year, I am shocked to have been a member of it. Nonetheless, we had created a mini-society that somehow served our needs.

⑧ At the beginning of the second semester, we found Benjamin packing up his room. Marc, who was walking down the hall, stopped by and said something like: "Hey buddy, the kitchen get too hot for you?" I was there, and I saw Benjamin turn around and say: "Do you practice at being such a _____, or does it come naturally? I've never met anybody who felt so good about making other people feel lousy. You'd better get yourself a job in the army or in the prison system, because no one else is going to put up with your _____." Marc said something in a raised voice. I stepped between them, and Benjamin said: "Get out." I was cheering.

⑨ Benjamin moved into an off-campus apartment with his girlfriend. This astonished us, first because of his effeminate manner (we didn't know he had a girlfriend) and second because none of the rest of us had been seeing girls much (though we talked about it constantly). Here was Benjamin, the gentlest among us, and he blew a hole in our macho society. Our social order never really recovered, which suggests its flimsy values. People in the dorm mostly went their own ways during the second semester. I'm not surprised, and I was more than a little grateful. Like most people in the dorm, save for Eric and Marc, I both got my lumps and I gave them, and I never felt good about either. Like Benjamin, I wanted to fit in with my new social surroundings. Unlike him, I didn't have the courage to challenge the unfairness of what I saw.

By chance, six of us were thrown together into a dorm and were expected, on the basis of proximity alone, to develop a friendship. What we did was sink to the lowest possible denominator. Lacking any real basis for friendship, we allowed the forceful, macho personalities of Marc and Eric to set the rules, which for one semester we all subscribed to—even those who suffered. ⑩

The macho rudeness couldn't last, and I'm glad it was Benjamin who brought us down. By leaving, he showed a different and a superior kind of power. I doubt he was reading Randall Collins at the time, but he somehow had come to Collins's same insight: As long as he played by the rules of our group, he suffered because those rules placed him far down in the dorm's pecking order. Even by participating in pleasant activities, like going out for pizza, Benjamin supported a social system that ridiculed him. Some systems are so oppressive and small-minded that they can't be changed from the inside. They've got to be torn down. Benjamin had to move, and in moving he made me (at least) question the basis of my dorm friendships. ⑪

Works Cited

Collins, Randall. *Sociological Insight: An Introduction to Non-obvious Sociology*. 2nd ed. New York: Oxford UP, 1992. Print.

Reading Critically: Peselman

What is the function of paragraph 1? Though Peselman does not use the word *sociology*, what signals does he give that this will be a paper that examines the social interactions of a group? Peselman introduces Collins in paragraph 2. Why? What does Peselman accomplish in paragraphs 3–4? How does his use of Collins in paragraph 5 logically follow the presentation in paragraphs 3–4? The actual analysis in this paper takes place in paragraphs 5–11. Point to where Peselman draws on the work of Randall Collins, and explain how he uses Collins to gain insight into dorm life.

HOW TO WRITE ANALYSES

Consider Your Purpose

Whether you are assigned a topic to write on or are left to your own devices, you inevitably face this question: What is my idea? Like every paper, an analysis has at its heart an idea you want to convey. For Edward Peselman, it was the idea that a social order based on flimsy values is not strong enough to sustain a direct challenge to its power and thus will fall apart eventually. From beginning to end, Peselman advances this one idea: first, by introducing readers to the dorm society he will analyze; next, by introducing principles of analysis (from Randall Collins); and finally, by examining his dorm relationships in light of those principles. The entire set of analytical insights coheres as a paper because the insights are *related* and point to Peselman's single idea.

Peselman's paper offers a good example of the personal uses to which analysis can be put. Notice that he gravitates toward events in his life that confuse him and about which he wants some clarity. Such topics can be especially fruitful for analysis because you know the particulars well and can provide readers with details; you view the topic with some puzzlement; and, through the application of your analytical tool, you may come to understand it. When you select topics to analyze from your own experience, you provide yourself with a motivation to write and learn. When you are motivated in this way, you spark the interest of readers.

Using Randall Collins as a guide, Edward Peselman returns again and again to the events of his freshman year in the dormitory. We sense that Peselman himself wants to understand what happened in that dorm. He writes, "I saw people hurt and in turn hurt others all for the sake of securing a place in the dorm's prized social order." Peselman does not approve of what happened, and the analysis he launches is meant to help him understand.

Locate an Analytical Principle

When you are given an assignment that asks for analysis, use two specific reading strategies to identify principles and definitions in source materials.

- **Look for a sentence that makes a general statement about the way something works.** The statement may strike you as a rule or a law. The line that Edward Peselman quotes from Randall Collins has this quality: "[A]ny social arrangement works because people avoid questioning it most of the time." Such statements are generalizations—conclusions to sometimes complicated and extensive arguments. You can use these conclusions to guide your own analyses as long as you are aware that for some audiences you will need to re-create and defend the arguments that resulted in these conclusions.

- **Look for statements that take this form: X can be defined as (or X consists of) A, B, and C.** The specific elements of the definition—A, B, and C—are what you use to identify and analyze parts of the object being studied. You've seen an example of this approach in Marie Winn's multipart definition of addiction, which she uses to analyze television viewing. As a reader looking for definitions suitable for conducting an analysis, you might come across Winn's definition of addiction and then use it for your own purposes, perhaps to analyze the playing of video games as an addiction.

Essential to any analysis is the validity of the principle or definition being applied, the analytical tool. Make yourself aware, as both writer and reader, of a tool's strengths and limitations. Pose these questions of the analytical principles and definitions you use: Are they accurate? Are they well accepted? Do *you* accept them? What are the arguments against them? What are their limitations? Since every principle or definition used in an analysis is the end product of an argument, you are entitled—even obligated—to challenge it. If the analytical tool is flawed, the analysis that follows from it will be flawed.

A page from Randall Collins's *Sociological Insight* follows; Edward Peselman uses a key sentence from this extract as an analytical tool in his essay on power relations in his dorm (see p. 118). Notice that Peselman underlines the sentence he will use in his analysis.

1. Try this experiment some time. When you are talking to someone, make them explain everything they say that isn't completely clear. The result, you will discover, is a series of uninterrupted interruptions:

   A: Hi, how are you doing?
   B: What do you mean when you say "how"?
   A: You know. What's happening with you?
   B: What do you mean, "happening"?
   A: Happening, you know, what's going on.
   B: I'm sorry. Could you explain what you mean by "what"?
   A: What do you mean, what do I mean? Do you want to talk to me or not?

2. It is obvious that this sort of questioning could go on endlessly, at any rate if the listener doesn't get very angry and punch you in the mouth. But it illustrates two important points. First, virtually

everything can be called into question. We are able to get along with other people not because everything is clearly spelled out, but because we are willing to take most things people say without explanation. Harold Garfinkel, who actually performed this sort of experiment, points out that there is an infinite regress of assumptions that go into any act of social communication. Moreover, some expressions are simply not explainable in words at all. A word like "you," or "here," or "now" is what Garfinkel calls "indexical." You have to know what it means already; it can't be explained.

3. "What do you mean by 'you'?"

4. "I mean *you, you!*" About all that can be done here is point your finger.

5. The second point is that people get mad when they are pressed to explain things that they ordinarily take for granted. This is because they very quickly see that explanations could go on forever and the questions will never be answered. If you really demanded a full explanation of everything you hear, you could stop the conversation from ever getting past its first sentence. The real significance of this for a sociological understanding of the way the world is put together is not the anger, however. It is the fact that people try to avoid these sorts of situations. They tacitly recognize that we have to avoid these endless lines of questioning. Sometimes small children will start asking an endless series of "whys," but adults discourage this.

6. In sum, any social arrangement works becuase people avoid questioning it most of the time. That does not mean that people do not get into arguments or disputes about just what ought to be done from time to time. But to have a dispute already implies there is a considerable area of agreement. An office manager may dispute with a clerk over just how to take care of some business letter, but they at any rate know more or less what they are disputing about. They do not get off into a...series of questions over just what is meant by everything that is said. You could very quickly dissolve the organization into nothingness if you followed that route: there would be no communication at all, even about what the disagreement is over.

7. Social organization is possible because people maintain a certain level of focus. If they focus on one thing, even if only to disagree about it, they are taking many other things for granted, thereby reinforcing their social reality.*

The statement that Peselman has underlined—"any social arrangement works because people avoid questioning it most of the time"—is the end result of an argument that takes Collins several paragraphs to develop. Peselman agrees with the conclusion and uses it in paragraph 7 of his analysis. Observe

*Randall Collins, *Sociological Insight: An Introduction to Non–obvious Sociology,* 2nd ed. (New York: Oxford UP, 1992) 73–74.

that for his own purposes Peselman does *not* reconstruct Collins's argument. He selects *only* Collins's conclusion and then imports that into his analysis, which concerns an entirely different subject. Once he identifies in Collins a principle he can use in his analysis, he converts the principle into questions that he then directs to his topic, life in his freshman dorm. Two questions follow directly from Collins's insight:

1. What was the social arrangement in the dorm?
2. How was this social arrangement questioned?

Peselman clearly defines his dormitory's social arrangement in paragraphs 3–6 (with the help of another principle borrowed from Collins). Beginning with paragraph 7, he explores how one member of his dorm questioned that arrangement:

> That is, until he left mid-year. According to Collins, "any social arrangement works because people avoid questioning it most of the time" (p. 74). The inverse of this principle is as follows: When a social arrangement is questioned, that arrangement can fall apart. The more fragile the arrangement (the flimsier the values on which it is based), the more quickly it will crumble. For the entire first semester, no one questioned our rude, macho rules, and because of them we pigeon-holed Benjamin as a wimp. In our dorm society, gentle men had no power. To say the least, ours was not a compassionate community. From a distance of one year, I am shocked to have been a member of it. Nonetheless, we had created a mini-society that somehow served our needs.

Formulate a Thesis

An analysis is a two-part argument. The first part states and establishes the writer's agreement with a certain principle or definition.

Part One of the Argument

This first part of the argument essentially takes this form:

Claim #1: Principle X (or definition X) is valuable.

Principle X can be a theory as encompassing and abstract as the statement that *myths are the enemy of truth*. Principle X can be as modest as the definition of a term such as *addiction* or *comfort*. As you move from one subject area to another, the principles and definitions you use for analysis will change, as these assignments illustrate:

Sociology: Write a paper in which you place yourself in American society by locating both your absolute position and relative rank on each single criterion of social stratification used by Lenski & Lenski. For each criterion, state whether you have attained your social position by yourself or if you have "inherited" that status from your parents.

Literature: Apply principles of Jungian psychology to Hawthorne's "Young Goodman Brown." In your reading of the story, apply Jung's principles of the shadow, persona, and anima.

Physics: Use Newton's second law (F = ma) to analyze the acceleration of a fixed pulley, from which two weights hang: m_1 (.45 kg) and m_2 (.90 kg). Explain in a paragraph the principle of Newton's law and your method of applying it to solve the problem. Assume your reader is not comfortable with mathematical explanations: Do not use equations in your paragraph.

Finance: Using Guidford C. Babcock's "Concept of Sustainable Growth" [Financial Analysis 26 (May–June 1970): 108–14], analyze the stock price appreciation of the XYZ Corporation, figures for which are attached.

The analytical tools to be applied in these assignments must be appropriate to the discipline. Writing in response to the sociology assignment, you

GUIDELINES FOR WRITING ANALYSES

Unless you are asked to follow a specialized format, especially in the sciences or the social sciences, you can present your analysis as a paper by following the guidelines below. As you move from one class to another, from discipline to discipline, the principles and definitions you use as the basis for your analyses will change, but the following basic components of analysis will remain the same.

- *Create a context for your analysis.* Introduce and summarize for readers the object, event, or behavior to be analyzed. Present a strong case about why an analysis is needed: Give yourself a motivation to write, and give readers a motivation to read. Consider setting out a problem, puzzle, or question to be investigated.
- *Introduce and summarize the key definition or principle that will form the basis of your analysis.* Plan to devote an early part of your analysis to arguing for the validity of this principle or definition if your audience is not likely to understand it or if they are likely to think that the principle or definition is not valuable.
- *Analyze your topic.* Systematically apply elements of this definition or principle to parts of the activity or object under study. You can do this by posing specific questions, based on your analytic principle or definition, about the object. Discuss what you find part by part (organized perhaps by question), in clearly defined sections of the essay.
- *Conclude by stating clearly what is significant about your analysis.* When considering your analytical paper as a whole, what new or interesting insights have you made concerning the object under study? To what extent has your application of the definition or principle helped you to explain how the object works, what it might mean, or why it is significant?

would use sociological principles developed by Lenski and Lenski. In your literature class, you would use principles of Jungian psychology; in physics, Newton's second law; and in finance, a particular writer's concept of "sustainable growth." But whatever discipline you are working in, the first part of your analysis will clearly state which (and whose) principles and definitions you are applying. For audiences unfamiliar with these principles, you will need to explain them; if you anticipate objections, you will need to argue that they are legitimate principles capable of helping you conduct the analysis.

Part Two of the Argument

In the second part of an analysis, you *apply* specific parts of your principle or definition to the topic at hand. Regardless of how it is worded, this second argument in an analysis can be rephrased to take this form:

> **Claim #2:** By applying principle (or definition) X, we can understand *(topic)* as *(conclusion based on analysis)*.

This is your thesis, the main idea of your analytical paper. Fill in the first blank with the specific object, event, or behavior you are examining. Fill in the second blank with your conclusion about the meaning or significance of this object, based on the insights you made during your analysis. Mary Winn completes the second claim of her analysis this way:

> By applying my multipart definition, we can understand *television viewing* as *an addiction.*

Develop an Organizational Plan

You will benefit enormously in the writing of a first draft if you plan out the logic of your analysis. Turn key elements of your analytical principle or definition into questions and then develop the paragraph-by-paragraph logic of the paper.

Turning Key Elements of a Principle or a Definition into Questions

Prepare for an analysis by phrasing questions based on the definition or principle you are going to apply, and then directing those questions to the activity or object to be studied. The method is straightforward: State as clearly as possible the principle or definition to be applied. Divide the principle or definition into its parts and, using each part, form a question. For example, Marie Winn develops a multipart definition of addiction, each part of which is readily turned into a question that she directs at a specific behavior: television viewing. Her analysis of television viewing can be understood as *responses* to each of her analytical questions. Note that, in her brief analysis, Winn does not first define addiction and then analyze television viewing. Rather, *as she* defines aspects of addiction, she analyzes television viewing.

Developing the Paragraph-by-Paragraph Logic of Your Paper

The following paragraph from Edward Peselman's essay illustrates the typical logic of a paragraph in an analytical essay:

> Up and down the pecking order, we exercised control through macho taunts and challenges. Collins writes that "individuals who manage to be powerful and get their own way must do so by going along with the laws of social organization, not by contradicting them" (p. 61). Until mid-year, our dorm motto could have read: "You win through rudeness and intimidation." Eric gained power with his frequent and brutal assessments of everyone's behavior. Marc gained power with his temper—which, when lost, made everyone run for cover. Those who were not rude and intimidating drifted to the bottom of our social world. Reggie was quiet and unemotional, which allowed us to take advantage of him because we knew he would back down if pressed in an argument. Yet Reggie understood that on a "power scale" he stood above Dozer and often shared in the group's tactics to get Dozer's food (his parents were forever sending him care packages). Dozer, in turn, seldom missed opportunities to take swipes at Benjamin, with references to his sexuality. From the very first week of school, Benjamin could never— and never wanted to—compete against Eric's bluntness or Marc's temper. Still, Benjamin hung out with us. He lived in our corner of the dorm, and he wanted to be friendly. But everyone, including Benjamin, understood that he occupied the lowest spot in the order.

We see in this paragraph the typical logic of analysis:

- *The writer introduces a specific analytical tool.* Peselman quotes a line from Randall Collins:

  > "[I]ndividuals who manage to be powerful and get their own way must do so by going along with the laws of social organization, not by contradicting them."

- *The writer applies this analytical tool to the object being examined.* Peselman states his dorm's law of social organization:

  > Until mid-year, our dorm motto could have read: "You win through rudeness and intimidation."

- *The writer uses the tool to identify and then examine the meaning of parts of the object.* Peselman shows how each member (the "parts") of his dorm society conforms to the laws of "social organization":

  > Eric gained power with his frequent and brutal assessments of everyone's behavior. Marc gained power with his temper—which, when lost, made everyone run for cover. Those who were not rude and intimidating drifted to the bottom of our social world.

An analytical paper takes shape when a writer creates a series of such paragraphs and then links them with an overall logic. Here is the logical organization of Edward Peselman's paper:

- Paragraph 1: Introduction states a problem—provides a motivation to write and to read.
- Paragraph 2: Randall Collins is introduced—the author whose work will provide principles for analysis.
- Paragraphs 3–4: Background information is provided—the cast of characters in the dorm.
- Paragraphs 5–9: The analysis proceeds—specific parts of dorm life are identified and found significant, using principles from Collins.
- Paragraphs 10–11: Summary and conclusion are provided—the freshman dorm society disintegrates for reasons set out in the analysis. A larger point is made: Some oppressive systems must be torn down.

Draft and Revise Your Analysis

You will usually need at least two drafts to produce a paper that presents your idea clearly. The biggest changes in your paper will typically come between your first and second drafts. No paper that you write, including an analysis, will be complete until you revise and refine your single compelling idea: your analytical conclusion about what the object, event, or behavior being examined means or how it is significant. You revise and refine by evaluating your first draft, bringing to it many of the same questions you pose when evaluating any piece of writing:

- Are the facts accurate?
- Are my opinions supported by evidence?
- Are the opinions of others authoritative?
- Are my assumptions clearly stated?
- Are key terms clearly defined?
- Is the presentation logical?
- Are all parts of the presentation well developed?
- Are significant opposing points of view presented?

Address these same questions to the first draft of your analysis, and you will have solid information to guide your revision.

Write an Analysis, Not a Summary

The most common error made in writing analyses—an error that is *fatal* to the form—is to present readers with a summary only. For analyses to succeed, you must *apply* a principle or definition and reach a conclusion about the object, event, or behavior you are examining. By definition, a summary (see Chapter 1) includes none of your own conclusions. Summary is naturally a part of analysis; you will need to summarize the object or activity being examined and, depending on the audience's needs, summarize the principle or definition being applied. But in an analysis you must take the next step and share insights that suggest the meaning or significance of some object, event, or behavior.

Make Your Analysis Systematic

Analyses should give the reader the sense of a systematic, purposeful examination. Marie Winn's analysis illustrates the point: She sets out specific elements of addictive behavior in separate paragraphs and then uses each, within its paragraph, to analyze television viewing. Winn is systematic in her method, and we are never in doubt about her purpose.

Imagine another analysis in which a writer lays out four elements of a definition and then applies only two, without explaining the logic for omitting the others. Or imagine an analysis in which the writer offers a principle for analysis but directs it to only a half or a third of the object being discussed, without providing a rationale for doing so. In both cases the writer would be failing to deliver on a promise basic to analyses: Once a principle or definition is presented, it should be thoroughly and systematically applied.

Answer the "So What?" Question

An analysis should make readers *want* to read. It should give readers a sense of getting to the heart of the matter, that what is important in the object or activity under analysis is being laid bare and discussed in revealing ways. If when rereading the first draft of your analysis, you cannot imagine readers saying, "I never thought of _____ this way," then something may be seriously wrong. Reread closely to determine why the paper might leave readers flat and exhausted, as opposed to feeling that they have gained new and important insights. Closely reexamine your own motivations for writing. Have *you* learned anything significant through the analysis? If not, neither will readers, and they will turn away. If you have gained important insights through your analysis, communicate them clearly. At some point, pull together your related insights and say, in effect, "Here's how it all adds up."

Attribute Sources Appropriately

In an analysis you work with one or two sources and apply insights from them to some object or phenomenon you want to understand more thoroughly. Because you are not synthesizing a great many sources, and because the strength of an analysis derives mostly from *your* application of a principle or definition, the opportunities for not appropriately citing sources are diminished. Take special care to cite and quote, as necessary, the one or two sources you use throughout the analysis.

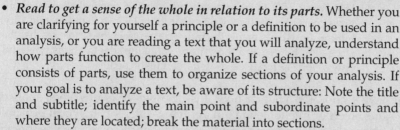

CRITICAL READING FOR ANALYSIS

- *Read to get a sense of the whole in relation to its parts.* Whether you are clarifying for yourself a principle or a definition to be used in an analysis, or you are reading a text that you will analyze, understand how parts function to create the whole. If a definition or principle consists of parts, use them to organize sections of your analysis. If your goal is to analyze a text, be aware of its structure: Note the title and subtitle; identify the main point and subordinate points and where they are located; break the material into sections.
- *Read to discover relationships within the object being analyzed.* Watch for patterns. When you find them, be alert—for they create an occasion to analyze, to use a principle or definition as a guide in discussing what the patterns may mean.

    In fiction, a pattern might involve responses of characters to events or to each other, the recurrence of certain words or phrasings, images, themes, or turns of plot (to name a few).

    In poetry, a pattern might involve rhyme schemes, rhythm, imagery, figurative or literal language, and more.

The challenge to you as a reader is first to see a pattern (perhaps using a guiding principle or definition to do so) and then to locate other instances of that pattern. Reading carefully in this way prepares you to conduct an analysis.

ANALYSIS: A TOOL FOR UNDERSTANDING

As this chapter has demonstrated, analysis involves applying principles as a way to probe and understand. With incisive principles guiding your analysis, you will be able to pose questions, observe patterns and relationships, and derive meaning. Do not forget that this meaning will be one of several possible meanings. Someone else, or even you, using different analytical tools, could observe the same phenomena and arrive at very different conclusions regarding meaning or significance. We end the chapter, then, as we began it: with the two brief analyses of *The Wizard of Oz*. The conclusions expressed in one look nothing like the conclusions expressed in the other, save for the fact that both seek to interpret the same movie. And yet we can say that both are useful, that both reveal meaning.

> At the dawn of adolescence, the very time she should start to distance herself from Aunt Em and Uncle Henry, the surrogate parents who raised her on their Kansas farm, Dorothy Gale experiences a hurtful

reawakening of her fear that these loved ones will be rudely ripped from her, especially her Aunt (Em—M for Mother!).*

[*The Wizard of Oz*] was originally written as a political allegory about grass-roots protest. It may seem harder to believe than Emerald City, but the Tin Woodsman is the industrial worker, the Scarecrow [is] the struggling farmer, and the Wizard is the president, who is powerful only as long as he succeeds in deceiving the people.†

You have seen in this chapter how it is possible for two writers, analyzing the same object or phenomenon but applying different analytical principles, to reach vastly different conclusions about what the object or phenomenon may mean or why it is significant. *The Wizard of Oz* is both an inquiry into the psychology of adolescence and a political allegory. What else the classic film may be awaits revealing with the systematic application of other analytical tools. The insights you gain as a writer of analyses depend entirely on your choice of tools and the subtlety with which you apply them.

---

*Greenberg, Movies.
†Dreier, "Politics."

Part II

An Anthology of Readings

Chapter 5

The Changing Landscape of Work in the Twenty-first Century

A long with the well-wishes of friends and family, you bring to college many expectations. Some involve your emergence as an independent thinker; others, your emergence as an adult, social being. But perhaps no expectations weigh so heavily as thoughts of future employment and the hope of financial independence—especially in an uncertain economy. On the far end of this journey you have begun in higher education, you will seek meaningful employment. If you already devote long hours to supporting your family or paying your way through school, then you know *exactly* why so many pursue a degree: the conviction that a diploma will ensure a better, more secure job. Learn, apply yourself, and succeed: This has always been the formula for achieving the American dream.

The times, however (to paraphrase Bob Dylan), are changing. In the second half of the twentieth century, the labor market rewarded the educated, conferring on those who attended college an "education premium." Even as the forces of globalization reshaped the American economy and workers began losing manufacturing jobs to competitors offshore in China and India, college-educated workers were generally spared severe disruptions. Today, education no longer promises such protection. The relentless search for cheap labor and plentiful raw materials, together with advances in technology, have opened the information-based service economy to foreign competition. According to economists and other analysts, the American, college-educated workforce will increasingly face the same pressures that decades ago so unsettled the automotive and manufacturing sectors. Employers are already offshoring computer coding, certain types of accounting, and medical consultation (the reading of X-rays, MRIs, CT scans, and such)—services that require extensive training.

Experts predict that more American jobs will be lost to foreign competition and fewer will entail a lifelong commitment between employer and employee (pensions, for instance, are quickly disappearing). What implications will these developments hold for you and your intended career? Will they affect the courses you take, the major (and minors) you choose, the summer jobs and internships you pursue? Could you undertake an analysis *now* that will help you anticipate and avoid major disruptions to your working life tomorrow?

This chapter gives you an opportunity to learn what economists, policy analysts, sociologists, historians, management consultants, statisticians, and educators are forecasting about the world of work in the twenty-first century. The readings set a broad context for your investigations. We open with varying definitions of *work* and the related terms *career, profession,* and *vocation.* As you will learn, *work* is not one thing and is not easily defined: Its meaning has shifted over time and across cultures. Next, an expert in international labor studies, Ursula Huws, examines the impact of twin "upheavals" that characterize the new economy: the migration of jobs to workers (think outsourcing on a global scale) and the migration of workers who sometimes travel great distances to find jobs. Sociologist Richard Sennett follows with a startling portrait of a man whose adaptability allowed him to succeed in a corporate culture of downsizing but at the same time "corroded" his character.

Many find reasons for optimism in the new economy. Management consultant Tom Peters sees "gargantuan opportunity" in the emerging business environment and offers six survival skills for success. Writing for a policy think tank, Richard Judy and Carol D'Amico offer a map to the twenty-first century workplace and project winners and losers. In an excerpt from *The World Is Flat,* Thomas Friedman advises that, if you expect your work life to flourish, you had better make yourself "untouchable." Next, former presidential advisor Alan Blinder traces the migration of service jobs (even those requiring a college degree) away from American shores. He, too, offers a strategy for succeeding in the global economy. Next, writers for the *Economist* argue that those worried about the loss of jobs to downsizing and globalization should relax: Through a process of "creative destruction," the economy inevitably adds more jobs than it destroys. Finally, any study of work in twenty-first century America should include a close look at the Bureau of Labor Statistics' "Occupational Outlook Handbook" and report on "Tomorrow's Jobs."

As you search for employment now and in the future, the selections in this chapter will inform your efforts at a doubly uncertain time—when the economy is struggling and when the very foundations of work itself are shifting.

DEFINITIONS: WORK, CAREER,
PROFESSION, VOCATION

The history of work is as old as the human race, and the meaning of the word has changed over time. Tracing the evolution of that meaning is a study unto itself. To ground the present discussion in a common vocabulary, we provide from that literature several definitions of work and related terms.

Work

1. Work has an end beyond itself, being designed to produce or achieve something; it involves a degree of obligation or necessity, being a task that others set us or that we set ourselves; and it is arduous, involving effort and persistence beyond the point at which the task ceases to be wholly pleasurable.

   Keith Thomas, The Oxford Book of Work, 1999 [qtd. in "Changing
   Boundaries and Definitions of Work Over Time and Space," Jurgen Kocka]

2. No, I don't like work. I had rather laze about and think of all the fine things that can be done. I don't like work—no man does—but I like what is in the work—the chance to find yourself. Your own reality—for yourself, not for others—what no other man can ever know. They can only see the mere show, and never can tell what it really means.

   Joseph Conrad, Heart of Darkness

3. The word *work* is not only a kind of activity but a set of ideas and values related to that activity. Consider why we say the following are performing work: a construction worker digging a ditch, an executive at a meeting, a professional basketball player practicing his shots, a critic watching a movie she has to review, a student reading a novel for class, a volunteer bathing a patient in a hospital, an artist painting a picture, a secretary typing a letter for the boss, a monk meditating, and a man washing his kitchen floor. What do these activities have in common? Essentially nothing, except for the fact that, as we say, all of these people are working. We usually don't term shooting baskets, watching movies, and reading short stories *work*. Some might say that getting paid for these activities makes them work. If I pay a group of noisy children to get out of the house and go to a movie, are they working? Students don't get paid to read stories, nor do hospital volunteers or people who wash their own floors get paid to do their tasks. And what about the monk? He doesn't seem to be doing anything.

   A common thread of necessity runs through all of these examples. There is a sense in which all the people *have* to do what they are doing or feel that they *must* do what they are doing. This is clear for the wage earners, including people who play games for a living. They have a particular agreement with their employers to be at a certain place at a certain time, and to perform a particular task. It's also true of the student who must read the book to pass the course, but the student has fewer restrictions on when and where she'll do her work. The floor washer also has few external restrictions. He can choose to let the floor remain dirty. However, if he finds the filth distasteful and doesn't want to live with it, he must wash the floor.

The painter seems to have the most amount of choice, particularly if he actually earns his living as a cabdriver. While external necessities such as bosses, agreements on time and uses of energy, and dirty floors are strong defining features of work, they do not account for the artist who paints from the internal necessity of his or her desire. It is tempting to say that he or she is not working, but as Karl Marx wrote, "Really free work, e.g., composing, is at the same time the most damned serious, the most intense exertion." Most artists would agree. The drive and motivation to work that come from inside a person can be far more powerful than outside forces. This is certainly true for the monk, who is driven by his spirituality.

Joanne B. Ciulla
The Working Life: The Promise and Betrayal of Modern Work

4. The story of work is a story of humanity's trials and triumphs—from the ordeal of hard work, sometimes under conditions of slavery with obedience mandated by the whip, to the development of tools and machines, which take the burdens off human backs and even human minds. These advances in technology, which are still taking place, extend the reach of the hand, expand muscle power, enlarge the senses, and multiply the capacities of the mind. This story of work is still unfolding, with great changes taking place throughout the world and in a more accelerated fashion than ever before.

But work involves more than the use of tools and techniques. The form and nature of the work process help determine the character of a civilization, but, in turn, a society's economic, political, and cultural characteristics shape the form and nature of the work process as well as the role and status of the worker within the society.

Work is essential in providing the basic physical needs of food, clothing, and shelter, and different explanations have been given at different times for its existence and purpose in human survival. Thus, in Chinese civilization, work became part of the Taoist flow of nature to which a person must adapt as part of the natural world. However, in the Judeo-Christian religious tradition (and in pagan religions as well), it was regarded as a punishment sent by God (or by the gods or spirits) to punish human beings for some deviation from the wishes or rules of the divine.

The human spirit, however, is too resilient and optimistic to face an eternal and damning process of hard physical labour, as most was during most of human history for most people, so more benign explanations of the meaning and purpose of work came into use. For example, in western Christendom the Benedictine monks enunciated the rule that "to work is to pray," to fulfill one's duty to God and thus achieve salvation. This notion of work bringing spiritual rewards, in addition to physical survival, was carried further during the 17th century by the Puritans, whose work ethic led them to regard the accumulation of material wealth through labour as a sign of God's favour as well as of the individual's religious fervour. This attitude still appears in the American expression, "You are what you do," implying that people define themselves by the nature of their work.

With the onset of the industrial Revolution and the development of powered machinery during the 18th and 19th centuries, much onerous physical effort was gradually removed from work in factories and fields. Work was still regarded, however, as something separate from pleasure, and the dichotomy between work and play persists even in today's highly industrialized society.

Melvin Kranzberg
"History of the Organization of Work"

Career

NINETEENTH CENTURY   The word career derives from forms meaning "carry." The original definitions of career all referred to rapid and continuous action, movement, and procedure. For instance, an 1819 American edition of Samuel Johnson's eighteenth century Dictionary of the English Language listed the following items: "1. The ground on which a race is run; the length of a course. 2. A course, a race. 3. Height of speed; swift motion. 4. Course of action; uninterrupted procedure." The most common usage of the word related to horse racing and falconry. As the nineteenth century progressed, however, the meaning of career took on a new dimension, cultural rather than physical, abstract rather than visual. The Oxford English Dictionary dated as 1803 the first example of the following usage: "A person's course for progress through life (or a distinct portion of life) so of a nation, party, etc. A profession affording opportunities of advancement." But it was not until midcentury that Oxford found an example of a person actively being told to "go and make a career for himself." The usage of the word was maturing. In American English by the late nineteenth century, to make the career meant to make a success, to become famous. The 1893 edition of the Funk and Wagnalls dictionary in America added the following definitions of career to the familiar ones: "1. A complete course or progress extending through the life or a portion of it, especially when abounding in remarkable actions or incidents, or when publicly conspicuous: said of persons, political parties, nations, etc. 2. A course of business activity, or enterprise; especially, a course of professional life or employment, that offers advancement or honor."

When speaking of occupational activities in the new usage of *career*, an individual no longer confined himself to the description of a random series of jobs, projects, or businesses which provided a livelihood. The individual could now speak of a larger and more absorbing experience—a career: a pre-established total pattern of organized professional activity, with up-ward movement through recognized preparatory stages, and advancement based on merit and bearing honor. By the late nineteenth century, *The Century Dictionary* and *Funk and Wagnalls* were acknowledging a new social concept.

Burton J. Bledstein
The Culture of Professionalism: The Middle Class
and the Development of Higher Education in America

Twenty-first century   Work has changed out of all recognition in less than a generation.

- Unprecedented change and uncertainty has led employers to seek flexible and adaptable employees.
- Globalization, competition and financial constraints have led to massive restructuring, more short-term contracts, and an emphasis on skills development. All sectors have been affected, including higher education.
- Employment in small organizations is more common.
- Continuous learning is vital to keep up with change.

How Careers Have Changed   If the future feels uncertain and you some-times wonder if you have a career, remember that the conventional idea of a "job for life," steadily rising up a hierarchy, is now less relevant. Careers now

- are less likely to be set within a single organization or even a single occupation over a lifetime;
- can include paid or unpaid work, part-time or full-time, within an employing organization or self-employment; and
- develop in a global job market.

The balance of responsibility for career management has shifted from employer to individual. As job opportunities in one specialty or geographic region fade, others blossom. To maintain employability, you need to be able to adapt to these changes by continuously developing and transferring your skills.

What shape is your career?   A range of career forms now coexist.

- **Linear career**—the conventional notion of upward progression through an organization. Now, with flatter organizations, promotions may be less available so you may have to move out to move up.
- **Professional career** (Dalton et al.)—career development is seen as series of stages (dependent apprentice, expert colleague, mentor/manager, figurehead). Again, movement between organizations may be neces-sary to gain experience for growth into the next professional stage.

- **Entrepreneurial career** (Rosabeth Moss Kanter)—career growth through creation of new income and capacity. Not only a feature of the private sector; this is as relevant to public sector organizations (including research) competing for funding.

- **Portfolio** (attributed to Charles Handy)—here the career is viewed as a project portfolio, each activity overlapping or running in parallel and using a slightly different mix of skills. Consultants typically grow their careers in this way.

- **Crazy paving or patchwork** (attributed to Robin Linnecar)—a career made up of a variety of different roles or even different occupations for which a pattern may only be apparent with hindsight. In periods of rapid change, this pattern is about adaptability and survival. It can create a rich career history.

- **Steady-state**—a career where work is enjoyed, development is related to keeping up to date to sustain employability and making an ongoing contribution, but desire for promotion is not significant.

A career can encompass several of these patterns. For example, higher education careers are based in bureaucratic organizations with linear career structures and progression is through stages identifiable with the professional career model. Growing a research group involves bidding competitively for funding providing entrepreneurial career growth, and experienced academics often carry out consultancy for a number of clients or develop spin-out activities giving portfolio career growth.... Contemporary careers can be viewed as a *journey through life, work and learning*. To ensure you are in control of this journey, learn how to manage your own career. How much you invest in your career and how fulfilling you find it is up to you.

> *Vitae: The Career and Development Organization**
> *http://www.vitae.ac.uk/1332/What-is-a-career.html*

Profession

Professions are one of the main forms of institutionalizing expertise in western societies. The term "profession" is a curious one. It immediately conjures up images drawn from television shows featuring lawyers or medical doctors. Such representations point to the hold that certain professions have on our imagination. In *Bleak House*, Charles Dickens's celebrated novel, Richard Carstone considers which profession he wants to take up. The realm of possibilities—according to the definitional criteria of the age—is the military, the clergy, the law, and medicine. Professions such as law and medicine have successfully maintained both their power and

---

*Vitae is a U.K.-based organization that champions the personal, professional, and career development of doctoral researchers and research staff in higher education institutions and research institutes. To find out more about Vitae, visit the organzation's Web site at www. vitae.ac.uk. © 2009 Careers Research and Advisory Centre (CRAC).

status across several centuries and are seen as quintessential examplars of what constitutes a profession. In the late nineteenth century and throughout the twentieth, a raft of new professions emerged. Some, like accountancy, have accured considerable power.

While the dazzling array of different professions renders a definition of a profession difficult,... research suggests that features of a profession include: a body of abstract and specialized knowledge; a professional's autonomy over the labor process; self-regulation by the profession; legal rights restricting those who can practice; control of the supply and licensing of practitioners by the professional body; altruism; and the enjoyment of high status within society. Such characteristics form an "ideal type" of professional labor—one which is rarely observed in professions themselves.

The professional associations of many so-called "new" professions, such as marketers and human resource specialists, have expended considerable effort in trying to emulate the traits of the more established professions. Professions are complex and variegated and there are crucial distinction in their relative status, the length of their history, and power.

Chris Carter
The Blackwell Encyclopedia of Sociology

Vocation

1. Vocation, or calling, is an answer to the question "for what purpose was I born?" The word vocation comes from the Latin *vocare*, to call. While many people are fortunate to find career tracks that make pursuit of their vocation easier, there are others who have careers in medicine and education, for example, who are not called to heal or to teach. In other words you *may* find a well-trod career path in which to live out your vocation and you may have to find a career or a job (job = anything you do for a paycheck) to support living out your vocation, at least in the early years. (Think of all the people waiting tables and doing auditions.)

Don't narrow the field too quickly when thinking of vocation. Try to separate vocation from job slots, to use the verb form rather than the noun: "I'm called to heal others," not, "I'm called to be a doctor." "Doctor" limits too quickly what you can imagine. Maybe a side interest in herbology will pull you into Chinese medicine, or your contemplative nature into spiritual direction.

Parker Palmer says your vocation is what you can't *not* do. I have a friend who understands her calling to be that of bringing love into the world. I can imagine very few jobs from the least to the greatest where this calling could not be lived out. "Liz" enjoys math and is a natural teacher, so teaching high school math was an easy first step. At some point it seemed right to take courses at the local seminary, as she was able; the school invited her to declare a degree when she nearly had enough courses to graduate. Taking clinical pastoral education, she felt pulled into training to be a pastoral counselor and during that time also worked with inner city girls at high-risk of becoming pregnant. A deeply spiritual person, Liz always worked hard to listen for the appropriate place to offer her gifts, whether or not she understood why. Discovering a gift for being present to the dying, she worked with hospice for a while and then as hospital chaplain. Still called to bring love into the world, Liz is now in higher education administration and in her spare time partners with a nurse to work with the ill and dying and their families. She cannot help but live her vocation in the places she finds herself.

Frederick Buechner defines vocation as "the place where your deep gladness and the world's deep hunger meet." Vocation is the thing that will make your heart sing while at the same time meeting a need for someone else.

Guilford College Web Site
http://www.guilford.edu/academics/vocation.html

2. Through work man must earn his daily bread[1] and contribute to the continual advance of science and technology and, above all, to elevating unceasingly the cultural and moral level of the society within which he lives in community with those who belong to the same family. And work means any activity by man, whether manual or intellectual, whatever its nature or circumstances; it means any human activity that can and must be recognized as work, in the midst of all the many activities of which man is capable and to which he is predisposed by his very natures, by virtue of humanity itself. Man is made to be in the visible universe and image and likeness of God himself,[2] and he is placed in it in order to subdue the earth.[3] From the beginning therefore he is *called to work. Work is one of the characteristics that distinguish* man from the rest of creatures, whose activity for sustaining their lives cannot be called work. Only man is capable of work, and only man works, at the same time by work occupying his existence on earth. Thus work bears a particular mark of man and of humanity, the mark of a person operating within a community of persons. And this mark decides its interior characteristics; in a sense it constitutes its very nature.

Pope John Paul II
Laborem exercens (On Human Work)

---

[1]Cf. Ps. 127 (128): 2; cf. also Gn. 3:17–19; Prv. 10:22; Ex. 1:8–14; Jer. 22:13.
[2]Cf. Gn. 1:26.
[3]Cf. Gn. 1:28.

Review Questions

1. Both Ciulla and Thomas use the word *necessity* in defining work. What do they mean by this word?

2. According to Kranzberg, what major transformation regarding attitudes toward work occurred in the Western Christian tradition?

3. What are major differences in the definition of *career* as the word was understood in the late nineteenth and much of the twentieth centuries and the word as it is understood today?

4. What are the defining characteristics of a profession?

5. What is a vocation?

Discussion and Writing Suggestions

1. Locate the definition of work in the *Oxford English Dictionary*. Read the entire entry. Report on what you find in a paragraph or two.

2. Write your own definition of work. Compare your effort to that of others in this selection. In the context of that comparison, consider Joanne Ciulla's observation that "[t]here may be no one particular feature present in everything we call work, but rather many characteristics that overlap and intersect" (*The Working Life* 23). To what extent does your comparison confirm Ciulla's statement?

3. Research the definition of a work-related word not defined in this selection. Possibilities include *toil, labor, job, drudgery, indentured servitude, slavery, livelihood, trade, craft, hobby,* and *occupation*. Report on the history of the word.

4. Consider an activity you know well in which it is possible to both play and work (e.g., tennis, basketball, or chess), and discuss the point at which play *becomes* work. Use Thomas's definition of work as involving "persistence beyond the point at which the task ceases to be wholly pleasurable" to clarify the distinction between play and work.

5. What work do you do that would qualify as a vocation, as opposed to a job? To what extent would you want your job to be your vocation? Do you see this combination as practical? desirable? Discuss.

6. According to the authors in this section, modern careers differ considerably from their historical counterparts. You may know of people who have pursued or are pursuing careers in the old sense of the word and the new. Discuss the advantages and disadvantages you find in each.

7. Describe differences between work that you do for yourself and work that you do for others. Build your description around two specific examples of work. Conrad writes that it is possible to "find yourself" in work. Consider working this idea into your response.

FIXED AND FOOTLOOSE: WORK AND IDENTITY IN THE TWENTY-FIRST CENTURY

Ursula Huws

Sociologist Ursula Huws, professor of international labor studies at the Working Lives Research Institute at London Metropolitan University, is the author of *Making of a Cybertariat: Virtual Work in a Real World* (2003). In this article, she reviews changes in the modern workplace that have left us "with a...shifting and largely uncharted landscape in which jobs are created (and disappear) with great rapidity, often without even a concrete designation—just a mix-and-match combination of 'skills,' 'aptitudes,' and 'competences.'" As you read, notice the structure of Huws's article: after a general introduction, she devotes paragraphs 6–11 to "fixed" jobs; paragraphs 12–15 to "footloose" jobs; and paragraphs 16–18 to "fractured" jobs. This article first appeared in *Monthly Review* (March 2006).

The combination of technological change and globalization is bringing about fundamental changes in who does what work where, when, and how. This has implications which are profoundly contradictory for the nature of jobs [and] for the people who carry them out....

On one hand, work which has previously been geographically tied to a particular place has become footloose to a historically unprecedented extent; on the other, there have been vast migrations of people crossing the planet in search of both jobs and personal safety. There has thus been a double uprooting—a movement of jobs to people and a movement of people to jobs. Between them, these upheavals are transforming the character of cities in both developed and developing countries.

In the process, they are also transforming social identities and structures. Most classic accounts of social stratification place a central importance on occupational identity. The basic building block of class identity has traditionally been the occupation, normally a stable identity acquired slowly either by inheritance or through a training process intended to equip the student or apprentice with skills for life. Once entered into this occupation and practicing those skills, the holder has a recognized position in the social division of labor which gives him or her a "place" in that society for life, barring some calamity such as illness, unemployment, or bankruptcy—risks against which the welfare states of most European countries provide some form of social insurance....

The unprecedented movements of people and jobs around the world have coincided with a breakdown of many traditional occupational identities. Specific skills linked to the use of particular tools or machinery have increasingly given way to more generic and fast-changing skills linked to the use of information and communications technologies (for work involving the processing of information) or to new labor-saving technologies for manual work, for instance in construction, manufacturing, packing, or cleaning. In many countries, this disintegration of occupational identities has also coincided with a collapse in the institutional forms of representation of workers, such as trade unions, which have in the past served to give some coherent shape and social visibility to these identities. We are left with a rapidly shifting and largely uncharted landscape in which jobs are created (and disappear) with great rapidity, often without even a concrete designation—just a mix-and-match combination of "skills," "aptitudes," and "competences."...

5   One of the ironies of the present situation is that many of the most fixed jobs are often carried out by the most footloose people, while some of the most footloose jobs may be carried out by people with deep ancestral roots in the location where they work.

Let us start with some of the fixed jobs. One of the most obvious characteristics of fixedness is the need for physical proximity to a particular spot, because the job directly involves the making, mending, cleaning, or moving of physical goods or the delivery of real personal services to people in real time and real space.

Starting with my own real space, I look around at the fixed jobs that sustain it. I live on a street of nineteenth-century three-story houses in London, where around a third of the houses are occupied by single middle-class households, the remainder having been converted into apartments or occupied by larger, poorer extended families. Most of the middle-class households employ a cleaner for three or four hours a week. Of the cleaners I know on this street, one is Bolivian, one Mauritian, one Ugandan, and one Colombian. Not a single one is white; not a single one was born in Europe, let alone London. At the end of the road there are two restaurants, a café, a fish-and-chip shop, and a fried chicken takeout outlet. One of the restaurants serves European-style dishes of various origins, mainly French. Its owner is a Montenegrin married to an Irish woman. The waitresses are Brazilian, Polish, and Russian. The other restaurant advertises an Italian menu but is owned and staffed (with the exception of one Albanian waitress) by Turkish men, as is the café. The fish-and-chip shop is staffed by Chinese men. The fried chicken outlet, which is open most of the night and caters to a rather rough clientele, is, despite its American name, staffed by a transient crew of exhausted-looking workers of African or Asian origins.

Periodically the houses on the street that are publicly owned (around 20 percent of the total) are renovated together. This happened last year, and for several weeks the neighborhood was filled with construction workers. This time, as far as we could tell, all the skilled workers were Polish; some of the less-skilled laborers were from various Balkan states. Apart from one surveyor (a black Londoner) I saw no women in the crew.

Not having a car, I make frequent use of a local minicab (cheap taxi) service. The drivers are constantly changing but include men from a large

umber of South Asian and African countries. To my knowledge there is
nly one woman driver, a feisty Nigerian who refuses to get out of her car
ut leans heavily on the horn to announce her arrival. I cannot remember
1e last time I was assigned a white driver.
This diversity of ethnic origin is not unique to manual work. The small
ompany that maintains my computer network is run by a Greek Cypriot
1an. His deputy is Syrian and when he is too busy he sends a Turkish
ngineer to attend to my problem. All are highly skilled and educated. The
eception desk in our local health center is staffed by two very efficient
omen—one Nigerian and one Somali.
Such examples could be multiplied many times, not just in London but
1 many cities across the globe where the maintenance of fixed infrastruc-
ure and customer-facing service activities are increasingly in the hands of
eople who were born in other countries or continents. Their presence as
ewcomers or temporary migrants has multiple effects on the shape and
haracter of the host cities now dependent on their labor, both in the areas
here they live and the areas where they work. As service workers and
ervice users they are often at the interface of consumption and production
1 both public and private services and in the process both are trans-
ormed: markets are created for new kinds of food and personal services;
ealth and educational institutions revise the hours and the languages in
vhich services are available; and new codes of dress or behavior, tacit or
xplicit, are introduced making multiple demands on both new and estab-
shed residents whose social survival depends on learning how to decode
1em....
So much for the fixed jobs; what of the footloose ones? The develop-
1ent of a global division of labor is not new. Regions have traded their
oods with each other for as long as recorded history, and raiding other
arts of the world for raw materials or slave labor is at least as old as colo-
ialism. At the end of the nineteenth century the British Empire exhibited
remarkably developed pattern of regional industrial specialization
nitted together into a global trade network. The twentieth century saw
1ultinational corporations operating with increasing independence of the
1terests of the nation states in which they were based, ushering in a
eriod after the Second World War that was characterized by Baran and
weezy as "monopoly capitalism."[1] By the 1970s, it was clear that a "new
lobal division of labor" was coming into being in manufacturing indus-
y with companies breaking down their production processes into
eparate subprocesses and redistributing these activities around the globe
 wherever conditions were most favorable.[2] These trends continued in
1e 1980s with industries as diverse as clothing, electronics, and auto man-
facture dispersing their production facilities away from developed
onomies with high labor costs and strong environmental controls to
eveloping countries, often in "free trade zones" where various tax incen-
ves were offered and labor and environmental-protection regulations
ere suspended in an effort to attract as much foreign direct investment

as possible. Workers in these zones were disproportionately young and female, and they received wages below subsistence level. Nevertheless, they were by no means passive and many actively organized to improve their lot.[3] This is one of the reasons why some of the regions once regarded as low wage, for instance Southeast Asia and Central America, are now seen as relatively high wage, and the companies have left them to exploit even cheaper workforces in places such as China, sub-Saharan Africa, and other parts of Latin America. . . .

Less well studied—at least until very recently—has been the new global division of labor in white-collar work. Nevertheless, this too has been progressing since the 1970s when low-skilled work such as data entry or typesetting began to be exported in bulk from North America and Europe to low-cost economies in the Caribbean, as well as South and Southeast Asia, while higher-skilled services, such as computer programming, started to be exported to the developed world from developing economies such as India, the Philippines, and Brazil.[4] . . .

Even more striking than the overall extent of "eWork" is the form it takes. Most literature on remote work, telecommuting, teleworking, or any of the other pseudonyms for "eWork" presupposes that the dominant form is home-based work. Yet these results show that the stereotypical "eWorker" employee based solely at home is in fact one of the least popular forms. Moreover, in-house "eWorking" is heavily outweighed by "eOutsourcing" as a mechanism for organizing work remotely, with some 43 percent of European employers and 26 percent of Australians making use of this practice. Much "eOutsourcing" is carried out within the region where the employer is based (34.5 percent), but substantial numbers (18.3 percent) outsource to other regions within the same country, and 5.3 percent outsource outside their national borders. These inter-regional and international (sometimes inter-continental) relocations of work provide clues to the geography of the emerging international division of labor in "eServices."

· · ·

15   What has happened since 2000? . . . What was still a risky experiment at the turn of the millennium had become normal, not to say routine, business practice three years later. Value chains were getting longer and more complex, with more and more intermediaries involved. The world was witnessing the emergence of huge new companies involved in the supply of business services, often many times bigger than their clients, with an internal global division of labor. When a large organization in the private or public sector decides to outsource a major contract to supply business services, it is increasingly not so much a case of choosing between India or Russia, Canada or China, but more a question of deciding on a particular company (for instance Accenture, EDS, or Siemens Business Services). Once that company has the contract, it may decide to divide up the work between teams

in many parts of the world, depending on the particular balance of skills, languages, cost, and quality criteria involved. This type of work could be regarded in many ways as a paradigmatic case of footlooseness, sliding without friction between teams across the globe who are linked by telecommunications networks and a common corporate culture but may nevertheless be physically located in strongly contrasting environments.

. . .

So far I have drawn a strongly dichotomous picture of a world in which the fixed is counterposed to the footloose in relation both to jobs and to people. For most of us, of course, the reality is much more complex than that, exhibiting both fixed and footloose features in complex configurations. I have termed this condition fractured. In a fractured existence, the characteristics of fixedness and footlooseness are in constant, tense interaction with each other. Rooted real-time activities (like putting the children to bed or eating a meal) are constantly interrupted by "virtual" ones (like the ringing of the telephone), while "virtual" activities (like checking one's e-mail) are disturbed by the physical realities of the situation in which one is placed (the pain of a stiff neck, for instance, or the impact of a power outage). The traditional diurnal rhythms of life are disrupted by requirements to respond to global demands. The interpenetration of time zones in one sphere of life leads inexorably to the development of a twenty-four-hour economy as people forced to work non-traditional hours then need to satisfy their needs as consumers during abnormal times, which in turn obliges another group to be on duty to provide these services, ratcheting up a process where-by opening hours are slowly extended right across the economy, and with them the expectation that it is normal for everything always to be open.

. . .

This fractured experience...is mirrored in the fracturing of occupational identities. Although many job descriptions retain a mix of fixed and footloose features, these are increasingly volatile. There has been an erosion of the clear boundaries of the workplace and the working day, with a spillover of many activities into the home or other locations, including an expectation that you should continue to be productive while traveling, whether you are a truck driver taking orders over a mobile phone during your lunch break or an executive working on a spreadsheet in an airport departure lounge. In a world in which the responsibilities for home and children are unevenly distributed between the sexes, these impacts are far from gender neutral and have contributed to an invisible redrawing of the boundaries between the jobs that can easily and safely be done by women and those that announce themselves subliminally as masculine.

Accompanying these dissolutions... there has also been a redesign of many work processes involving some subtle and other not-so-subtle shifts in responsibility for particular tasks within most workplaces. Some of these changes have the cumulative effect of tipping the balance between fixedness and footlooseness. For example, a job that previously combined meeting and greeting customers with more backroom activities might become wholly computerbased, making it easy to relocate it either wholly or in part to another location. If that other location is the existing worker's own home, then this might be experienced as quite liberating, but if the skills are not unique to the worker, the chances are the other location could be somebody else's desk on the other side of the world; far from being liberating this would then constitute a new source of precariousness....

It is easy to caricature as rigid and hierarchical the old world [of work] in which everyone knew "this task is what I do; that task is what you do; that task is reserved for new young trainees; that one is only done by very experienced older workers who know what can go wrong." Apart from anything else, it could easily lead to a set of unspoken rules which assigned certain tasks to women or to members of particular ethnic groups or people with a particular educational background. This would pose unacceptable barriers to social mobility and equality of opportunity. But [today] without [the old, hierarchical rules], what do we have? A world in which you are always only as good as last week's performance; where to keep your job you must always be prepared to learn new skills and change the old ways you were trained in (and in which you may have taken pride in the past); where you cannot know reliably in advance when you will be free and when you will have to work; where you can never say "no, that is not my responsibility" without fear of reprisal. A world without occupational boundaries could very easily become a world in which social solidarity is well-nigh impossible because you no longer have any clear way of defining who are your co-workers or your neighbors, and one where so many of your interactions are with strangers that it is hard to tell friend or ally from threat or enemy.

Notes

1. Paul Baran and Paul Sweezy, *Monopoly Capital: An Essay on the American Economic and Social Order* (New York: Monthly Review Press, 1966).
2. F. Froebel, J. Heinrichs, & O. Krey, *The New International Division of Labor* (Cambridge: Cambridge University Press, 1979).
3. See for instance *Women Working Worldwide, Common Interests: Women Organising in Global Electronics* (London: Women Working Worldwide, 1991).
4. Ursula Huws, *The Making of a Cybertariat: Virtual Work in a Real World* (New York: Monthly Review Press & London: Merlin Books, 2003).

Review Questions

1. Reread paragraphs 3 and 4 of Huws's article and the equally important final paragraph. These three paragraphs rest on the same set of facts, but the final paragraph is notably different. How so?

2. According to Huws, a worker's occupation has traditionally defined his or her personal identity and social identity. How so? How have changes in technology and globalization affected these identities?

3. What does Huws mean by "fixed" work? What changes have new technologies and globalization brought to fixed work?

4. What does Huws mean by "footloose" work, and what were its origins? How has footloose work changed in modern times? Specifically, what is the new "paradigmatic case of footlooseness"?

5. What does Huws mean by "fractured" work, and what are its implications?

Discussion and Writing Suggestions

1. What evidence do you find that we live in a world in which "jobs are created (and disappear) with great rapidity, often without even a concrete designation—just a mix-and-match combination of 'skills,' 'aptitudes,' and 'competences'"?

2. Would you expect the "rapidly shifting...landscape of work" that Huws describes to have the same effect on a worker of your generation as it might on a worker of your parents' generation? Explain.

3. What are some of the ways in which people are defined by their occupation—both individually and as members of a group? In developing your answer, describe someone you know well and the work he or she does.

4. One of the assumptions on which Huws builds her article is the "classic" view of occupation as having "central importance" in the individual's identity and position in the larger social order (see paragraph 3). Assume for a moment that identity is based less on "what you do" than on "what kind of person you are" and on "how other people see you." (On this point, see the story of Enrico that follows below.) In what ways would this new, competing assumption change Huws's argument?

5. Huws claims (in paragraph 4) that "[t]he unprecedented movements of people and jobs around the world have coincided with a breakdown of many traditional occupational identities." By the end of her paper, Huws comes to regard this breakdown with alarm—evidence of which we find in her final paragraph. What is your response to the breakdown? Do you expect, for instance, that the world of work you will enter post-college will be incoherent and anxiety provoking? (Note that other writers in this chapter find reasons for optimism in this same "rapidly shifting...landscape.")

No Long Term: New Work and the Corrosion of Character

Richard Sennett

Richard Sennett, a sociologist best known for his writing about cities, labor, and culture, is Centennial Professor of Sociology at the London School of Economics and Professor of the Humanities at New York University. During the 1980s he served as president of the American Council on Work. He is the author of three novels and numerous scholarly studies, including the much-cited *The Corrosion of Character: The Personal Consequences of Work in the New Capitalism* (1998), in which the following passage initially appeared. *Corrosion* is the first in a series of four books that explores "modern capitalism [and]...its personal consequences for workers."

Recently I met someone in an airport whom I hadn't seen for fifteen years. I had interviewed the father of Rico (as I shall call him) a quarter century ago when I wrote a book about blue-collar workers in America, *The Hidden Injuries of Class*. Enrico, his father, then worked as a janitor, and had high hopes for this boy, who was just entering adolescence, a bright kid good at sports. When I lost touch with his father a decade later, Rico had just finished college. In the airline lounge, Rico looked as if he had fulfilled his father's dreams. He carried a computer in a smart leather case, dressed in a suit I couldn't afford, and sported a signet ring with a crest.

Enrico had spent twenty years by the time we first met cleaning toilets and mopping floors in a downtown office building. He did so without complaining, but also without any hype about living out the American Dream. His work had one single and durable purpose, the service of his family. It had taken him fifteen years to save the money for a house, which he purchased in a suburb near Boston, cutting ties with his old Italian neighborhood because a house in the suburbs was better for the kids. Then his wife, Flavia, had gone to work, as a presser in a dry-cleaning plant; by the time I met Enrico in 1970, both parents were saving for the college education of their two sons.

What had most struck me about Enrico and his generation was how linear time was in their lives: year after year of working in jobs which seldom varied from day to day. And along that line of time, achievement was cumulative: Enrico and Flavia checked the increase in their savings every week, measured their domesticity by the various improvements and additions they had made to their ranch house. Finally, the time they lived was predictable. The upheavals of the Great Depression and World War II had faded, unions protected their jobs; though he was only forty when I first met him, Enrico knew precisely when he would retire and how much money he would have.

Time is the only resource freely available to those at the bottom of society. To make time accumulate, Enrico needed what the sociologist Max Weber called an "iron cage," a bureaucratic structure which rationalized the use of time; in Enrico's case, the seniority rules of his union about pay and the regulations organizing his government pension provided this scaffolding. When he added to these resources his own self-discipline, the result was more than economic.

He carved out a clear story for himself in which his experience accumulated materially and psychically; his life thus made sense to him as a linear narrative. Though a snob might dismiss Enrico as boring, he experienced the years as a dramatic story moving forward repair by repair, interest payment by interest payment. The janitor felt he became the author of his life, and though he was a man low on the social scale, this narrative provided him a sense of self-respect.

Though clear, Enrico's life story was not simple. I was particularly struck by how Enrico straddled the worlds of his old immigrant community and his new suburban-neutral life. Among his suburban neighbors he lived as a quiet, self-effacing citizen; when he returned to the old neighborhood, however, he received much more attention as a man who had made good on the outside, a worthy elder who returned each Sunday for Mass followed by lunch followed by gossipy coffees. He got recognition as a distinctive human being from those who knew him long enough to understand his story; he got a more anonymous kind of respect from his new neighbors by doing what everyone else did, keeping his home and garden neat, living without incident. The thick texture of Enrico's particular experience lay in the fact that he was acknowledged in both ways, depending in which community he moved: two identities from the same disciplined use of his time.

If the world were a happy and just place, those who enjoy respect would give back in equal measure the regard which has been accorded them. This was Fichte's idea in "The Foundations of National Law"; he spoke of the "reciprocal effect" of recognition. But real life does not proceed so generously.

Enrico disliked blacks, although he had labored peaceably for many years with other janitors who were black; he disliked non-Italian foreigners like the Irish, although his own father could barely speak English. He could not acknowledge kindred struggles; he had no class allies. Most of all, however, Enrico disliked middle-class people. We treated him as though he were invisible, "as a zero," he said; the janitor's resentment was complicated by his fear that because of his lack of education and his menial status, we had a sneaking right to do so. To his powers of endurance in time he contrasted the whining self-pity of blacks, the unfair intrusion of foreigners, and the unearned privileges of the bourgeoisie.

Though Enrico felt he had achieved a measure of social honor, he hardly wanted his son Rico to repeat his own life. The American dream of upward mobility for the children powerfully drove my friend. "I don't understand a word he says," Enrico boasted to me several times when Rico had come home from school and was at work on math. I heard many other parents of sons and daughters like Rico say something like "I don't understand him" in harder tones, as though the kids had abandoned them. We all violate in some way the place assigned us in the family myth, but upward mobility gives that passage a peculiar twist. Rico and other youngsters headed up the social ladder sometimes betrayed shame about their parents' working-class accents and rough manners, but more often felt suffocated by the endless strategizing over pennies and the reckoning of time in tiny steps. These favored children wanted to embark on a less constrained journey.

10   Now, many years later, thanks to the encounter at the airport, I had the chance to see how it had turned out for Enrico's son. In the airport lounge, I must confess, I didn't much like what I saw. Rico's expensive suit could have been just business plumage, but the crested signet ring—a mark of elite family background—seemed both a lie and a betrayal of the father. However, circumstances threw Rico and me together on a long flight. He and I did not have one of those American journeys in which a stranger spills out his or her emotional guts to you, gathers more tangible baggage when the plane lands, and disappears forever. I took the seat next to Rico without being asked, and for the first hour of a long flight from New York to Vienna had to pry information out of him.

Rico, I learned, has fulfilled his father's desire for upward mobility, but has indeed rejected the way of his father. Rico scorns "time-servers" and others wrapped in the armor of bureaucracy; instead he believes in being open to change and in taking risks. And he has prospered; whereas Enrico had an income in the bottom quarter of the wage scale, Rico's has shot up to the top 5 percent. Yet this is not an entirely happy story for Rico.

After graduating from a local university in electrical engineering, Rico went to a business school in New York. There he married a fellow student, a young Protestant woman from a better family. School prepared the young couple to move and change jobs frequently, and they've done so. Since graduation, in fourteen years at work Rico has moved four times.

Rico began as a technology adviser to a venture capital firm on the West Coast, in the early, heady days of the developing computer industry in Silicon Valley; he then moved to Chicago, where he also did well. But the next move was for the sake of his wife's career. If Rico were an ambition-driven character out of the pages of Balzac, he would never have done it, for he gained no larger salary, and he left hotbeds of high-tech activity for a more retired, if leafy, office park in Missouri. Enrico felt somewhat ashamed when Flavia went to work; Rico sees Jeannette, his wife, as an equal working partner, and has adapted to her. It was at this point, when Jeannette's career took off, that their children began arriving.

In the Missouri office park, the uncertainties of the new economy caught up with the young man. While Jeannette was promoted, Rico was downsized—his firm was absorbed by another, larger firm that had its own analysts. So the couple made a fourth move, back East to a suburb outside New York. Jeannette now manages a big team of accountants, and he has started a small consulting firm.

Prosperous as they are, the very acme of an adaptable, mutually supportive couple, both husband and wife often fear they are on the edge of losing control over their lives. This fear is built into their work histories.

In Rico's case, the fear of lacking control is straightforward: it concerns managing time. When Rico told his peers he was going to start his own consulting firm, most approved; consulting seems the road to independence. But in getting started he found himself plunged into many menial tasks, like doing his own photocopying, which before he'd taken for granted. He found himself plunged into the sheer flux of networking; every call had to be answered, the slightest acquaintance pursued. To find work, he has fallen subservient to the schedules of people who are in no way obliged to respond to him. Like other consultants, he wants to work in accordance with contracts setting out just what the consultant will do. But these contracts, he says, are largely fictions. A consultant usually has to tack one way and another in response to the changing whims or thoughts of those who pay; Rico has no fixed role that allows him to say to others, "This is what I do, this is what I am responsible for."

Jeannette's lack of control is more subtle. The small group of accountants she now manages is divided among people who work at home, people usually in the office, and a phalanx of low-level back-office clerks a thousand miles away connected to her by computer cable. In her present corporation, strict rules and surveillance of phones and e-mail disciplines the conduct of the accountants who work from home; to organize the work of the back-office clerks a thousand miles away, she can't make hands-on, face-to-face judgments, but instead must work by formal written guidelines. She hasn't experienced less bureaucracy in this seemingly flexible work arrangment; indeed, her own decisions count for less than in the days when she supervised workers who were grouped together, all the time, in the same office.

As I say, at first I was not prepared to shed many tears for this American Dream couple. Yet as dinner was served to Rico and me on our flight, and he began to talk more personally, my sympathies increased. His fear of losing control, it developed, went much deeper than worry about losing power in his job. He feared that the actions he needs to take and the way he has to live in order to survive in the modern economy have set his emotional, inner life adrift.

Rico told me that he and Jeannette have made friends mostly with the people they see at work, and have lost many of these friendships during the moves of the last twelve years, "though we stay 'netted.' " Rico looks to electronic communications for the sense of community which Enrico most enjoyed when he attended meetings of the janitors' union, but the son finds communications on-line short and hurried. "It's like with your kids—when you're not there, all you get is news later."

In each of his four moves, Rico's new neighbors have treated his advent as an arrival which closes past chapters of his life; they ask him about Silicon Valley or the Missouri office park, but, Rico says, "they don't *see* other places"; their imaginations are not engaged. This is a very American fear. The classic American suburb was a bedroom community; in the last generation a different kind of suburb has arisen, more economically independent of the urban core, but not really town or village either; a place springs into life with the wave of a developer's wand, flourishes, and begins to decay all within a generation. Such communities are not empty of sociability or neighborliness, but no one in them becomes a long-term witness to another person's life.

The fugitive quality of friendship and local community form the background to the most important of Rico's inner worries, his family. Like Enrico, Rico views work as his service to the family; unlike Enrico, Rico finds that the demands of the job interfere with achieving the end. At first I thought he was talking about the all too familiar conflict between work time and time for family. "We get home at seven, do dinner, try to find an hour for the kids' homework, and then deal with our own paperwork." When things get tough for months at a time in his consulting firm, "it's like I don't know who my kids are." He worries about the frequent anarchy into which his family plunges, and about neglecting his children, whose needs can't be programmed to fit into the demands of his job.

Hearing this, I tried to reassure him; my wife, stepson, and I had endured and survived well a similarly high-pressure life. "You aren't being fair to yourself," I said. "The fact you care so much means you are doing the best for your family you can." Though he warmed to this, I had misunderstood.

As a boy, I already knew, Rico had chafed under Enrico's authority; he had told me then he felt smothered by the small-minded rules which governed the janitor's life. Now that he is a father himself, the fear of a lack of ethical discipline haunts him, particularly the fear that his children will become "mall rats," hanging out aimlessly in the parking lots of shopping centers in the afternoons while the parents remain out of touch at their offices.

He therefore wants to set for his son and daughters an example of resolution and purpose, "but you can't just tell kids to be like that"; he has to set an example. The objective example he could set, his upward mobility, is something they take for granted, a history that belongs to a past not their own, a story which is over. But his deepest worry is that he cannot offer the substance of his work life as an example to his children of how they should conduct themselves ethically. The qualities of good work are not the qualities of good character.

25   As I came later to understand, the gravity of this fear comes from a gap separating Enrico and Rico's generations. Business leaders and journalists emphasize the global marketplace and the use of new technologies as the hallmarks of the capitalism of our time. This is true enough, but misses another dimension of change: new ways of organizing time, particularly working time.

The most tangible sign of that change might be the motto "No long term." In work, the traditional career progressing step by step through the corridors of one or two institutions is withering; so is the deployment of a single set of skills through the course of a working life. Today, a young American with at least two years of college can expect to change jobs at least eleven times in the course of working, and change his or her skill base at least three times during those forty years of labor.

An executive for ATT points out that the motto "No long term" is altering the very meaning of work:

> In ATT we have to promote the whole concept of the work force being contingent, though most of the contingent workers are inside our walls. "Jobs" are being replaced by "projects" and "fields of work."[1]

Corporations have also farmed out many of the tasks they once did permanently in-house to small firms and to individuals employed on short-term contracts. The fastest-growing sector of the American labor force, for instance, is people who work for temporary job agencies.[2]

"People are hungry for [change]," the management guru James Champy argues, because "the market may be 'consumer-driven' as never before in history."[3] The market, in this view, is too dynamic to permit doing things the same way year after year, or doing the same thing. The economist Bennett Harrison believes the source of this hunger for change is "impatient capital," the desire for rapid return; for instance, the average length of time stocks have been held on British and American exchanges has dropped 60 percent in the last fifteen years. The market believes rapid market return is best generated by rapid institutional change.

The "long-term" order at which the new regime takes aim, it should be said, was itself short-lived—the decades spanning the mid-twentieth century. Nineteenth-century capitalism lurched from disaster to disaster in the stock markets and in irrational corporate investment; the wild swings of the business cycle provided people little security. In Enrico's generation after World War II, this disorder was brought somewhat under control in most advanced economies; strong unions, guarantees of the welfare state, and large-scale corporations combined to produce an era of relative stability. This span of thirty or so years defines the "stable past" now challenged by a new regime.

A change in modern institutional structure has accompanied short-term, contract, or episodic labor. Corporations have sought to remove layers of bureaucracy, to become flatter and more flexible organizations. In place of organizations as pyramids, management wants now to think of organizations as networks. "Networklike arrangements are lighter on their feet" than pyramidal hierarchies, the sociologist Walter Powell declares; "they are more readily decomposable or redefinable than the fixed assets of hierarchies."[4] This means that promotions and dismissals tend not to be based on clear, fixed rules, nor are work tasks crisply defined; the network is constantly redefining its structure.

An IBM executive once told Powell that the flexible corporation "must become an archipelago of related activities."[5] The archipelago is an apt image for communications in a network, communication occurring like travel between islands—but at the speed of light, thanks to modern technologies. The computer has been the key to replacing the slow and clogged communications which occur in traditional chains of command. The fastest-growing sector of the labor force deals in computer and data-processing services, the area in which Jeanette and Rico work; the computer is now used in virtually all jobs, in many ways, by people of all ranks....

For all these reasons, Enrico's experience of long-term, narrative time in fixed channels has become dysfunctional. What Rico sought to explain to me—and perhaps to himself—is that the material changes embodied in the motto "No long term" have become dysfunctional for him too, but as guides to personal character, particularly in relation to his family life.

Take the matter of commitment and loyalty. "No long term" is a principle which corrodes trust, loyalty, and mutual commitment. Trust can, of course, be a purely formal matter, as when people agree to a business deal or rely on another to observe the rules in a game. But usually deeper experiences of trust are more informal, as when people learn on whom they can rely when given a difficult or impossible task. Such social bonds take time to develop, slowly rooting into the cracks and crevices of institutions.

The short time frame of modern institutions limits the ripening of informal trust. A particularly egregious violation of mutual commitment often occurs when new enterprises are first sold. In firms starting up, long hours and intense effort are demanded of everyone; when the firms go public—that is, initially offer publicly traded shares—the founders are apt to sell out and cash in, leaving lower-level employees behind. If an organization whether new or old operates as a flexible, loose network structure rather than by rigid command from the top, the network can also weaken social bonds. The sociologist Mark Granovetter says that modern institutional networks are marked by "the strength of weak ties," by which he partly means that fleeting forms of association are more useful to people than long-term connections, and partly that strong social ties like loyalty have ceased to be compelling.[6] These weak ties are embodied in teamwork, in which the team moves from task to task and the personnel of the team changes in the process.

35   Strong ties depend, by contrast, on long association. And more personally they depend on a willingness to make commitments to others. Given the typically short, weak ties in institutions today, John Kotter, a Harvard Business School professor, counsels the young to work "on the outside rather than on the inside" of organizations. He advocates consulting rather than becoming "entangled" in long-term employment; institutional loyalty is a trap in an economy where "business concepts, product designs, competitor intelligence, capital equipment, and all kinds of knowledge have shorter credible life spans."[7] A consultant who managed a recent IBM job shrinkage declares that once employees "understand [they can't depend on the corporation] they're marketable."[8] Detachment and superficial

cooperativeness are better armor for dealing with current realities than behavior based on values of loyalty and service.

It is the time dimension of the new capitalism, rather than high-tech data transmission, global stock markets, or free trade, which most directly affects people's emotional lives outside the workplace. Transposed to the family realm, "No long term" means keep moving, don't commit yourself, and don't sacrifice. Rico suddenly erupted on the plane, "You can't imagine how stupid I feel when I talk to my kids about commitment. It's an abstract virtue to them; they don't see it anywhere." Over dinner I simply didn't understand the outburst, which seemed apropos of nothing. But his meaning is now clearer to me as a reflection upon himself. He means the children don't see commitment practiced in the lives of their parents or their parents' generation.

Similarly, Rico hates the emphasis on teamwork and open discussion which marks an enlightened, flexible workplace once those values are transposed to the intimate realm. Practiced at home, teamwork is destructive, marking an absence of authority and of firm guidance in raising children. He and Jeannette, he says, have seen too many parents who have talked every family issue to death for fear of saying "No!," parents who listen too well, who understand beautifully rather than lay down the law; they have seen as a result too many disoriented kids.

"Things have to hold together," Rico declared to me. Again, I didn't at first quite get this, and he explained what he meant in terms of watching television. Perhaps unusually, Rico and Jeannette make it a practice to discuss with their two sons the relation between movies or sitcoms the boys watch on the tube and events in the newspapers. "Otherwise it's just a jumble of images." But mostly the connections concern the violence and sexuality the children see on television. Enrico constantly spoke in little parables to drive home questions of character; these parables he derived from his work as a janitor—such as "You can ignore dirt but it won't go away." When I first knew Rico as an adolescent, he reacted with a certain shame to these homely snippets of wisdom. So now I asked Rico if he too made parables or even just drew ethical rules from his experience at work. He first ducked answering directly—"There's not much on TV about that sort of thing"—then replied, "And well, no, I don't talk that way."

Behavior which earns success or even just survival at work thus gives Rico little to offer in the way of a parental role model. In fact, for this modern couple, the problem is just the reverse: how can they protect family relations from succumbing to the short-term behavior, the meeting mind-set, and above all the weakness of loyalty and commitment which mark the modern workplace? In place of the chameleon values of the new economy, the family—as Rico sees it—should emphasize instead formal obligation, trustworthiness, commitment, and purpose. These are all long-term virtues.

This conflict between family and work poses some questions about adult experience itself. How can long-term purposes be pursued in a short-term society? How can durable social relations be sustained? How can a human being develop a narrative of identity and life history in a society composed of episodes and fragments? The conditions of the new economy feed instead on experience which drifts in time, from place to place, from job to job. If I could state Rico's dilemma more largely, short-term capitalism threatens to corrode his character, particularly those qualities of character which bind human beings to one another and furnishes each with a sense of sustainable self.

• • •

Rico's experiences with time, place, and work are not unique; neither is his emotional response. The conditions of time in the new capitalism have created a conflict between character and experience, the experience of disjointed time threatening the ability of people to form their characters into sustained narratives.

At the end of the fifteenth century, the poet Thomas Hoccleve declared in *The Regiment of Princes*, "Allas, wher ys this worldes stabylnesse?"—a lament that appears equally in Homer or in Jeremiah in the Old Testament.[9] Through most of human history, people have accepted the fact that their lives will shift suddenly due to wars, famines, or other disasters, and that they will have to improvise in order to survive. Our parents and grandparents were filled with anxiety in 1940, having endured the wreckage of the Great Depression and facing the looming prospect of a world war.

What's peculiar about uncertainty today is that it exists without any looming historical disaster; instead it is woven into the everyday practices of a vigorous capitalism. Instability is meant to be normal, Schumpeter's entrepreneur served up as an ideal Everyman. Perhaps the corroding of character is an inevitable consequence. "No long term" disorients action over the long term, loosens bonds of trust and commitment, and divorces will from behavior.

I think Rico knows he is both a successful and a confused man. The flexible behavior which has brought him success is weakening his own character in ways for which there exists no practical remedy. If he is an Everyman for our times, his universality may lie in that dilemma.

Notes

1. Quoted in *New York Times,* Feb. 13, 1996, pp. D1, D6.

2. Corporations like Manpower grew 240 percent from 1985 to 1995. As I write, the Manpower firm, with 600,000 people on its payroll, compared with the 400,000 at General Motors and 350,000 at IBM, is now the country's largest employer.

3. James Champy, *Re-engineering Management* (New York: HarperBusiness, 1995) p. 119, pp. 39–40.

4. Walter Powell and Laurel Smith-Doerr, "Networks and Economic Life," in Neil Smelser and Richard Swedberg, eds., *The Handbook of Economic Sociology* (Princeton: Princeton University Press, 1994), p. 381.

5. Ibid.

6. Mark Granovetter, "The Strength of Weak Ties, " *American Journal of Sociology* 78 (1973), 1360–80.

7. John Kotter, *The New Rules* (New York: Dutton, 1995) pp. 81, 159.

8. Anthony Sampson, *Company Man* (New York: Random House, 1995), pp. 226–27.

9. Quoted in Ray Pahl, *After Success: Fin de Siècle Anxiety and Identity* (Cambridge, U.K.: Polity Press, 1995), pp. 163–64.

● Review Questions

1. What does "No long term" mean—as compared with "Long term"? How does Sennett use "No long term" as a "motto" to describe changes in the new economy?

2. Sennett describes Rico and his father, Enrico, as having different life narratives. What are these narratives? How do they differ? How do they lead to Rico's distress?

3. In the new economy, what changes have occurred in the structure of businesses and the ways in which workers are assigned and do work?

4. Why does Rico feel that he needs to protect his family from behavior patterns and values now commonplace in the new economy?

5. Reread paragraphs 39 through 43, in which Sennett summarizes Rico's "dilemma." What is that dilemma?

● Discussion and Writing Suggestions

1. Rico's "deepest worry," according to Sennett, "is that he cannot offer the substance of his work life as an example to his children of how they should conduct themselves ethically. The qualities of good work are not the qualities of good character" (paragraph 24). As a reader, you are obliged to accept Sennett's description of Rico's "deepest worry." At the same time, Rico's turmoil need not be yours. In your experience, how closely tied are the qualities of "good character" to your activities at a job? Can doing a job well elicit from a worker good character? How so?

2. To what extent have you seen evidence that the behaviors demanded of both employees and employers in the new economy jeopardize the link between good work and good character?

3. According to Sennett, "a young American with at least two years of college can expect to change jobs at least eleven times in the course of working, and change his or her skill base at least three times during those forty years

of labor" (paragraph 26). What is your "gut-level" response to these projections concerning changes in jobs and skill bases?

4. As an undergraduate, how do you *prepare* for a working life characterized by the changes Sennett projects?

5. In describing the life of Rico, Sennett shows us how identity is tied to work—an important correlation among sociologists. (See, for instance, paragraph 3 in the selection by Ursula Huws, who makes the same assumption about the relationship of identity, social status, and occupation.) Reflect on your experiences of work and the working lives of people you know well. Is the assumption concerning the relationship between work and identity true? Is it possible to have a self-respecting identity if you do not respect what you do (or how you must do what you do) on the job?

6. Sennett contrasts "No long term" and "Long term" employment and also the lives of Enrico and his son, Rico. For Sennett, "Long term" equals stable employment, stable values, and a stable identity; "No long term" equals the instability of all three. Enrico's life in long-term employment was stable; Rico's life in short-term employment is not. Is Sennett proposing some sort of "law" here? That is, *if* identity is tied to occupation (as many sociologists believe) *and* the "qualities of good work are not the qualities of good character" (paragraph 24), then must one's identity be in crisis, as Rico's is? Given the demands on workers in the new economy, must the identities of all or most workers be thrown into crisis? If you don't think so, then where does Sennett's argument break down?

I FEEL SO DAMN LUCKY!

Tom Peters

Tom Peters, a well-known management consultant, prolific writer, and much sought-after speaker, coauthored the influential In *Search of Excellence* (1982). The selection that follows, originally titled "The New Wired World of Work: A More Transparent Workplace Will Mean More White-collar Accountability and Less Tolerance for Hangers-on," first appeared in *Business Week* (August 28, 2008). The new title is taken from the last line of the selection itself.

You're hiking along near the Grand Canyon in August, 2000, but fretting about the progress your virtual partner in Kuala Lumpur has made in the past 24 hours? No problem! Your local Kampgrounds of America campsite now has Internet access.

Call it the new wired world of work. Depending on how you view it, it's intrusive, pervasive, or merely ubiquitous. But it's definitely not your dad's office. And this perpetually plugged-in existence is just the beginning of the changes we'll see in the 21st century white-collar workplace.

Work in the '50s and '60s meant trudging to the same office for decades. Same colleagues. Same processes, mostly rote. Former MCI Communications Chief Bill McGowan called yesterday's middle managers "human message switches." And the information was laughably dated. Closing the account books at month's end could drag on for weeks. Customer data were nonexistent, or hopelessly unreliable.

But in the next few years, whether at a tiny company or behemoth, we will be working with an eclectic mix of contract teammates from around the globe, many of whom we'll never meet face-to-face. Every project will call for a new team, composed of specially tailored skills. Info that's more than hours old will be viewed with concern.

Every player on this team will be evaluated—pass by pass, at-bat by at-bat—for the quality and uniqueness and timeliness and passion of her or his contribution. And therein lies the peril, and the remarkable opportunity, of this weird, wired, wild new age of work. White-collar accountability has until now been mostly an oxymoron. Show up, suck up, process your paper flow with a modicum of efficiency, and you could count on a pretty decent end-of-year evaluation, a cost-of-living-plus raise, and a sure-as-death-and-taxes 40-year tenure at Desk No. 263.

Now you are like a New York Yankees or Los Angeles Dodgers closer. A couple of blown saves following a night on the town and your pressured and performance-driven teammates, more than your manager, are ready to show you the exit. This will hold for the freshly minted University of Wisconsin grad as well as the 56-year-old who had envisioned himself on a pain-free coast toward retirement. There may be a tight labor market for stellar performers, but the flip side is much less tolerance for hangers-on.

As enterprise resource-planning software and other such systems wreak havoc on the vast majority of staff jobs in the next decade, what will it take for you and me to navigate and win? Here's a list of minimal survival skills for the 21st century office worker:

- Mastery: To thrive in tomorrow's transparent team environment, the typical white-collar worker will have to be noticeably good at something the world values. "HR guy" doesn't cut it. Nor does "CPA." What subset of, say, techie recruiting skills or international accountancy excellence makes you a clearly valued contributor? I firmly believe that if you can't describe your distinction in the space of a one-sixteenth-page Yellow Pages ad, you will be doomed.

- Who Do You Know?: The new Rolodex will deemphasize bosses and traditional power figures, focusing more on peers (future project mates!) who appreciate your clear-cut contributions. I consider my own electronic Rolodex to be my Extended Global University, colleagues I can call upon (and who can call upon me) to further my current and future projects.

- Entrepreneurial Instinct: You do not have to start your own business. But as I see it, all these projects are entrepreneurial. So you must act as if you were running your own business. Think of yourself as Maggie Inc., who happens to be at General Electric Capital Services Inc. at the moment. And speaking of which, I fully expect women to dominate managerial roles. I think they tend to handle ambiguity better than we guys do. The new world is a floating crap game, with new projects, new teammates, and a constant need to adjust. Those who can operate in the absence of laid-out bounds will be the leaders.

- Love of Technology: Technology is changing everything. Believe the hype—if anything, it's understated. You need not be a technologist per se, but you must embrace technology. "Coping" with it is not enough.
- Marketing: You do not have to become a shameless self-promoter, a la Martha Stewart. But you must get your story out on the airwaves. Do it via your personal Web site. Do it by telling your project's story at a trade show.
- Passion for Renewal: You've got to constantly improve and, on occasion, reinvent yourself. My bread and butter—at age 57—are my lectures. But I imagine that the Internet will devour many conventional meetings in a few years. Hence I am madly working with several groups that will deliver my message via the new technologies.

I love to read Dilbert and usually choke with laughter. But I have a problem with the subtext: My company stinks, my boss stinks, my job stinks. If that's your take—at this moment of monumental change and gargantuan opportunity—then I can only feel sad for you. We get to reinvent the world. I feel so damn lucky!

Review Questions

1. What are some of the main differences between "your dad's office" and the workplace of the twenty-first century?

2. In the view of Tom Peters, what are the minimal survival skills for office workers in the twenty-first century?

3. Peters uses a sports analogy in this selection. To what end?

Discussion and Writing Suggestions

1. "The new world is a floating crap game, with new projects, new teammates, and a constant need to adjust. Those who can operate in the absence of laid-out bounds will be the leaders." How significant a departure is the world described here from the world of work just a generation ago? (See, for instance, the example of Enrico in Richard Sennett's article.) How comfortable are you operating "in the absence of laid-out bounds"?

2. Age 57 when writing this piece, Tom Peters is an unabashed optimist comfortable with the changing landscape of work he describes. Fifty-seven is close to the traditional age of retirement. Do you know other fifty-somethings in the workforce? Contact them and ask how they're adapting to recent changes on the job. What accounts for the anxiety of some in the face of these changes and the optimism of others?

3. Peters regards workers of the twenty-first century as occupying a "moment of monumental change and gargantuan opportunity" in which he and his readers get to "reinvent the world." Peters is thrilled at the prospect. Do you feel up to the challenge? Do you have an appetite to continually renew and promote yourself in the ways he is suggesting? Explain.

4. Peters suggests that in the new world of work you will be evaluated on a what-have-you-done-for-me-lately basis, much as an athlete is. In your view, what is lost and what is gained in such an intensely performance-driven view of the workplace?

WORK AND WORKERS IN THE TWENTY-FIRST CENTURY

Richard W. Judy and Carol D'Amico

The selection that follows forms the opening section of the Hudson Institute's *Workforce 2020* (published in 1997), which appeared ten years after its predecessor, *Workforce 2000* (published in 1987). That book challenged policymakers and employers to consider and respond to trends that were revolutionizing the landscape of work at the end of the twentieth century. In this update, Hudson analysts Richard Judy and Carol D'Amico similarly ask us to project current trends into the near future so that we can respond meaningfully. The Hudson Institute describes itself as "a non-partisan policy research organization dedicated to innovative research and analysis that promotes global security, prosperity, and freedom."

You have before you a map, one that describes the journey America's labor force is now beginning. It lays out the general contours of the employment landscape, not the fine details or the specific landmarks, depicting the many roads to what we call "Workforce 2020." Some will be superhighways and some will be dead ends for American workers. Although immense forces shape the employment landscape, we believe that we know the difference between the superhighways and the dead ends.

Skilled cartographers in the guise of economists, education experts, and policy researchers at Hudson Institute helped prepare this map. It offers our best ideas about what lies ahead and what Americans—collectively and individually, in large and small firms, in federal agencies and in small-town development commissions—should do to prepare for the journey to Workforce 2020.

Our map is needed because American workers at the threshold of the twenty-first century are embarking on mysterious voyages. They seek glittering destinations but travel along roads with numerous pitfalls and unexpected diversions. Many workers—more than at any time in America's history—will reach the glittering destinations. They will enjoy incomes unimaginable to their parents, along with working and living conditions more comfortable than anyone could have dreamed of in centuries past. But many other workers will be stymied by the pitfalls along the road or baffled by the diversions. Their standard of living may stagnate or even decline. Much is already known today about what will divide the hopeful from the anxious along these roads, and we will share that knowledge here.

What makes America's voyage to the workforce of 2020 unique is not merely the heights to which some will climb or the difficulties others will endure. Two qualities give a truly unprecedented character to the roads ahead. First, the gates have lifted before almost every American who wishes to embark on the journey of work. Age, gender, and race barriers to employment opportunity have broken down. What little conscious discrimination remains will be swept away soon—not by government regulation but by the enlightened self-interest of employers. Second, more and more individuals now undertake their own journeys through the labor force, rather than "hitching rides" on the traditional mass transportation provided by unions, large corporations, and government bureaucracies. For most workers, this "free agency" will be immensely liberating. But for others, it will provoke anxiety and anger. For all workers, the premium on education, flexibility, and foresight has never been greater than it will be in the years ahead.

5   What explains the immense satisfactions and dangers ahead? What makes possible the unprecedented expansion of opportunities in the labor force? What forces conspire, for better or worse, to demand that we compete as individuals and contend with ever-changing knowledge and skill requirements? We highlight four forces in particular.

First, the pace of technological change in today's economy has never been greater. It will accelerate still further, in an exponential manner. Innovations in biotechnology, computing, telecommunications, and their confluences will bring new products and services that are at once marvelous and potentially frightening. And the "creative destruction"* wrought by this technology on national economies, firms, and individual workers will be even more powerful in the twenty-first century than when economist Joseph Schumpeter coined the phrase fifty years ago. We cannot know what

---

*In *Capitalism, Socialism and Democracy* (1942), Joseph Schumpeter coined the term "creative destruction" to describe the process by which capitalism, operating through "new consumers, goods, the new methods of production or transportation, the new markets, [and] the new forms of industrial organization,…incessantly revolutionizes the economic structure *from within*, incessantly destroying the old one, incessantly creating a new one" (New York, Harper: 1975, pp. 82–85; http://transcriptions.english.ucsb.edu/archive/courses/liu/english25/materials/schumpeter.html).

innovations will transform the global economy by 2020, any more than analysts in the mid-1970s could have foreseen the rise of the personal computer or the proliferation of satellite, fiber-optic, and wireless communications. However, the computer and telecommunications revolutions enable us to speculate in an informed manner on the implications of today's Innovation Age for the American workforce:

- Automation will continue to displace low-skilled or unskilled workers in America's manufacturing firms and offices. Indeed, machines will substitute for increasingly more sophisticated forms of human labor. Even firms that develop advanced technology will be able to replace some of their employees with technology (witness the "CASE tools" that now assist in writing routine computer code) or with lower-paid workers in other countries (witness the rise of India's computer programmers and data processors).

- However, experience suggests that the development, marketing, and servicing of ever more sophisticated products—and the use of those products in an ever richer ensemble of personal and professional services—almost certainly will create more jobs than the underlying technology will destroy. On the whole, the new jobs will also be safer, more stimulating, and better paid than the ones they replace.

- The best jobs created in the Innovation Age will be filled by Americans (and workers in other advanced countries) to the extent that workers possess the skills required to compete for them and carry them out. If jobs go unfilled in the U.S., they will quickly migrate elsewhere in our truly global economy.

- Because the best new jobs will demand brains rather than brawn, and because physical presence in a particular location at a particular time will become increasingly irrelevant, structural barriers to the employment of women and older Americans will continue to fall away. Americans of all backgrounds will be increasingly able to determine their own working environments and hours.

Second, the rest of the world matters to a degree that it never did in the past. We can no longer say anything sensible about the prospects for American workers if we consider only the U.S. economy or the characteristics of the U.S. labor force. Fast-growing Asian and Latin American economies present us with both opportunities and challenges. Meanwhile, communications and transportation costs have plummeted (declining to almost zero in the case of information exchanged on the Internet), resulting in what some have called "the death of distance." Whereas the costs of shipping an automobile or a heavy machine tool remain consequential, the products of the world's most dynamic industries—such as biological formulas, computers, financial services, microchips, and software—can cross the globe for a pittance. Investment capital is also more abundant and more mobile than ever before, traversing borders with abandon in search of the best ideas, the savviest entrepreneurs, and the most productive economies. The implications of this globalization for U.S. workers are no less complex than the implications of new technology:

- Manufacturing will continue to dominate U.S. exports. Almost 20 percent of U.S. manufacturing workers now have jobs that depend on exports; that figure will continue to escalate. America's growing export dependence in the early twenty-first century will benefit most of America's highly productive workers, because many foreign economies will continue to expand more rapidly than our own, thereby generating massive demand for U.S. goods. Skilled workers whose jobs depend on exports are better paid than other U.S. manufacturing workers as a rule, because the U.S. enjoys a comparative advantage in the specialized manufacturing and service sectors that create their jobs. These workers also tend to earn more than similar workers in other countries.

- But globalization will affect low-skilled or unskilled American workers very differently. They will compete for jobs and wages not just with their counterparts across town or in other parts of the U.S., but also with low-skilled workers around the globe. As labor costs become more important to manufacturers than shipping costs, the U.S. will retain almost no comparative advantage in low-skilled manufacturing. Jobs in that sector will disappear or be available only at depressed wages. Second or third jobs and full-time employment for both spouses—already the norm in households headed by low-skilled workers—will become even more necessary.

- Manufacturing's share of total U.S. employment will continue to decline, due to the combined effects of automation and globalization. But the millions of high-productivity manufacturing jobs that remain will be more highly skilled and therefore better paid than at any other time in U.S. history. Employment growth, meanwhile, will remain concentrated in services, which also will benefit increasingly from export markets and will offer high salaries for skilled workers.

- Globalization and technological change will make most segments of the U.S. economy extremely volatile, as comparative advantages in particular market segments rise and then fall away. Small- and medium-sized firms will be well situated to react to this volatility, and their numbers will grow. Labor unions will cope badly with this rapidly evolving economy of small producers, and their membership and influence will shrink. Individual workers will change jobs frequently over time. For those who maintain and improve their skills, the changes should bring increasing rewards. But the changes may be traumatic for those who fall behind the skills curve and resist retraining.

Third, America is getting older. At some level, all of us are aware of this. Our parents and grandparents are living longer, and we are having fewer children. But U.S. public policy as well as many employers have yet to come to grips with the full implications of America's aging. The oldest among America's so-called baby boomers—the massive cohort born between 1945 and 1965—will begin to reach age 65 in 2010. By 2020, almost 20 percent of the U.S. population will be 65 or older. There will be as many Americans of "retirement age" as there are 20–35-year-olds. America's aging baby boomers will decisively affect the U.S. workforce, through their departure from and continued presence in it, and as recipients of public entitlements and purchasers of services:

- America's taxpayer-funded entitlements for its aging population— Medicare and Social Security—are likely to undergo profound changes in the next two decades. The tax rates necessary to sustain the current "pay-as-you-go" approach to funding these programs as the baby boomers retire will rise, perhaps precipitously, unless the expectations of retirees regarding their benefits become more modest, the economy grows more strongly than expected, or the programs receive fundamental overhauls.

- Depending on how the funding of entitlement programs is resolved and how well individual baby boomers have prepared for retirement, some who reach age 65 will continue to require outside income and will be unable to retire. Many others will not want to retire and will seek flexible work options. As average life expectancies extend past 80 years of age, even many of the well-heeled will conclude that twenty years on golf courses and cruise ships do not present enough of a challenge.

- Whether they continue working or simply enjoy the fruits of past labors, America's aging baby boomers will constitute a large and powerful segment of the consumer market. Their resulting demand for entertainment, travel, and other leisure-time pursuits; specialized health care; long-term care facilities; and accounting, home-repair, and other professional services will fuel strong local labor markets throughout the U.S., but particularly in cities and regions that attract many retirees. The jobs created by this boom in the service sector in local economies may replace many of the low-skilled or unskilled manufacturing jobs the U.S. stands to lose, though not always at comparable wages.

Fourth, the U.S. labor force continues its ethnic diversification, though at a fairly slow pace. Most white non-Hispanics entering America's early twenty-first century workforce simply will replace exiting white workers; minorities will constitute slightly more than half of net new entrants to the U.S. workforce. Minorities will account for only about a third of total new entrants over the next decade. Whites constitute 76 percent of the total labor force today and will account for 68 percent in 2020. The share of African-Americans in the labor force probably will remain constant, at

11 percent, over the next twenty years. The Asian and Hispanic shares will grow to 6 and 14 percent, respectively. Most of this change will be due to the growth of Asian and Hispanic workforce representation in the South and West. The changes will not be dramatic on a national scale. The aging of the U.S. work-force will be far more dramatic than its ethnic shifts.

10   In summary, Hudson Institute's *Workforce 2020* offers a vision of a bifurcated U.S. labor force in the early twenty-first century. As we envision the next twenty-plus years, the skills premium appears even more powerful to us than it did to our predecessors who wrote *Workforce 2000*. Millions of Americans with proficiency in math, science, and the English language will join a global elite whose services will be in intense demand. These workers will command generous and growing compensation. Burgeoning local markets for services in some parts of the U.S. will continue to sustain some decent-paying, low-skill jobs. But other Americans with inadequate education and no technological expertise—how many depends in large part on what we do to improve their training—will face declining real wages or unemployment, particularly in manufacturing.

● Review Questions

1. What two qualities give an "unprecedented character" to the prospects for work in America in the coming years?

2. What major factors do researchers at the Hudson Institute think will shape the employment landscape in the coming years?

3. The writers claim that "the best new jobs will demand brains rather than brawn." Explain what they mean.

4. What are the implications of globalization for U.S. workers?

5. What are the implications of an aging American population for U.S. workers?

6. What is the "skills premium"?

● Discussion and Writing Suggestions

1. How appropriate and how effective do you find the "map" metaphor in the opening of the selection? Trace its use throughout the piece, and comment.

2. Given the Hudson Institute's forecast for work in the coming decades, how well do think your education to date, and your intended field of study, prepare you to take your place in the global economy? To what extent are you poised to join what the authors anticipate will be "a global elite"?

3. Those who endorse the principle of "creative destruction" (see paragraph 6) expect that the loss of industries and jobs to mechanization, computerization, or outsourcing will in time create new industries and jobs. Cite one example of a job category or industry lost. Do you see evidence of new jobs or industries forming?

4. Judy and D'Amico write that "more and more individuals [will] undertake their own journeys through the labor force, rather than 'hitching rides' on the traditional mass transportation provided by unions, large corporations, and government bureaucracies. For most workers, this 'free agency' will be immensely liberating. But for others, it will provoke anxiety and anger." What do you imagine your response will be to the likely "free agency" of working life? Do you expect to (or do you already) feel liberated? Angry or anxious? Explain.

5. Locate the Hudson Institute's *Workforce 2000*, written in 1987. Assess its accuracy in predicting contours of our present-day workforce.

THE UNTOUCHABLES

Thomas L. Friedman

Thomas Friedman, an investigative reporter and a columnist for the *New York Times*, won the National Book Award for *From Beirut to Jerusalem* (1989) and three Pulitzer Prizes for international reporting and commentary. Most recently he has written *Hot, Flat, and Crowded* (2008). The selection that follows appears in his best seller *The World Is Flat: A Brief History of the Twenty-First Century* (2005), in which Friedman explores the opportunities and dangers associated with globalization. Friedman uses the word "flat" to describe "the stunning rise of middle classes all over the world." In this newly flat world, "we are now connecting all the knowledge centers on the planet together into a single global network, which—if politics and terrorism do not get in the way—could usher in an amazing era of prosperity, innovation, and collaboration, by companies, communities, and individuals."

If the flattening of the world is largely (but not entirely) unstoppable, and if it holds out the potential to be as beneficial to American society in general as past market evolutions have been, how does an individual get the best out of it? What do we tell our kids?

My simple answer is this: There will be plenty of good jobs out there in the flat world for people with the right knowledge, skills, ideas, and self-motivation to seize them. But there is no sugar-coating the new challenge: Every young American today would be wise to think of himself or herself as competing against every young Chinese, Indian, and Brazilian. In Globalization 1.0, countries had to think globally to thrive, or at least survive. In Globalization 2.0, companies had to think globally to thrive, or at least survive. In Globalization 3.0, individuals have to think globally to thrive, or at least survive. This requires not only a new level of technical skills but also a certain mental flexibility, self-motivation, and psychological mobility. I am certain that we Americans can indeed thrive in this world. But I am also certain that it will not be as easy as it was in the last fifty years. Each of us, as an individual, will have to work a little harder and run a little faster to keep our standard of living rising.

"Globalization went from globalizing industries to globalizing individuals," said Vivek Paul, the Wipro president.* "I think today that people working in most jobs can sense how what they are doing integrates globally: 'I am working with someone in India. I am buying from someone in China. I am selling to someone in England.' As a result of the ability to move work around, we have created an amazing awareness on the part of every individual that says: 'Not only does my work have to fit into somebody's global supply chain, but I myself have to understand how I need to compete and have the skill sets required to work at a pace that fits the supply chain. And I had better be able to do that as well or better than anyone else in the world.'" That sense of responsibility for one's own advancement runs deeper than ever today. In many global industries now, you have got to justify your job every day with the value you create and the unique skills you contribute. And if you don't, that job can fly away farther and faster than ever.

In sum, it was never good to be mediocre in your job, but in a world of walls, mediocrity could still earn you a decent wage. You could get by and then some. In a flatter world, you *really* do not want to be mediocre or lack any passion for what you do. You don't want to find yourself in the shoes of Willy Loman in *Death of a Salesman*, when his son Biff dispels his idea that the Loman family is special by declaring, "Pop! I'm a dime a dozen, and so are you!" An angry Willy retorts, "I am not a dime a dozen! I am Willy Loman, and you are Biff Loman!"

5   I don't care to have that conversation with my girls, so my advice to them in this flat world is very brief and very blunt: "Girls, when I was growing up, my parents used to say to me, 'Tom, finish your dinner—people in China and India are starving.' My advice to you is: Girls, finish your homework—people in China and India are starving for your jobs." And in a flat world, they can have them, because in a flat world there is no such thing as an American job. There is just a job, and in more cases than ever before it will go to the best, smartest, most productive, or cheapest worker—wherever he or she resides.

The New Middle

It is going to take more than just doing your homework to thrive in a flat world, though. You are going to have to do the *right kind* of homework as well. Because the companies that are adjusting best to the flat world are not just making minor changes, they are changing the whole model of the work they do and how they do it—in order to take advantage of the flat-world

---

*Wipro is a global technology company that provides "integrated business, technology, and process solutions" in North and South America, Europe, the Middle East, Asia, and Australia.

platform and to compete with others who are doing the same. What this means is that students also have to fundamentally reorient what they are learning and educators how they are teaching it. They can't just keep the same old model that worked for the past fifty years, when the world was round. This set of issues is what I will explore in this and the next chapter: What kind of good middle-class jobs are successful companies and entrepreneurs creating today? How do workers need to prepare themselves for those jobs, and how can educators help them do just that?

Let's start at the beginning. The key to thriving, as an individual, in a flat world is figuring out how to make yourself an "untouchable." That's right. When the world goes flat, the caste system gets turned upside down. In India, untouchables are the lowest social class, but in a flat world everyone should want to be an untouchable. "Untouchables," in my lexicon, are people whose jobs cannot be outsourced, digitized, or automated. And remember, as analyst David Rothkopf notes, most jobs are not lost to outsourcing to India or China—most lost jobs are "outsourced to the past." That is, they get digitized and automated. *The New York Times*'s Washington bureau used to have a telephone operator–receptionist. Now it has a recorded greeting and voice mail. That reception job didn't go to India; it went to the past or it went to a microchip. The flatter the world gets, the more anything that can be digitized, automated, or outsourced will be digitized, automated, or outsourced. As Infosys CEO Nandan Nilekani likes to say, in a flat world there is "fungible and nonfungible work." Work that can be easily digitized, automated, or transferred abroad is fungible. One of the most distinguishing features of the flat world is how many jobs—not just blue-collar manufacturing jobs but now also *white-collar service jobs*—are becoming fungible. Since more of us work in those service jobs than ever before, more of us will be affected.

• • •

[W]ho will the untouchables be? What jobs are not likely to become fungible, easy to automate, digitize, or outsource? I would argue that the untouchables in a flat world will fall into three broad categories. First are people who are really "special or specialized." This label would apply to Michael Jordan, Madonna, Elton John, J. K. Rowling, your brain surgeon, and the top cancer researcher at the National Institutes of Health. These people perform functions in ways that are so special or specialized that they can never be outsourced, automated, or made tradable by electronic transfer. They are untouchables. They have a global market for their goods and services and can command global wages.

Second are people who are really "localized" and "anchored." This category includes many, many people. They are untouchables because their jobs must be done in a specific location, either because they involve some specific local knowledge or because they require face-to-face, personalized contact or interaction with a customer, client, patient, colleague, or audience. All these people are untouchables because they are anchored: my barber, the waitress at lunch, the chefs in the kitchen, the plumber, nurses, my dentist, lounge singers, masseurs, retail sales clerks, repairmen, electricians, nannies, gardeners, cleaning ladies, and divorce lawyers. Note that these people can be working in high-end jobs (divorce lawyer, dentist), vocational jobs (plumber, carpenter), or low-end jobs (garbage collector, maid). Regardless of that worker's level of sophistication, their wages will be set by the local market forces of supply and demand.

10   That then brings me to the third broad category. This category includes people in many formerly middle-class jobs—from assembly line work to data entry to securities analysis to certain forms of accounting and radiology—that were once deemed nonfungible or nontradable and are now being made quite fungible and tradable thanks to the ten flatteners.* Let's call these the "old middle" jobs. Many of them are now under pressure from the flattening of the world. As Nandan Nilekani puts it: "The problem [for America] is in the middle. Because the days when you could count on being an accounts-payable clerk are gone. And a lot of the middle class are where that [old] middle is.... This middle has not yet grasped the competitive intensity of the future. Unless they [do], they will not make the investments in reskilling themselves and you will end up with a lot of people stranded on an island."

That is not something we want. The American economy used to look like a bell curve, with a big bulge in the middle. That bulge of middle-class jobs has been the foundation not only of our economic stability but of our political stability as well. Democracy cannot be stable without a broad and deep middle class. We cannot afford to move from a bell curve economy to a barbell economy—with a big high end and a bigger low end and nothing in the middle. It would be economically unfair and politically unstable. As former Clinton national economic adviser Gene Sperling rightly argues, "We either grow together or we will grow apart."

So if the next new thing is the automation and outsourcing of more and more old middle-class jobs, then the big question for America—and every other developed country—is this: What will be the jobs of the new middle, and what skills will they be based on? In the United States, new middle jobs are coming into being all the time; that is why we don't have large-scale unemployment, despite the flattening of the world. But to get and keep these new middle jobs you need certain skills that are suited to the flat world—skills that can make you, at least temporarily, special, specialized, or anchored, and therefore, at least temporarily, an untouchable. In the new middle, we are all temps now.

---

*In *The World Is Flat*, Friedman argues that ten forces have "flattened" the world. These forces include the fall of the Berlin Wall (November 1989), the emergence of Internet connectivity, and the outsourcing of work.

Review Questions

1. Why in a "flat" world do you not want to be mediocre in your work?

2. Why does one want to be "untouchable" in a flat world, according to Friedman?

3. What kinds of workers are likely to remain untouchable in the global economy?

4. What are the differences between a bell-curve and a barbell economy? What implications do these differences hold for the future?

Discussion and Writing Suggestions

1. Read Alan S. Blinder's "Will Your Job Be Exported?" (summary, p. 174; article, pp. 8–13). Compare and contrast his analysis of the future job market with Friedman's.

2. Tell the story of someone you know well—a grandparent, perhaps— who has never quite felt comfortable in the digital age. Maybe remote controls, cell phones, or computers are a challenge to this individual. Speculate on the ways in which retraining for the new economy might also be a challenge.

3. Consider your work history and the work you intend to do in the future. Use Friedman's distinction of fungible/nonfungible as a lens to analyze your past and intended work. What observations can you make?

4. Having read this piece, to what extent are you inclined at all to rethink your course selections in the coming semesters? Has Friedman's argument prompted you to reconsider your major? Explain.

5. Friedman writes: "In Globalization 3.0, individuals have to think globally to thrive, or at least survive. This requires not only a new level of technical skills but also a certain mental flexibility, self-motivation, and psychological mobility." What technical skills do you plan to develop in college? How mentally flexible do you see yourself? Self-motivated? Psychologically mobile? Aside from the technical, how does one *learn* these attributes?

6. Do you find challenges in "thinking globally" about your intended work? As you prepare yourself to take on rewarding work in the twenty-first century, to what degree do you anticipate competition from workers in India or China?

WILL YOUR JOB BE EXPORTED?
[SUMMARY]

Alan S. Blinder

Alan S. Blinder is the Gordon S. Rentschler Memorial Professor of Economics at Princeton University. He has served as vice chairman of the Federal Reserve Board and was a member of President Clinton's original Council of Economic Advisers. This article first appeared in *The American Prospect* in November 2006. The following summary of "Will Your Job Be Exported?" appears in Chapter 1, in the context of a discussion on how to write summaries. See pp. 8–13 for the complete text of this important article.

In "Will Your Job Be Exported?" economist Alan S. Blinder argues that the quality and security of future jobs in America's services sector will be determined by how "offshorable" those jobs are. For the past 25 years, the greater a worker's skill or level of education, the better and more stable the job. No longer. Advances in technology have brought to the service sector the same pressures that forced so many manufacturing jobs offshore to China and India. The rate of offshoring in the service sector will accelerate, and jobs requiring both relatively little education (like call-center staffing) and extensive education (like software development) will increasingly be lost to workers overseas.

These losses will "eventually exceed" losses in manufacturing, but not all service jobs are equally at risk. While "personal services" workers (like barbers and surgeons) will be relatively safe from offshoring because their work requires close physical proximity to customers, "impersonal services" workers (like call-center operators and radiologists), regardless of their skill or education, will be at risk because their work can be completed remotely without loss of quality and then delivered via phone or computer. "[T]he relative demand for labor in the United States will [probably] shift away from impersonal services and toward personal services."

Blinder recommends three courses of action. He advises young people to plan for "a high-end personal services occupation that is not offshorable." He urges educators to prepare the future workforce by anticipating the needs of a personal services economy and redesigning classroom instruction and vocational training accordingly. Finally, he urges the government to adopt policies that will improve existing personal services jobs by increasing wages for low-wage workers; retraining workers to take on better jobs; and increasing opportunities in high-demand, well-paid areas like nursing and carpentry. Ultimately, Blinder wants America to prepare a new generation to "lead and innovate" in an economy that will continue exporting jobs that require "following and copying."

Review Questions

1. What is "offshoring"? Why have service jobs been thought "immune to foreign competition"?

2. Explain Blinder's distinction between "personal services" and "impersonal services." Why is this distinction important?

3. In the past twenty-five years, what role has education played in preparing people for work? How does Blinder see that role changing in the coming decades?

4. What advice does Blinder offer to young people preparing for future work in the coming decades?

5. Why will the United States eventually lose more service-sector than manufacturing-sector jobs?

Discussion and Writing Suggestions

1. Identify a worker (real or imagined) in a job that may be at risk for offshoring, according to Blinder. Write a letter to that person, apprising him or her of the potential danger and offering advice you think appropriate.

2. What is your reaction to Blinder's claim that educational achievement, in and of itself, will be less of a predictor of job quality and security than it once was?

3. Describe a well-paying job that would not require a college education but that should, according to Blinder, be immune to offshoring. Compare your responses to those of your classmates.

4. What work can you imagine doing in ten years? Describe that work in a concise paragraph. Now analyze your description as Blinder might. How secure is your future job likely to be?

5. Approach friends who have not read the Blinder article with his advice on preparing for future work (see Review Question 4). Report on their reactions.

6. What were your *emotional* reactions to Blinder's article? Did the piece leave you feeling hopeful, anxious, apprehensive, excited? Explain.

INTO THE UNKNOWN

The Economist

The following piece first appeared in the *Economist* (November 13, 2004).

Where will the jobs of the future come from?

"Has the machine in its last furious manifestation begun to eliminate workers faster than new tasks can be found for them?" wonders Stuart

Chase, an American writer. "Mechanical devices are already ousting skilled clerical workers and replacing them with operators....Opportunity in the white-collar services is being steadily undermined." The anxiety sounds thoroughly contemporary. But Mr. Chase's publisher, MacMillan, "set up and electrotyped" his book, *Men and Machines,* in 1929.

The worry about "exporting" jobs that currently grips America, Germany and Japan is essentially the same as Mr. Chase's worry about mechanization 75 years ago. When companies move manufacturing plants from Japan to China, or call-center workers from America to India, they are changing the way they produce things. This change in production technology has the same effect as automation: some workers in America, Germany and Japan lose their jobs as machines or foreign workers take over. This fans fears of rising unemployment.

What the worriers always forget is that the same changes in production technology that destroy jobs also create new ones. Because machines and foreign workers can perform the same work more cheaply, the cost of production falls. That means higher profits and lower prices, lifting demand for new goods and services. Entrepreneurs set up new businesses to meet demand for these new necessities of life, creating new jobs.

5   As Alan Greenspan, chairman of America's Federal Reserve Bank, has pointed out, there is always likely to be anxiety about the jobs of the future, because in the long run most of them will involve producing goods and services that have not yet been invented.* William Nordhaus, an economist at Yale University, has calculated that under 30% of the goods and services consumed at the end of the 20th century were variants of the goods and services produced 100 years earlier. "We travel in vehicles that were not yet invented that are powered by fuels not yet produced, communicate through devices not yet manufactured, enjoy cool air on the hottest days, are entertained by electronic wizardry that was not dreamed of and receive medical treatments that were unheard of," writes Mr. Nordhaus. What hardy late 19th-century American pioneer would have guessed that, barely more than a century later, his country would find employment for (by the government's latest count) 139,000 psychologists, 104,000 floral designers and 51,000 manicurists and pedicurists?

Even relatively short-term labor-market predictions can be hazardous. In 1988, government experts at the Bureau of Labor Statistics confidently predicted strong demand in America over the next 12 years for, among others, travel agents and [gas]-station attendants. But by 2000, the number of travel agents had fallen by 6% because more travellers booked online, and the number of pump attendants was down to little more than half because drivers were filling up their cars themselves. Of the 20 occupations that the government predicted would suffer the most job losses between 1988 and 2000, half actually gained jobs. Travel agents have now joined the

---

*Alan Greenspan served as chairman of the Federal Reserve Bank from 1987 to 2006.

government's list of endangered occupations for 2012. May be they are due for a modest revival. You never know.

The bureau's statisticians are now forecasting a large rise in the number of nurses, teachers, salespeople, "combined food preparation and serving workers, including fast food" (a fancy way of saying burger flippers), waiters, truck drivers and security guards over the next eight years. If that list fails to strike a chord with recent Stanford graduates, the bureau also expects America to create an extra 179,000 software-engineering jobs and 185,000 more places for computer-systems analysts over the same period.

Has the bureau forgotten about Bangalore? Probably not. Catherine Mann of the Institute for International Economics points out that the widely quoted number of half a million for [Information Technology] jobs "lost" to India in the past couple of years takes as its starting point the year 2001, the top of the industry's cycle. Most of the subsequent job losses were due to the recession in the industry rather than to an exodus to India. Measured from 1999 to 2003, the number of IT-related white-collar jobs in America has risen. . . .

Ms. Mann thinks that demand will continue to grow as falling prices help to spread IT more widely through the economy, and as American companies demand more tailored software and services. Azim Premji, the boss of Wipro,* is currently trying to expand his business in America. "IT professionals are in short supply in America," says Mr. Premji. "Within the next few months, we will have a labor shortage."

If that seems surprising, it illustrates a larger confusion about jobs and work. Those who worry about the migration of white-collar work abroad like to talk about "lost jobs" or "jobs at risk." Ashok Bardhan, an economist at the University of California at Berkeley, thinks that 14 [million] Americans, a whopping 11% of the workforce, are in jobs "at risk to outsourcing." The list includes computer operators, computer professionals, paralegals and legal assistants. But what Mr. Bardhan is really saying is that some of this work can now also be done elsewhere.

What effect this has on jobs and pay will depend on supply and demand in the labor market and on the opportunity, willingness and ability of workers to retrain. American computer professionals, for instance, have been finding recently that certain skills, such as maintaining standard business-software packages, are no longer in such demand in America, because there are plenty of Indian programmers willing to do this work more cheaply. On the other hand, IT firms in America face a shortage of skills in areas such as tailored business software and services. There is a limited supply of fresh IT graduates to recruit and train in America, so companies such as IBM and Accenture are having to retrain their employees in these sought-after skills.

---

*See footnote on p. 170.

Moreover, Mr. Bardhan's list of 14 [million] jobs at risk features many that face automation anyway, regardless of whether the work is first shipped abroad. Medical transcriptionists, data-entry clerks and a large category of 8.6 [million] miscellaneous "office support" workers may face the chop as companies find new ways of mechanizing paperwork and capturing information.

Indeed, the definition of the sort of work that Indian outsourcing firms are good at doing remotely—repetitive and bound tightly by rules—sounds just like the sort of work that could also be delegated to machines. If offshoring is to be blamed for this "lost" work, then mechanical diggers should be blamed for usurping the work of men with shovels. In reality, shedding such lower-value tasks enables economies to redeploy the workers concerned to jobs that create more value.

Stuart Chase understood the virtuous economics of technological change, but he still could not stop himself from fretting. "An uneasy suspicion has gathered that the saturation point has at last been reached" he reflected darkly. Could it be that, with the invention of the automobile, central heating, the phonograph and the electric refrigerator, entrepreneurs had at long last emptied the reservoir of human desires? He need not have worried. Today's list of human desires includes instant messaging, online role-playing games and internet dating services, all unknown in the 1920s. And there will be many more tomorrow.

Review Questions

1. What is the main mechanism by which the economy creates jobs even as it eliminates jobs through automation, computerization, and outsourcing?

2. *The Economist* believes that, while our anxiety at being unable to identify future jobs that will replace current jobs lost to outsourcing is understandable, our apprehensions are not warranted. Why not?

3. What types of jobs are most easily outsourced, and how does such outsourcing create opportunities for American companies and their employees?

4. What is the role of human desire in fueling the economy?

Discussion and Writing Suggestions

1. The writers open this article by playing a trick of sorts on readers: quoting Stuart Chase on the topic of job loss to advancing technology. Discuss this strategy. Did you find it effective?

2. *The Economist* trusts the economy to create new jobs. Do you? In developing your response, reread paragraphs 3 and 4.

3. How would you describe the mood of this piece—relatively optimistic or pessimistic? Explain.

4. How does the economic news of the day color your reading of the piece? In your view, does the validity of the *Economist's* basic argument change at all in tough economic times?

5. Briefly research the term "market fundamentalism." What does it mean, and to what extent does it apply to the *Economist's* position in this essay?

OCCUPATIONAL OUTLOOK HANDBOOK, 2010–11 EDITION

Bureau of Labor Statistics

The Bureau of Labor Statistics, a division of the U.S. Department of Labor, regularly publishes its *Occupational Outlook Handbook,* which for hundreds of occupations provides current, thorough information on the following: "the training and education needed, earnings, expected job prospects, what workers do on the job, and working conditions." Use these categories to learn more about the occupations that interest you. And draw on the *OOH* Web site as a dependable resource while writing papers associated with this chapter.

Access the OOH Web site at http://www.bls.gov/oco/. To prepare for more detailed use later, devote fifteen or twenty minutes to exploring the site and its offerings.

OVERVIEW OF JOBS: THE 2008–18 PROJECTIONS

Bureau of Labor Statistics

An important document that can be accessed from the *Occupational Outlook Handbook* Web site is the BLS overview of jobs. The U.S. Department of Labor releases these ten-year employment projections every two years as part of a "60-year tradition of providing information to individuals who are making education and training choices, entering the job market, or changing careers." This is not likely a report you will read in its entirety. The more appropriate strategy would be to download the pdf file (or browse the Web site online) and skim its contents, returning to sections as needed when writing your papers. You will find statistically backed projections on changes in the age and ethnic makeup of the labor pool and expanding and shrinking employment opportunities by industry sector.

Access "Tomorrow's Jobs" at http://www.bls.gov/oco/oco2003.htm.

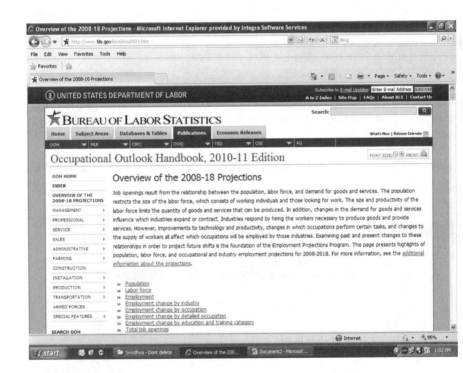

Review Questions

Go the Web site http://www.bls.gov/oco and answer these questions:

1. How is the *Occupational Outlook Handbook (OOH)* organized?

2. What nine specific types of information can a researcher find for every job listed in the *OOH* database?

3. From the *OOH* page for a particular occupation, follow a link to an associated Occupational Employment Statistics (OES) page. What information do you find there?

Find the Bureau of Labor Statistics (BLS) Web site at http://www.bls.gov/oco/oco2003.htm. Answer these questions:

4. What is the purpose of the BLS report?

5. How is the report organized?

6. Under the heading of "Labor Force," find the BLS projection for the youth labor force's share of the overall labor force by 2018.

7. Under the "Employment Change by Industry" heading, what do you learn about the goods-producing economy of the United States? Offer an example of an industry that is expected to grow between now and 2018. Offer an example of an industry expected to decline.

Discussion and Writing Suggestions

1. Your evaluation of every Web site can begin (but should not necessarily end) with a close reading of the site's "About" page, which most reputable sites will list on their top-level (or home) pages. Locate the "About BLS" Web page and report on what you find. How, for instance, does BLS gather the statistics you might use in a paper?

2. Describe the ways in which you might use these Bureau of Labor Statistics Web sites to investigate either broad career areas or specific jobs within a broad area.

3. The *Occupational Outlook Handbook* is a vast resource that can provide you with credible statistical information as you complete writing assignments associated with this chapter. Take a moment to skim the synthesis activities on pages 181–183. For any *one* activity, locate on these Web pages a statistic that might prove useful in your writing.

4. Peruse the Teacher's Guide to the *Occupational Outlook Handbook*, which you can access from the OOH main page or directly at http://www.bls.gov/oco/teachers_guide.htm. The guide will introduce you to the Web site and provide additional resources for research related to this chapter.

SYNTHESIS ACTIVITIES

1. Write an explanatory synthesis that reviews the developments responsible for the accelerating changes in the American workplace and the jobs that are most—and least—at risk from these changes. What are these changes? How did they come about? How do they affect workers?

2. According to the authors in this chapter, what are the attributes of workers likeliest to succeed in the new economy? Consult Peters, Judy and D'Amico, Blinder, and Friedman. Given this information, how likely is it that you will succeed? No one has a crystal ball, of course, but take stock of your character: Use your answer to the first question as a lens to analyze your attributes as a worker, and make a projection from there. How prepared would Peters or Friedman, for instance, find you to take on a job that would not likely be lost to outsourcing or rendered obsolete by technology?

3. Use any of the definitions from the first selection of this chapter, or one of the definitions from the articles by Blinder or Friedman, to analyze a job that interests you. First, carefully research that job (or a similar one) at the Bureau of Labor Statistics Web site. Recall that in your analysis you can use a definition or principle to generate questions, which you can then use as a lens to study key features of the object under analysis—in this case, a particular job. What insights does your analysis yield?

4. Sennett concludes that the skills needed to succeed in the new economy may "corrode" one's character. Use his insight as a principle to analyze the working life of someone you know well, much as Sennett has analyzed the life of Rico.

5. Both Sennett and Huws suggest that developments in the new economy can assault a worker's identity. If identity is tied to occupation (a common assumption among sociologists—see Huws, paragraph 3) and the "qualities of good work [in the new economy] are not the qualities of good character" (see Sennett, paragraph 24), then are you as a worker in the new economy destined to become as conflicted as Rico? Where does the Sennett/Huws argument break down? In a synthesis that draws on selections in this chapter for support, critique the Sennett/Huws argument.

6. In the articles by Sennett and Huws, you may have detected a tone of lament—a sense that something of value from the old world of work has been lost in the new economy. Other writers, like Peters, Judy and D'Amico, Blinder, Friedman, and the *Economist,* sound more hopeful notes. Compare and contrast the degrees of optimism and pessimism among authors in this chapter, considering their reasons (stated or not) for taking the positions they do. This paper could be an explanatory or an argument synthesis. If an argument, agree or disagree that an author's optimism or pessimism is warranted; conclude with a statement of your own regarding optimism or pessimism. Remember to organize your synthesis by idea, not by source.

7. Sennett writes that "a young American with at least two years of college can expect to change jobs at least eleven times in the course

of working, and change his or her skill base at least three times during those forty years of labor" (paragraph 26). Assuming this claim to be true, how will you prepare for a working life in which change is the one constant? What mix of knowledge and skills will you pursue? Develop your response into an argument synthesis that draws on Sennett, Judy and D'Amico, Blinder, Friedman, and any other selections you think pertinent. You may enjoy framing your argument around either of the following statements:

a. College years are not only a preparation for the world of work; they are also a safe harbor from it—a time to think broadly, impractically even, and look beyond the narrow needs of the workplace. Because no one can predict the future with certainty, a college student is best served by training broadly, developing core skills (such as critical thinking, writing, and speaking), and later meeting the challenges of the future workplace as they arise.

b. A favorite uncle or aunt tells you: "You'd better be realistic about your studies. Changes are coming, and you need to be prepared....A college education is expensive. It's unconscionable to spend all that money and not get the training you need for a good job immediately after graduation."

8. Define work and its essential features. Recall the multiple definitions that open this chapter (and there are many that were not included in the opening selection); recall also the definitions either assumed or stated explicitly by various writers in the chapter. Your definition will necessarily be an argument: one claim among many, the purpose of which will be to convince readers that the way you define work is reasonable, even compelling.

9. Reread, in the first selection of this chapter, the definitions of work and vocation. Consider the differences between approaching work as a livelihood and approaching it as a vocation. How might a confusion concerning these words complicate your working life?

RESEARCH ACTIVITIES

1. Interview several workers you know who are in their forties or, preferably, in their fifties. Ask them to describe changes they've seen in the workplace and ask how they're adapting to these changes. Frame the results of your interview in the context of several of the readings in this chapter. That is, use the readings to help make sense of the information you record in the interviews. Your research paper could take the form of an argument or an analysis.

2. Take a thorough accounting of the *Occupational Outlook Handbook* at the Bureau of Labor Statistics Web site, as previewed in this chapter. Prepare a report that presents (1) the range of information available at the OOH site—and closely linked sites—and (2) a strategy for mining useful information. Essentially, you will be preparing a "User's Guide" to the OOH.

3. Find a copy of Studs Terkel's *Working*, select one of the interviewees reporting on his or her experiences at a particular job, and research the current status of this job or career field at the Bureau of Labor Statistics Web site. Compare and contrast the experiences of the Terkel subject (mid-1970s) with those of a present-day worker.

4. Visit the career counseling office at your school. Interview one or more of the staff people there, and survey the publications available at the office to determine facts about the interests and employment prospects of the student body at your school. Write a report on the success your fellow students have had in securing internships at local businesses or job placements with local employers.

5. Writing for the Hudson Institute, Judy and D'Amico claim that the emergence of new jobs and services will "almost certainly...create more jobs than the underlying [emerging] technology will destroy." This view on the "creative destruction" in the economy is shared by the *Economist* and also Blinder, who cautions that we must do our best to anticipate coming changes and train the U.S. workforce accordingly. Research the work of Joseph Schumpeter, originator of the concept of creative destruction, and report on the acceptance of this concept by present-day economists.

6. Trace the changing attitudes toward work in Western culture. Authors of interest will likely include Herbert Applebaum, Melvin Kranzberg and Joseph Gies, Richard Donkin, and Joanne Ciulla.

7. Research the origins of the Puritan work ethic and its persistence in American culture. Puritans, writes Melvin Kranzberg, "regard[ed] the accumulation of material wealth through labor as a sign of God's favor as well as of the individual's religious fervor." Be sure, in your research, to look at *The Protestant Ethic and the Spirit of Capitalism* by economist and sociologist Max Weber.

Chapter 6

Green Power

Our wealth, our society, our being is driven by oil and carbon. And when we say that we have to make a shift, that is extremely difficult. It is intellectually dishonest to say that we can get some lightbulbs, or we can get a Prius, and we're all done. No— this is going to take massive technological innovation. It's going to take changes in the way we live and work. It's going to take cooperation of unprecedented degrees among businesses and government and among countries. That's where we are. There's no other word except "daunting."

—Jerry Brown, Attorney General of California

In 2006 climber and filmmaker David Breashears made his way up to a Himalayan outcrop on a steep ridge 19,000 feet high. From that familiar vantage point he had a clear view of the Rongbuk Glacier in Tibet, a frozen river of ice that flows from the north slope of Mount Everest. Comparing what he was seeing to a photograph taken in 1921 from the same vantage point by British explorer George Mallory, he was appalled by how much the ice had melted. "The glacier's just gone," he remarked to *Frontline* producer Martin Smith. It had, in fact, lost some 40 percent of its mass in the past 85 years.

The shrunken Himalayan glacier is but one more indication— along with collapsing ice shelves in Antarctica and polar bears stranded on ice floes—of the extent of climate change since the middle of the twentieth century. Climate experts warn of nothing short of an apocalypse unless current global warming trends are reversed. The earth's population faces the prospect of more frequent and severe hurricanes, fires, declining agricultural yields, the extinction of species, and rising ocean levels that threaten to flood coastal cities. Author and *New York Times* columnist Thomas Friedman quotes environmental consultant Rob Watson on the nature of the challenge we confront: "People don't seem to realize...that it is not like we're on the *Titanic* and we have to avoid the iceberg. *We've already hit the iceberg.* The water is rushing in below. But some people just don't want to leave the dance floor; others don't want to give up on the buffet."

What's causing climate change? Experts point to inceasing levels of greenhouse gases—chiefly carbon dioxide or CO_2. (Other greenhouse gases include methane, ozone, and water vapor.) These gases trap the sun's heat in the atmosphere by preventing infrared rays from escaping into space—and therefore, they keep living things from freezing to death. (Like cholesterol, a certain quantity of greenhouse gases is essential to survival.) For most of human history, greenhouse gases have remained at a life-supporting equilibrium. But accelerating levels of industrialization during the nineteenth and twentieth centuries have changed this equilibrium by measurably increasing atmospheric levels of CO_2, a byproduct of burning fossil fuels such as coal and oil, energy sources that are integral to the existence of modern civilization. More than half of the nation's electricity is generated by burning coal. It takes nine and a half tons of coal to produce the quantity of electricity used by the average American each year. And, of course, the overwhelming majority of the world's vehicles are fueled by gasoline, or refined petroleum.

The internal-combustion, CO_2-spewing engine that has powered vehicles of every type since the dawn of the automobile era in the early twentieth century has long been viewed as one of the greatest culprits in creating air pollution—and, more recently, in contributing to climate change. And bad as the situation is now, it is expected to get far worse. The number of cars in the world, about 625 million, is anticipated to double by 2020. China and India—whose populations account for a third of humanity—will soon replace the United States as the world's biggest importers of oil, a development that will generate significantly increased levels of CO_2 in the atmosphere.

In recent years, interest in and development of alternative energy sources that do not release CO_2 (or, at least, as *much* CO_2) into the atmosphere—and thus that serve to slow, if not reverse, the pace of global climate change—have intensified. Automakers are taking the first serious steps away from gasoline powered vehicles. The popularity of the Toyota Prius hybrid, the development of the all-electric Chevrolet Volt, ongoing research into hydrogen fuel-cell vehicles, and the increased use of biofuels and natural gas to power cars and buses are all evidence of the slow greening of the transportation industry. And wind and solar power are gaining ground as sources of electricity for home and industry. In 2008 Texas oilman T. Boone Pickens launched a highly visible public relations campaign explaining his plan to build the world's largest wind farm in the Texas Panhandle, which would generate and transmit enough electricity to power one million homes. Pickens also proposed conversion of all of the nation's automobiles to run on natural gas, instead of gasoline. As the recession that began later that year deepened, however, the scarcity of credit and the fall-off in natural gas prices (making wind power less economically attractive) forced Pickens to scale back his ambitious project in favor of a series of smaller wind farms in the Midwest.

More controversial than wind power is nuclear power, owing chiefly to questions of safety and cost. Building a nuclear power plant costs between $5 billion and $10 billion, and no application for a new nuclear power plant has been approved since 1979 (the year of the Three Mile Island reactor accident). Other renewable sources of electrical power include hydroelectric (generated by the force of flowing water); geothermal (generated by heat from the earth's core, transmitted to the surface); and biomass (generated by the burning of organic matter such as wood, leaves, manure, and crops). As of 2007, however, according to the U.S. Department of Energy's Energy Information Administration (EIA), only about 7 percent of the nation's energy consumption was being generated from renewable sources—as opposed to 40 percent from fossil fuels like petroleum and 22 percent from coal. (Natural gas provides 23 percent of the total consumption; nuclear power provides 8 percent.)

The development of green power, of renewable energy sources, is not only a global imperative; it is also a matter of public policy. That is, it involves questions of what government does or does not do to encourage or discourage particular activities by businesses, nonprofit organizations, educational institutions, and individuals. Governments issue regulations, pass laws, tax and spend, subsidize, make grants, reward those who comply with their rules, and penalize those who do not. In the 1970s, the U.S. government attempted to impose Corporate Average Fuel Efficiency Standards (CAFE) regulations mandating minimum fuel efficiency standards for vehicles. But automakers have long resisted such standards and have pressured the government to ease or abandon them. Other government efforts to curb greenhouse gas emissions have not survived industry opposition. In 2007 Senators Joseph Lieberman (ID-CT) and John Warner (R-VA) proposed the Climate Security Act, which would have imposed caps on CO_2 emissions; penalized companies for exceeding their allowable emissions limits; and mandated a 60 percent reduction in greenhouse gases by 2050. That measure, too, was resisted by business interests, and the matter never came to a vote.

The election of the environmentally conscious Barack Obama as president in 2008 (who, in his inaugural address, called for the country to "harness the sun and the winds and the soil to fuel our cars and run our factories") raised new hopes that public policy would now favor dramatic steps to reverse climate change, to encourage the development of renewable energy sources, and to reduce the nation's reliance on fossil fuels. In his campaign Obama supported cap-and-trade programs, which impose gradually reduced limits on the quantities of carbon dioxide that large industries may emit. Environmentalists were also encouraged by Obama's announced intent to raise federal fuel economy standards, to provide government subsidies for the development of more fuel-efficient vehicles, and to make significant federal investments in green technologies—including the construction of a national "smart grid" to transmit electrical power from wind and solar generators to energy-hungry cities.

The selections in this chapter offer multiple perspectives on how we can reduce (if not entirely eliminate) our dependence on fossil fuels and support the development of alternative, renewable energy sources. As you might expect, experts disagree not only about the nature of the problem and its causes but also about needed solutions. In this chapter, we present some of these disagreements, which will give you ample opportunity to evaluate, respond, and form your own informed opinions.

The chapter is organized into two sections. The first lays out the more general challenges we face in addressing a carbon emissions–related climate crisis and in working to reduce our dependence on fossil fuels. The second section considers particular alternative, renewable energy sources such as nuclear, wind, and solar power.

The chapter begins with two contrasting perspectives on energy independence. First is *Thomas Friedman's "205* Easy Ways to Save the Earth," a chapter in his book *Hot, Flat, and Crowded: Why We Need a Green Revolution—And How it Can Save America* (2008). Friedman argues that, contrary to his ironic title, there are no easy ways to save the earth: The task ahead is both gigantic and daunting. "If we can pull this off," he declares, "it will be the biggest single peacetime project humankind will ever have undertaken."

Next, in "The Dangerous Delusions of Energy Independence," Robert Bryce throws cold water on those who believe that we can free ourselves of reliance upon oil produced in other countries. "Energy independence is hogwash," he declares. "Worse yet, the inane obsession with the idea of energy independence is preventing the U.S. from having an honest and effective discussion about the energy challenges it now faces."

The rest of the chapter focuses on various types of carbon and non-carbon-based energy sources. In "Why the Gasoline Engine Isn't Going Away Any Time Soon," *Wall Street Journal* reporter Joseph B. White cautions that the challenges facing alternative energy vehicles like the Volt are sufficiently daunting that there is no prospect in the near term of their supplanting vehicles powered by internal-combustion. Next, in "The Case for and Against Nuclear Power," Michael Totty argues both sides of the issue while striving for objectivity. See if you can decide which case he finds stronger. Two pairs of pro-con pieces follow. In "The Island in the Wind" *New Yorker* writer Elizabeth Kolbert reports on the fascinating case of the Danish island of Samso, whose citizens decided to convert to electrical power generated entirely by wind turbines. Their experience raises intriguing questions about what might be done in this country, given the will. However, in "Wind Power Puffery," another doubter, H. Sterling Burnett, dismisses the prospect of wind power as a significant response to our energy problems. Next, in "State Solar Power Plans Are as Big as All Outdoors," *Los Angeles Times* reporter Marla Dickerson discusses what the state of California, facing new mandates on renewable power, has done to convert a significant part of its power generation from coal to solar. In the final selection, "Environmentalists Against Solar Power," the *New York Times'* Peter Maloney reports on a split in the environmentalist ranks between big solar and small solar. Big solar is represented by power companies that build large, ground-based solar projects capable of producing thousands of megawatts, and small solar is represented by individual homeowners who install rooftop solar panels. The small solar advocates object to the toll taken by the industrial solar projects on the environment and on wildlife.

And so the debate continues, not only between business people and environmentalists, but also among environmentalists themselves. To return to Thomas Friedman, "there is no 'Easy' button we can press to make the world green."

---

205 EASY WAYS TO SAVE THE EARTH

Thomas L. Friedman

Thomas Friedman, foreign affairs columnist for the *New York Times,* has won three Pulitzer Prizes for his books, which include *From Beirut to Jerusalem* (1989), *The Lexus and the Olive Tree* (1999), and *The World Is Flat* (2005). (We offer an excerpt from *The World Is Flat* in Chapter 5, "The Changing Landscape of Work in the Twenty-first Century.") The following passage is from his most recent book: *Hot, Flat, and Crowded: Why We Need a Green Revolution—And How It Can Renew America* (2008). Friedman expresses his opinions forcefully and is not afraid of initially offending readers with his tongue-in-cheek dismissal of quick-fix solutions to the climate crisis. But he also has the ability—and the facts—to make people reconsider their basic assumptions about important issues, whether or not they end up agreeing with him.

> *"Oh God, here they come—act green."*
> –A husband and wife speaking as another couple approaches them at a cocktail party. Cartoon in *The New Yorker*, August 20, 2007

> *A recent study found the average American golfer walks about 900 miles a year. Another study found American golfers drink, on average, 22 gallons of alcohol a year. That means, on average, American golfers get about 41 miles to the gallon. Kind of makes you proud.*
>
> —From the Internet

What do you mean? We're not having a green revolution? But I just picked up *Working Mother* magazine at the doctor's office and read the cover story: "205 Easy Ways to Save the Earth" (November 2007). It so whetted my appetite for easy ways to save the planet that I Googled for more books and magazine articles on this topic—and boy, did I find more: "20 Easy Ways You Can Help the Earth," "Easy Ways to Protect Our Planet," "Simple Ways to Save the Earth," "10 Ways to Save the Earth," "20 Quick and Easy Ways to Save the Planet," "Five Ways to Save the Earth," "The 10 Easiest Ways to Green Your Home," "365 Ways to Save the Earth," "100 Ways You Can Save the Earth," "1001 Ways to Save the Earth," "101 Ways to Heal the Earth," "10 Painless Ways to Save the Planet," "21 Ways to Save the Earth and Make More Money," "14 Easy Ways to Be an Everyday Environmentalist," "Easy Ways to Go Green," "40 Easy Ways to Save the Planet," "10 Simple Ways to

Save the Earth," "Help Save the Planet: Easy Ways to Make a Difference," "50 Ways to Save the Earth," "50 Simple Ways to Save the Earth and Get Rich Trying," "Top Ten Ways to Green Up Your Sex Life" (vegan condoms, solar vibrators—I'm not making this up), "Innovative Ways to Save Planet Earth," "101 Thing Designers Can Do to Save the Earth," "Five Weird and Wacky Ways to Save the Earth," "Five Ways to Save the World," and for those with a messianic streak but who are short of both cash and time: "10 Ways to Save the Earth (& Money) in Under a Minute."

Who knew that saving the earth could be so easy—and in under a minute!

There is some good news in this trend. Thinking about how to live and work in a greener fashion—with cleaner electrons, greater energy and resource productivity, and an ethic of conservation—is being popularized and democratized. It is no longer an elite issue for those living on the West and East coasts or in the backwoods of Colorado or Vermont.

If you are in the technology business today and you have not been invited to a green-tech conference somewhere, you must not be breathing, or everybody has lost your e-mail address. To say that green is the color du jour is an understatement. "Green" was actually the single most trade-marked term in 2007, according to the U.S. Patent and Trademark office. Environmental reporters in newsrooms, who used to sit in the corner far-thest from the editor's desk, are suddenly cool. Universities are adding classes on environmentalism and looking to shrink their carbon footprints, as are more and more companies. No candidate can get elected today with-out uttering the trilogy: I will support cleaner fuels. I will liberate America from its oil dependence. I will combat climate change.

5   The politics of this issue have shifted so much that even al-Qaeda sup-porters, who always have their fingers on the global pulse, are getting in on the green branding thing. *Newsweek* (September 10, 2007) reported that in July 2007 "an umbrella group of Islamists that advocates a Sharia state in Indonesia—and whose leaders have publicly supported Osama bin Laden—hoisted placards bearing the name Friends of the Earth-Indonesia at a rally protesting a U.S. mining company and the Bush Administration... [The real] Friends of the Earth denounced the unauthorized use of their logo and denied any links. But don't be surprised if radical Islamists make more attempts to cloak their work in the garb of social activism."

Not to be outdone by the Muslims, the Jews are also getting in on the act. UPI reported (December 5, 2007): "A group of Israeli environmentalists has launched an Internet campaign encouraging Jews around the world to light at least one fewer candle this Hanukkah ... The founders of the Green Hanukkia campaign say each candle burning all the way down produces 15 grams of carbon dioxide," and that many candles multiplied around Jewish households all over the world starts to add up to a kosher carbon footprint. "'The campaign calls for Jews around the world to save the last candle and save the planet, so we won't need another miracle,' Liad Ortar, a founder of the campaign, told *The Jerusalem Post*." (One blog I saw said in response: Why not ask everyone in the world to stop smoking cigarettes?)

You'll pardon me, though, if I've become a bit cynical about all of this. I have read or heard so many people saying, "We're having a green revolution." Of course, there is certainly a lot of green buzz out there. But whenever I hear that "we're having a green revolution" line I can't resist firing back: "Really? Really? A green revolution? Have you ever seen a revolution where no one got hurt? That's the green revolution we're having." In the green revolution we're having, everyone's a winner, nobody has to give up anything, and the adjective that most often modifies "green revolution" is "easy." That's not a revolution. That's a party. We're actually having a green party. And, I have to say, it's a lot of fun. I get invited to all the parties. But in America, at least, it is mostly a costume party. It's all about *looking* green—and everyone's a winner. There are no losers. The American farmers are winners. They're green. They get to grow ethanol and garner huge government subsidies for doing so, even though it makes no real sense as a CO_2-reduction strategy. Exxon Mobil says it's getting green and General Motors does too. GM put yellow gas caps on its cars that are flex-fuel, meaning they can run on a mix of gasoline and ethanol. For years, GM never bothered to highlight that its cars were flex-fuel, or use it as a selling point with customers, because the only reason GM made a certain number of cars flex-fuel was that, if it did so, the government would allow it to build even more gas-guzzling Hummers and pickup trucks and still remain under the CAFE fuel economy standard mandated by Congress—but why quibble?

Coal companies are going green by renaming themselves "energy" companies and stressing how sequestration of CO_2, something none of them has ever done, will give us "clean coal." I am sure Dick Cheney is green. He has a home in Wyoming, where he goes hunting, and he favors liquefied coal. We're all green. "Yes, step right up, ladies and gentlemen, in the green revolution we're having in America today, everybody gets to play, everybody's a winner, nobody gets hurt, and nobody has to do anything hard."

As I said, that's not the definition of a revolution. That's the definition of a party.

Thankfully, more than a few people are onto this green party. A blogger at Greenasathistle.com, which tracks environmental issues, wryly observed:

> Raising awareness about global warming, enviro-friendly products and people doing green deeds is obviously a good thing—but does every single magazine on the rack have to come out with a green issue? I'm starting to believe that there actually can be too much publicity when it comes to climate change, especially when it reaches the fashion world. Seriously, if I read the word "eco-chic" one more time, I'll jab my eyes out with my biodegradable pen…I just fear that as soon as all the magazines get these green issues out of the way, they'll feel like it's out of their system, over and done with, like any other passing trend. By next month they'll probably declare … gas guzzling "in" and earnest recycling "out," with headlines like "Littering is the new black!"

The amount of time, energy, and verbiage being spent on making people "aware" of the energy-climate problem, and asking people to make symbolic gestures to call attention to it, is out of all proportion to the time, energy, and effort going into designing a systemic solution. We've had too many Live Earth concerts and Barneys "Have a Green Holiday" Christmas catalogs and too few focused lobbying efforts to enact transformational green legislation. If the money and mobilization effort spent on Live Earth had gone into lobbying the U.S. Congress for more generous and longer-term production and investment tax credits for renewable energy, and for other green legislation, the impact would have been vastly more meaningful. Moving from the symbolic to the substantive is not easy. I live in Montgomery County, Maryland, which is chock-full of people who identify themselves as green and recycle and do all the other good things. But when I wanted to install two solar arrays in my side yard, I was told that it was against the law. Too unsightly. Zoning laws said they could go only in the backyard. Our backyard doesn't get enough sun. Our solar firm had to hire a lawyer and appeal to get the law changed, which we managed to do after almost a year.

Pentagon planners like to say: "A vision without resources is a hallucination." Right now we are having a green hallucination, not a green revolution. Because we are offering ourselves and our kids a green vision without the resources—without a systemic response shaped by an intelligent design and buttressed by market forces, higher efficiency standards, tougher regulations, and an ethic of conservation that might have a chance of turning that vision into reality. We have willed the ends, but not the means.

Sure, if you look at how far we have come in just the last five years, it can feel like we're having a green revolution. But if you look at where we have to go in the next ten years, we're having a party. No one has said it better than Michael Maniates, a professor of political science and environmental science at Allegheny College, who wrote in *The Washington Post* (November 22, 2007): "Never has so little been asked of so many at such a critical moment."

Several best-selling books "offer advice about what we must ask of ourselves and one another," Maniates noted.

> Their titles suggest that we needn't break much of a sweat: "It's Easy Being Green," "The Lazy Environmentalist," or even "The Green Book: The Everyday Guide to Saving the Planet One Simple Step at a Time."
> Although each offers familiar advice ("reuse scrap paper before recycling" or "take shorter showers"), it's what's left unsaid by these books that's intriguing. Three assertions permeate the pages: (1) We should look for easy, cost-effective things to do in our private lives as consumers, since that's where we have the most power and control; these are the best things to do because (2) if we all do them the cumulative effect of these individual choices will be a safe planet; which is fortunate indeed because (3) we, by nature, aren't terribly interested in doing anything that isn't private, individualistic, cost-effective and, above all, easy. This glorification of easy isn't limited to the newest environmental self-help books. The Web sites of the big U.S. environmental groups, the Environmental Protection Agency and even the American Association for the Advancement of Science offer markedly similar lists of actions that tell us we can change the world through our consumer choices, choices that are economic, simple, even stylish.

Of course, we are not going to consume our way out of this problem. And there is no "Easy" button we can press to make the world green. Maniates went on:

> The hard facts are these: If we sum up the easy, cost-effective, eco-efficiency measures we should all embrace, the best we get is a slowing of the growth of environmental damage...Obsessing over recycling and installing a few special light bulbs won't cut it. We need to be looking at fundamental change in our energy, transportation and agricultural systems rather than technological tweaking on the margins, and this means changes and costs that our current and would-be leaders seem afraid to discuss. Which is a pity, since Americans are at their best when they're struggling together, and sometimes with one another, toward difficult goals...Surely we must do the easy things: They slow the damage and themselves become enabling symbols of empathy for future generations. But we cannot permit our leaders to sell us short. To stop at "easy" is to say that the best we can do is accept an uninspired politics of guilt around a parade of uncoordinated individual action.

The problem is, the minute we leave the comforting realm of "the easy ways to go green," whatever facile consensus for action exists around this issue breaks down. The truth is, for all that we talk about going green, "we have not agreed as a society on what being 'green' actually means," remarked Peter Gleick, the climate expert from the Pacific Institute. That opens a door to everyone claiming to be green, without any benchmarks.

What I hope to do in the remainder of this book is lay out what a systemic green strategy would look like. But before we go there, we need to stop for just one moment at the weight scale.

You know how after you put on a few pounds, you stop weighing yourself—or at least I do—because you just don't want to know how many pounds you are going to have to shed? Well, the same has been true of the green issue. People tend to talk about it in the total abstract, without any connection to the actual scale of the challenge we have to meet in order to significantly reduce CO_2 emissions and become more energy and resource efficient. So before we take another step, we need to put this challenge on the scale, look down at the digital readout, and behold, without blinking, just how big a project this really is.

For starters, let's remember what we're trying to do: *We're trying to change the climate system—to avoid the unmanageable and manage the unavoidable!* We are trying to affect how much the rain falls, how strong the winds blow, how fast the ice melts. In addition to all that, *we're trying to preserve and restore the world's rapidly depleting ecosystems*—our forests, rivers, savannahs, oceans, and the cornucopia of plant and animal species they contain. Finally, we are trying to break a collective addiction to gasoline that is having not only profound climate effects, but also geopolitical ones. It doesn't get any bigger than this. This is not something you do as a hobby, and the adjective "easy" should never—ever, ever—accompany this task.

The truth is: Not only are there not 205 easy ways to *really go green,* there isn't *one easy way to really go green*! If we can pull this off, it will be the biggest single peacetime project humankind will have ever undertaken. Rare is the political leader anywhere in the world who will talk straight about the true size of this challenge.

20   As a result, the task often falls to oil, gas, and coal company executives. They are happy to tell us about the scale of the problem—but usually with secret delight, because they want us to believe that a real green revolution is impossible to pull off, so we have no choice but to remain addicted to oil, gas, and coal. They want to break our will to resist. Their hidden message is: "Surrender now, give in to your inner gas guzzler; the scale of what we need to do to really make a difference is too great. Surrender now, surrender now, surrender now…"

I am instinctively wary of their analysis—but I do make exceptions, for companies that have actually made substantial bets in renewable energy and are actually looking to build real businesses there—if there is a market. Chevron, for instance, is the world's biggest private producer of electricity from clean geothermal sources (steam, heat, and hot water produced underground by volcanic material from the earth's core, which provides the force to spin turbine generators and produce electricity.) Here's how Chevron's CEO, David O'Reilly, sees the scope and scale of our clean energy challenge:

"There is a problem with energy literacy," O'Reilly argues. "If you look at energy consumption in the world each day and convert it all into oil equivalent, we are consuming ten million barrels an hour—that is 420 million gallons per hour. Think about that. That means if we take all the hydro, coal, oil, and renewables—everything—and put them together, that is how much we are using. To really make a difference, there are three issues: There is the scale of the demand, the scale of the investment needed to produce alternatives at scale, and the scale of time it takes to produce alternatives. Many alternatives are just at the embryonic phase.

"Now let's look at the rising demand. I've heard people talk about 'the golden billion'—the billion people on the planet who [already] have the quality of life and standard of living we [Americans] are used to. But there are another two billion on the way up and three billion still in poverty. The two billion who are moving up want to get to where we are, and then the three billion want to move up—and from a global prosperity point of view, we want them to move up. Then there's another three billion coming along who have not even been born yet [but will be here by 2050]. This energy supply we have today is focused on meeting the demands of the one billion and the two billion—not the three billion who are still in poverty, let alone the three billion who have not been born yet. So this ten million barrels per hour [that we are consuming] is not static," said O'Reilly. "It is going to rise, because there is an inexorable connection between energy use and well-being."

Now, said O'Reilly, let's look at the challenge of creating new ways to produce and use energy. "People are overestimating the ability of the alternatives that are out there to get to scale," he explained. "Let's talk about efficiency: If you shut down the whole transportation system—I am talking about every car, truck, train, ship, and plane, anything that flies or is on wheels—and another vehicle never moved on planet earth, you would reduce carbon emission by 14 percent, globally. If you shut down all industrial activity, all commercial activity, all residential activity—shut everything off to every home—you would reduce carbon emissions by 68 percent...So efficiency can help, but let's not make false promises. We still need oil and natural gas. We need to make coal work, and we need to make energy efficiency work more."

As if that scenario doesn't already boggle the mind, O'Reilly argues that, absent some unexpected breakthrough, it will take decades for alternatives to be brought to scale. "I want my grandchildren to live in a world that has energy, environment, and economy in balance. But you cannot get there overnight," he insisted. "The system we have today is the product of over a hundred years of investments, and the next one will require a hundred years of investments. [So,] these quick promises that we hear in Washington and other places—be careful. My prediction [is that] global greenhouse gases will be higher ten years from now than they are today, but when my grandchildren are in my stage of life—their sixties—they could be substantially lower. We need leaders who will stand up and say this is hard, this is big, and it [requires] massive amounts of investment."

What about the $5 billion or so that I keep reading about that went into green venture capital investing in 2007? I asked O'Reilly. That would not even buy a sophisticated new oil refinery, he snapped. "If you want to really change the path we are on, you need a number that starts with a T in front of it"—T for *trillion*. "Otherwise we will stay on the path we are on."

But let's say you are an optimist. You believe that the renewable energy technologies available today, and opportunities for energy efficiency, are advanced enough to make a fundamental impact on both climate change and energy prices. What exactly would we have to do by way of deploying these existing clean power technologies and energy-efficiency programs—starting today—to make that fundamental impact?

The answer to that question—and another way to look at the scale of the problem—is offered by Robert Socolow, an engineering professor at Princeton, and Stephen Pacala, an ecology professor there, who together lead the Carbon Mitigation Initiative, a consortium that has set out to design scalable solutions for the climate problem. Socolow and Pacala first argued in a now famous paper published by the journal *Science* (August 2004) that human beings can emit only so much carbon dioxide into the atmosphere before the buildup of CO_2 reaches a level unknown in recent geologic history, and the earth's climate system starts to go haywire. Like the Intergovernmental Panel on Climate Change, they argued that the risk of really weird global weirding grows rapidly as CO_2 levels approach a doubling of the concentration of CO_2 that was in the atmosphere before the Industrial Revolution, which was 280 parts per million (ppm).

"Think of the climate-change issue as a closet, and behind the door are lurking all kinds of monsters—and there's a long list of them," Pacala said.

All of our scientific work says the most damaging monsters start to come out from behind that door when you hit the doubling of CO_2 levels."

30   So, as a simple goal everyone can understand, the doubling of CO_2 is what we want to avoid. Here's the problem: If we basically do nothing, and global CO_2 emissions continue to grow at the current trajectory, we will easily pass the doubling level—an atmospheric concentration of carbon dioxide of 560 ppm—around mid-century, and we'll likely hit a tripling sometime around 2075, said Pacala. You don't want to live in a 560 ppm world, let alone an 800 ppm world. To avoid that—and still leave room for developed countries to grow, while using less carbon, and for developing countries like India and China to grow, emitting double or triple their current carbon levels, until they climb out of poverty and are able to become more energy efficient—will require a huge global industrial energy project.

To convey the scale involved, Socolow and Pacala created a pie chart with fifteen different wedges. Some wedges represent carbon-free or carbon-diminishing power-generating technologies; other wedges represent efficiency programs that could conserve large amounts of energy and prevent CO_2 emissions. Socolow and Pacala argue that beginning today—right now—the world needs to deploy any eight of these fifteen wedges on a grand scale, or sufficient amounts of all fifteen, in order to generate enough clean power, conservation, and energy efficiency to grow the world economy and still avoid the doubling of CO_2 in the atmosphere by mid-century.

Each of these wedges, when phased in over fifty years, would avoid the release of twenty-five billion tons of carbon, for a total of 200 billion tons of carbon avoided between now and mid-century, which is the amount that Pacala and Socolow believe would keep us below the doubling. To qualify as one of the fifteen wedges, though, the technology must exist today and must be capable of large-scale deployment, and the emissions reductions it offers have to be measurable.

So now we have a target: We want to avoid the doubling of CO_2 by mid-century, and to do it we need to avoid the emission of 200 billion tons of carbon as we grow between now and then. So let's get to the wedges. Choose your favorite "easy" eight:

- Double fuel efficiency of two billion cars from 30 miles per gallon to 60 mpg.
- Drive two billion cars only 5,000 miles per year rather than 10,000, at 30 miles per gallon.
- Raise efficiency at 1,600 large coal-fired plants from 40 to 60 percent.
- Replace 1,400 large coal-fired electric plants with natural-gas-powered facilities.
- Install carbon capture and sequestration capacity at eight hundred large coal-fired plants, so that the CO_2 can be separated and stored underground.
- Install carbon capture and sequestration at new coal plants that would produce hydrogen for 1.5 billion hydrogen-powered vehicles.

- Install carbon capture and sequestration at 180 coal gasification plants.
- Add twice today's current global nuclear capacity to replace coal-based electricity.
- Increase wind power fortyfold to displace all coal-fired power.
- Increase solar power seven-hundred-fold to displace all coal-fired power.
- Increase wind power eightyfold to make hydrogen for clean cars.
- Drive two billion cars on ethanol, using one-sixth of the world's cropland to grow the needed corn.
- Halt all cutting and burning of forests.
- Adopt conservation tillage, which emits much less CO_2 from the land, in all agricultural soils worldwide.
- Cut electricity use in homes, offices, and stores by 25 percent, and cut carbon emissions by the same amount.

If the world managed to take just one of those steps, it would be a miracle. Eight would be the miracle of miracles, but this is the scale of what will be required. "There has never been a deliberate industrial project in history as big as this," Pacala said. Through a combination of clean power technology and conservation, "we have to get rid of 200 billion tons of carbon over the next fifty years—and still keep growing. It is possible to accomplish this if we start today. But every year that we delay, the job becomes more difficult. Because every year you delay, you have to do that much more the next year—and if we delay a decade or two, avoiding the doubling or more will become impossible."

Nate Lewis, the California Institute of Technology chemist and energy expert, uses a somewhat different set of calculations than Socolow and Pacala, but his approach is also useful in conveying the challenge. Lewis puts it this way: In the year 2000, the world's total average rate of energy usage was roughly 13 trillion watts (13 terawatts). That means that at any given moment, on average, the world was using about 13 trillion watts. That is what the world's electric meter would read. Even with aggressive conservation, that figure is expected to double by 2050 to around 26 trillion watts. But if we want to avoid the doubling of CO_2 in the atmosphere, and accommodate our own growth and that of India and China and other developing countries, we would actually have to cut global CO_2 emissions by 2050 by close to 80 percent, relative to current levels—starting today.

That means by 2050 we could use only about 2.6 trillion watts from carbon-emitting energy sources. But we know total demand is going to double by then, to about 26 terawatts. "That means, roughly speaking," said Lewis, "between now and 2050 we have to conserve almost as much energy as we are currently using, by becoming more energy efficient, and we also have to make almost as much clean energy as we currently use, by developing non-carbon-emitting energy sources."

An average nuclear power plant today produces about a billion watts— one gigawatt—of electricity at any given time. So if we tried to get all the new clean power we would need between now and 2050 (almost 13 trillion watts) just from nuclear power, we would have to build 13,000 new nuclear reactors, or roughly one new reactor every day for the next thirty-six years— starting today.

"It will take all of our investment capital and intellectual capital to meet this challenge," said Lewis. "Some people say it will ruin our economy and is a project which we can't afford to do. I'd say it is a project at which we simply can't afford to fail."

And make no mistake: We are failing right now. For all the talk of a green revolution, said Lewis, "things are not getting better. In fact, they are actually getting worse. From 1990 to 1999, global CO_2 emissions increased at a rate of 1.1 percent per year. Then everyone started talking about Kyoto, so we buckled up our belts, got serious, and we showed 'em what we could do: In the years 2000 to 2006, we *tripled* the rate of global CO_2 emission increases, to an average [increase] for that period of over 3 percent a year! That'll show 'em that we mean business! Hey, look what we can do when we're serious—we can emit even more carbon even faster."

This is where politics meets climate meets energy meets technology. Do we have the political energy—does anyone have the political energy—to undertake and deploy an industrial project of this scale?

40   Of course, being green at the rhetorical level we're at right now is not inconsistent with the broadly professed principles of either the Democratic or the Republican party. But implementing a green revolution at speed and scale is going to mean confronting some of the economic, regional, and corporate vested interests that live at the heart of both parties—from farmers in Iowa to coal lobbies in West Virginia. Therefore, without a real clash within the Republican and Democratic parties on this issue, there will be no real green revolution in America.

"When everyone—Democrats and Republicans, corporations and consumers—claims to embrace your cause, you should suspect that you have not really defined the problem, or framed it as a real political question," said the Harvard philosopher Michael J. Sandel. "Serious social, economic, and political change is controversial. It is bound to provoke argument and opposition. Unless you think there is a purely technological fix, meeting the energy challenge will require shared sacrifice, and political will. There is no real politics without disagreement and competing interests. Politics is about hard choices, not feel-good posturing. Only when a real debate breaks out—between or within the political parties—will we be on our way to a politically serious green agenda."

You can't call something a revolution when the maximum changes that are politically feasible still fall well short of the minimum needed to start making even a dent in the problem. The challenges posed by the Energy-Climate Era "can't be solved at the level of current political thinking," said Hal Harvey, an energy expert at the William and Flora Hewlett Foundation. "You cannot solve a problem from the same level of thinking that created it."

Rob Watson, the environmental consultant, said to me one day that meeting this challenge—for real—reminded him of an experience he had in the Boy Scouts. "I was overweight, and there were things I thought I could do in my head that I couldn't always do in real life," he explained. "Once my Boy Scout troop had a fifty-mile hike. And to prepare we had to do a series of training hikes. So I took hikes on my own. I thought I was going nine to twelve miles each time to prepare, but actually I was just going three or four. When I finally got out in the wilderness with my troop, I collapsed with heat-stroke, because I was not really in shape. I endangered myself and everyone in my group, because I was not being real. I know the need to want to feel that you are doing well and doing right—but if we are not real about where we are, we are not going to do what we need to do to survive in this wilderness."

People don't seem to realize, he added, that it is not like we're on the *Titanic* and we have to avoid the iceberg. *We've already hit the iceberg.* The water is rushing in down below. But some people just don't want to leave the dance floor; others don't want to give up on the buffet. But if we don't make the hard choices, nature will make them for us. Right now, that acute awareness of the true scale and speed of this problem remains confined largely to the expert scientific community, but soon enough it will be blindingly obvious to everyone.

Don't get me wrong: I take succor from the number of young people being engaged by this issue. And as the Greenasathistle.com blogger rightly observed, "it's better to be hypocritical than apathetic when it comes to the environment"—as long as you know that's what you're doing, as long as you keep moving in the right direction, and as long as you don't prematurely declare victory. It's planting our flag prematurely that will get us in the most trouble. And that's what we've started doing lately—a green brand, some green buzz, a green concert, and we're on our way to solving the problem. Not a chance.

"It is as if we were climbing Mount Everest and we reached base camp six, the lowest rung on the mountain climb, and decided to look around, put down our gear, pat our Sherpas on the back, and open a celebratory brandy," said Jack Hidary, the energy entrepreneur. "But meanwhile, Mount Everest, all 29,000 feet of it, still looms before us."

Review Questions

1. Why is Friedman "cynical" about all of the "green buzz"?

2. What does Friedman propose in place of a "green hallucination"?

3. What is the scale problem, discussed by Chevron CEO David O'Reilly?

4. Explain the purpose of Socolow and Pacala's fifteen-wedge pie chart.

5. Why are China and India mentioned so often by Friedman and others in discussions of the global climate problem?

● Discussion and Writing Suggestions

1. Friedman appears to make fun of the "205 Easy Ways to Save the Earth" approach to climate change. Why? To what extent do you agree with him? To what extent have you bought into the kind of "eco-chic" for which Friedman has such scorn? Do you think he is not sufficiently appreciative of well-intentioned (if ineffectual) efforts on the part of individuals?

2. Throughout this piece, Friedman writes in a breezy, punchy style. (See, for example, the opening of paragraph 4). Was this style effective for you? Cite examples of sentences that worked for you (in advancing Friedman's argument) or that didn't.

3. Write a critique of this selection. Use as guidelines the principles discussed in Chapter 2. Consider first the main questions: (1) To what extent does Friedman succeed in his purpose? (2) To what extent do you agree with him? Then move to the specifics: Do you find Friedman's strategies (for example, dismissing the effectiveness of what he calls "easy ways to save the earth") effective? Has he argued logically? What are his assumptions, and how do you assess their validity?

4. Friedman lays partial blame on the government—and, particularly, the Bush administration—for not effectively responding to the threat of climate change. Based on what you have seen and read so far about the Obama administration's approach to global warming, to what extent do you believe that the current administration is responding effectively to this crisis? Explain.

5. Locate a specific principle or definition that Friedman uses in this selection. For example, in paragraph 6 in which he discusses the "green revolution," Friedman asks, "Have you ever seen a revolution where no one got hurt?" The underlying principle here is that in real revolutions people *do* get hurt—not necessarily physically, but perhaps economically, or in such a way as to significantly change their preferred lifestyle. Write an analysis in which you apply this or another of Friedman's principles or definitions to a particular situation of which you have personal knowledge or about which you have read. See the guidelines and model analyses in Chapter 4 for ideas on how to proceed.

6. Toward the end of this selection (paragraph 41), Friedman quotes philosopher Michael J. Sandel as follows: "Serious social, economic, and political change is controversial. It is bound to provoke argument and opposition.... There is no real politics without disagreement and competing interests." (You may wish to reread the rest of this paragraph.) Assuming that you agree, why do you think that this is the case?

7. At the end of this selection, Friedman makes use of vivid imagery: Boy Scouts on a fifty-mile hike, the *Titanic* hitting the iceberg, mountain climbers on Everest. What does he achieve with such imagery? To what extent do you find it effective?

THE DANGEROUS DELUSIONS OF ENERGY INDEPENDENCE

Robert Bryce

In the following selection, Robert Bryce argues that it is neither possible nor desirable for the United States to become independent of foreign energy supplies. Those who advocate such independence, he claims, are "woefully ignorant about the fundamentals of energy and the energy business." Bryce's provocative conclusion flies in the face of often unexamined assumptions held by many politicians, as well as environmentalists.

Robert Bryce, a fellow at the Institute for Energy Research, and a managing editor of the *Energy Tribune*, has written about energy for more than two decades. His articles have appeared in such publications as the *Atlantic Monthly*, the *Guardian*, and the *Nation*. His books include *Cronies: Oil, the Bushes, and the Rise of Texas, America's Superstate* (2004) and *Pipe Dreams: Greed, Ego, and the Death of Enron* (2002). This selection is excerpted from the Introduction ("The Persistent Delusion") to his book *Gusher of Lies: The Dangerous Delusions of "Energy Independence"* (2008).

Americans love independence.

Whether it's financial independence, political independence, the Declaration of Independence, or grilling hotdogs on Independence Day, America's self-image is inextricably bound to the concepts of freedom and autonomy. The promises laid out by the Declaration—life, liberty, and the pursuit of happiness—are the shared faith and birthright of all Americans.

Alas, the Founding Fathers didn't write much about gasoline.

Nevertheless, over the past 30 years or so—and particularly over the past 3 or 4 years—American politicians have been talking as though Thomas Jefferson himself warned about the dangers of imported crude oil. Every U.S. president since Richard Nixon has extolled the need for energy independence. In 1974, Nixon promised it could be achieved within 6 years.[1] In 1975, Gerald Ford promised it in 10.[2] In 1977, Jimmy Carter warned Americans that the world's supply of oil would begin running out within a decade or so and that the energy crisis that was then facing America was "the moral equivalent of war."[3]

The phrase "energy independence" has become a prized bit of meaningful-sounding rhetoric that can be tossed out by candidates and political operatives eager to appeal to the broadest cross section of voters. When the U.S. achieves energy independence, goes the reasoning, America will be a self-sufficient Valhalla, with lots of good-paying manufacturing jobs that will come from producing new energy technologies. Farmers will grow fat, rich, and happy by growing acre upon acre of corn and other plants that can be turned into billions of gallons of oil-replacing ethanol. When America arrives at the promised land of milk, honey, and supercheap motor fuel, then U.S. soldiers will never again need visit the Persian Gulf, except, perhaps, on vacation. With energy independence, America can finally dictate terms to those rascally Arab sheikhs from troublesome countries. Energy independence will mean a thriving economy, a positive balance of trade, and a stronger, better America.

The appeal of this vision of energy autarky has grown dramatically since the terrorist attacks of September 11. That can be seen through an analysis of news stories that contain the phrase "energy independence." In 2000, the Factiva news database had just 449 stories containing that phrase. In 2001, there were 1,118 stories. By 2006, that number had soared to 8,069.

The surging interest in energy independence can be explained, at least in part, by the fact that in the post–September 11 world, many Americans have been hypnotized by the conflation of two issues: oil and terrorism. America was attacked, goes this line of reasoning, because it has too high a profile in the parts of the world where oil and Islamic extremism are abundant. And buying oil from the countries of the Persian Gulf stuffs petrodollars straight into the pockets of terrorists like Mohammad Atta and the 18 other hijackers who committed mass murder on September 11.

Americans have, it appears, swallowed the notion that all foreign oil—and thus, presumably, all foreign energy—is bad. Foreign energy is a danger to the economy, a danger to America's national security, a major source of funding for terrorism, and, well, just not very patriotic. Given these many assumptions, the common wisdom is to seek the balm of energy independence. And that balm is being peddled by the Right, the Left, the Greens, Big Agriculture, Big Labor, Republicans, Democrats, senators, members of the House, [former president] George W. Bush, the opinion page of the *New York Times*, and the neoconservatives. About the only faction that dismisses the concept is Big Oil. But then few people are listening to Big Oil these days.

Environmental groups like Greenpeace and Worldwatch Institute continually tout energy independence.[4] The idea has long been a main talking point of Amory Lovins, the high priest of the energy-efficiency movement and the CEO of the Rocky Mountain Institute.[5] One group, the Apollo Alliance, which represents labor unions, environmentalists, and other left-leaning groups, says that one of its primary goals is "to achieve sustainable American energy independence within a decade."[6]

10   Al Gore's 2006 documentary about global warming, *An Inconvenient Truth*, implies that America's dependence on foreign oil is a factor in global warming.[7] The film, which won two Academy Awards (for best documentary feature and best original song), contends that foreign oil should be replaced with domestically produced ethanol and that this replacement will reduce greenhouse gases.[8] (In October 2007, Gore was awarded the Nobel Peace Prize.)

The leading Democratic candidates for the White House in 2008 have made energy independence a prominent element of their stump speeches. [Former] Illinois senator Barack Obama has declared that "now is the time for serious leadership to get us started down the path of energy independence."[9] In January 2007, in the video that she posted on her Website that kicked off her presidential campaign, New York senator Hillary Clinton said she wants to make America "energy independent and free of foreign oil."[10]

The Republicans are on board, too. In January 2007, shortly before Bush's State of the Union speech, one White House adviser declared that the president would soon deliver "headlines above the fold that will knock your socks off in terms of our commitment to energy independence."[11] In February 2007, Arizona senator and presidential candidate John McCain told voters in Iowa, "We need energy independence. We need it for a whole variety of reasons."[12] In March 2007, former New York mayor Rudolph Giuliani insisted that the federal government "must treat energy independence as a matter of national security." He went on, saying that "we've been talking about energy independence for over 30 years and it's been, well, really, too much talk and virtually no action....I'm impatient and I'm single-minded about my goals, and we will achieve energy independence."[13]

• • •

Polls show that an overwhelming majority of Americans are worried about foreign oil. A March 2007 survey by Yale University's Center for Environmental Law and Policy found that 93 percent of respondents said imported oil is a serious problem and 70 percent said it was "very" serious.[14] That finding was confirmed by an April 2007 poll by Zogby International, which found that 74 percent of Americans believe that cutting oil imports should be a high priority for the federal government. And a majority of those surveyed said that they support expanding the domestic production of alternative fuels.[15]

The energy independence rhetoric has become so extreme that some politicians are even claiming that lightbulbs will help achieve the goal. In early 2007, U.S. Representative Jane Harman, a California Democrat, introduced a bill that would essentially outlaw incandescent bulbs by requiring all bulbs in the U.S. to be as efficient as compact fluorescent bulbs. Writing about her proposal in the *Huffington Post*, Harman declared that such bulbs could "help transform America into an energy efficient and energy independent nation."[16]

While Harman may not be the brightest bulb in the chandelier, there's no question that the concept of energy independence resonates with American voters and explains why a large percentage of the American populace believes that energy independence is not only doable but desirable.

But here's the problem: It's not and it isn't.

Energy independence is hogwash. From nearly any standpoint—economic, military, political, or environmental—energy independence makes no sense. Worse yet, the inane obsession with the idea of energy independence is preventing the U.S. from having an honest and effective discussion about the energy challenges it now faces.

[Let's] acknowledge, and deal with, the difference between rhetoric and reality. The reality is that the world—and the energy business in particular—is becoming ever more interdependent. And this interdependence will likely only accelerate in the years to come as new supplies of fossil fuel become more difficult to find and more expensive to produce. While alternative and renewable forms of energy will make minor contributions to America's overall energy mix, they cannot provide enough new supplies to supplant the new global energy paradigm, one in which every type of fossil fuel—crude oil, natural gas, diesel fuel, gasoline, coal, and uranium—gets traded and shipped in an ever more sophisticated global market.

Regardless of the ongoing fears about oil shortages, global warming, conflict in the Persian Gulf, and terrorism, the plain, unavoidable truth is that the U.S., along with nearly every other country on the planet, is married to fossil fuels. And that fact will not change in the foreseeable future, meaning the next 30 to 50 years. That means that the U.S. and the other countries of the world will continue to need oil and gas from the Persian Gulf and other regions. Given those facts, the U.S. needs to accept the reality of *energy interdependence.*

20   The integration and interdependence of the $5-trillion-per-year global energy business can be seen by looking at Saudi Arabia, the biggest oil producer on the planet.[17] In 2005, the Saudis *imported* 83,000 barrels of gasoline and other refined oil products per day.[18] It can also be seen by looking at Iran, which imports 40 percent of its gasoline needs. Iran also imports large quantities of natural gas from Turkmenistan.[19] If the Saudis, with their 260 billion barrels of oil reserves, and the Iranians, with their 132 billion barrels of oil and 970 trillion cubic feet of natural gas reserves, can't be energy independent, why should the U.S. even try?[20]

An October 2006 report by the Council on Foreign Relations put it succinctly: "The voices that espouse 'energy independence' are doing the nation a disservice by focusing on a goal that is unachievable over the foreseeable future and that encourages the adoption of inefficient and counterproductive policies."[21]

America's future when it comes to energy—as well as its future in politics, trade, and the environment—lies in accepting the reality of an increasingly interdependent world. Obtaining the energy that the U.S. will need in future decades requires American politicians, diplomats, and business people to be actively engaged with the energy-producing countries of the world, particularly the Arab and Islamic producers. Obtaining the country's future energy supplies means that the U.S. must embrace the global market while acknowledging the practical limits on the ability of wind power and solar power to displace large amounts of the electricity that's now generated by fossil fuels and nuclear reactors.

The rhetoric about the need for energy independence continues largely because the American public is woefully ignorant about the fundamentals of energy and the energy business.[22] It appears that voters respond to the phrase, in part, because it has become a type of code that stands for foreign policy isolationism—the idea being that if only the U.S. didn't buy oil from the Arab and Islamic countries, then all would be better. The rhetoric of energy independence provides political cover for protectionist trade policies, which have inevitably led to ever larger subsidies for politically connected domestic energy producers, the corn ethanol industry being the most obvious example.

But going it alone with regard to energy will not provide energy security or any other type of security. Energy independence, at its root, means protectionism and isolationism, both of which are in direct opposition to America's long-term interests in the Persian Gulf and globally.

Once you move past the hype and the overblown rhetoric, there's little or no justification for the push to make America energy independent. And that's the purpose of this book: to debunk the concept of energy independence and show that none of the alternative or renewable energy sources now being hyped—corn ethanol, cellulosic ethanol, wind power, solar power, coal-to-liquids, and so on—will free America from imported fuels. America's appetite is simply too large and the global market is too sophisticated and too integrated for the U.S. to secede.

Indeed, America is getting much of the energy it needs because it can rely on the strength of an ever-more-resilient global energy market. In 2005, the U.S. bought crude oil from 41 different countries, jet fuel from 26 countries, and gasoline from 46.[23] In 2006, it imported coal from 11 different countries and natural gas from 6 others.[24] American consumers in some border states rely on electricity imported from Mexico and Canada.[25] Tens of millions of Americans get electricity from nuclear power reactors that are fueled by foreign uranium. In 2006, the U.S. imported the radioactive element from 8 different countries.[26]

Yes, America does import a lot of energy. But here's an undeniable truth: It's going to continue doing so for decades to come. Iowa farmers can turn all of their corn into ethanol, Texas and the Dakotas can cover themselves in windmills, and Montana can try to convert all of its coal into motor fuel, but none of those efforts will be enough. America needs energy, and lots of it. And the only way to get that energy is by relying on the vibrant global trade in energy commodities so that each player in that market can provide the goods and services that it is best capable of producing.

Notes

1. Richard Nixon, State of the Union address, January 30, 1974. Available: http://www.thisnation.com/library/sotu/1974rn.html.

2. Gerald Ford, State of the Union address, January 15, 1975. Available: http://www.ford.utexas.edu/LIBRARY/SPEECHES/750028.htm.

3. Jimmy Carter, televised speech on energy policy, April 18, 1977. Available: http://www.pbs.org/wgbh/amex/carter/filmmore/ps_energy.html.

4. Greenpeace is perhaps the most insistent of the environmental groups regarding energy independence. This 2004 statement is fairly representative: http://www.greenpeace.org/international/campaigns/no-war/war-on-iraq/it-s-about-oil. For Worldwatch, see its press release after George W. Bush's 2007 State of the Union speech, which talks about "increased energy independence." Available: http://www.worldwatch.org/node/4873.

5. See any number of presentations by Lovins on energy independence. One sample: his presentation before the U.S. Senate Committee on Energy and Natural Resources on March 7, 2006. Available: http://energy.senate.gov/public/index.cfm? FuseAction=Hearings.Testimony&Hearing_ID=1534& Witness_ID=4345. Or see *Winning the Energy Endgame*, by Lovins et al., 228, discussing the final push toward "total energy independence" and the move to the hydrogen economy.

6. National Apollo Alliance Steering Committee statement. Available: http://www. apolloalliance.org/about_the_alliance/who_we_are/steeringcommittee.cfm.

7. At approximately 1:32 into the movie, in a section that discusses what individuals can do to counter global warming, a text message comes onto the screen: "Reduce our dependence on foreign oil, help farmers grow alcohol fuels."

8. AMPAS data. Available: http://www.oscars.org/79academyawards/ nomswins.html.

9. Barack Obama, "Energy Security Is National Security," Remarks of Senator Barack Obama to the Governor's Ethanol Coalition, February 28, 2006. Available: http://obama.senate.gov/speech/060228-energy_security_is_ national_security/index.html.

10. Original video at www.votehillary.org. See also, http://www.washingtonpost .com/wp-dyn/content/article/2007/01/20/AR2007012000426.html.

11. *New York Times*, "Energy Time: It's Not about Something for Everyone," January 16, 2007.

12. Shailagh Murray, "Ethanol Undergoes Evolution as Political Issue," *Washington Post*, March 13, 2007, A06. Available: http://www.washingtonpost.com/ wp-dyn/content/article/2007/03/12/AR2007031201722_pf.html.

13. Richard Perez-Pena, "Giuliani Focuses on Energy," *The Caucus: Political Blogging from the New York Times*, March 14, 2007. Available: http://thecaucus. blogs.nytimes.com/2007/03/14/giuliani-focuses-on-energy.

14. Yale Center for Environmental Law and Policy, 2007 Environment survey. Available: http://www.yale.edu/envirocenter/YaleEnvironmentalPoll2007 Keyfindings.pdf.

15. UPI, "Americans Want Energy Action, Poll Says," April 17, 2007. Available: http://www.upi.com/Energy/Briefing/2007/04/17/americans_want_energy_ action_poll_says.

16. Jane Harman, "A Bright Idea for America's Energy Future," *Huffington Post*, March 15, 2007. Available: http://www.huffingtonpost.com/rep-jane-harman/ a-bright-idea-for-america_b_43519.html.

17. http://www.infoplease.com/ipa/A0922041.html.

18. Organization of Arab Petroleum Exporting Countries (OPEC), *Annual Statistical Report 2006*, 75. Available: http://www.oapecorg.org/images/A% 20S%20R%202006.pdf.

19. Nazila Fathi and Jad Mouawad, "Unrest Grows amid Gas Rationing in Iran," *New York Times*, June 29, 2007. According to this story, Iran imports gasoline from 16 countries. Iran has been importing natural gas from Turkmenistan since the late 1990s. In 2008, those imports will likely be about 1.3 billion cubic feet of natural gas per day. The fuel will be used to meet demand in northern Iran. For more, see, David Wood, Saeid Mokhatab, and Michael J. Economides, "Iran Stuck in Neutral," *Energy Tribune*, December 2006, 19.

20. EIA oil reserve data for Saudi Arabia available: http://www.eia.doe.gov/ emeu/cabs/saudi.html. EIA oil reserve data for Iran available: http:// www.eia.doe.gov/emeu/cabs/Iran/Oil.html. EIA natural gas data for Iran available: http://www.eia.goe.gov/emeu/cabs/Iran/NaturalGas.html.

21. Council on Foreign Relations, "National Security Consequences of U.S. Oil Dependency," October 2006, 4. Available: http://www.cfr.org/content/publications/attachments/EnergyTFR.pdf.

22. A June 2007 survey done by Harris Interactive for the American Petroleum Institute found that only 9 percent of the respondents named Canada as America's biggest supplier of oil for the year 2006. For more on this, see Robert Rapier, "America's Energy IQ," R-Squared Energy Blog, June 29, 2007. Available: http://i-r-squared.blogspot.com/2007/06/americas-energy-iq.html#links. For the results of the entire survey, see: http://www.energytomorrow.org/energy_issues/energy_iq/energy_iq_survey.html.

23. EIA crude import data available: http://tonto.eia.doe.gov/dnav/pet/pet_move_impcus_a2_nus_epc0_im0_mbbl_a.htm. EIA data for jet fuel available: http://tonto.eia.doe.gov/dnav/pet/pet_move_impcus_a2_nus_EPJK_im0_mbbl_a.htm. EIA data for finished motor gasoline available: http://tonto.eia.doe.gov/dnav/pet/pet_move_impcus_a2_nus_epm0f_im0_mbbl_a.htm.

24. EIA coal data available: http://www.eia.doe.gov/cneaf/coal/quarterly/html/t18p01p1.html. For gas imports, EIA data available: http://tonto.eia.doe.gov/dnav/ng/ng_move_impc_sl_a.htm.

25. EIA data available: http://www.eia.doe.gov/cneaf/electricity/epa/epat6p3.html.

26. Information from 2006, EIA data available: http://www.eia.doe.gov/cneaf/nuclear/umar/table3.html.

Review Questions

1. Why are Americans so obsessed with independence, according to Bryce?

2. Why does Bryce believe that renewable energy sources such as wind power and solar power cannot supplant fossil fuels in the foreseeable future?

3. How does Bryce explain the American public's (and its leaders') rhetoric about independence?

Discussion and Writing Suggestions

1. What is Bryce's chief objection to the premise that the United States should strive to become energy independent? To what extent do you agree with his objection?

2. To what extent do you believe that Bryce is overly pessimistic about the prospects for renewable energy sources supplanting fossil fuels in the near term? Explain.

3. Bryce employs sarcasm plentifully throughout this piece. Cite examples. Do you think that he uses this rhetorical device effectively? Explain.

4. Bryce argues that "the U.S. needs to accept the reality of *energy interdependence.*" What implications does such an acceptance have for (1) domestic suppliers of fossil fuels (coal, oil, natural gas); (2) domestic consumption of energy from both fossil and renewable sources; and (3) our relations with oil-supplying nations of the Middle East?

5. Critique Bryce's argument. Use as guidelines the principles discussed in Chapter 2. Consider first the main questions: (1) To what extent does Bryce succeed in his purpose? (2) To what extent do you agree with him? Then move to the specifics: Do you find Bryce's arguments compelling? Has he argued logically? What are his assumptions, and how do you assess their validity? You may want to draw upon other authors in this chapter—for example, Friedman—to provide support in your critique of Bryce. Keep in mind that this selection by Bryce is part of the Introduction to a book-length treatment of the subject during which he goes into much greater detail and a more extended argument than you will find in this relatively brief excerpt. Nevertheless, the heart of Bryce's argument is contained in this passage.

6. Locate a specific principle or definition that Bryce uses in this selection. For example, in paragraph 1, he asserts that "Americans love independence" and in paragraph 18 he contends that "the world—and the energy business in particular—is becoming ever more interdependent. And this interdependence will likely only accelerate in the years to come ..." Write an analysis in which you apply this or another principle or definition by Bryce to a particular situation of which you have personal knowledge or about which you have read. See the guidelines and model analyses in Chapter 4 for ideas on how to proceed.

WHY THE GASOLINE ENGINE ISN'T GOING AWAY ANY TIME SOON

Joseph B. White

In the following article, Joseph B. White, who covers automobile and energy-related stories for the *Wall Street Journal*, explains why, despite its numerous critics and its massive carbon footprint, the internal-combustion engine still has miles to go before it sleeps. This article first appeared in the *Journal* on September 15, 2008.

An automotive revolution is coming—but it's traveling in the slow lane.

High oil prices have accomplished what years of pleas from environmentalists and energy-security hawks could not: forcing the world's major auto makers to refocus their engineers and their capital on devising mass-market alternatives to century-old petroleum-fueled engine technology.

With all the glitzy ads, media chatter and Internet buzz about plug-in hybrids that draw power from the electric grid or cars fueled with hydrogen, it's easy to get lulled into thinking that gasoline stations soon will be as rare as drive-in theaters. The idea that auto makers can quickly execute a revolutionary transition from oil to electricity is now a touchstone for both major presidential candidates.

That's the dream. Now the reality: This revolution will take years to pull off—and that's assuming it isn't derailed by a return to cheap oil. Anyone who goes to sleep today and wakes up in five years will find that most cars for sale in the U.S. will still run on regular gas—with a few more than today taking diesel fuel. That will likely be the case even if the latter-day Rip Van Winkle sleeps until 2020.

Free to Drive

Cars aren't iPods or washing machines. They are both highly complex machines and the enablers of a way of life that for many is synonymous with freedom and opportunity—not just in the U.S., but increasingly in rising nations such as China, India and Russia.

Engineering and tooling to produce a new vehicle takes three to five years—and that's without adding the challenge of major new technology. Most car buyers won't accept "beta" technology in the vehicles they and their families depend on every day. Many senior industry executives—including those at Japanese companies—have vivid memories of the backlash against the quality problems that resulted when Detroit rushed smaller cars and new engines into the market after the gas-price shocks of the 1970s. The lesson learned: Technological change is best done incrementally.

Integral to Modern Life

Technological inertia isn't the only issue. Cars powerful enough and large enough to serve multiple functions are integral to modern life, particularly in suburban and rural areas not well served by mass transit.

Ditching the internal-combustion engine could mean ditching the way of life that goes with it, and returning to an era in which more travel revolves around train and bus schedules, and more people live in smaller homes in dense urban neighborhoods.

Economic and cultural forces—high gas prices and empty-nest baby boomers bored with the suburbs—are encouraging some Americans to return to city life, but by no means all. In rising economies such as China, meanwhile, consumers are ravenous for the mobility and freedom that owning a car provides.

Desire Isn't Enough

That doesn't mean auto makers and their technology suppliers aren't serious about rethinking the status quo. But displacing internal-combustion engines fueled by petroleum won't be easy and it won't be cheap.

It also may not make sense. Over the past two decades, car makers have at times declared the dawn of the age of ethanol power, hydrogen power and electric power—only to wind up back where they started: confronting the internal-combustion engine's remarkable combination of low cost, durability and power. One effect of higher oil prices is that car makers now have strong incentives to significantly improve the technology they already know.

"There are a lot of improvements coming to the internal-combustion engine," says John German, manager for environmental and energy analysis at Honda Motor Co.'s U.S. unit.

Refinements to current gasoline motors, driven by advances in electronic controls, could result in motors that are a third to half the size and weight of current engines, allowing for lighter, more-efficient vehicles with comparable power. That, Mr. German says, "will make it harder for alternative technologies to succeed."

By 2020, many mainstream cars could be labeled "hybrids." But most of these hybrids will run virtually all the time on conventional fuels. The "hybrid" technology will be a relatively low-cost "micro hybrid" system that shuts the car off automatically at a stop light, and then restarts it and gives it a mild boost to accelerate.

Cheaper Than Water

15 Gasoline and diesel are the world's dominant motor-vehicle fuels for good reasons. They are easily transported and easily stored. They deliver more power per gallon than ethanol or other biofuels. And until recently petroleum fuels were a bargain, particularly for consumers in the U.S. Even now, gasoline in the U.S. is cheaper by the gallon than many brands of bottled water.

Car makers have made significant advances in technology to use hydrogen as a fuel, either for a fuel cell that generates electricity or as a replacement for gasoline in an internal-combustion engine. But storing and delivering hydrogen remains a costly obstacle to mass marketing of such vehicles.

Natural gas has enjoyed a resurgence of interest in the wake of big new gas finds in the U.S., and Honda markets a natural-gas version of its Civic compact car.

But there are only about 1,100 natural-gas fueling stations around the country, of which just half are open to the public, according to the Web site for Natural Gas Vehicles for America, a group that represents various natural-gas utilities and technology providers.

Among auto-industry executives, the bet now is that the leading alternative to gasoline will be electricity. Electric cars are a concept as old as the industry itself. The big question is whether battery technology can evolve to the point where a manufacturer can build a vehicle that does what consumers want at a cost they can afford.

20 "The No. 1 obstacle is cost," says Alex Molinaroli, head of battery maker Johnson Controls Inc.'s Power Solutions unit. Johnson Controls is a leading maker of lead-acid batteries—standard in most cars today—and is working to develop advanced lithium-ion automotive batteries in a joint venture with French battery maker Saft Groupe SA.

The Costs Add Up

Cost is a problem not just with the advanced batteries required to power a car for a day's driving. There's also the cost of redesigning cars to be lighter and more aerodynamic so batteries to power them don't have to be huge.

There's the cost of scrapping old factories and the workers that go with them—a particular challenge for Detroit's Big Three auto makers, which have union agreements that make dismissing workers difficult and costly.

A world full of electricity-driven cars would require different refueling infrastructure but the good news is that it's already largely in place, reflecting a century of investment in the electric grid.

The refueling station is any electric outlet. The key will be to control recharging so it primarily happens when the grid isn't already stressed, but controllers should be able to steer recharging to off-peak hours, likely backed by discount rates for electricity.

Big utilities in the two most populous states, California and Texas, are adding millions of smart meters capable of verifying that recharging happens primarily in periods when other electricity use is slack. Studies show the U.S. could easily accommodate tens of millions of plug-in cars with no additional power plants. Three big utilities in California are planning to install smart meters capable of managing off-peak recharging. The estimated cost: $5 billion over the next five years.

Remembering the Past

Americans often reach for two analogies when confronted with a technological challenge: The Manhattan Project, which produced the first atomic bomb during World War II, and the race to put a man on the moon during the 1960s. The success of these two efforts has convinced three generations of Americans that all-out, spare-no-expense efforts will yield a solution to any challenge.

This idea lives today in General Motors Corp.'s crash program to bring out the Chevrolet Volt plug-in hybrid by 2010—even though the company acknowledges the battery technology required to power the car isn't ready.

Even if GM succeeds in meeting its deadline for launching the Volt, the Volt won't be a big seller for years, especially if estimates that the car will be priced at $40,000 or more prove true.

Moon-shot efforts like the Volt get attention, but the most effective ways to use less energy may have less to do with changing technology than with changing habits.

A 20-mile commute in an electric car may not burn gasoline, but it could well burn coal—the fuel used to fire electric power plants in much of the U.S. The greener alternative would be to not make the drive at all, and fire up a laptop and a broadband connection instead.

[The following table accompanied White's article.]

The Road Ahead

Gasoline has powered the vast majority of the world's automobiles for the past century. But now amid rising oil prices and increasing concern about tailpipe emissions and global warming, new types of propulsion technologies are starting to emerge. Here's an overview of what's here now, and what's ahead.

—Kelly McDaniel-Timon

	Pros	Cons	Vehicles	Availability/Starting Prices
Hybrids Have a battery and electric motor to power the car at low speeds and a gas engine for accelerating and highway driving.	Increases fuel-economy significantly, especially in heavy stop-and-go driving.	Price premium over standard models can be $2,500 or more for a Toyota Prius, $8,000 and up for large hybrid SUVs. Mileage improvements modest in some larger vehicles.	Toyota Prius, Ford Escape Hybrid, GMC Yukon Hybrid, Lexus LS600h, Lexus RX400h, Chrysler Aspen Hybrid, Dodge Durango Hybrid.	On the market now. Prius $23,375, Yukon $50,920, Lexus RX400h $43,480.
Mild Hybrids Electric motor only assists the gasoline engine; it can't drive wheels on its own.	Cost. Generally less expensive than full hybrids.	Only modest improvement in fuel economy.	Honda Civic Hybrid, Chevrolet Malibu Hybrid, Saturn Aura Hybrid.	On the market now. Honda Civic $22,600, Chevy Malibu $24,695, Saturn Aura $24,930.
Plug-In Hybrids A full hybrid with a large battery that drivers can recharge by plugging the car into an AC outlet.	Dramatic boost in fuel economy-can go up to perhaps 120 miles on the battery alone.	The advanced batteries required are not yet available. They are also expensive and can overheat.	None on the market today. Some "hackers" can convert Priuses to plug-ins.	Many auto makers working to offer them in 2-4 years.

Flex Fuel Vehicles Have standard internal combustion engines that can run on gasoline or a mix of gasoline and ethanol.	No price premium, can be used in vehicles of all sizes. Reduces greenhouse gas emissions.	Ethanol not widely available. A gallon of ethanol has less energy than a gallon of gas, so mile per gallon is lower.	Almost all GM, Ford and Chrysler models.	On the market now.
Fuel Cell Vehicles Use hydrogen gas and a chemical process to generate electricity that powers an electric motor.	Uses no fossil fuel, hydrogen is widely available and the only tailpipe emission is water vapor.	Still in experimental stage, hydrogen not widely available as fuel, technology still far too expensive for commercial use.	Models now in tests include Honda FCX Clarity and Chevrolet Equinox among others.	Small number of Clarity and Equinox available for lease through test programs.
Electric Car Powered by a long-lasting battery and electric motor. Can have a small gas engine on board to charge the battery.	Practically no emission or engine noise. Can be recharged from AC outlet.	Technology still unproven. Batteries not available.	GM working on Chevy Volt. Also start-up electric car makers Tesla, Fisker and others.	Volt due by 2011. Tesla, Fisker and others possibly sooner.
Clean Diesel New, advanced diesel engines that burn fuel more cleanly and use low-sulfur fuel.	20% to 40% more miles per gallon and more torque than gas engines, reduced greenhouse gas emissions.	More expensive than models with gas engines. Diesel fuel more expensive than gasoline. Unclear if Americans will embrace diesel.	Jeep Grand Cherokee and Volkswagen Jetta are two examples. BMW and Mercedes-Benz also offering clean diesel models.	VW Jetta diesel $21,999, Grand Cherokee $31,390.

Source: WSJ Reporting

Review Questions

1. Summarize White's answer to the implied question in the title of his article.

2. What are the main stumbling blocks, according to White, to broad consumer acceptance of alternative energy vehicles?

3. What are the chief drawbacks of hydrogen and natural gas as automobile fuels? To what extent do electric-powered vehicles share such drawbacks?

Discussion and Writing Suggestions

1. White argues, "Most car buyers won't accept 'beta' [developmental] technology in the vehicles that they and their families depend on every day." To what extent do you agree with this assertion as it applies to alternative energy vehicles? Would you be hesitant to buy a first-generation Chevy Volt or any other plug-in hybrid vehicle if there were no guarantee of its reliability?

2. White cites "mobility and freedom" as one reason that the internal-combustion engine will persist for the foreseeable future. To what extent are such values sufficiently important that you would hesitate to purchase or refuse to consider purchasing an all-electric vehicle?

3. Locate a specific principle or definition that White uses in this selection. For example, he asserts in paragraph 5 that cars "are both highly complex machines and the enablers of a way of life that for many is synonymous with freedom and opportunity." Write an analysis in which you apply this or another principle or definition by White to a particular situation of which you have personal knowledge or about which you have read. See the guidelines and model analyses in Chapter 4 for ideas on how to proceed.

4. If the next generation of gasoline-powered vehicles were built with motors "a third to half the size and weight of [motors in] current vehicles" (and, therefore, with an equivalent decrease in their carbon footprint), would there be any reason to convert the nation's vehicle fleet to electric, fuel-cell, or other forms of power?

5. Toward the end of this article, White suggests that "the most effective ways to use less energy may have less to do with changing technology than with changing habits." To what extent do you agree with this conclusion? Is the goal of using less energy better achieved by changing our habits than by changing our technology? In what particular ways might changing our habits affect the way we live and work?

THE CASE FOR AND AGAINST NUCLEAR POWER

Michael Totty

In the following article, *Wall Street Journal* staff reporter Michael Totty attempts the tricky task of arguing on both sides of the same issue: whether or not we should build more nuclear reactors to help satisfy our energy needs. Can you determine which argument Totty himself finds more persuasive? This article appeared in a special energy section of the *Journal* on June 30, 2008.

Is nuclear power the answer for a warming planet? Or is it too expensive and dangerous to satisfy future energy needs?

Interest in nuclear power is heating up, as the hunt intensifies for "green" alternatives to fossil fuels like coal and natural gas. Even some environmentalists have come on board, citing the severity of the global-warming threat to explain their embrace of the once-maligned power source.

But the issue is far from settled. Proponents insist that nuclear is a necessary alternative in an energy-constrained world. They say that the economics make sense—and that the public has a warped image of the safety risks, thanks to Three Mile Island, Chernobyl and *The China Syndrome*. [See paragraph 25.] Opponents, meanwhile, are convinced that the costs are way too high to justify the safety hazards, as well as the increased risks of proliferation.

Has nuclear's time come? The debate rages on.

Nuclear's the Answer

The argument for nuclear power can be stated pretty simply: We have no choice.

If the world intends to address the threat of global warming and still satisfy its growing appetite for electricity, it needs an ambitious expansion of nuclear power.

Scientists agree that greenhouse gases, mainly carbon dioxide, are building up in the atmosphere and contributing to a gradual increase in global average temperatures. At the same time, making electricity accounts for about a third of U.S. greenhouse emissions, mostly from burning fossil fuels to produce power.

Nuclear power plants, on the other hand, emit virtually no carbon dioxide—and no sulfur or mercury either. Even when taking into account "full life-cycle emissions"—including mining of uranium, shipping fuel, constructing plants and managing waste—nuclear's carbon-dioxide discharges are comparable to the full life-cycle emissions of wind and hydropower and less than solar power.

Nuclear power, of course, isn't the only answer. We need to get more energy from other nonpolluting sources such as solar and wind. Conservation is crucial. So is using technology to make more efficient use of fossil-fuel power.

But we have to be realistic about the limits of these alternatives. As it is, the 104 nuclear power plants in the U.S. generate about a fifth of the nation's

HOW A NUCLEAR REACTOR WORKS

All power plants convert a source of energy or fuel into electricity. Most large plants do that by heating water to create steam, which turns a turbine that drives an electric generator. Inside the generator, a large electromagnet spins within a coil of wire, producing electricity.

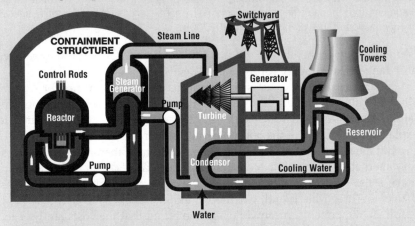

A fossil plant burns coal or oil to make the heat that creates the steam. Nuclear power plants...make the steam from heat that is created when atoms split apart—called fission.

The fuel for nuclear power plants is uranium, which is made into pellets and sealed inside long metal tubes, called fuel rods. The rods are located in the reactor vessel.

The fission process takes place when the nucleus of a uranium atom is split when struck by a neutron. The "fissioning" of the nucleus releases two or three new neutrons and energy in the form of heat. The released neutrons then repeat the process, releasing more neutrons and producing more nuclear energy. The repeating of the process is called a chain reaction and creates the heat needed to turn water into steam.

In a pressurized water reactor...water is pumped through the reactor core and heated by the fission process. The water is kept under high pressure inside the reactor so it does not boil.

The heated water from the reactor passes through tubes inside four steam generators, where the heat is transferred to water flowing around the tubes. The water boils and turns to steam.

The steam is piped to the turbines. The force of the expanding steam drives the turbines, which spin a magnet in coil of wire—the generator—to produce electricity.

After passing through the turbines, the steam is converted back to water by circulating it around tubes carrying cooling water in the condenser. The condensed steam—now water—is returned to the steam generators to repeat the cycle.

The cooling water from the condenser is sprayed into the air inside the cooling tower and falls about 60 feet, which cools it before it is continuously recycled to condense more steam. Water in the vapor rising from the cooling tower is replenished to the condenser cooling system using [pumped-in water, generally from a nearby river].

The three water systems at [a nuclear power plant] are separate from each other, and the radioactive water is not permitted to mix with other non-radioactive water systems.

Adapted from "How Sequoyah Works," Tennessee Valley Authority, http://www. tva.gov/power/nuclear/sequoyah_howworks.htm.

energy. Wind accounts for about 1%, and solar even less than that. Any increase in the number of nuclear power plants can help—even if they won't solve the whole problem.

More important from the standpoint of displacing fossil fuel, nuclear can meet power demand 24 hours a day. Solar and wind can't do that. Nuclear is the only current technology that fits the bill.

The Real Economics   So, what's the case against nuclear power? It boils down to two things: economics and safety.

Neither holds up to scrutiny.

First, economics. Critics argue that the high cost of building and financing a new plant makes nuclear power uneconomical when compared with other sources of power.

But that's misleading on a number of levels. One reason it's so expensive at this point is that no new plant has been started in the U.S. since the last one to begin construction in 1977. Lenders—uncertain how long any new plant would take because of political and regulatory delays—are wary of financing the first new ones. So financing costs are unusually high. As we build more, the timing will be more predictable, and financing costs will no doubt come down as lenders become more comfortable.

Loan guarantees and other federal incentives are needed to get us over this hump. They are not permanent subsidies for uneconomical ventures. Instead, they're limited to the first half dozen of plants as a way to reassure investors that regulatory delays won't needlessly hold up construction. It's important to remember that although nuclear energy has been around a while, it's hardly a "mature" industry, as some critics say. Because of the lack of new plants in so many years, nuclear in many ways is more like an emerging technology, and so subsidies make sense to get it going.

It's also true that a shortage of parts and skills is raising the cost of new plants. But if we start building more plants, the number of companies supplying parts will increase to meet the demand, lowering the price.

Most important, nuclear power appears economically uncompetitive primarily because the price of "cheaper" fossil fuels, mainly coal, don't reflect the high cost that carbon emissions pose for the environment. Add those costs, and suddenly, nuclear power will look like a bargain.

That's likely to happen soon. Governments are expected to assign a cost to greenhouse gases, through either a direct tax (based on the carbon content of a fuel) or a so-called cap-and-trade system, which would set a limit on emissions while allowing companies whose discharges are lower than the cap to sell or trade credits to companies whose pollution exceeds the cap.

20   Suddenly, big carbon polluters like coal-produced electricity are going to look a lot more expensive compared with low-carbon sources—in particular, nuclear, wind and hydropower.

It's estimated that a carbon "price" of between $25 and $50 a ton makes nuclear power economically competitive with coal. That should be enough to ease investor concerns about utilities that build new nuclear plants.

Even without a carbon tax, rising natural-gas prices are beginning to make nuclear power more competitive. That's true even in some deregulated markets, such as Texas.

NRG Energy Inc., based in Princeton, New Jersey has filed an application to build a reactor adjacent to an existing plant in Texas. Though it's too early to know how much the plant will eventually cost—or even if it ultimately will get built—high natural-gas prices alone are enough to justify construction, according to NRG.

One other point on cost: Solar and wind advocates say these sources are cheaper than nuclear—and getting cheaper. But again, even if true, the intermittent nature of these sources make them flawed replacements for carbon-emitting sources. Nuclear is the only clean-energy way to address that gap.

25 *No 'China Syndrome'*   Let's turn to the critics' other argument: safety. We're still living in a world whose viewpoints have been warped by the 1979 accident at the Three Mile Island plant in Pennsylvania and the 1986 explosion at the Chernobyl plant in the Ukraine, as well as by the anti-nuclear movie *The China Syndrome.*

The truth is that there's little doubt that in the U.S., at least, plants are much safer now than they were in the past. Those accidents led regulators and the industry to bolster safety at U.S. nuclear plants. There are more safety features at the plants, plant personnel are better trained and reactors have been redesigned so that accidents are far less likely to occur. For instance, every U.S. plant has an on-site control-room simulator where employees can hone their skills and handle simulated emergencies, and plant workers spend one week out of every six in the simulator or in the classroom.

The next generation of plants is designed to be even safer, using fewer pumps and piping and relying more on gravity to move water for cooling the hot nuclear core. This means fewer possible places where equipment failure could cause a serious accident.

And even if a serious accident does occur, U.S. plants are designed to make sure that no radiation is released into the environment. Reactors are contained inside a huge structure of reinforced concrete with walls that are as much as four feet thick; the Chernobyl reactor lacked such a structure.

What's more, you can't look at safety in a vacuum. Consider the hazards of the world's reliance on coal-fired plants: Coal mining world-wide results in several thousand deaths every year, most of them in China, and burning coal is a leading source of mercury in the atmosphere.

Furthermore, look at safety more broadly—from an environmental perspective. The death and destruction stemming from global warming far exceed what is likely to happen if there is a nuclear accident. And yet, when we talk about safety, we seem to focus only on the risks of nuclear power.

Politics of Disposal   The long-term disposal of nuclear waste is also a problem—but it's mainly a policy issue, not a technical one.

Most experts agree that the best way to dispose of waste is deep underground, where radioactive materials can be prevented from entering the environment and where it can be guarded against theft or terrorist attack. In the U.S., the Energy Department picked Yucca Mountain in southwestern Nevada for a repository, but political wrangling has so far blocked proceeding with the site, and final approval is considered a long shot. Even if approved, it won't be able to begin accepting waste for a decade or more.

In the meantime, interim storage in deep pools next to nuclear plants is considered sufficiently safe to meet the industry's needs until well into the future. The amount of waste produced is relatively small; all the waste produced so far in the U.S. would only cover a football field about five yards deep. Older, cooler fuel can also be stored for decades in dry casks.

Longer term, advanced fuel recycling and reprocessing can reduce the amount of waste that needs to be stored. While reprocessing wouldn't eliminate the need for a long-term repository, it can reduce the amount, heat and radioactivity of the remaining waste.

Stopping the Spread   Finally, critics say that an expansion of nuclear power will increase the danger that potentially hostile nations will use nuclear material from a power program to develop atomic weapons, or that rogue states or terrorists will steal nuclear material to make bombs.

While nonproliferation is an important consideration, the proliferation problem won't be solved by turning away from nuclear power.

To curtail these risks, governments need to strengthen current international anti-proliferation efforts to, among other things, give the International Atomic Energy Agency more information about a country's nuclear-related activities and IAEA inspectors greater access to suspect locations. Further, current fuel-reprocessing techniques are limited and new processing technologies are being developed to limit the amount and accessibility of weapons-grade materials (by, for instance, producing a form of plutonium that needs further reprocessing before it could be used in bombs).

One final point about security: One of the biggest dangers to our security is from oil nations providing support to anti-U.S. terrorist groups. The faster we can move away from carbon-based energy, the faster we take away that funding source. Nuclear energy offers the fastest and most direct path to that safer future.

No to Nuclear

Nuclear power isn't a solution to global warming. Rather, global warming is just a convenient rationale for an obsolete energy source that makes no sense when compared to the alternatives.

40   Sure, nuclear power generates lots of electricity while producing virtually no carbon dioxide. But it still faces the same problems that have stymied the development of new nuclear plants for the past 20 years—exorbitant costs, the risks of an accident or terrorist attack, the threat of proliferation and the challenge of disposing of nuclear waste.

The cost issue alone will mean that few if any new nuclear power stations will get built in the next few years, at least in the U.S., and any that do will require expensive taxpayer subsidies. Instead of subsidizing the development of new plants that have all these other problems, the U.S. would be better off investing in other ways to meet growing energy demands and reduce carbon-dioxide emissions.

In fact, the sheer number of nuclear plants needed to make a major dent in greenhouse emissions means the industry hasn't a prayer of turning nuclear power into the solution to global warming. One study from last year determined that to make a significant contribution toward stabilizing atmospheric carbon dioxide, about 21 new 1,000-megawatt plants would have to be built each year for the next 50 years, including those needed to replace existing reactors, all of which are expected to be retired by 2050. That's considerably more than the most ambitions industry growth projections.

Too Expensive   But let's start with the biggest problem with nuclear power: the cost.

While no one knows what a new reactor will cost until one gets built, estimates for new construction continue to rise. Building a new plant could cost as much as $6,000 a kilowatt of generating capacity, up from estimates of about $4,000 a kilowatt just a year ago. FPL Group, of Juno Beach, Florida, estimates that two new reactors planned for southeast Florida would cost between $6 billion and $9 billion each.

45   Part of the reason for the rising cost estimates is the small number of vendors able to supply critical reactor components, as well as shortage of engineering and construction skills in the nuclear industry. Perhaps the biggest bottleneck is in the huge reactor vessels that contain a plant's radioactive core. Only one plant in the world is capable of forging the huge vessels in a single piece, and it can produce only a handful of the forgings a year. Though the plant intends to expand capacity in the next couple of years, and China has said it plans to begin making the forgings, this key component is expected to limit development for many years.

The only way to make nuclear power economically competitive would be the imposition of steep "prices" on carbon-emitting power sources. Nobody knows precisely how high those prices would have to go—there are too many variables to consider. But estimates range as high as $60 a ton of carbon dioxide. This imposes an unacceptably high price on consumers.

More important, though, there are less-costly ways of weaning ourselves off these carbon-emitting energy sources. Even if a high price of carbon makes nuclear economical, the costs of renewable energy such as wind and solar power are cheaper, and getting cheaper all the time. By contrast, nuclear is more expensive, and getting more expensive all the time.

Solving a Problem   And yes, it's true that wind and solar suffer from the problem of not being available 24 hours a day. But new technology is already beginning to solve that problem. And we'd be better off—from both an economic and safety standpoint—if we used natural gas to fill in the gaps, rather than nuclear.

Subsidies to the industry distort the financial picture further. In the U.S., Washington assumes liability for any catastrophic damages above $10.5 billion for an accident, and has taken on responsibility for the disposal of nuclear waste. The 2005 federal Energy Policy Act also provides loan guarantees for as much as 80% of the cost of new reactors and additional financial guarantees of up to $2 billion for costs arising from regulatory delays.

The 2005 act saw subsidies as a way to prime the pump of a nuclear-energy revival in the U.S.; increased demand and a stable regulatory environment would ultimately reduce the cost of building new plants. However, the industry for 50 years has shown only a trend toward higher costs, and there's no evidence that subsidies will spur any reduction in those costs.

And besides, if nuclear power is such a great deal, it should be able to stand on its own, and not require such subsidies from the taxpayer. Government subsidies should sponsor research and development into new or emerging energy technologies where prices are already falling and the subsidies can jump-start demand to help further bring down costs. They're inappropriate for mature industries, like nuclear power, where market forces should be allowed to do their work.

The Safety Issue   Cost isn't the only reason an expansion of nuclear power is a bad idea.

The safety of nuclear plants has certainly improved, thanks to changes adopted in the wake of the Three Mile Island accident. But safety problems persist, because the U.S. Nuclear Regulatory Commission isn't adequately enforcing existing safety standards. What's more, countries where nuclear power is likely to expand don't have a strong system for regulating nuclear safety.

The important thing to remember about safety is this: The entire nuclear power industry is vulnerable to the safety standards of its worst performers, because an accident anywhere in the world would stoke another antinuclear backlash among the public and investors.

55   There's also the question of waste disposal. Proponents of nuclear power say disposal of the industry's waste products is a political problem. That's true. But it doesn't make the problem any less real. California, for instance, won't allow construction of more plants until the waste issue is resolved.

Opposition to a long-term waste repository at Yucca Mountain shows how difficult it will be to come up with a politically acceptable solution. Yucca Mountain has been plagued by questions about the selection process and its suitability as a repository, and even if it is ultimately approved, it won't be available for at least another decade—and it will be filled to capacity almost immediately. If it isn't approved, any replacement site will face the same opposition from neighbors and local political leaders.

Proliferation Threat   By far the greatest risk is the possibility that an expansion of nuclear power will contribute to the proliferation of nuclear weapons. Plants that enrich uranium for power plants can also be used to enrich for bombs; this is the path Iran is suspected of taking in developing a weapons program. An ambitious expansion of nuclear power would require a lot more facilities for enriching uranium, broadening this risk. Facilities for reprocessing spent nuclear fuel for reuse pose the danger that the material can be diverted for weapons.

Expansion of nuclear power in the U.S. doesn't pose a great proliferation risk, but a nuclear renaissance will put a strain on the current anti-proliferation system. Most of the growth world-wide is expected to be in countries—such as those in the Middle East and Africa—where a nuclear-energy program could give cover to surreptitious weapons development and create the local expertise in handling and processing nuclear materials.

The dangers of nuclear proliferation would be heightened if a nuclear revival turned to reprocessing of spent fuel to reduce the amount of high-level waste that builds up and to maintain adequate fuel supplies. Reprocessing is a problem because it can produce separated plutonium—which is easier to steal or divert for weapons production, as North Korea has done, than plutonium contained in highly radioactive fuel. And commercial reprocessing plants produce so much plutonium that keeping track of it all is difficult, making it easier to divert enough for weapons without the loss being detected.

60   If nuclear power really were able to make a big dent in greenhouse emissions, then it would be worth the time and resources necessary to address all these problems. Instead, though, the magnitude of these difficulties will keep any nuclear renaissance too small to make a difference, and will require expensive government support just to achieve modest gains. Those resources are better spent elsewhere.

Review Questions

1. Why is nuclear power seen as a viable way of dealing with the global warming problem?

2. Summarize the chief arguments against nuclear power.

3. Why are current nuclear power plant designs safer than older designs?

4. In outline form, summarize the pro-con arguments regarding (1) costs of nuclear power plants; (2) safety of nuclear power plants; and (3) nuclear proliferation.

Discussion and Writing Suggestions

1. Totty argues (rather than summarizes) both the pros and cons of nuclear power. To what extent, if any, can you detect his own position on the subject as he attempts to present the arguments made by each side?

2. Which arguments for or against nuclear power presented by Totty are the most persuasive to you? The least persuasive? Since the same author presents both sides of the case, how is one to determine whether the pro or the con argument is the stronger one?

3. Which of the concerns about nuclear power do you most share? To what extent do Totty's arguments rebutting these concerns in the first section of his article allay your concerns? Explain.

4. Many solutions to social or technological problems, while appealing in theory, fall victim to the NIMBY (not in my back yard) syndrome. People who vigorously support building more prisons often don't want a prison built in or near their own home town, citing safety concerns. The same appears to apply to nuclear power plants. If you were convinced that building more nuclear power plants would significantly decrease carbon emissions caused by power generation, would you be willing to see one constructed several miles away from where you live? Explain, offering alternatives if your answer is in the negative.

5. In "205 Easy Ways to Save the Earth," Thomas Friedman notes that, if we were to try to derive all the renewable energy we need between now and the year 2050 from nuclear power, "we would have to build 13,000 new nuclear reactors or roughly one new reactor every day for the next thirty-six years—starting today." Given the obstacles noted by Totty to building even one nuclear power plant, is it unrealistic to expect that nuclear power can play a significant role in reducing carbon emissions over the next few decades? Assuming that what Friedman says is true, do such considerations doom nuclear power as a viable power source?

THE ISLAND IN THE WIND

Elizabeth Kolbert

In the following selection, excerpted from a longer article in the New Yorker, Elizabeth Kolbert describes in vivid imagery "an unlikely social movement": how the people of the Danish island of Samsø got all their homes and farms to run on electricity generated entirely by wind power. Their experience is a testament to determination and "people power"—though whether that experience can be duplicated in other areas is an open question.

Kolbert is a journalist who specializes in environmental issues. She wrote for the *New York Times* from 1984 to 1999 and has been a staff reporter for the *New Yorker* since 1999. She is the author of *Field Notes from a Catastrophe: Man and Nature and Climate Change* (2006).

Jørgen Tranberg is a farmer who lives on the Danish island of Samsø. He is a beefy man with a mop of brown hair and an unpredictable sense of humor. When I arrived at his house, one gray morning this spring, he was sitting in his kitchen, smoking a cigarette and watching grainy images on a black-and-white TV. The images turned out to be closed-circuit shots from his barn. One of his cows, he told me, was about to give birth, and he was keeping an eye on her. We talked for a few minutes, and then, laughing, he asked me if I wanted to climb his wind turbine. I was pretty sure I didn't, but I said yes anyway.

We got into Tranberg's car and bounced along a rutted dirt road. The turbine loomed up in front of us. When we reached it, Tranberg stubbed out his cigarette and opened a small door in the base of the tower. Inside were eight ladders, each about twenty feet tall, attached one above the other. We started up, and were soon huffing. Above the last ladder, there was a trapdoor, which led to a sort of engine room. We scrambled into it, at which point we were standing on top of the generator. Tranberg pressed a button, and the roof slid open to reveal the gray sky and a patchwork of green and brown fields stretching toward the sea. He pressed another button. The rotors, which he had switched off during our climb, started to turn, at first sluggishly and then much more rapidly. It felt as if we were about to take off. I'd like to say the feeling was exhilarating; in fact, I found it sickening. Tranberg looked at me and started to laugh.

Samsø, which is roughly the size of Nantucket, sits in what's known as the Kattegat, an arm of the North Sea. The island is bulgy in the south and narrows to a bladelike point in the north, so that on a map it looks a bit like a woman's torso and a bit like a meat cleaver. It has twenty-two villages that hug the narrow streets; out back are fields where farmers grow potatoes and wheat and strawberries. Thanks to Denmark's peculiar geography, Samsø is smack in the center of the country and, at the same time, in the middle of nowhere.

For the past decade or so, Samsø has been the site of an unlikely social movement. When it began, in the late nineteen-nineties, the island's forty-three hundred inhabitants had what might be described as a conventional attitude toward energy: as long as it continued to arrive, they weren't much interested in it. Most Samsingers heated their houses with oil, which was brought in on

Catching the wind

Alternative energy sources are getting a new look as demand for fossil fuels increases worldwide, and as technical innovations help reduce the costs of alternatives. California produces more wind-generated electricity than any state except Texas and Iowa. A look at wind farms:

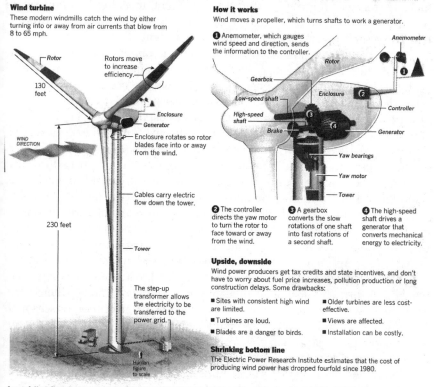

Wind turbine

These modern windmills catch the wind by either turning into or away from air currents that blow from 8 to 65 mph.

Rotor

Rotors move to increase efficiency.

130 feet

WIND DIRECTION

230 feet

Enclosure
Generator

Enclosure rotates so rotor blades face into or away from the wind.

Cables carry electric flow down the tower.

Tower

The step-up transformer allows the electricity to be transferred to the power grid.

Human figure to scale

How it works

Wind moves a propeller, which turns shafts to work a generator.

❶ Anemometer, which gauges wind speed and direction, sends the information to the controller.

Anemometer

Rotor

Gearbox

Low-speed shaft

Enclosure ❷

High-speed shaft

Brake ❸ ❹

Controller

Generator

Yaw bearings

Yaw motor

Tower

❷ The controller directs the yaw motor to turn the rotor to face toward or away from the wind.

❸ A gearbox converts the slow rotations of one shaft into fast rotations of a second shaft.

❹ The high-speed shaft drives a generator that converts mechanical energy to electricity.

Upside, downside

Wind power producers get tax credits and state incentives, and don't have to worry about fuel price increases, pollution production or long construction delays. Some drawbacks:

- Sites with consistent high wind are limited.
- Turbines are loud.
- Blades are a danger to birds.
- Older turbines are less cost-effective.
- Views are affected.
- Installation can be costly.

Shrinking bottom line

The Electric Power Research Institute estimates that the cost of producing wind power has dropped fourfold since 1980.

Sources: California Energy Commission, National Wind Technology Center, U.S. Department of Energy's Energy Information Administration, National Renewable Energy Laboratory

DOUG STEVENS Los Angeles Times

tankers. They used electricity imported from the mainland via cable, much of which was generated by burning coal. As a result, each Samsinger put into the atmosphere, on average, nearly eleven tons of carbon dioxide annually.

Then, quite deliberately, the residents of the island set about changing this. They formed energy coöperatives and organized seminars on wind power. They removed their furnaces and replaced them with heat pumps. By 2001, fossil-fuel use on Samsø had been cut in half. By 2003, instead of importing electricity, the island was exporting it, and by 2005 it was producing from renewable sources more energy than it was using.

The residents of Samsø that I spoke to were clearly proud of their accomplishment. All the same, they insisted on their ordinariness. They were, they noted, not wealthy, nor were they especially well educated or idealistic. They weren't even terribly adventuresome. "We are a conservative farming community" is how one Samsinger put it. "We are only normal people," Tranberg told me. "We are not some special people."

This year, the world is expected to burn through some thirty-one billion barrels of oil, six billion tons of coal, and a hundred trillion cubic feet of natural gas. The combustion of these fossil fuels will produce, in aggregate, some four hundred quadrillion B.T.U.s of energy. It will also yield around thirty billion tons of carbon dioxide. Next year, global consumption of fossil fuels is expected to grow by about two per cent, meaning that emissions will rise by more than half a billion tons, and the following year consumption is expected to grow by yet another two per cent.

When carbon dioxide is released into the air, about a third ends up, in relatively short order, in the oceans. (CO_2 dissolves in water to form a weak acid; this is the cause of the phenomenon known as "ocean acidification.") A quarter is absorbed by terrestrial ecosystems—no one is quite sure exactly how or where—and the rest remains in the atmosphere. If current trends in emissions continue, then sometime within the next four of five decades the chemistry of the oceans will have been altered to such a degree that many marine organisms—including reef-building corals—will be pushed toward extinction. Meanwhile, atmospheric CO_2 levels are projected to reach five hundred and fifty parts per million—twice pre-industrial levels—virtually guaranteeing an eventual global temperature increase of three or more degrees. The consequences of this warming are difficult to predict in detail, but even broad, conservative estimates are terrifying: at least fifteen and possibly as many as thirty per cent of the planet's plant and animal species will be threatened; sea levels will rise by several feet; yields of crops like wheat and corn will decline significantly in a number of areas where they are now grown as staples; regions that depend on glacial runoff or seasonal snowmelt—currently home to more than a billion people—will face severe water shortages; and what now counts as a hundred-year drought will occur in some parts of the world as frequently as once a decade.

Today, with CO_2 levels at three hundred and eighty-five parts per million, the disruptive impacts of climate change are already apparent. The Arctic ice cap, which has shrunk by half since the nineteen-fifties, is melting at an annual rate of twenty-four thousand square miles, meaning that an expanse of ice the size of West Virginia is disappearing each year. Over the past ten years, forests covering a hundred and fifty million acres in the United States and Canada have died from warming-related beetle infestations. It is believed that rising temperatures are contributing to the growing number of international refugees—"Climate change is today one of the main drivers of forced displacement," the United Nations' high commissioner for refugees, António Guterres, said recently—and to armed conflict: some experts see a link between the fighting in Darfur, which has claimed as many as three hundred thousand lives, and changes in rainfall patterns in equatorial Africa.

10   "If we keep going down this path, the Darfur crisis will be only one crisis among dozens of other," President Nicolas Sarkozy, of France, told a meeting of world leaders in April. The Secretary-General of the United Nations, Ban Ki-moon, has called climate change "the defining challenge of our age."

In the context of this challenge, Samsø's accomplishments could be seen as trivial. Certainly, in numerical terms they don't amount to much: all the island's avoided emissions of the past ten years are overwhelmed by the CO_2 that a single coal-fired power plant will emit in the next three weeks, and China is building new coal-fired plants at the rate of roughly four a month. But it is also in this context that the island's efforts are most significant. Samsø transformed its energy systems in a single decade. Its experience suggests how the carbon problem, as huge as it is, could be dealt with, if we were willing to try.

Samsø set out to reinvent itself thanks to a series of decisions that it had relatively little to do with. The first was made by the Danish Ministry of Environment and Energy in 1997. The ministry, looking for ways to promote innovation, decided to sponsor a renewable-energy contest. In order to enter, a community had to submit a plan showing how it could wean itself off fossil fuels. An engineer who didn't actually live on Samsø thought the island would make a good candidate. In consultation with Samsø's mayor, he drew up a plan and submitted it. When it was announced that Samsø had won, the general reaction among residents was puzzlement. "I had to listen twice before I believed it," one farmer told me.

The brief surge of interest that followed the announcement soon dissipated. Besides its designation as Denmark's "renewable-energy island," Samsø received basically nothing—no prize money or special tax breaks, or even government assistance. One of the few people on the island to think the project was worth pursuing was Søren Hermansen.

Hermansen, who is now forty-nine, is a trim man with close-cropped hair, ruddy cheeks, and dark-blue eyes. He was born on Samsø and, save for a few stints away, to travel and go to university, has lived there his entire life. His father was a farmer who grew, among other things, beets and parsley. Hermansen, too, tried his hand at farming—he took over the family's hundred acres when his father retired—but he discovered he wasn't suited to it. "I like to talk, and vegetables don't respond," he told me. He leased his fields to a neighbor and got a job teaching environmental studies at a local boarding school. Hermansen found the renewable-energy-island concept intriguing. When some federal money was found to fund a single staff position, he became the project's first employee.

For months, which stretched into years, not much happened. "There was this conservative hesitating, waiting for the neighbor to do the move," Hermansen recalled. "I know the community and I know this is what usually happens." Rather than working against the islanders' tendency to look to one another, Hermansen tried to work with it.

"One reason to live here can be social relations," he said. "This renewable-energy project could be a new kind of social relation, and we used that." Whenever there was a meeting to discuss a local issue—any local issue—Hermansen attended and made his pitch. He asked Samsingers to think about what it would be like to work together on something they could all be proud of. Occasionally, he brought free beer along to the discussions. Meanwhile, he began trying to enlist the support of the island's opinion leaders. "This is where the hard work starts, convincing the first movers to be active," he said. Eventually, much as Hermansen had hoped, the social dynamic that had stalled the project began to work in its favor. As more people got involved, that prompted others to do so. After a while, enough Samsingers were participating that participation became the norm.

"People on Samsø started thinking about energy," Ingvar Jørgensen, a farmer who heats his house with solar hot water and a straw-burning furnace, told me. "It became a kind of sport."

"It's exciting to be a part of this," Brian Kjæ, an electrician who installed a small-scale turbine in his back yard, said. Kjæ's turbine, which is seventy-two feet tall generates more current than his family of three can use, and also more than the power lines leading away from his house can handle, so he uses the excess to heat water, which he stores in a tank that he rigged up in his garage. He told me that one day he would like to use the leftover electricity to produce hydrogen, which could potentially run a fuel-cell car.

"Søren, he has talked again and again, and slowly it's spread to a lot of people," he said.

20   Since becoming the "renewable energy island," Samsø has increasingly found itself an object of study. Researchers often travel great distances to get there, a fact that is not without its own irony. The day after I arrived, from New York via Copenhagen, a group of professors from the University of Toyama, in Japan, came to look around. They had arranged a tour with Hermansen, and he invited me to tag along. We headed off to meet the group in his electric Citroën, which is painted blue with white puffy clouds on the doors. It was a drizzly day, and when we got to the dock the water was choppy. Hermansen commiserated with the Japanese, who had just disembarked from the swaying ferry; then we all boarded a bus.

Our first stop was a hillside with a panoramic view of the island. Several wind turbines exactly like the one I had climbed with Tranberg were whooshing nearby. In the wet and the gray, they were the only things stirring. Off in the distance, the silent fields gave way to the Kattegat, where another group of turbines could be seen, arranged in a soldierly line in the water.

All told, Samsø has eleven large land-based turbines. (It has about a dozen additional micro-turbines.) This is a lot of turbines for a relatively small number of people, and the ratio is critical to Samsø's success, as is the fact that the wind off the Kattegat blows pretty much continuously; flags on Samsø, I noticed, do not wave—they stick straight out, as in children's drawings. Hermansen told us that the land-based turbines are a hundred and fifty feet tall, with rotors that are eighty feet long. Together, they produce some twenty-six million kilowatt-hours a year, which is just about enough to meet all the island's demands for electricity. (This is true in an arithmetic sense; as a practical matter, Samsø's production of electricity and its needs fluctuate, so that sometimes it is feeding power into the grid and sometimes it is drawing power from it.) The offshore turbines, meanwhile, are even taller—a hundred and ninety-five feet high, with rotors that extend a hundred and twenty feet. A single offshore turbine generates roughly eight million kilowatt-hours of electricity a year, which, at Danish rates of energy use, is enough to satisfy the needs of some two thousand homes. The offshore turbines—there are ten of them—were erected to compensate for Samsø's continuing use of fossil fuels in its cars, trucks, and ferries. Their combined output, of around eighty million kilowatt-hours a year, provides the energy equivalent of all the gasoline and diesel oil consumed on the island, and then some; in aggregate, Samsø generates about ten per cent more power than it consumes.

"When we started, in 1997, nobody expected this to happen," Hermansen told the group. "When we talked to local people, they said, Yes, come on, maybe in your dreams." Each land-based turbine cost the equivalent of eight hundred and fifty thousand dollars. Each offshore turbine cost around three million dollars. Some of Samsø's turbines were erected by a single investor, like Tranberg; others were purchased collectively. At least four hundred and fifty island residents own shares in the onshore turbines, and a roughly equal number own shares in those offshore. Shareholders, who also include many nonresidents, receive annual dividend checks based on the prevailing price of electricity and how much their turbine has generated.

"If I'm reduced to being a customer, then if I like something I buy it, and if I don't like it I don't buy it," Hermansen said. "But I don't care about the production. We care about the production, because we own the wind turbines. Every time they turn around, it means money in the bank. And, being part of it, we also feel responsible." Thanks to a policy put in place by Denmark's government in the late nineteen-nineties, utilities are required to offer ten-year fixed-rate contracts for wind power that they can sell to customers elsewhere. Under the terms of these contracts, a turbine should—barring mishap—repay a shareholder's initial investment in about eight years.

From the hillside, we headed to the town of Ballen. There we stopped at a red shed-shaped building made out of corrugated metal. Inside, enormous bales of straw were stacked against the walls. Hermansen explained that the building was a district heating plant that had been designed to run on biomass. The bales, each representing the equivalent of fifty gallons of oil, would be fed into a furnace, where water would be heated to a hundred and fifty-eight degrees. This hot water would then be piped underground to two hundred and sixty houses in Ballen and in the neighboring town of Brundby. In this way, the energy of the straw burned at the plant would be transferred to the homes, where it could be used to provide heat and hot water.

Samsø has two other district heating plants that burn straw—one in Tranebjerg, the other in Onsbjerg—and also a district plant, in Nordby, that burns wood chips. When we visited the Nordby plant, later that afternoon, it was filled with what looked like mulch. (The place smelled like a potting shed.) Out back was a field covered in rows of solar panels, which provide additional hot water when the sun is shining. Between the rows, sheep with long black faces were munching on the grass. The Japanese researchers pulled out their cameras as the sheep snuffled toward them, expectantly.

Of course, burning straw or wood, like burning fossil fuels, produces CO_2. The key distinction is that while fossil fuels release carbon that otherwise would have remained sequestered, biomass releases carbon that would have entered the atmosphere anyway, through decomposition. As long as biomass regrows, the CO_2 released in its combustion should be reabsorbed, meaning that the cycle is—or at least can be—carbon neutral. The wood chips used in the Nordby plant come from fallen trees that previously would have been left to rot. The straw for the Ballen-Brundby plant comes mainly from wheat stalks that would previously have been burned in the fields. Together, the biomass heating plants prevent the release of some twenty-seven hundred tons of carbon dioxide a year.

In addition to biomass, Samsø is experimenting on a modest scale with biofuels: a handful of farmers have converted their cars and tractors to run on canola oil. We stopped to visit one such farmer, who grows his own seeds, presses his own oil, and feeds the leftover mash to his cows. The farmer couldn't be located, so Hermansen started up the press himself. He stuck a finger under the spout, then popped it into his mouth. "The oil is very good," he announced. "You can use it in your car, and you can use it on your salad."

After the tour, I went back with Hermansen to his office, in a building known as the Energiakademi. The academy, which looks like a Bauhaus interpretation of a barn, is covered with photovoltaic cells and insulated with shredded newspapers. It is supposed to serve as a sort of interpretive center, though when I visited, the place was so new that the rooms were mostly empty. Some high-school students were kneeling on the floor, trying to put together a miniature turbine.

30   I asked Hermansen whether there were any projects that hadn't worked out. He listed several, including a plan to use natural gas produced from cow manure and an experiment with electric cars that failed when one of the demonstration vehicles spent most of the year in the shop. The biggest disappointment, though, had to do with consumption.

"We made several programs for energy savings," he told me. "But people are acting—what do you call it?—irresponsibly. They behave like monkeys." For example, families that insulated their homes better also tended to heat more rooms, "so we ended up with zero." Essentially, he said, energy use on the island has remained constant for the past decade.

I asked why he thought the renewable-energy-island effort had got as far as it did. He said he wasn't sure, because different people had had different motives for participating. "From the very egoistic to the more over-all perspective, I think we had all kinds of reasons."

Finally, I asked what he thought other communities might take from Samsø's experience.

"We always hear that we should think globally and act locally," he said. "I understand what that means—I think we as a nation should be part of the global consciousness. But each individual cannot be part of that. So 'Think locally, act locally' is the key message for us."

35   "There's this wish for showcases," he added. "When we are selected to be the showcase for Denmark, I feel ashamed that Denmark doesn't produce anything bigger than that. But I feel proud because we are the showcase. So I did my job, and my colleagues did their job, and so did the people of Samsø."

●   Review Questions

1. Locate the one or two sentences in Kolbert's article that make the connection between Samsø's experience with wind power and the reduction of global CO_2 emissions.

2. How did Samsø's geographical circumstances play a role in the success of its conversion to renewable energy?

3. Why is the process of burning biomass substances, such as bales of straw or wood chips, more carbon-neutral than burning coal, according to Kolbert?

●   Discussion and Writing Suggestions

1. Why do you think Kolbert begins this article as she does, with a verbal picture of Jørgen Tranberg, rather than with, say, the data on CO_2 emissions in paragraph 7 or the consequences of heightened levels of CO_2 in the atmosphere in paragraphs 8 and 9?

2. Kolbert describes a "social dynamic" through which one committed citizen convinced a number of his fellow citizens to participate in a community project, and they in turn convinced others, some with particular skills, until the committed few became a community-wide movement dedicated to productive change. Have you witnessed or been a part of such a movement in your own or another community? Describe what happened and the conclusions you draw from this experience. What obstacles did you face? How were they overcome? Which factors or events were most helpful? Most surprising? Most frustrating? Most rewarding? What advice do you have for others considering such community projects?

3. To what extent do you think the experience of Samsø concerning renewable energy sources such as wind is repeatable elsewhere, particularly in the United States? In what ways might the different geographical, cultural, and political circumstances in the United States make it difficult to repeat Samsø's experience here? In what respects might the circumstances be similar?

4. What conclusions, if any, can you draw from the Samsø experience with wind power about the role of government in encouraging the use of renewable energy? About the role of entrepreneurship? The role of individual initiative? The role of civic duty?

WIND POWER PUFFERY

H. Sterling Burnett

In this op-ed, H. Sterling Burnett discusses the limitations and drawbacks of wind power. Burnett is a senior fellow with the National Center for Policy Analysis. In 2000 he served as a member of the Environment and Natural Resources Task Force in the Texas Comptroller's e-Texas commission. His articles and opinion pieces have been published in *Environmental Ethics, International Studies in Philosophy,* and daily newspapers nation-wide. This piece appeared in the *Washington Times* on February 4, 2004.

Whenever there is a discussion of energy policy, many environmentalists and their political allies tout wind power as an alternative to burning fossil fuels. Even if electricity from wind power is more expensive than conventional fuel sources, and it is, wind advocates argue its environmental benefits are worth it. In particular, proponents claim increased reliance on wind power would reduce air pollution and greenhouse gas emissions.

But is this assertion correct? No, the truth is wind power's environmental benefits are usually overstated, while its significant environmental harms are often ignored.

Close inspection of wind power finds the promised air pollution improvements do not materialize. There are several reasons, the principal one being that wind farms generate power only when the wind blows within a certain range of speed. When there is too little wind, wind towers don't generate power. Conversely, when the wind is too strong, they must be shut off for fear of being blown down.

Due to this fundamental limitation, wind farms need conventional power plants to supplement the power they supply and to replace a wind farm's expected supply to the grid when the towers are not turning. After all, the power grid requires a regulated constant flow of energy to function properly.

5   Yet bringing a conventional power plant on line to supply power is not as simple as turning on a switch. Most "redundant" fossil fuel power stations must run, even if at reduced levels, continuously. When these factors are combined with the emissions of pollutants and CO_2 caused by the manufacture and maintenance of wind towers and their associated infrastructure, very little of the air quality improvements actually result from expansion of wind power.

There are other problems. A recent report from Great Britain—where wind power is growing even faster than in the U.S.—says that as wind farms grow, wind power is increasingly unpopular. Why? Wind farms are noisy, land-intensive and unsightly. The industry has tricked its way into unspoiled countryside in "green" disguise by portraying wind farms as "parks." In reality, wind farms are more similar to highways, industrial buildings, railways and industrial farms. This wouldn't be a major consideration if it weren't that, because of the prevailing wind currents, the most favorable locations for wind farms usually are areas with particularly spectacular views in relatively wild places.

Worse, wind farms produce only a fraction of the energy of a conventional power plant but require hundreds of times the acreage. For instance, two of the biggest wind "farms" in Europe have 159 turbines and cover thousands of acres between them. But together they take a year to produce less than four days' output from a single 2,000-megawatt conventional power station—which takes up 100 times fewer acres. And in the U.S., a proposed wind farm off the coast of Massachusetts would produce only 450 megawatts of power but require 130 towers and more than 24 square miles of ocean.

Perhaps the most well-publicized harmful environmental impact of wind power relates to its effect on birds and bats. For efficiency, wind farms must be located where the wind blows fairly constantly. Unfortunately, such locations are prime travel routes for migratory birds, including protected species like Bald and Golden Eagles. This motivated the Sierra Club to label wind towers "the Cuisinarts of the air."

Indeed, scientists estimate as many as 44,000 birds have been killed over the past 20 years by wind turbines in the Altamont Pass, east of San Francisco. The victims include kestrels, red-tailed hawks and golden eagles—an average of 50 golden eagles are killed each year.

These problems are exacerbated explains one study as "Wind farms have been documented to act as both bait and executioner—rodents taking shelter at the base of turbines multiply with the protection from raptors, while in turn their greater numbers attract more raptors to the farm."

Deaths are not limited to the United States or to birds. For example, at Tarif, Spain, thousands of birds from more than 13 species protected under European Union law have been killed by the site's 269 wind turbines. During last fall's migration, at least 400 bats, including red bats, eastern pipistrelles, hoary bats and possible endangered Indiana bats, were killed at a 44-turbine wind farm in West Virginia.

As a result of these problems and others, lawsuits are either pending or being considered to prevent expansion of wind farms in West Virginia and California and to prevent the construction of offshore wind farms in a number of New England states.

Indeed, the Audubon society has called for a moratorium on new wind development in bird-sensitive areas—which, because of the climatic conditions needed for wind farms, includes the vast majority of the suitable sites for proposed construction.

Wind power is expensive, doesn't deliver the environmental benefits it promises and has substantial environmental costs. In short, wind power is no bargain. Accordingly, it doesn't merit continued government promotion or funding.

Discussion and Writing Suggestions

1. To what extent do you view the problems with wind power cited by Burnett as serious enough to rule out this energy source as viable? To what extent do you think we should proceed with large-scale construction of wind farms, considering the realities of (1) intermittent power that must be periodically supplemented by conventional power plants; (2) the poor ratio of power generated to acreage of land consumed by wind turbines; and (3) the danger to birds?

2. Conduct a brief Google (or other database) search, and then respond to some of Burnett's concerns about wind power with the information you

find. To what extent are Burnett's objections well founded? To what extent might it be possible to deal effectively with the problems he discusses?

3. The danger to birds posed by spinning wind turbines is analogous to the danger to whales posed by sonar tests conducted by Navy submarines. In one case, the benefit is renewable energy; in the other case, the benefit is (according to the military and civilian Department of Defense officials) enhanced national security. How should we weigh such conflicting interests and decide between them?

4. Critique Burnett's argument. Use as guidelines the principles discussed in Chapter 2. Consider first the main questions: (1) To what extent does Burnett succeed in his purpose? (2) To what extent do you agree with him? Then move to the specifics: for example, to what extent do you agree with his contention that wind turbines pose too great a risk to birds? Before writing your critique, you may want to reread what Elizabeth Kolbert and other authors in this chapter have written about wind power.

STATE SOLAR PLANS ARE AS BIG AS ALL OUTDOORS

Marla Dickerson

In the following selection, Marla Dickerson reports on the expansion of solar power construction in California in compliance with that state's mandate to generate 20 percent of its electricity from renewable power sources by 2010. In a more recent article ("Solar Farm Cuts Gap with Fossil Fuel"), Dickerson reported that Sempra Energy, a San Diego–based power company that recently installed a 10-megawatt solar farm in Nevada, has employed a new form of panel technology that has enabled it to achieve the critical goal of "grid parity"—that is, to produce renewable energy at a cost equal to or lower than the cost of a comparable amount of power generated from carbon-based fuels such as coal or natural gas. The key to this "Wal-Mart of solar panels" is an array of solar cells made from a cadmium telluride semiconductor that is less expensive to make than its silicon-based equivalent.

Dickerson is an economics and business writer for the *Los Angeles Times*, where this article appeared on December 3, 2008. Previously, Dickerson wrote for the *Detroit News* and the *Rochester Times-Union*.

Just up the road, past pump jacks bobbing in California's storied oil patch, look sharp and you'll catch a glimpse of the state's energy future.

Rows of gigantic mirrors covering an area bigger than two football fields have sprouted alongside almond groves near California 99. This is a power plant that uses the sun's heat to produce electricity for thousands of homes.

Owned by Palo Alto-based Ausra Inc., it's the first so-called solar thermal facility to open in California in nearly two decades. It's part of a drive to build clean electricity generation using the sun, wind and other renewable sources with an urgency not seen since the days of environmentalist Gov. Jerry Brown. Add President-elect Barack Obama's stated intention to push for more renewable power, and you've got the equivalent of a green land rush.

At least 80 large solar projects are on the drawing board in California, more than in any other place in the country. The scale of some is unrivaled on the planet. One facility planned for the Mojave Desert is projected to take up a land mass the size of Inglewood.*

"The expectation is that renewables will transform California's electricity system," said Terry O'Brien, who helps vet sites for new facilities for the California Energy Commission.

It's a daunting challenge for the world's eighth-largest economy. Despite the nation's toughest mandates for boosting green energy and reducing greenhouse gases, California remains addicted to burning fossil fuels to keep the lights on.

Excluding large hydroelectric operations, less than 12% of the state's electricity came from renewable sources in 2007, according to the commission. Solar ranked last, supplying just 0.2% of California's needs. Rooftop photovoltaic panels are unaffordable or impractical for most Californians even with generous state incentives.

Enter Big Solar.

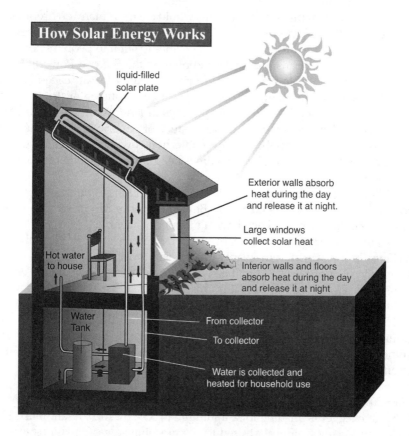

How Solar Energy Works

liquid-filled solar plate

Exterior walls absorb heat during the day and release it at night.

Large windows collect solar heat

Interior walls and floors absorb heat during the day and release it at night

Hot water to house

Water Tank

From collector

To collector

Water is collected and heated for household use

---

*Inglewood: a city in southwestern Los Angeles County; area: 9.1 square miles.

Proponents say utility-scale solar is a way to get lots of clean megawatts online quickly, efficiently and at lower costs. Solar thermal plants such as Ausra's are essentially giant boilers made of glass and steel. They use the sun's heat to create steam to power turbines that generate electricity.

10   Costing about 18 cents a kilowatt-hour at present, solar thermal power is roughly 40% cheaper than that generated by the silicon-based panels that sit on the roofs of homes and businesses, according to a June report by Clean Edge Inc. and the Co-op American Foundation. Analysts say improved technology and economies of scale should help lower the cost of solar thermal to about 5 cents a kilowatt-hour by 2025. That would put it on par with coal, the cheap but carbon-spewing fuel that generates about half the nation's electricity.

Size matters, said Sun Microsystems Inc. co-founder-turned-venture-capitalist Vinod Khosla, whose Khosla Ventures has invested more than $30 million in Ausra. A square patch of desert about 92 miles long on each side blanketed with Ausra's technology could generate enough electricity to meet the entire nation's demand, company executives say. "Utility-scale solar is probably the only way to achieve real scale...and reduce our carbon emissions" significantly, Khosla said.

Critics fear that massive solar farms would create as many environmental problems as they purport to solve. This new-age electricity still requires old-fashioned power towers and high-voltage lines to get it to people's homes. A proposed 150-mile transmission line known as the Sunrise Powerlink that would carry renewable power from Imperial County to San Diego has run into stiff resistance from grass-roots groups and environmentalists.

Solar plants require staggering amounts of land, which could threaten fragile ecosystems and mar the stark beauty of America's deserts. And in contrast to rooftop panels, which enable homeowners to pursue energy independence, these centralized facilities keep consumers tethered to utility companies.

"They are trying to perpetuate the old Big Energy paradigm into the renewable-energy era," said Sheila Bowers, a Santa Monica attorney and environmental activist. "They have a monopoly agenda."

15   California already has the largest operating collection of solar thermal facilities in the world: nine plants totaling just over 350 megawatts in San Bernardino County. Built in the 1980s, they were part of a drive toward energy self-sufficiency stemming from the '70s oil shocks. The boom ended when California dropped requirements forcing utilities to buy renewable power.

The push is back. The 2000–01 energy crisis exposed California's continued dependence on outsiders—more than 30% of its electricity still comes from out of state. Renewable forms of energy are once again central to efforts to shore up supply and fight global warming.

State lawmakers have told investor-owned utilities that they must procure 20% of their electricity from renewable sources by 2010; Gov. Arnold Schwarzenegger is pushing for a minimum of 33% by 2020. A landmark 2006 state law forcing California to reduce its greenhouse gas emissions to 1990 levels within 12 years also is boosting green generation. Most of the proposed utility-scale solar plants are slated for San Bernardino and Riverside counties, whose vast deserts offer abundant sunshine and plenty of open space for the behemoths. The U.S. Bureau of Land Management is juggling so many requests from companies looking to build on federal land—79 at last count, covering more than 690,000 acres—that it had to stop accepting applications for a few weeks last summer. Many of these facilities may never get built. Environmentalists are mobilizing. U.S. credit markets are in a deep freeze. Oil and natural gas prices are falling, reducing some of the urgency to go green.

Still, the obstacles haven't clouded the ambitions of solar start-ups such as Ausra.

"Our investors perceive there is a huge opportunity here," said Bob Fishman, Ausra's president and chief executive. A group of dignitaries that included Schwarzenegger gathered near here in October to get a close-up look at the 5-megawatt operation Ausra opened.

The company uses a technology known as a compact linear Fresnel reflector. Acres of mirrors are anchored to metal frames and held roughly 6 feet off the ground in parallel rows. Controlled by computers, these panels make hundreds of barely perceptible movements throughout the day, tracking the sun's path across the sky.

The mirrors catch the sun's rays and reflect them onto a cluster of water pipes overhead. The intense heat—it can reach 750 degrees—generates pressurized steam inside the pipes. That steam is then fed into a turbine whose spinning generates electricity.

"It's like when you were a kid and you used a magnifying glass to fry a bug" on a sunny day, said Dave DeGraaf, vice president of product development. "We're focusing all that energy."

Despite its mammoth size, this pilot plant generates a modest amount of electricity, enough to power just 3,500 homes when the sun is shining. Ausra is thinking much bigger.

It has set up a manufacturing facility in Nevada that will supply a 177-megawatt solar plant planned for a site near Carrizo Plain National Monument in eastern San Luis Obispo County.

The facility's mirrors will occupy a full square mile of terrain. The project is still in the permitting process. Ausra has never tried something on this scale. But Pacific Gas & Electric is confident enough that is has agreed to buy the power from Carrizo to help it meet its green energy needs.

Other companies looking to shine in California with utility-scale plants include Solel Inc., whose proposed 553-megawatt project in the Mojave Desert would span nine square miles; BrightSource Energy Inc. of Oakland; SunPower Corp. of San Jose; OptiSolar Inc. of Hayward, Calif.; Stirling Energy Systems Inc. of Phoenix; and FPL Energy of Juno Beach, Fla.

"Climate change is the greatest challenge that mankind has ever faced," said Peter Darbee, president and chief executive of Pacific Gas & Electric and head of its parent, San Francisco-based PG&E Corp. "It's imperative to seek out the most cost-effective solutions."

Review Questions

1. "Size matters," says Sun Microsystems co-founder Vinod Khosla, referring to solar power systems. What does he mean?

2. What are the disadvantages of the solar thermal power systems of the kind described by Dickerson?

3. What forces are helping to spur the development of solar power, especially in California?

Discussion and Writing Suggestions

1. How do you think Thomas Friedman would feel about the kind of solar projects described in this article? Might such projects fall into the category of "205 Easy Ways to Save the Earth"? Why or why not?

2. Dickerson contrasts the key features of "massive solar farms" with rooftop solar panels. Considering the pros and cons of each system, which type of solar power generation do you believe the government should most encourage, through subsidies, tax credits, etc.? Explain your reasoning.

3. The NIMBY (not in my backyard) issue raised in Discussion and Writing Suggestion no. 4 for Michael Totty's article on nuclear power (p. 223) applies equally to large-scale solar power projects, as the following article by Peter Maloney also makes clear. Would you be prepared to live in an area near one of the large-scale solar facilities described in this article, knowing that the generation of solar power in large quantities could significantly reduce the volume of carbon dioxide released into the atmosphere from the burning of coal? Explain.

ENVIRONMENTALISTS AGAINST SOLAR POWER

Peter Maloney

One might think that environmentalists would be all for solar power generation, but as Peter Maloney indicates, this is not necessarily so. There is the concept of solar power and there is the engineering reality of actual solar powered generators. Writing for the *New York Times* in a story published on September 24, 2008, Maloney explains the difference.

What's not to like about solar power? Sunlight is clean, quiet and abundant. If enough of it were harnessed and turned into electricity, it could be the solution to the energy crisis. But surprisingly, solar power projects are running into mounting opposition—and not from hard-nosed, coal-fired naysayers, but from environmentalists.

The opposition is particularly strong in Southern California. Aside from abundant sunshine and virtually cloudless skies, the California desert has altitude, so there is less atmospheric interference for the sun's rays, as well as broad swaths of level land for installing equipment, and proximity to large, electricity-hungry cities.

But it is also home to the Mojave ground squirrel, the desert tortoise and the burrowing owl, and to human residents who describe themselves as desert survivors and who are unhappy about the proliferation of solar projects planned for their home turf.

"We're tired of everyone looking at the desert like a wasteland," said Donna Charpied, who lives with her husband, Larry, in Desert Center, California, where they have been farming jojoba, a native shrub cultivated for its oil, for 27 years. She is also the policy advocate for the Desert Communities Protection Campaign of the Center for Community Action and Environmental Justice.

The United States Bureau of Land Management said it had applications for solar power projects that would cover 78,490 acres in the area around the Charpieds' farm, which abuts Joshua Tree National Park. For the entire United States, the total number of applications is far greater, growing from zero less than two years ago to more than 125 projects with a combined electrical potential of 70,000 megawatts, the equivalent of the electrical capacity of about 70 large coal-fired power plants.

Investors, developers and speculators filed so many applications with the bureau that in May it declared a moratorium on new ones. On July 2, overwhelmed by protests, it reversed itself and ended the moratorium.

The land rush is being driven in large part by a California law that calls for 20 percent of the state's electricity to come from renewable resources by 2010.

The California Public Utilities Commission said the state was falling behind in meeting that goal. It estimated that California's electric utilities would have to build or buy 3,000 megawatts of renewable resources over the next two years to meet the 20 percent target. So the utilities are scrambling to find renewable resources, and developers are working furiously to build projects.

Last month, Pacific Gas and Electric, based in San Francisco, signed contracts to buy the electricity produced by projects under development in San Luis Obispo County by two companies, OptiSolar and the SunPower Corporation, which are expected to come on line between 2010 and 2013.

This sudden flood of solar power projects not only caught the staff of the Bureau of Land Management off guard, it also surprised some environmentalists. "Many community groups are up in arms" about the projects planned in the Mojave Desert and Coachella Valley regions, said D'Anne Albers, the California desert associate for Defenders of Wildlife, citing plans by OptiSolar, BrightSource Energy and FPL Energy.

Jim Harvey, a founder of the Alliance for Responsible Energy Policy, an environmental group in Joshua Tree, said: "Our position is that none of this is needed. We support renewable energy, and we support California's renewable energy targets, but we think it can be done through rooftop solar."

Mr. Harvey said that if Germany, which is as far north as the Canadian city of Calgary, could have a successful solar power program that relies heavily on rooftops, so could the United States. Germany's solar program works, he said, because the government offers so-called feed-in tariffs—fixed-rate payments for electricity generated from solar panels.

The tariff is the equivalent of about 50 cents a kilowatt hour. The average residential retail rate in the United States is about 11 cents a kilowatt hour, according to the Department of Energy.

Mr. Harvey said the tariff would not have to be that high in the United States. Matching wholesale rates would be sufficient to spur a rush to small solar power. "It's all about policy," he said. "Our lawmakers have sold out to the big solar lobby."

15   In addition to obstructing views and disrupting habitats, large solar power projects take a toll on the desert's scarce water supply, environmentalists like Mr. Harvey said. Mirrors and solar panels have to be washed, and some solar projects incorporate steam turbines, which require even more water.

In addition, some solar projects call for grading the land and spraying it with chemicals to inhibit dust or plant growth that can reduce the efficiency of solar panels. Others require backup generators powered by fossil fuels.

These environmentalists favor "distributed generation," like solar panels on rooftops, and they argue that the leadership of national environmental organizations such as the Sierra Club and the Natural Resources Defense Council has gone in the wrong direction.

Terry Frewin, the chairman of the Sierra Club's California/Nevada desert committee, wrote to the club's executive director, Carl Pope, in July, criticizing him for backing large-scale solar projects.

"Remote solar arrays destroy all native resources on site, and have indirect and irreversible impacts on surrounding wildernesses," Mr. Frewin wrote. He urged the Sierra Club to embrace distributed generation as an alternative to the "industrial renewable" option.

20   Carl Zichella, Western renewable projects director for the Sierra Club, said in response to the letter, "We don't take a back seat to anyone in caring for the desert." But he said the group's position was unchanged.

At the current rate of adding 200 megawatts of rooftop solar power a year, it would take 100 years to meet the 20 percent renewable target that California must meet by 2010, Mr. Zichella said. "What they are proposing is not a solution at all."

One of the first tests of public land use for large, privately owned solar projects is likely to be over BrightSource Energy's planned 400-megawatt solar project, which would occupy 3,400 acres on the California border near Primm, Nev.

The project would use an array of mirrors to concentrate the sun's rays on a boiler. Steam produced in the boiler would turn a turbine that would generate enough electricity to power 250,000 homes.

John Woolard, the chief executive of BrightSource, cited several ways in which the company was trying to have as little impact as possible on the desert. He said the project would use "dry cooling" technology to condense the steam in the turbines for reuse, keeping water usage to a minimum, and that BrightSource had purposely sought out already disrupted land (it had been used for cattle grazing) for its project.

But in the end, the scale of BrightSource's project is driven by the efficiencies of the technology. "You get half as much bang for your buck from rooftop solar" as with concentrating solar technology, Mr. Woolard said, adding, "Rooftop solar will never put a dent in California's renewable targets."

Currently available commercial photovoltaic technology converts sunlight to electricity at an efficiency rate of 12 percent to 14 percent. (The most efficient power plants can achieve efficiencies of nearly 60 percent.)

Absent an economic incentive, solar power just does not make sense, said Al Forte, principal and director of the clean energy solutions practice at Nexant, an energy industry consulting firm. Lucrative incentives like Germany's feed-in tariff "tend to warp the reality of the market," he said.

One of the first battles over a large solar power project was fought on the outskirts of Victorville, California, on the western edge of the Mojave. Inland Energy is building a "hybrid" project on 250 acres there for the city of Victorville that will combine solar panels with conventional technology.

In compliance with state law, Inland hired a firm to look for endangered species, including the Mojave ground squirrel and the desert tortoise. No squirrels were found, but three or four tortoises were found. Because no squirrels were found, Inland proposed to the California Department of Fish and Game that it buy one acre of land to offset every acre of lost habitat, said Tom Barnett, executive vice president at Inland. But the department insisted on the three-to-one ratio its rules call for, he said.

"Time is more important than anything else" in project development, Mr. Barnett said, explaining why Inland agreed to the three-to-one ratio. But he noted that it would cost $6.5 million to $10 million to buy and maintain the offsetting acreage for the tortoises.

A family—of human beings—was also living on the site. Inland reached a deal to relocate them at a total cost of $250,000.

"One of the biggest concerns we have," Mr. Barnett said, "is that ours is just a 50-megawatt project."

The much larger projects being proposed will be that much more complicated, but Mr. Barnett, who has a master's degree in environmental science, is not giving up easily. He has begun work on an identical project in Palmdale, California, where the wildlife survey, once again, found no squirrels. He said he was prepared to fight the habitat battle again.

Meanwhile, on the other side off the desert, south of Joshua Tree National Park, Donna Charpied said desert residents of California and Nevada were planning some unspecified action within two months. "The desert will not go quietly into that dark night," she said.

Review Questions

1. Summarize the chief objections of some environmentalists to large-scale solar power farms.

2. What is the "feed-in" tariff used in Germany and recommended for use here by some environmentalists as a way of offering incentives to homeowners to install rooftop solar panels?

3. Contrast the key benefits of ground-based solar power plants to rooftop panels.

Discussion and Writing Suggestions

1. Maloney's article develops more fully some of the environmental concerns about solar power raised in Dickerson's article immediately preceding. To what extent do you take such objections seriously? How should we weigh the competing interests—both ultimately involving the environment—of (1) the need for large-scale renewable energy and (2) the need to protect the environment?

2. Currently, California law mandates that 20 percent of the state's electricity must be generated from renewable resources by 2010. To what extent do you favor a policy that imposes government mandates on power generation?

3. Maloney quotes environmentalist Tim Harvey: "We support renewable energy, and we support California's renewable energy targets, but we think it can be done through rooftop solar." To what extent do you agree? In developing your response, draw upon Dickerson's article, preceding, as well as Maloney's.

SYNTHESIS ACTIVITIES

1. Write an explanatory synthesis, as if it were a cover story for a weekly newsmagazine, in which you discuss the range of alternative, renewable energy sources available now or in the near future.

   Begin by drawing on Friedman and Bryce to discuss some of the opposing view points on green power. Then, summarize information and arguments about some of the particular forms of renewable energy—nuclear, wind, and solar power, as well as the prospect of plug-in hybrid vehicles, drawing upon the authors represented in the second half of this chapter.

   Conclude by indicating which of these forms of green energy, and which policies, appear to the authors of your sources as the most promising or practical.

2. Write an argument synthesis in which you advocate a policy or a set of policies that you believe should govern the nation's use of energy over the next fifty years. Respond to some of the chief concerns expressed by Friedman and Bryce. Some of the articles in the latter section of the chapter cover policies already in place (such as California's mandate to derive 20 percent of the state's energy sources from renewable energy by 2010, as reported by Marla Dickerson).

   Based on your reading in this chapter and elsewhere, as well as on your your own sense of what must be done, make the case for your policies. Remember that it is not sufficient to simply advocate broad goals (we must steadily convert to renewable energy sources): You must also indicate what government, industry, smaller business, and individuals must *do* to achieve significant reductions in greenhouse gas emissions.

3. How, in the years ahead, are green technologies likely to change our daily lives? Write an article for a magazine dated December 2025 (or 2050) on the subject of how the national quest to address the climate crisis and to develop alternative energy sources has, since 2000, changed the way Americans live and work. Draw upon as many sources in this chapter as are helpful, but use your imagination (and a reasonable degree of probability) to analyze how the world of the near future developed from policy decisions and technological innovations being made now and over the next few years.

4. Given what you have read about the need for renewable energy, what do you believe are an *individual's* responsibilities, if any, in reducing energy use? Thomas Friedman appears to believe that the climate crisis cannot effectively be addressed by individuals, arguing that unless solutions are "scaled" to a massive degree, they are token and inconsequential in resolving the larger problem. What, amid all this incoming data, is your position? Is it necessary or useful for an individual to have an energy policy? What would your policy be? How effective would this policy be in reducing carbon emissions? If it is symbolic only (or mostly), is that still important and necessary? Draw upon whichever authors in this chapter seem most relevant to you.

5. Imagine that you work for an advertising agency that is competing for a contract with a large company that generates either nuclear, wind, or solar power for a particular state or a particular region. Your job is to try to win the contract by preparing a brief plan that lays out to the power company execs a potential advertising campaign. Draw upon some of the authors in this chapter to prepare your written prospectus. (Include a Works Cited list on a separate page at the end of the document.) Indicate the key idea

of your proposed campaign that will sell nuclear/wind/solar power. Explain why the type of energy the company is offering is superior to other types of energy. Do not misrepresent or distort the information presented by the authors in this chapter, but use their information and their arguments to best advantage. Organize your plan so that it has an introductory section, a body section containing specifics and a persuasive argument, and a conclusion.

6. Explain how some of the selections in this chapter may have changed your perception of the way you and those around you use energy, and how your life may be affected by the necessity of developing alternative sources of energy. Which authors' analyses have done the most to impress upon you the seriousness of the challenge? Which have most concerned you? For example, when Friedman asks, "Have you ever seen a revolution where no one got hurt?" he implies that saving the earth will require considerable sacrifice. To what extent are you prepared to make sacrifices: to pay increased taxes to help ensure a cleaner, safer environment and a more stable climate; to give up a degree of ease of movement; to take different jobs; to buy different cars, homes, and appliances; to live in places located near power generation stations, whether wind, solar, or nuclear? Draw upon whichever authors in the chapter seem best suited to help you grapple with such questions.

7. In the latter part of his article, Thomas Friedman discusses the scope of the environmental problems facing us by describing the fifteen-wedge pie chart created by engineering professor Robert Socolow and ecology professor Stephen Pacala. Discuss the prospects of achieving the goals in some of these wedges by drawing upon information in the latter half of this chapter about nuclear, wind, and solar power by authors like White, Totty, Kolbert, and Maloney.

8. Robert Bryce forcefully argues that we should not succumb to the "delusions of energy independence." Much as we would prefer, he asserts, there is no prospect of achieving independence from Middle Eastern oil during the next few decades. Which other authors in this chapter might support that position? Write an argument supporting or refuting Bryce's conclusion, based on arguments made and information presented by other authors in the second part of this chapter.

9. Thomas Friedman and others have argued that the most effective way to spur the development of energy-efficient vehicles and alternative fuels for transportation is to make gasoline so expensive that it becomes financially painful to drive vehicles powered by internal-combustion engines. "As long as gas is cheap," he writes, "people will go out and buy used SUVs and Hummers." Imposing a steep gas tax will force people to change their habits and their preferred

modes of transportation. In an editorial, argue for or against the federal government's imposing a gas tax sufficient to make gasoline in the United States as expensive as it is in Europe—between $5 and $7 a gallon. Draw upon some of the authors in this chapter to help you make the case for or against such a tax.

10. Many hope that electric vehicles like the Chevy Volt, along with other forthcoming plug-in hybrids, may go a long way toward helping the nation break its dependence upon Middle Eastern oil—or not. Drawing upon Joseph B. White ("Why the Gasoline Engine Isn't Going Away Any Time Soon"), compare and contrast the features, advantages, and disadvantages of electric, fuel cell, and internal-combustion (*gasoline-powered) vehicles.*

11. You have read about the conflicts between those who would pursue renewable energy projects (such as solar power in California) and locals who scream NIMBY (not in my backyard). Many people live in remote areas, away from cities and suburbs, because they like the view, and they don't want to see wind turbines or solar power arrays cluttering the landscape. The construction of a national electric power grid, necessary to send electricity from a wind farm in Texas to office buildings in Los Angeles, may be delayed, according to a recent *Los Angeles Times* article, because "municipalities and landowners have protested plans to string transmission networks through their backyards."

   What can we do to get beyond the NIMBY syndrome? Draw particularly upon the readings in the latter part of this chapter, as well as any others that seem relevant.

RESEARCH ACTIVITIES

1. After the presidential election of 2008, many people were hopeful that the policies of the incoming Obama administration would be far more responsive to environmental concerns than the policies of the previous administration. The new president campaigned partially on the promise to take climate change seriously, to transform the automobile industry to make more energy-efficient vehicles, and to build a high-tech energy infrastructure to transmit electricity from wind and solar power plants in rural areas to the cities. The president also promised to push for higher federal fuel-economy standards and to support a cap-and-trade program with the goal of reducing carbon emissions by 80 percent by mid-century.

   Investigate what the Obama administration has done so far to achieve these goals. What policies and programs have been proposed, what regulations have been issued, and what laws have been passed? What kind of hurdles has the federal government encountered as it attempts to achieve its green energy goals?

2. Robert Bryce is one of many who dismiss as impractical the goal of energy independence. To what degree are we more independent of Middle Eastern oil than we were five or ten years ago? To what degree are plug-in hybrids more of a reality than they were at the turn of the present century? To what extent has the amount of power generated by wind and solar power significantly supplanted coal-fired electricity during the last few years? Write a report summarizing your findings.

3. In the report "American's Energy 'Independence'" published on the Web (http://www.abc.net.au/unleashed/stories/s2274315.htm), Dennis Phillips, a professor of foreign policy at the University of Sydney in Australia, notes that the environmental agenda often clashes with the economic and employment agenda, particularly in developing countries. He argues:

   All the world's poor are entitled to a much higher standard of living, but in order to progress, the world's poorest three billion will need to access and consume vastly increased quantities of energy. "Renewables" like wind and solar power are not going to do the job in the short term.

   Do we tell the world's poor to be patient and wait? In the "ethanol fiasco" we have done worse than that. We have processed staple crops like corn and soybeans to pour into our fuel tanks, forcing up food prices that ignited riots around the world.

   Research the energy situation in one or two non-European countries to determine (1) energy requirements for sustainability and economic development; (2) chief energy sources; (3) carbon footprints; and (4) prospects for developing and using clean, renewable energy. How, if at all, have governments and businesses in these countries attempted to reconcile the environmental costs of increased energy use, on the one hand, and the need for increased energy to spur economic development, on the other?

4. To what extent are other countries, particularly in Europe, further along in developing and using clean energy than the United States? Select one European country and research its government's energy policy, its patterns of energy use, and its development of renewable energy plants and infrastructure. Determine the extent to which the experiences of this country, particularly its successes, may be transferable to the United States.

5. In 2008 Texas oilman T. Boone Pickens, declaring that "the United States is the Saudi Arabia of wind power," attempted to counteract our dependence on foreign oil by launching an ambitious plan to build the world's largest wind farm in Texas. Investing millions of

dollars of his own money, Pickens founded Mesa Power to oversee the project, which involved more than 2,500 wind turbines, sufficient, he anticipated, to eventually produce electricity to power 1.3 million homes. Launching a nationwide publicity campaign on television, in newspapers, and in magazines to promote his plan, Pickens also proposed that natural gas—which is abundant in this country and which does not produce CO_2—should replace gasoline as the fuel for all automobiles. Pickens's plan ran into a snag with the credit crunch of late 2008 (it was difficult for him to get the necessary financing), but he remained hopeful that the setback would be temporary.

Research the Pickens plan and its current status and prospects. How many wind turbines have been built? How much power is being supplied? What kind of progress has been made converting automobiles to use natural gas? To what extent do energy experts and environmentalists view the Pickens plan as offering a viable solution to the environmental crisis?

6. Opponents of nuclear power argue that previous nuclear accidents such as occurred at the Three Mile Island reactor in Pennsylvania (1979) and at the Chernobyl reactor in the former Soviet Union (1986) risk a cataclysm that makes nuclear power generation too dangerous. Others point to the perfect safety record of nuclear reactors in France, where, after a twenty-five-year conversion process, 80 percent of the country's energy comes from nuclear reactors. Investigate the safety factor of nuclear reactors used for power generation. What steps have been taken since Three Mile Island and Chernobyl to decrease the risks of radioactive particles being released into the atmosphere following a nuclear accident? Have experts arrived at a consensus about the safety issues, or is there still significant controversy over this issue?

7. Investigate the attempts to discourage use of fossil fuels and to encourage renewable power generation by one of the following methods: (1) cap and trade; (2) carbon taxes; (3) increased gasoline taxes. Consider not only proposed U.S. government programs but also state programs, such as California's mandate to generate at least 20 percent of its power from renewable sources by 2010. Consider also policies proposed at international environmental conferences such as occurred at the United Nations Conference on Environment and Development (the "Earth Summit," Rio de Janeiro, 1992), in Kyoto (the Kyoto Protocol, 1997), and at the United Nations Climate Change Conference (Bali, 2007). Which proposals and programs to discourage carbon greenhouse gas pollution and to encourage green energy generation have met with most success? Which have been the most controversial?

To what extent can successful programs in one state (or one country) be transferred, in the opinion of experts, to other states (or other countries)?

8. Research the latest developments in either (1) plug-in hybrid technology or (2) hydrogen fuel cell technology. If you choose to study plug-in hybrid technology, pay particular attention to the quest to develop relatively low-cost, long-range batteries. If you choose hydrogen fuel cell technology, pay particular attention to the quest to separate pure hydrogen from its other bound elements, as well as to store and distribute hydrogen through a national infrastructure.

9. Investigate the latest developments in either wind or solar power. For the energy source you select, investigate the actual growth of this technology over the past decade or so and the projected growth over the next ten years. How much of the nation's power requirements are currently being supplied by this particular technology? How much is projected to be supplied ten, twenty, or fifty years down the road? What government incentives are available for the construction and operation of wind power or solar power? If you research solar power, to what extent are large-scale ground arrays overtaking rooftop solar panels in popularity? To what extent are environmental concerns, political wrangling, and bureaucratic roadblocks hindering the development of wind or solar power?

10. For many years there was great excitement about ethanol, an alcohol-based fuel that is blended with gasoline. The most popular formulation, known as E85, consists of 85 percent corn ethanol and 15 percent gasoline. Presidential candidates campaigning in Iowa felt compelled to express their undying support for ethanol because Iowan and other Midwestern farmers grew and sold the corn necessary for its manufacture. More recently, ethanol's stock has fallen. Research the history of ethanol as an alternative fuel, focusing on the economic and political aspects of its role in the search for alternatives to straight gasoline.

11. Research another form of alternative energy not significantly covered in this chapter: biomass, diesel, biodiesel, geothermal, natural gas, algae. To what extent does this form of energy promise to help us achieve a greater degree of energy independence? To what degree is it likely to supplant fossil fuels, such as oil and coal? What are its advantages and disadvantages? What are the implications for the environment of large-scale use of this form of energy? What major players currently control or are likely to control the supply of this energy? Which parties stand most to gain by such large-scale use? Which stand most to lose?

Chapter 7

Marriage and Family in America

Between 40 and 50 percent of all American marriages will fail. An even higher percentage of second marriages will end in divorce. Failed marriages of young couples have become cynically known as "starter marriages." Cohabitation is on the rise, and more people than ever before are choosing to stay single. A survey released by the U.S. Census Bureau in October 2006 found that domiciles led by married couples were now in the minority—just 49.7 percent of all households. Yet marriage continues to fascinate and inspire us—as it has every known culture throughout human history. The wedding industry generates over $60 billion a year in expenses ranging from embossed invitations to rented tuxedos to $10,000 video shoots. Newsstands are choked with bridal magazines. Tabloids splash celebrity weddings across their covers, and most Hollywood comedies still end with the prospect of a wedding. Everybody, it seems, plans on getting married. According to one set of statistics, 85 percent of Americans will marry at some point in their lives, and 99 percent say they plan to do so.

Why? What is it about the marital state that is so universally appealing? Why do we continue to wed, despite the fact that most of us, statistically, have experienced or witnessed divorce? For some young people, marriage is simply another fact of life—perhaps part of a dimly glimpsed future, along with 401(k) plans, 9-to-5 jobs, and other pillars of adulthood. Others may see the institution in more specific terms—for instance, a teenage girl obsessing over the color of her future bridesmaids' dresses and the merits of white versus pink roses for the centerpieces.

Whether marriage fuels our childhood fantasies or fulfills (or frustrates) our expectations as adults, very few of us can describe what it means to be married—if it ever occurred to us to do so. Doesn't this seem odd? After all, most people have no trouble describing "friendship" as a form of human relationship or "employment" or "citizenship." Yet marriage, an institution to which nearly all of us aspire, and a condition in which most of us will spend many years of our lives, resists easy interpretation. If pressed, most of us would probably characterize the marriage relationship as primarily romantic. The most idealistic and starry-eyed of us, who see marriage as a way for soul mates to pledge unending devotion to one another, dwell at one end of this spectrum. Others, aware that love can be fickle and ephemeral, sense that marriage must be about other things: maturity and commitment, an indication that one has "settled down," perhaps even a rite of passage to adulthood. (Yes, you are marrying someone you love, but you loved at twenty and didn't marry. What changed? *You* did.)

Sociologists Maria Kefalas and Kathryn Edin have demonstrated how, among poorer Americans, marriage has become a luxury item, to be purchased only when a couple has "arrived" financially, last on a "to-do" list, behind a home mortgage and new furniture. And at least some of us suspect that marriage involves pragmatic considerations of a social, political, or even avaricious nature. As they say, it's just as easy to fall in love with and marry a rich girl (or guy) as a poor one.

As the selections in this chapter will show, these conflicting and tangled motives for marrying are no accident. The very meaning of marriage has been changing over the centuries, an evolution that can be traced to broad cultural, intellectual, and economic trends. If anything, these changes seem to be accelerating. (To borrow from Hemingway—the changes seem to be happening slowly, and all at once.) But what significance can we draw from this evolution? Conservative cultural commentators point to the muddled state of contemporary marriage as proof that our society has taken a wrong turn. Yet a wrong turn from what—some historical, universally acclaimed ideal of marriage? As marriage historian Stephanie Coontz notes:

> Everyone agrees that marriage isn't what it used to be, and everyone is quite right. But most of what "everyone knows" about what matrimony used to be and just how it has changed is wrong.

With Coontz's observation as our starting point, this chapter examines the state of marriage and family in contemporary America. Historians, sociologists, anthropologists, political scientists, legal scholars, political activists, and journalists have studied marriage from their various perspectives, and they have offered observations about its impact on our culture, our lives, and indeed our very sense of who we are. Some call marriage a vital public institution that must be safeguarded for the civic good (we allude, here, to the debate over gay marriage). Others view marriage as a private concern between two consenting adults. Some venerate marriage as the ultimate partnership between the sexes. Others charge that marriage forces men and women into rigid—and unequal—gender roles.

The selections in this chapter reveal an institution in flux, the mutable nature of which forces Americans to create their own definitions—not just of marriage and family, but also of what it means to be a wife, a husband, a mother, and a father. The viewpoint in these selections ranges from the scholarly to the personal. A common theme, as you will notice, revolves around the female half of the marriage equation. Debates over the role of women, both in families and in society as a whole, underlie the most contentious debates regarding modern marriages and families. We will examine two of these disputes—working versus stay-at-home mothers, and the continued gender divide between women and men over the subject of child care and housework. As you read the selections, think about your own experiences with marriage and family. You may not be married yourself, or have even thought much about marriage, but certainly you have witnessed the marriages of family members and of friends. Ask yourself whether the viewpoint being expressed in the selections squares with your own observations and your own beliefs on the subject.

In our first selection, historian Stephanie Coontz challenges some of your assumptions about marriage by describing the incomprehension with which many societies have treated "The Radical Idea of Marrying for Love"—a concept most of us now take for granted. The next two selections take on the contentious topic of gay marriage as debated by two prominent cultural commentators. First, Andrew Sullivan argues why conservatives ought to support gay marriage. Then, conservative commentator William Bennett charges that opening marriage to homosexuals would destroy the institution itself.

The chapter next turns to an examination of two ongoing debates regarding marriage: working mothers versus stay-at-home mothers (often referred to as the "Mommy Wars" or the "opt-out debate") and the "stalled revolution"—the feminist complaint that, in an age of working women, men still refuse to shoulder their share of the housework or childcare. First, we offer two opposing perspectives, written twenty-nine years apart, by one woman, Terri Martin Hekker, on the subject of stay-at-home mothers. Taken together, these essays paint a stark portrait of marital disillusionment and personal despair that you are unlikely to forget anytime soon. Next, linguist Deborah Tannen challenges her mother's traditional assumptions about whether or not wives should work—or want to work—at professional careers, but she then attempts to see things from her mother's point of view.

Then, two selections detail another skirmish on the marital front: housework. According to recent research, the amount of time men spend on housework has not changed in forty years. While an increasing number of women have joined the workforce, often earning more than their husbands, women still do the bulk of the cooking, laundry, and child-rearing. Naturally, this state of affairs has occasioned anger and bitterness among wives. Is this a private issue among spouses or a more systemic, feminist one? The next two selections, by Hope Edelman and Eric Bartels, offer personal perspectives on married life that range across several of the issues raised by previous selections in the chapter. Their writings provide a raw, honest look at the daily reality of married life.

In the chapter's final selection, Aviva Patz reports on a study that responds to the key question confronting many hopeful engaged couples: Can success in marriage be predicted? The answer may surprise you.

These selections on marriage are intended to be provocative—to challenge assumptions about what marriage and family mean to you. After all, if you are like 90 percent of Americans, one day you too will be married.

THE RADICAL IDEA OF MARRYING FOR LOVE

Stephanie Coontz

One of the bedrock assumptions of modern marriage is the once-radical idea that newlyweds be in love. Marriage and love have existed through the ages, of course. But according to historian Stephanie Coontz, only in the relatively recent past, beginning in the eighteenth century, did the political and economic institution of marriage take on romantic associations. Reminding us through historical and cultural examples that many people were (and still are) horrified by the idea of marrying for love, and loving the one you marry, Coontz traces the intellectual development of this subversive notion back to the Enlightenment. She then hints at the long-term consequences it held for the institution of marriage.

Stephanie Coontz teaches history and family studies at The Evergreen State College in Olympia, Washington, and has written numerous books on marriage and family in America, including *The Way We Never Were: American Families and the Nostalgia Trap* (1992) and *The Way We Really Are: Coming to Terms with America's Changing Families* (1998). The following selection first appeared in *Marriage: A History: From Obedience to Intimacy, or How Love Conquered Marriage* (2005).

George Bernard Shaw described marriage as an institution that brings together two people "under the influence of the most violent, most insane, most delusive, and most transient of passions. They are required to swear that they will remain in that excited, abnormal, and exhausting condition continuously until death do them part."

Shaw's comment was amusing when he wrote it at the beginning of the twentieth century, and it still makes us smile today, because it pokes fun at the unrealistic expectations that spring from a dearly held cultural ideal— that marriage should be based on intense, profound love and a couple should maintain their ardor until death do them part. But for thousands of years the joke would have fallen flat.

For most of history it was inconceivable that people would choose their mates on the basis of something as fragile and irrational as love and then focus all their sexual, intimate, and altruistic desires on the resulting marriage. In fact, many historians, sociologists, and anthropologists used to think romantic love was a recent Western invention. This is not true.

People have always fallen in love, and throughout the ages many couples have loved each other deeply.

But only rarely in history has love been seen as the main reason for getting married. When someone did advocate such a strange belief, it was no laughing matter. Instead, it was considered a serious threat to social order.

In some cultures and times, true love was actually thought to be incompatible with marriage. Plato believed love was a wonderful emotion that led men to behave honorably. But the Greek philosopher was referring not to the love of women, "such as the meaner men feel," but to the love of one man for another.

Other societies considered it good if love developed after marriage or thought love should be factored in along with the more serious considerations involved in choosing a mate. But even when past societies did welcome or encourage married love, they kept it on a short leash. Couples were not to put their feelings for each other above more important commitments, such as their ties to parents, siblings, cousins, neighbors, or God.

In ancient India, falling in love before marriage was seen as a disruptive, almost antisocial act. The Greeks thought lovesickness was a type of insanity, a view that was adopted by medieval commentators in Europe. In the Middle Ages the French defined love as a "derangement of the mind" that could be cured by sexual intercourse, either with the loved one or with a different partner. This cure assumed, as Oscar Wilde once put it, that the quickest way to conquer yearning and temptation was to yield immediately and move on to more important matters.

In China, excessive love between husband and wife was seen as a threat to the solidarity of the extended family. Parents could force a son to divorce his wife if her behavior or work habits didn't please them, whether or not he loved her. They could also require him to take a concubine if his wife did not produce a son. If a son's romantic attachment to his wife rivaled his parents' claims on the couple's time and labor, the parents might even send her back to her parents. In the Chinese language the term *love* did not traditionally apply to feelings between husband and wife. It was used to describe an illicit, socially disapproved relationship. In the 1920s a group of intellectuals invented a new word for love between spouses because they thought such a radical new idea required its own special label.

In Europe, during the twelfth and thirteenth centuries, adultery became idealized as the highest form of love among the aristocracy. According to the Countess of Champagne, it was impossible for true love to "exert its powers between two people who are married to each other."

In twelfth-century France, Andreas Capellanus, chaplain to Countess Marie of Troyes, wrote a treatise on the principles of courtly love. The first rule was that "marriage is no real excuse for not loving." But he meant loving someone outside the marriage. As late as the eighteenth century the French essayist Montaigne wrote that any man who was in love with his wife was a man so dull that no one else could love him.

Courtly love probably loomed larger in literature than in real life. But for centuries, noblemen and kings fell in love with courtesans rather than the wives they married for political reasons. Queens and noblewomen had to be more discreet than their husbands, but they too looked beyond marriage for love and intimacy.

This sharp distinction between love and marriage was common among the lower and middle classes as well. Many of the songs and stories popular among peasants in medieval Europe mocked married love.

The most famous love affair of the Middle Ages was that of Peter Abelard, a well-known theologian in France, and Héloïse, the brilliant niece of a fellow churchman at Notre Dame. The two eloped without marrying, and she bore him a child. In an attempt to save his career but still placate Héloïse's furious uncle, Abelard proposed they marry in secret. This would mean that Héloïse would not be living in sin, while Abelard could still pursue his church ambitions. But Héloïse resisted the idea, arguing that marriage would not only harm his career but also undermine their love.

"Nothing Is More Impure Than to Love One's Wife as if She Were a Mistress"

Even in societies that esteemed married love, couples were expected to keep it under strict control. In many cultures, public displays of love between husband and wife were considered unseemly. A Roman was expelled from the Senate because he had kissed his wife in front of his daughter. Plutarch conceded that the punishment was somewhat extreme but pointed out that everyone knew that it was "disgraceful" to kiss one's wife in front of others.

15   Some Greek and Roman philosophers even said that a man who loved his wife with "excessive" ardor was "an adulterer." Many centuries later Catholic and Protestant theologians argued that husbands and wives who loved each other too much were committing the sin of idolatry. Theologians chided wives who used endearing nicknames for their husbands, because such familiarity on a wife's part undermined the husband's authority and the awe that his wife should feel for him. Although medieval Muslim thinkers were more approving of sexual passion between husband and wife than were Christian theologians, they also insisted that too much intimacy between husband and wife weakened a believer's devotion to God. And, like their European counterparts, secular writers in the Islamic world believed that love thrived best outside marriage.

Many cultures still frown on placing love at the center of marriage. In Africa, the Fulbe people of northern Cameroon do not see love as a legitimate emotion, especially within marriage. One observer reports that in conversations with their neighbors, Fulbe women "vehemently deny emotional attachment to a husband." In many peasant and working-class communities, too much love between husband and wife is seen as disruptive because it encourages the couple to withdraw from the wider web of dependence that makes the society work.

As a result, men and women often relate to each other in public, even after marriage, through the conventions of a war between the sexes, disguising the fondness they may really feel. They describe their marital behavior, no matter how exemplary it may actually be, in terms of convenience, compulsion, or self-interest rather than love or sentiment. In Cockney rhyming slang, the term for *wife* is *trouble and strife.*

Whether it is valued or not, love is rarely seen as the main ingredient for marital success. Among the Taita of Kenya, recognition and approval of married love are widespread. An eighty-year-old man recalled that his fourth wife "was the wife of my heart....I could look at her and no words would pass, just a smile." In this society, where men often take several wives, women speak wistfully about how wonderful it is to be a "love wife." But only a small percentage of Taita women experience this luxury, because a Taita man normally marries a love wife only after he has accumulated a few more practical wives.

In many cultures, love has been seen as a desirable outcome of marriage but not as a good reason for getting married in the first place. The Hindu tradition celebrates love and sexuality in marriage, but love and sexual attraction are not considered valid reasons for marriage. "First we marry, then we'll fall in love" is the formula. As recently as 1975, a survey of college students in the Indian state of Karnataka found that only 18 percent "strongly" approved of marriages made on the basis of love, while 32 percent completely disapproved.

Similarly, in early modern Europe most people believed that love developed after marriage. Moralists of the sixteenth and seventeenth centuries argued that if a husband and wife each had a good character, they would probably come to love each other. But they insisted that youths be guided by their families in choosing spouses who were worth learning to love. It was up to parents and other relatives to make sure that the woman had a dowry or the man had a good yearly income. Such capital, it was thought, would certainly help love flower.

"[I]t Made Me Really Sick, Just as I Have Formerly Been When in Love with My Wife"

I don't believe that people of the past had more control over their hearts than we do today or that they were incapable of the deep love so many individuals now hope to achieve in marriage. But love in marriage was seen as a bonus, not as a necessity. The great Roman statesman Cicero exchanged many loving letters with his wife, Terentia, during their thirty-year marriage. But that didn't stop him from divorcing her when she was no longer able to support him in the style to which he had become accustomed.

Sometimes people didn't have to make such hard choices. In seventeenth-century America, Anne Bradstreet was the favorite child of an indulgent father who gave her the kind of education usually reserved for elite boys. He later arranged her marriage to a cherished childhood friend who eventually became the governor of Massachusetts. Combining love, duty, material security, and marriage was not the strain for her that it was for many men and women of that era. Anne wrote love poems to her husband that completely ignored the injunction of Puritan ministers not to place one's spouse too high in one's affections. "If ever two were one," she wrote him, "then surely we; if ever man were loved by wife, then thee....I prize thy love more than whole mines of gold, or all the riches that the East doth hold; my love is such that rivers cannot quench, nor ought but love from thee, give recompense."

The famous seventeenth-century English diarist Samuel Pepys chose to marry for love rather than profit. But he was not as lucky as Anne. After hearing a particularly stirring piece of music, Pepys recorded that it "did wrap up my soul so that it made me really sick, just as I have formerly been when in love with my wife." Pepys would later disinherit a nephew for marrying under the influence of so strong yet transient an emotion.

There were always youngsters who resisted the pressures of parents, kin, and neighbors to marry for practical reasons rather than love, but most accepted or even welcomed the interference of parents and others in arranging their marriages. A common saying in early modern Europe was "He who marries for love has good nights and bad days." Nowadays a bitter wife or husband might ask, "Whatever possessed me to think I loved you enough to marry you?" Through most of the past, he or she was more likely to have asked, "Whatever possessed me to marry you just because I loved you?"

"Happily Ever After"

25 Through most of the past, individuals hoped to find love, or at least "tranquil affection," in marriage. But nowhere did they have the same recipe for marital happiness that prevails in most contemporary Western countries. Today there is general agreement on what it takes for a couple to live "happily ever after." First, they must love each other deeply and choose each other unswayed by outside pressure. From then on, each must make the partner the top priority in life, putting that relationship above any and all competing ties. A husband and wife, we believe, owe their highest obligations and deepest loyalties to each other and the children they raise. Parents and in-laws should not be allowed to interfere in the marriage. Married couples should be best friends, sharing their most intimate feelings and secrets. They should express affection openly but also talk candidly about problems. And of course they should be sexually faithful to each other.

This package of expectations about love, marriage, and sex, however, is extremely rare. When we look at the historical record around the world, the customs of modern America and Western Europe appear exotic and exceptional.

Leo Tolstoy once remarked that all happy families are alike, while every unhappy family is unhappy in its own way. But the more I study the history of marriage, the more I think the opposite is true. Most unhappy marriages in history share common patterns, leaving their tear-stained—and sometimes bloodstained—records across the ages. But each happy, successful marriage seems to be happy in its own way. And for most of human history, successful marriages have not been happy in *our* way.

A woman in ancient China might bring one or more of her sisters to her husband's home as backup wives. Eskimo couples often had cospousal arrangements, in which each partner had sexual relations with the other's spouse. In Tibet and parts of India, Kashmir, and Nepal, a woman may be married to two or more brothers, all of whom share sexual access to her.

In modern America, such practices are the stuff of trash TV: "I caught my sister in bed with my husband"; "My parents brought their lovers into our home"; "My wife slept with my brother"; "It broke my heart to share my husband with another woman." In other cultures, individuals often find such practices normal and comforting. The children of Eskimo cospouses felt that they shared a special bond, and society viewed them as siblings. Among Tibetan brothers who share the same wife, sexual jealousy is rare.

In some cultures, cowives see one another as allies rather than rivals. In Botswana, women add an interesting wrinkle to the old European saying "Woman's work is never done." There they say: "Without cowives, a woman's work is never done." A researcher who worked with the Cheyenne Indians of the United States in the 1930s and 1940s told of a chief who tried to get rid of two of his three wives. All three women defied him, saying that if he sent two of them away, he would have to give away the third as well.

Even when societies celebrated the love between husband and wife as a pleasant by-product of marriage, people rarely had a high regard for marital intimacy. Chinese commentators on marriage discouraged a wife from confiding in her husband or telling him about her day. A good wife did not bother her husband with news of her own activities and feelings but treated him "like a guest," no matter how long they had been married. A husband who demonstrated open affection for his wife, even at home, was seen as having a weak character.

In the early eighteenth century, American lovers often said they looked for "candor" in each other. But they were not talking about the soul-baring intimacy idealized by modern Americans, and they certainly did not believe that couples should talk frankly about their grievances. Instead candor meant fairness, kindliness, and good temper. People wanted a spouse who did *not* pry too deeply. The ideal mate, wrote U.S. President John Adams in his diary, was willing "to palliate faults and Mistakes, to put the best Construction upon Words and Action, and to forgive Injuries."

Modern marital advice books invariably tell husbands and wives to put each other first. But in many societies, marriage ranks very low in the hierarchy of meaningful relationships. People's strongest loyalties and emotional connections may be reserved for members of their birth families. On the North American plains in the 1930s, a Kiowa Indian woman commented to a researcher that "a woman can always get another husband, but she has only one brother." In China it was said that "you have only one family, but you can always get another wife." In Christian texts prior to the seventeenth century, the word *love* usually referred to feelings toward God or neighbors rather than toward a spouse.

In Confucian philosophy, the two strongest relationships in family life are between father and son and between elder brother and younger brother, not between husband and wife. In thirteenth-century China the bond between father and son was so much stronger than the bond between husband and wife that legal commentators insisted a couple do nothing if the patriarch of the household raped his son's wife. In one case, although the judge was sure that a woman's rape accusation against her father-in-law was true, he ordered the young man to give up his sentimental desire "to grow old together" with his wife. Loyalty to parents was paramount, and therefore the son should send his wife back to her own father, who could then marry her to someone else. Sons were sometimes ordered beaten for siding with their wives against their father. No wonder that for 1,700 years women in one Chinese province guarded a secret language that they used to commiserate with each other about the griefs of marriage.

35   In many societies of the past, sexual loyalty was not a high priority. The expectation of mutual fidelity is a rather recent invention. Numerous cultures have allowed husbands to seek sexual gratification outside marriage. Less frequently, but often enough to challenge common preconceptions, wives have also been allowed to do this without threatening the marriage. In a study of 109 societies, anthropologists found that only 48 forbade extramarital sex to both husbands and wives.

When a woman has sex with someone other than her husband and he doesn't object, anthropologists have traditionally called it wife loaning. When a man does it, they call it male privilege. But in some societies the choice to switch partners rests with the woman. Among the Dogon of West Africa, young married women publicly pursued extramarital relationships with the encouragement of their mothers. Among the Rukuba of Nigeria, a wife can take a lover at the time of her first marriage. This relationship is so embedded in accepted custom that the lover has the right, later in life, to ask his former mistress to marry her daughter to his son.

Among the Eskimo of northern Alaska, as I noted earlier, husbands and wives, with mutual consent, established comarriages with other couples. Some anthropologists believe cospouse relationships were a more socially acceptable outlet for sexual attraction than was marriage itself. Expressing open jealousy about the sexual relationships involved was considered boorish.

Such different notions of marital rights and obligations made divorce and remarriage less emotionally volatile for the Eskimo than it is for most modern Americans. In fact, the Eskimo believed that a remarried person's partner had an obligation to allow the former spouse, as well as any children of that union, the right to fish, hunt, and gather in the new spouse's territory.

Several small-scale societies in South America have sexual and marital norms that are especially startling for Europeans and North Americans. In these groups, people believe that any man who has sex with a woman during her pregnancy contributes part of his biological substance to the child. The husband is recognized as the primary father, but the woman's lover or lovers also have paternal responsibilities, including the obligation to share food with the woman and her child in the future. During the 1990s researchers taking life histories of elderly Bari women in Venezuela found that most had taken lovers during at least one of their pregnancies. Their husbands were usually aware and did not object. When a woman gave birth, she would name all the men she had slept with since learning she was pregnant, and a woman attending the birth would tell each of these men: "You have a child."

In Europe and the United States today such an arrangement would be a surefire recipe for jealousy, bitter breakups, and very mixed-up kids. But among the Bari people this practice was in the best interests of the child. The secondary fathers were expected to provide the child with fish and game, with the result that a child with a secondary father was twice as likely to live to the age of fifteen as a brother or sister without such a father.

Few other societies have incorporated extramarital relationships so successfully into marriage and child rearing. But all these examples of differing marital and sexual norms make it difficult to claim there is some universal model for the success or happiness of a marriage.

About two centuries ago Western Europe and North America developed a whole set of new values about the way to organize marriage and sexuality, and many of these values are now spreading across the globe. In this Western model, people expect marriage to satisfy more of their psychological and social needs than ever before. Marriage is supposed to be free of the coercion, violence, and gender inequalities that were tolerated in the past. Individuals want marriage to meet most of their needs for intimacy and affection and all their needs for sex.

Never before in history had societies thought that such a set of high expectations about marriage was either realistic or desirable. Although many Europeans and Americans found tremendous joy in building their relationships around these values, the adoption of these unprecedented goals for marriage had unanticipated and revolutionary consequences that have since come to threaten the stability of the entire institution.

•   •   •

[B]y the beginning of the seventeenth century a distinctive marriage system had taken root in Western Europe, with a combination of features that together not only made it different from marriage anywhere else in the world but also made it capable of very rapid transformation. Strict divorce laws made it difficult to end a marriage, but this was coupled with more individual freedom to choose or refuse a partner. Concubinage had no legal status. Couples tended to marry later and to be closer to each other in age. And upon marriage a couple typically established an independent household.

45   During the eighteenth century the spread of the market economy and the advent of the Enlightenment wrought profound changes in record time. By the end of the 1700s personal choice of partners had replaced arranged marriage as a social ideal, and individuals were encouraged to marry for love. For the first time in five thousand years, marriage came to be seen as a private relationship between two individuals rather than one link in a larger system of political and economic alliances. The measure of a successful marriage was no longer how big a financial settlement was involved, how many useful in-laws were acquired, or how many children were produced, but how well a family met the emotional needs of its individual members. Where once marriage had been seen as the fundamental unit of work and politics, it was now viewed as a place of refuge from work, politics, and community obligations.

The image of husbands and wives was also transformed during the eighteenth century. The husband, once the supervisor of the family labor force, came to be seen as the person who, by himself, provided for the family. The wife's role was redefined to focus on her emotional and moral contributions to family life rather than her economic inputs. The husband was the family's economic motor, and the wife its sentimental core.

Two seismic social changes spurred these changes in marriage norms. First, the spread of wage labor made young people less dependent on their parents for a start in life. A man didn't have to delay marriage until he inherited land or took over a business from his father. A woman could more readily earn her own dowry. As day labor replaced apprenticeships and provided alternatives to domestic service, young workers were no longer obliged to live in a master's home for several years. They could marry as soon as they were able to earn sufficient wages.

Second, the freedoms afforded by the market economy had their parallel in new political and philosophical ideas. Starting in the mid-seventeenth century, some political theorists began to challenge the ideas of absolutism. Such ideas gained more adherents during the eighteenth-century Enlightenment, when influential thinkers across Europe championed individual rights and insisted that social relationships, including those between men and women, be organized on the basis of reason and justice rather than force. Believing the pursuit of happiness to be a legitimate goal, they advocated marrying for love rather than wealth or status. Historian Jeffrey Watts writes that although the sixteenth-century Reformation had already "enhanced the dignity of married life by denying the superiority of celibacy," the eighteenth-century Enlightenment "exalted marriage even further by making love the most important criterion in choosing a spouse."

The Enlightenment also fostered a more secular view of social institutions than had prevailed in the sixteenth and seventeenth centuries. Marriage came to be seen as a private contract that ought not be too closely regulated by church or state. After the late eighteenth century, according to one U.S. legal historian, marriage was increasingly defined as a private agreement with public consequences, rather than as a public institution whose roles and duties were rigidly determined by the family's place in the social hierarchy.

The new norms of the love-based, intimate marriage did not fall into place all at once but were adopted at different rates in various regions and social groups. In England, the celebration of the love match reached a fever pitch as early as the 1760s and 1770s, while the French were still commenting on the novelty of "marriage by fascination" in the mid-1800s. Many working-class families did not adopt the new norms of marital intimacy until the twentieth century.

But there was a clear tipping point during the eighteenth century. In England, a new sentimentalization of wives and mothers pushed older anti-female diatribes to the margins of polite society. Idealization of marriage reached such heights that the meaning of the word *spinster* began to change. Originally an honorable term reserved for a woman who spun yarn, by the 1600s it had come to mean any woman who was not married. In the 1700s the word took on a negative connotation for the first time, the flip side of the new reverence accorded to wives.

In France, the propertied classes might still view marriage as "a kind of joint-stock affair," in the words of one disapproving Englishwoman, but the common people more and more frequently talked about marriage as the route to "happiness" and "peace." One study found that before the 1760s fewer than 10 percent of French couples seeking annulments argued that a marriage should be based on emotional attachment to be fully valid, but by the 1770s more than 40 percent thought so.

Romantic ideals spread in America too. In the two decades after the American Revolution, New Englanders began to change their description of an ideal mate, adding companionship and cooperation to their traditional expectations of thrift and industriousness.

These innovations spread even to Russia, where Tsar Peter the Great undertook westernizing the country's army, navy, bureaucracy, and marriage customs all at once. In 1724 he outlawed forced marriages, requiring bride and groom to swear that each had consented freely to the match. Russian authors extolled "the bewitchment and sweet tyranny of love."

The court records of Neuchâtel, in what is now Switzerland, reveal the sea change that occurred in the legal norms of marriage. In the sixteenth and seventeenth centuries, judges had followed medieval custom in forcing individuals to honor betrothals and marriage contracts that had been properly made, even if one or both parties no longer wanted the match. In the eighteenth century, by contrast, judges routinely released people from unwanted marriage contracts and engagements, so long as the couple had no children. It was no longer possible for a man to force a woman to keep a marriage promise.

In contrast to the stories of knightly chivalry that had dominated secular literature in the Middle Ages, late eighteenth-century and early nineteenth-century novels depicted ordinary lives. Authors and audiences alike were fascinated by domestic scenes and family relations that had held no interest for medieval writers. Many popular works about love and marriage were syrupy love stories or melodramatic tales of betrayals. But in the hands of more sophisticated writers, such as Jane Austen, clever satires of arranged marriages and the financial aspects of courtship were transformed into great literature.

One result of these changes was a growing rejection of the legitimacy of domestic violence. By the nineteenth century, male wife-beaters rather than female "scolds" had become the main target of village shaming rituals in much of Europe. Meanwhile, middle- and upper-class writers condemned wife beating as a "lower-class" vice in which no "respectable" man would indulge.

Especially momentous for relations between husband and wife was the weakening of the political model upon which marriage had long been based. Until the late seventeenth century the family was thought of as a miniature monarchy, with the husband king over his dependents. As long as political absolutism remained unchallenged in society as a whole, so did the hierarchy of traditional marriage. But the new political ideals fostered by the Glorious Revolution in England in 1688 and the even more far-reaching revolutions in America and France in the last quarter of the eighteenth century dealt a series of cataclysmic blows to the traditional justification of patriarchal authority.

In the late seventeenth century John Locke argued that governmental authority was simply a contract between ruler and ruled and that if a ruler exceeded the authority his subjects granted him, he could be replaced. In 1698 he suggested that marriage too could be seen as a contract between equals. Locke still believed that men would normally rule their families because of their greater strength and ability, but another English writer, Mary Astell, pushed Locke's theories to what she thought was their logical conclusion, "If Absolute Sovereignty be not necessary in a State," Astell asked, "how comes it to be so in a Family?" She answered that not only was absolutism unnecessary within marriage, but it was actually "more mischievous in Families than in kingdomes," by exactly the same amount as "100,000 tyrants are worse than one."

60   During the eighteenth century people began to focus more on the mutual obligations required in marriage. Rejecting analogies between the absolute rights of a husband and the absolute rights of a king, they argued that marital order should be based on love and reason, not on a husband's arbitrary will. The French writer the Marquis de Condorcet and the British author Mary Wollstonecraft went so far as to call for complete equality within marriage.

Only a small minority of thinkers, even in "enlightened" circles, endorsed equality between the sexes. Jean Jacques Rousseau, one of the most enthusiastic proponents of romantic love and harmonious marriage, also wrote that a woman should be trained to "docility...for she will always be in subjection to a man, or to man's judgment, and she will never be free to set her own opinion above his." The German philosopher J. G. Fichte argued in 1795 that a woman could be "free and independent only as long as she had no husband." Perhaps, he opined, a woman might be eligible to run for office if she promised not to marry. "But no rational woman can give such a promise, nor can the state rationally accept it. For woman is destined to love, and…when she loves, it is her duty to marry."

In the heady atmosphere of the American and French revolutions of 1776 and 1789, however, many individuals dared draw conclusions that anticipated feminist demands for marital reform and women's rights of the early twentieth century. And even before that, skeptics warned that making love and companionship the core of marriage would open a Pandora's box.

The Revolutionary Implications of the Love Match

The people who pioneered the new ideas about love and marriage were not, by and large, trying to create anything like the egalitarian partnerships that modern Westerners associate with companionship, intimacy, and "true love." Their aim was to make marriage more secure by getting rid of the cynicism that accompanied mercenary marriage and encouraging couples to place each other first in their affections and loyalties.

But basing marriage on love and companionship represented a break with thousands of years of tradition. Many contemporaries immediately recognized the dangers this entailed. They worried that the unprecedented idea of basing marriage on love would produce rampant individualism.

Critics of the love match argued—prematurely, as it turns out, but correctly—that the values of free choice and egalitarianism could easily spin out of control. If the choice of a marriage partner was a personal decision, conservatives asked, what would prevent young people, especially women, from choosing unwisely? If people were encouraged to expect marriage to be the best and happiest experience of their lives, what would hold a marriage together if things went "for worse" rather than "for better"?

If wives and husbands were intimates, wouldn't women demand to share decisions equally? If women possessed the same faculties of reason as men, why would they confine themselves to domesticity? Would men still financially support women and children if they lost control over their wives' and children's labor and could not even discipline them properly? If parents, church, and state no longer dictated people's private lives, how could society make sure the right people married and had children or stop the wrong ones from doing so?

Conservatives warned that "the pursuit of happiness," claimed as a right in the American Declaration of Independence, would undermine the social and moral order. Preachers declared that parishioners who placed their husbands or wives before God in their hierarchy of loyalty and emotion were running the risk of becoming "idolaters." In 1774 a writer in England's *Lady Magazine* commented tartly that "the idea of matrimony" was not "for men and women to be always taken up with each other" or to seek personal self-fulfillment in their love. The purpose of marriage was to get people "to discharge the duties of civil society, to govern their families with prudence and to educate their children with discretion."

There was a widespread fear that the pursuit of personal happiness could undermine self-discipline. One scholar argues that this fear explains the extraordinary panic about masturbation that swept the United States and Europe at the end of the eighteenth century and produced thousands of tracts against "the solitary vice" in the nineteenth. The threat of female masturbation particularly repelled and fascinated eighteenth-century social critics. To some it seemed a short step from two people neglecting their social duties because they were "taken up with each other" to one person pleasuring herself without fulfilling a duty to anyone else at all.

As it turned out, it took another hundred years for the contradictions that gave rise to these fears to pose a serious threat to the stability of the new system of marriage.

Review Questions

1. What are the two main reasons, according to Coontz, that the norms about the relationship between love and marriage began to change in the eighteenth century?

2. According to Coontz, what was the aim of people who championed the "love match" model of marriage in the eighteenth century?

3. What did a conservative writer in a 1774 issue of England's *Lady Magazine* claim was the purpose of marriage?

4. Describe the two values that critics of the "love match" feared could lead to widespread individualism. Cite at least one feared consequence of each value.

Discussion and Writing Suggestions

1. Coontz begins the selection with a cynical observation of marriage by George Bernard Shaw: that marriage brings together two people "under the influence of the most violent, most insane, most delusive, and most transient of passions. They are required to swear that they will remain in that excited, abnormal, and exhausting condition until death do them part." To what extent—before your reading of this selection—would you (or others you know) have subscribed to the assumptions about marriage that are the object of Shaw's scorn? To what extent do you think that Shaw is overstating the case? Explain.

2. Coontz notes that only a "small minority" of the Enlightenment thinkers who called for greater equality within marriage actually endorsed equality between the sexes. Is there a difference between equality within marriage and equality between the sexes? Is it contradictory to believe in one but not the other? Explain your answer.

3. Coontz writes that with the advent of the love-based marriage, "The measure of a successful marriage was no longer how big a financial settlement was involved, how many useful in-laws were acquired, or how many children were produced, but how well a family met the emotional needs of its individual members." To what degree would you agree that this statement describes the reality of modern marriages? Do you feel that issues such as money, number of offspring, and in-laws can or should be separated from the "emotional needs" of husband and wife? If possible, when stating your opinion, cite specific examples of marriages you have known about or witnessed.

4. Critics of the love match argued that allowing people to choose their mates would also allow them to choose badly. But presumably some arranged marriages also resulted in bad matches. Do you feel that one sort of bad match is worse than the other? And what does a "bad match" mean, exactly?

5. In her historical and cultural survey of attitudes toward love in marriage, Coontz notes that many cultures have believed that married people should "love" one another. But these cultures have also differentiated married love from romantic love, which they felt was transitory and fleeting. Do you see any distinction(s) between married love and romantic love?

A DEBATE ON GAY MARRIAGE

There are few more hot-button topics in American politics today than gay marriage. In the Defense of Marriage Act of 1996, the federal government defined marriage as the legal union of a man as husband and a woman as wife. Similar legislation has been passed in 38 states. In November 2003, however, the Massachusetts Supreme Court ruled that denying marriage licenses to gay couples violated the state's Equal Protection Clause. The following year, the city of San Francisco began issuing marriage licenses to gay couples. Hundreds of same-sex couples were legally married in the aftermath of these rulings. Responding in outrage, many conservative state legislatures rushed to pass or reaffirm laws banning gay marriage. In July 2006, court rulings in New York, Nebraska, and Washington limited marriage to unions between a man and a woman. In November 2008, Proposition 8, an initiative to ban gay marriage in California, was passed by 52% of voters; the initiative was subsequently upheld by California's Supreme Court and then (in August 2010) struck down by a federal judge.

For Gay Marriage

Andrew Sullivan

The debate over gay marriage highlights a vast cultural divide that typically hinges on core beliefs regarding the nature of marriage itself. In the following selection from Andrew Sullivan's book *Virtually Normal: An Argument about Homosexuality* (1995), Sullivan articulates a vision of marriage as a public contract that should be available to any two citizens. Andrew Sullivan is a former editor of the *New Republic* magazine who writes on a wide range of political and social topics, including gay and lesbian issues. He lives in Washington, D.C.

Marriage is not simply a private contract; it is a social and public recognition of a private commitment. As such, it is the highest public recognition of personal integrity. Denying it to homosexuals is the most public affront possible to their public equality.

This point may be the hardest for many heterosexuals to accept. Even those tolerant of homosexuals may find this institution so wedded to the notion of heterosexual commitment that to extend it would be to undo its very essence. And there may be religious reasons for resisting this that, within certain traditions, are unanswerable. But I am not here discussing what churches do in their private affairs. I am discussing what the allegedly neutral liberal state should do in public matters. For liberals, the case for homosexual marriage is overwhelming. As a classic public institution, it should be available to any two citizens.

Some might argue that marriage is by definition between a man and a woman; and it is difficult to argue with a definition. But if marriage is articulated beyond this circular fiat, then the argument for its exclusivity to one man and one woman disappears. The center of the public contract is an emotional, financial, and psychological bond between two people; in this respect, heterosexuals and homosexuals are identical. The heterosexuality of marriage is intrinsic only if it is understood to be intrinsically procreative; but that definition has long been abandoned in Western society. No civil marriage license is granted on the condition that the couple bear children; and the marriage is no less legal and no less defensible if it remains childless. In the contemporary West, marriage has become a way in which the state recognizes an emotional commitment by two people to each other for life. And within that definition, there is no public way, if one believes in equal rights under the law, in which it should legally be denied homosexuals.

Of course, no public sanctioning of a contract should be given to people who cannot actually fulfill it. The state rightly, for example, withholds marriage from minors, or from one adult and a minor, since at least one party is unable to understand or live up to the contract. And the state has also rightly barred close family relatives from marriage because familial emotional ties are too strong and powerful to enable a marriage contract to be entered into freely by two autonomous, independent individuals, and because incest poses a uniquely dangerous threat to the trust and responsibility that the family needs to survive. But do homosexuals fall into a similar category? History and experience strongly suggest they don't. Of course, marriage is characterized by a kind of commitment that is rare—and perhaps declining—even among heterosexuals. But it isn't necessary to prove that homosexuals or lesbians are less—or more—able to form long-term relationships than straights for it to be clear that at least *some* are. Moreover, giving these people an equal right to affirm their commitment doesn't reduce the incentive for heterosexuals to do the same.

In some ways, the marriage issue is exactly parallel to the issue of the military. Few people deny that many homosexuals are capable of the sacrifice, the commitment, and the responsibilities of marriage. And indeed, for many homosexuals and lesbians, these responsibilities are already enjoined—as they have been enjoined for centuries. The issue is whether these identical relationships should be denied equal legal standing, not by virtue of anything to do with the relationships themselves but by virtue of the internal, involuntary nature of the homosexuals involved. Clearly, for liberals, the answer to this is clear. Such a denial is a classic case of unequal protection of the laws.

But perhaps surprisingly,...one of the strongest arguments for gay marriage is a conservative one. It's perhaps best illustrated by a comparison with the alternative often offered by liberals and liberationists to legal gay marriage, the concept of "domestic partnership." Several cities in the United States have domestic partnership laws, which allow relationships that do not fit into the category of heterosexual marriage to be registered with the city and qualify for benefits that had previously been reserved for heterosexual married couples. In these cities, a variety of interpersonal arrangements qualify for health insurance, bereavement leave, insurance, annuity and pension rights, housing rights (such as rent-control apartments), adoption, and inheritance rights. Eventually, the aim is to include federal income tax and veterans' benefits as well. Homosexuals are not the only beneficiaries; heterosexual "live-togethers" also qualify.

The conservative's worries start with the ease of the relationship. To be sure, potential domestic partners have to prove financial interdependence, shared living arrangements, and a commitment to mutual caring. But they don't need to have a sexual relationship or even closely mirror old-style marriage. In principle, an elderly woman and her live-in nurse could qualify, or a pair of frat buddies. Left as it is, the concept of domestic partnership could open a Pandora's box of litigation and subjective judicial decision making about who qualifies. You either are or you're not married; it's not a complex question. Whether you are in a domestic partnership is not so clear.

More important for conservatives, the concept of domestic partnership chips away at the prestige of traditional relationships and undermines the priority we give them. Society, after all, has good reasons to extend legal advantages to heterosexuals who choose the formal sanction of marriage over simply living together. They make a deeper commitment to one another and to society; in exchange, society extends certain benefits to them. Marriage provides an anchor, if an arbitrary and often weak one, in the maelstrom of sex and relationships to which we are all prone. It provides a mechanism for emotional stability and economic security. We rig the law in its favor not because we disparage all forms of relationship other than the nuclear family, but because we recognize that not to promote marriage would be to ask too much of human virtue.

For conservatives, these are vital concerns. There are virtually no conservative arguments either for preferring no social incentives for gay relationships or for preferring a second-class relationship, such as domestic partnership, which really does provide an incentive for the decline of traditional marriage. Nor, if conservatives are concerned by the collapse of stable family life, should they be dismayed by the possibility of gay parents. There is no evidence that shows any deleterious impact on a child brought up by two homosexual parents, and considerable evidence that such a parental structure is clearly preferable to single parents (gay or straight) or no effective parents at all, which, alas, is the choice many children now face. Conservatives should not balk at the apparent radicalism of the change involved, either. The introduction of gay marriage would not be some sort of leap in the dark, a massive societal risk. Homosexual marriages have always existed, in a variety of forms; they have just been euphemized. Increasingly they exist in every sense but the legal one. As it has become more acceptable for homosexuals to acknowledge their loves and commitments publicly, more and more have committed themselves to one another for life in full view of their families and friends. A law institutionalizing gay marriage would merely reinforce a healthy trend. Burkean conservatives should warm to the idea.

10   It would also be an unqualified social good for homosexuals. It provides role models for young gay people, who, after the exhilaration of coming out can easily lapse into short-term relationships and insecurity with no tangible goal in sight. My own guess is that most homosexuals would embrace such a goal with as much (if not more) commitment as heterosexuals. Even in our society as it is, many lesbian and gay male relationships are virtual textbooks of monogamous commitment; and for many, "in sickness and in health" has become a vocation rather than a vow. Legal gay marriage could also help bridge the gulf often found between homosexuals and their parents. It could bring the essence of gay life—a gay couple—into the heart of the traditional family in a way the family can most understand and the gay offspring can most easily acknowledge. It could do more to heal the gay-straight rift than any amount of gay rights legislation.

More important, perhaps, as gay marriage sank into the subtle background consciousness of a culture, its influence would be felt quietly but deeply among gay children. For them, at last, there would be some kind of future; some older faces to apply to their unfolding lives, some language in which their identity could be properly discussed, some rubric by which it could be explained—not in terms of sex, or sexual practices, or bars, or subterranean activity, but in terms of their future life stories, their potential loves, their eventual chance at some kind of constructive happiness. They would be able to feel by the intimation of myriad examples that in this respect their emotional orientation was not merely about pleasure, or sin, or shame, or otherness (although it might always be involved in many of those things), but about the ability to love and be loved as complete, imperfect human beings. Until gay marriage is legalized, this fundamental element of personal dignity will be denied a whole segment of humanity. No other change can achieve it.

Any heterosexual man who takes a few moments to consider what his life would be like if he were never allowed a formal institution to cement his relationships will see the truth of what I am saying. Imagine life without a recognized family; imagine dating without even the possibility of marriage. Any heterosexual woman who can imagine being told at a young age that her attraction to men was wrong, that her loves and crushes were illicit, that her destiny was singlehood and shame, will also appreciate the point. Gay marriage is not a radical step; it is a profoundly humanizing, traditionalizing step. It is the first step in any resolution of the homosexual question—more important than any other institution, since it is the most central institution to the nature of the problem, which is to say, the emotional and sexual bond between one human being and another. If nothing else were done at all, and gay marriage were legalized, 90 percent of the political work necessary to achieve gay and lesbian equality would have been achieved. It is ultimately the only reform that truly matters.

So long as conservatives recognize, as they do, that homosexuals exist and that they have equivalent emotional needs and temptations as heterosexuals, then there is no conservative reason to oppose homosexual marriage and many conservative reasons to support it. So long as liberals recognize, as they do, that citizens deserve equal treatment under the law, then there is no liberal reason to oppose it and many liberal reasons to be in favor of it. So long as intelligent people understand that homosexuals are emotionally and sexually attracted to the same sex as heterosexuals are to the other sex, then there is no human reason on earth why it should be granted to one group and not the other.

Review Questions

1. According to Sullivan, what definition of marriage prohibits any public way for marriage to be legally denied to homosexuals "if one believes in equal rights under the law"?

2. Which two classes of people, according to Sullivan, does the state believe cannot fulfill the contract of marriage?

3. Summarize Sullivan's "conservative" arguments preferring gay marriage to "domestic partnership."

4. How does Sullivan believe that gay marriage will "bridge the gulf" that is often found between homosexuals and their parents?

● Discussion and Writing Suggestions

1. Write a critique of Sullivan's argument in favor of gay marriage. To what extent do you agree, for example, that "the marriage issue [for gays] is exactly parallel to the issue of the military"? Or that "[l]egal gay marriage could ... help bridge the gulf often found between homosexuals and their parents"? Follow the principles discussed in Chapter 2.

2. Sullivan makes the surprising case that conservatives should support, rather than oppose, gay marriage because marriage is a fundamentally conservative institution (more conservative, for instance, than domestic partnership). To what extent do you agree with his reasoning?

3. Imagine for a moment, as Sullivan suggests, that you belong to a class of people that has been denied the right to marry or have a recognized family. To what extent do you feel that this restriction would affect your approach to life? For example, do you feel that you would be drawn more to short-term relationships—as Sullivan suggests is true of some young gays? To what extent do you feel that the lack of these rights would adversely affect your life?

4. Sullivan writes: "[G]iving [homosexuals] an equal right to affirm their commitment doesn't reduce the incentive for heterosexuals to do the same." However, many antigay marriage activists make precisely that argument—that gay marriage "devalues" heterosexual marriage, by implication making it less attractive to men and women. To what degree does the value you place on marriage depend on its being an institution reserved for a heterosexual man and woman?

5. Sullivan writes that marriage provides a bulwark against the "maelstrom of sex and relationships to which we are all prone." Do you agree that people who have undertaken the public commitment of marriage are less likely to yield to temptation than, say, people who have made a private commitment that has not been publicly recognized? If so, describe what it is about the public nature of the commitment that would tend to encourage fidelity.

6. Noting that "it is difficult to argue with a definition," Sullivan bypasses the argument that marriage is by definition between a man and a woman. Instead, he insists on articulating for the sake of his argument a broader and more complex definition of the nature of marriage: as a public contract that has, at its center, an "emotional, financial, and psychological bond between two people." However, because other relationships—such as that between a father and son—are often characterized by emotional, financial, and psychological bonds, clearly more is needed before this definition could be called comprehensive. In a sentence beginning "Marriage is ...," craft your own comprehensive definition of marriage, one that reflects your own beliefs.

AGAINST GAY MARRIAGE

William J. Bennett

In the following selection, William J. Bennett, a prominent cultural conservative, explains why he thinks that allowing gays to marry would damage the institution of marriage. Note that Bennett attempts to rebut Andrew Sullivan's pro-gay marriage arguments. Bennett served as chairman of the National Endowment for the Humanities (1981–85) and secretary of education (1985–88) under President Ronald Reagan, and as President George H. W. Bush's "drug czar" (1989–90). His writings on cultural issues in America include *The Book of Virtues* (1997) and *The Broken Hearth: Reversing the Moral Collapse of the American Family* (2001). He has served as senior editor of the conservative journal *National Review* and is codirector of Empower America, a conservative advocacy organization. This piece first appeared as an op-ed column in the *Washington Post* on May 21, 1996.

We are engaged in a debate which, in a less confused time, would be considered pointless and even oxymoronic: the question of same-sex marriage.

But we are where we are. The Hawaii Supreme Court has discovered a new state constitutional "right"—the legal union of same-sex couples. Unless a "compelling state interest" can be shown against them, Hawaii will become the first state to sanction such unions. And if Hawaii legalizes same-sex marriages, other states might well have to recognize them because of the Constitution's Full Faith and Credit Clause. Some in Congress recently introduced legislation to prevent this from happening.*

Now, anyone who has known someone who has struggled with his homosexuality can appreciate the poignancy, human pain and sense of exclusion that are often involved. One can therefore understand the effort to achieve for homosexual unions both legal recognition and social acceptance. Advocates of homosexual marriages even make what appears to be a sound conservative argument: Allow marriage in order to promote faithfulness and monogamy. This is an intelligent and politically shrewd argument. One can even concede that it might benefit some people. But I believe that overall, allowing same-sex marriages would do significant, long-term social damage.

Recognizing the legal union of gay and lesbian couples would represent a profound change in the meaning and definition of marriage. Indeed, it would be the most radical step ever taken in the deconstruction of society's most important institution. It is not a step we ought to take.

The function of marriage is not elastic; the institution is already fragile enough. Broadening its definition to include same-sex marriages would

---

*As of September 2009, six states (Massachusetts, Connecticut, Vermont, New Hampshire, Maine, and Iowa) and the District of Columbia have recognized the right of same-sex couples to marry. Nine states (including Oregon, Washington, and New Jersey) recognize some form of civil union for same-sex couples. Legislatures in several other states are actively debating the issue.

stretch it almost beyond recognition—and new attempts to broaden the definition still further would surely follow. On what principled grounds could the advocates of same-sex marriage oppose the marriage of two consenting brothers? How could they explain why we ought to deny a marriage license to a bisexual who wants to marry two people? After all, doing so would be a denial of that person's sexuality. In our time, there are more (not fewer) reasons than ever to preserve the essence of marriage.

Marriage is not an arbitrary construct; it is an "honorable estate" based on the different, complementary nature of men and women—and how they refine, support, encourage and complete one another. To insist that we maintain this traditional understanding of marriage is not an attempt to put others down. It is simply an acknowledgment and celebration of our most precious and important social act.

Nor is this view arbitrary or idiosyncratic. It mirrors the accumulated wisdom of millennia and the teaching of every major religion. Among worldwide cultures, where there are so few common threads, it is not a coincidence that marriage is almost universally recognized as an act meant to unite a man and a woman.

To say that same-sex unions are not comparable to heterosexual marriages is not an argument for intolerance, bigotry or lack of compassion (although I am fully aware that it will be considered so by some). But it is an argument for making distinctions in law about relationships that are themselves distinct. Even Andrew Sullivan, among the most intelligent advocates of same-sex marriage, has admitted that a homosexual marriage contract will entail a greater understanding of the need for "extramarital outlets." He argues that gay male relationships are served by the "openness of the contract," and he has written that homosexuals should resist allowing their "varied and complicated lives" to be flattened into a "single, moralistic model."

But this "single, moralistic model" is precisely the point. The marriage commitment between a man and a woman does not—it cannot—countenance extramarital outlets. By definition it is not an open contract; its essential idea is fidelity. Obviously that is not always honored in practice. But it is normative, the ideal to which we aspire precisely because we believe some things are right (faithfulness in marriage) and others are wrong (adultery). In insisting that marriage accommodate the less restrained sexual practices of homosexuals, Sullivan and his allies destroy the very thing that supposedly has drawn them to marriage in the first place.

10   There are other arguments to consider against same-sex marriage—for example, the signals it would send, and the impact of such signals on the shaping of human sexuality, particularly among the young. Former Harvard professor E. L. Pattullo has written that "a very substantial number of people are born with the potential to live either straight or gay lives." Societal indifference about heterosexuality and homosexuality would cause a lot of confusion. A remarkable 1993 article in *The Post* supports this point. Fifty teenagers and dozens of school counselors and

parents from the local area were interviewed. According to the article, teenagers said it has become "cool" for students to proclaim they are gay or bisexual—even for some who are not. Not surprisingly, the caseload of teenagers in "sexual identity crisis" doubled in one year. "Everything is front page, gay and homosexual," according to one psychologist who works with the schools. "Kids are jumping on it ... [counselors] are saying, 'What are we going to do with all these kids proclaiming they are bisexual or homosexual when we know they are not?' "

If the law recognizes homosexual marriages as the legal equivalent of heterosexual marriages, it will have enormous repercussions in many areas. Consider just two: sex education in the schools and adoption. The sex education curriculum of public schools would have to teach that heterosexual and homosexual marriage are equivalent. "Heather Has Two Mommies" would no longer be regarded as an anomaly; it would more likely become a staple of a sex education curriculum. Parents who want their children to be taught (for both moral and utilitarian reasons) the privileged status of heterosexual marriage will be portrayed as intolerant bigots; they will necessarily be at odds with the new law of matrimony and its derivative curriculum.

Homosexual couples will also have equal claim with heterosexual couples in adopting children, forcing us (in law at least) to deny what we know to be true: that it is far better for a child to be raised by a mother and a father than by, say, two male homosexuals.

The institution of marriage is already reeling because of the effects of the sexual revolution, no-fault divorce and out-of-wedlock births. We have reaped the consequences of its devaluation. It is exceedingly imprudent to conduct a radical, untested and inherently flawed social experiment on an institution that is the keystone in the arch of civilization. That we have to debate this issue at all tells us that the arch has slipped. Getting it firmly back in place is, as the lawyers say, a "compelling state interest."

Review Questions

1. What is the "intelligent and politically shrewd" conservative argument for marriage, according to Bennett?

2. What "enormous repercussion" does Bennett predict in the area of sex education, if the law recognizes homosexual marriage?

3. Summarize two of Bennett's arguments against broadening "the meaning and definition" of marriage to include same-sex marriages.

4. According to Bennett, what distinguishes the sexual behavior of heterosexuals from that of homosexuals?

Discussion and Writing Suggestions

1. Write a critique of Bennett's arguments against gay marriage. Follow the principles discussed in Chapter 2. For example, to what extent do you agree with Bennett's assertion that one argument against same-sex marriage is that it sends "the wrong signals"? Or his assertion that "it is far better for a child to be raised by a mother and a father than by, say, two male homosexuals"? You may wish to include some of Andrew Sullivan's points in your discussion.

2. Contending that homosexual relationships involve "less restrained sexual practices" than heterosexual ones, Bennett quotes Andrew Sullivan, who admits that a homosexual marriage contract will need to feature an acknowledgment of the need for "extramarital outlets." Propose a definition of marriage that allows for such outlets.

3. Imagine that you are one of the advocates of same-sex marriage to whom Bennett refers in the fifth paragraph of his op-ed column. In a brief paragraph, argue why same-sex marriages should be allowed but not the marriage of two consenting brothers.

THE SATISFACTIONS OF HOUSEWIFERY AND MOTHERHOOD/PARADISE LOST (DOMESTIC DIVISION)

Terry Martin Hekker

We begin with a matched set of op-ed columns written nearly 30 years apart for the *New York Times* by the same author. At the time her December 20, 1977, column "The Satisfactions of Housewifery and Motherhood" was published, Terry Martin Hekker was a housewife living in South Nyack, New York, who had been married 22 years to her husband, John Hekker, a lawyer and South Nyack village judge. The column deals with Hekker's experiences as a "stay-at-home" mom at a time—the late 1970s—when many women were opting to enter the workforce rather than stay home to raise their children. As a result of the extraordinary response to Hekker's column—some of which she describes in her follow-up 2006 piece, "Paradise Lost"—she expanded the essay into a book, *Ever Since Adam and Eve*, published by William Morrow in 1979. "Paradise Lost" was published on January 1, 2006. Like her first column, it aroused much comment in op-ed pieces and blogs around the nation.

(1977)

My son lied about it on his college application. My husband mutters it under his breath when asked. And I had grown reluctant to mention it myself.

The problem is my occupation. But the statistics on women that have come out since the Houston conference have given me a new outlook. I have ceased thinking of myself as obsolete and begun to see myself as I really am—an endangered species. Like the whooping crane and the snow leopard, I deserve attentive nurturing and perhaps a distinctive metal tag on my foot. Because I'm one of the last of the dying breed of human females designated, "Occupation: Housewife."

I know it's nothing to crow about. I realize that when people discuss their professions at parties I am more of a pariah than a hooker or a loan shark is. I have been castigated, humiliated and scorned. In an age of do-your-own-thing, it's clear no one meant me. I've been told (patiently and a little louder than necessary, as one does with a small child) that I am an anachronism (except that they avoid such a big word). I have been made to feel so outmoded that I wouldn't be surprised to discover that, like a carton of yogurt, I have an expiration date stamped on my bottom.

I once treasured a small hope that history might vindicate me. After all, nursing was once just such a shameful occupation, suitable for only the lowest women. But I abandoned any thought that my occupation would ever become fashionable again, just as I had to stop counting on full-figured women coming back into style. I'm a hundred years too late on both counts.

Now, however, thanks to all these new statistics, I see a brighter future for myself. Today, fewer than 16 percent of American families have a full-time housewife-mother. Comparing that with previous figures, at the rate it's going I calculate I am less than eight years away from being the last housewife in the country. And then I intend to be impossible.

I shall demand enormous fees to go on talk shows, and will charge for my autograph. Anthropologists will study my feeding and nesting habits through field glasses and keep notebooks detailing my every move. That is, if no one gets the bright idea that I'm so unique that I must be put behind sealed glass like the Book of Kells. In any event, I can expect to be a celebrity and to be pampered. I cannot, though, expect to get even.

There's no getting even for years of being regarded as stupid or lazy, or both. For years of being considered unproductive (unless you count five children, which no one does). For years of being viewed as a parasite, living off a man (except by my husband whose opinion doesn't seem to matter). For years of fetching other women's children after they'd thrown up in the lunchroom, because I have nothing better to do, or probably there is nothing I do better, while their mothers have "careers." (Is clerking in a drug store a bona fide career?) For years of caring for five children and a big house and constantly being asked when I'm going to work.

I come from a long line of women, most of them more Edith Bunker* than Betty Friedan,† who never knew they were unfulfilled. I can't testify

---

*Edith Bunker (wife of Archie Bunker) was a character in the 1970s sitcom *All in the Family;* in the first few years of the series, she was a traditional stay-at-home housewife.

†Betty Friedan (1921–2006) was an author and activist; her 1963 book *The Feminine Mystique,* documenting the stifling and vaguely dissatisfied lot of the mid-20th century traditional housewife, launched the "second wave" feminist revolution.

that they were happy, but they *were* cheerful. And if they lacked "meaningful relationships," they cherished relations who meant something. They took pride in a clean, comfortable home and satisfaction in serving a good meal because no one had explained to them that the only work worth doing is that for which you get paid.

They enjoyed rearing their children because no one ever told them that little children belonged in church basements and their mothers belonged somewhere else. They lived, very frugally, on their husbands' paychecks because they didn't realize that it's more important to have a bigger house and a second car than it is to rear your own children. And they were so incredibly ignorant that they died never suspecting they'd been failures.

10   That won't hold true for me. I don't yet perceive myself as a failure, but it's not for want of being told I am.

The other day, years of condescension prompted me to fib in order to test a theory. At a party where most of the guests were business associates of my husband, a Ms. Putdown asked me who I was. I told her I was Jack Hekker's wife. That had a galvanizing effect on her. She took my hand and asked if that was all I thought of myself—just someone's wife? I wasn't going to let her in on the five children but when she persisted I mentioned them but told her that they weren't mine, that they belonged to my dead sister. And then I basked in the glow of her warm approval.

It's an absolute truth that whereas you are considered ignorant to stay home to rear *your* children, it is quite heroic to do so for someone else's children. Being a housekeeper is acceptable (even to the Social Security office) as long as it's not *your* house you're keeping. And treating a husband with attentive devotion is altogether correct as long as he's not *your* husband.

Sometimes I feel like Alice in Wonderland. But lately, mostly, I feel like an endangered species.

PARADISE LOST (DOMESTIC DIVISION)

(2006)

A while back, at a baby shower for a niece, I overheard the expectant mother being asked if she intended to return to work after the baby was born. The answer, which rocked me, was, "Yes, because I don't want to end up like Aunt Terry."

That would be me.

In the continuing case of Full-Time Homemaker vs. Working Mother, I offer myself as Exhibit A. Because more than a quarter-century ago I wrote an Op-Ed article for *The New York Times* on the satisfaction of being a full-time housewife in the new age of the liberated woman. I wrote it from my heart, thoroughly convinced that homemaking and raising my children was the most challenging and rewarding job I could ever want.

"I come from a long line of women," I wrote, "most of them more Edith Bunker than Betty Friedan, who never knew they were unfulfilled. I can't testify that they were happy, but they were cheerful. They took pride in a clean, comfortable home and satisfaction in serving a good meal because no one had explained that the only work worth doing is that for which you get paid."

I wasn't advocating that mothers forgo careers to stay home with their children; I was simply defending my choice as a valid one. The mantra of the age may have been "Do your own thing," but as a full-time home-maker, that didn't seem to mean me.

The column morphed into a book titled *Ever Since Adam and Eve*, fol-lowed by a national tour on which I, however briefly, became the authority on homemaking as a viable choice for women. I ultimately told my story on *Today* and to Dinah Shore, Charlie Rose and even to Oprah, when she was the host of a local TV show in Baltimore.

In subsequent years I lectured on the rewards of homemaking and housewifery. While others tried to make the case that women like me were parasites and little more than legalized prostitutes, I spoke to rapt audi-ences about the importance of being there for your children as they grew up, of the satisfactions of "making a home," preparing family meals and supporting your hard-working husband.

So I was predictably stunned and devastated when, on our 40th wed-ding anniversary, my husband presented me with a divorce. I knew our first anniversary would be paper, but never expected the 40th would be papers, 16 of them meticulously detailing my faults and flaws, the reason our marriage, according to him, was over.

We had been married by a bishop with a blessing from the pope in a country church filled with honeysuckle and hope. Five children and six grandchildren later we were divorced by a third-rate judge in a suburban courthouse reeking of dust and despair.

Our long marriage had its full share of love, complications, illnesses, joy and stress. Near the end we were in a dismal period, with my husband in treatment for alcoholism. And although I had made more than my share of mistakes, I never expected to be served with divorce papers. I was stunned to find myself, at this stage of life, marooned. And it was small comfort that I wasn't alone. There were many other confused women of my age and circumstance who'd been married just as long, sharing my situation.

I was in my teens when I first read Dickens's *Great Expectations*, with the tale of Miss Haversham, who, stood up by her groom-to-be, spent decades in her yellowing wedding gown, sitting at her cobweb-covered bridal banquet table, consumed with plotting revenge. I felt then that to be left waiting at the altar with a church full of people must be the most crushing thing that could happen to a woman.

I was wrong. No jilted bride could feel as embarrassed and humiliated as a woman in her 60's discarded by her husband. I was confused and scared, and the pain of being tossed aside by the love of my life made bitterness unavoidable. In those first few bewildering months, as I staggered and wailed through my life, I made Miss Haversham look like a good sport.

Sitting around my kitchen with two friends who had also been dumped by their husbands, I figured out that among the three of us we'd been married 110 years. We'd been faithful wives, good mothers, cooks and housekeepers who'd married in the 50's, when "dress for success" meant a wedding gown and "wife" was a tenured position.

Turns out we had a lot in common with our outdated kitchen appliances. Like them we were serviceable, low maintenance, front loading, self-cleaning and (relatively) frost free. Also like them we had warranties that had run out. Our husbands sought sleeker models with features we lacked who could execute tasks we'd either never learned or couldn't perform without laughing.

15   Like most loyal wives of our generation, we'd contemplated eventual widowhood but never thought we'd end up divorced. And "divorced" doesn't begin to describe the pain of this process. "Canceled" is more like it. It began with my credit cards, then my health insurance and checkbook, until, finally, like a used postage stamp, I felt canceled too.

I faced frightening losses and was overwhelmed by the injustice of it all. He got to take his girlfriend to Cancun, while I got to sell my engagement ring to pay the roofer. When I filed my first nonjoint tax return, it triggered the shocking notification that I had become eligible for food stamps.

The judge had awarded me alimony that was less than I was used to getting for household expenses, and now I had to use that money to pay bills I'd never seen before: mortgage, taxes, insurance and car payments. And that princely sum was awarded for only four years, the judge suggesting that I go for job training when I turned 67. Not only was I unprepared for divorce itself, I was utterly lacking in skills to deal with the brutal aftermath.

I read about the young mothers of today—educated, employed, self-sufficient—who drop out of the work force when they have children, and I worry and wonder. Perhaps it is the right choice for them. Maybe they'll be fine. But the fragility of modern marriage suggests that at least half of them may not be.

Regrettably, women whose husbands are devoted to their families and are good providers must nevertheless face the specter of future abandonment. Surely the seeds of this wariness must have been planted, even if they can't believe it could ever happen to them. Many have witnessed their own mothers jettisoned by their own fathers and seen divorced friends trying to rear children with marginal financial and emotional support.

These young mothers are often torn between wanting to be home with their children and the statistical possibility of future calamity, aware that one of the most poverty-stricken groups in today's society are divorced older women. The feminine and sexual revolutions of the last few decades have had their shining victories, but have they, in the end, made things any easier for mothers?

I cringe when I think of that line from my Op-Ed article about the long line of women I'd come from and belonged to who were able to find fulfillment as homemakers "because no one had explained" to us "that the only work worth doing is that for which you get paid." For a divorced mother, the harsh reality is that the work for which you do get paid is the only work that will keep you afloat.

These days couples face complex negotiations over work, family, child care and housekeeping. I see my children dealing with these issues in their marriages, and I understand the stresses and frustrations. It becomes evident that where traditional marriage through the centuries had been a partnership based on mutual dependency, modern marriage demands greater self-sufficiency.

While today's young women know from the start they'll face thorny decisions regarding careers, marriage and children, those of us who married in the 50's anticipated lives similar to our mothers' and grandmothers'. Then we watched with bewilderment as all the rules changed, and the goal posts were moved.

If I had it to do over again, I'd still marry the man I married and have my children: they are my treasure and a powerful support system for me and for one another. But I would have used the years after my youngest started school to further my education. I could have amassed two doctorates using the time and energy I gave to charitable and community causes and been better able to support myself.

But in a lucky twist, my community involvement had resulted in my being appointed to fill a vacancy on our Village Board. I had been serving as titular deputy mayor of my hometown (Nyack, N.Y.) when my husband left me. Several weeks later the mayor chose not to run again because of failing health, and I was elected to succeed him, becoming the first female mayor.

I held office for six years, a challenging, full-time job that paid a whopping annual salary of $8,000. But it consumed me and gave me someplace to go every day and most nights, and as such it saved my sanity. Now, mostly retired except for some part-time work, I am kept on my toes by 12 amazing grandchildren.

My anachronistic book was written while I was in a successful marriage that I expected would go on forever. Sadly, it now has little relevance for modern women, except perhaps as a cautionary tale: never its intended purpose. So I couldn't imagine writing a sequel. But my friend Elaine did come up with a perfect title: "Disregard First Book."

Discussion and Writing Suggestions

1. Hekker discovered that events have a way of reversing our most cherished beliefs. To what extent, based on your own life and on your observations of others, does Hekker's sadder-but-wiser experience appear to be universal? Can one—should one—prepare for such reversals in life? What is gained, and what is lost, by such preparation?

2. In her 1977 column, Hekker writes that traditional mothers "lived, very frugally, on their husbands' paychecks because they didn't realize that it's more important to have a bigger house and a second car than it is to rear your own children." Based on your own observations of working mothers, to what extent do you feel that Hekker's suggestion that most mothers choose to work in order to maintain an affluent lifestyle is fair and/or accurate?

3. In her 2006 column, Hekker writes, "It becomes evident that where traditional marriage through the centuries had been a partnership based on mutual dependency, modern marriage demands greater self-sufficiency." Assuming the truth of this statement, which type of marriage would you prefer—traditional or modern? Why?

4. In 2006, notwithstanding her divorce and the bitter lessons learned, Hekker maintained that she would still have stayed at home with her children until the youngest was school-age. Presumably that choice in 2006, as in the 1970s, would have involved some sacrifice of money and/or career goals. Assume that you faced this same choice. That is, assume that you are married, have a career you care about, yet also want to raise a family. Based on your values regarding childrearing, would you stay at home until the youngest is school-age? What financial and career sacrifices would you be willing to make in order to maintain this arrangement? Describe your ideal child-care arrangement.

5. In her 2006 column, Hekker writes, "Women whose husbands are devoted to their families and are good providers must nevertheless face the specter of future abandonment." To what extent do you agree with this statement? Assuming it is true, would you want to live in this way—either being a suspicious woman or an implicitly distrusted man?

6. To what extent do you feel that the self-confident Hekker of the 1977 column got her comeuppance? To what extent do you feel that she deserves your sympathy and support? On a blog site in response to the 2006 column, one poster criticized Hekker as self-pitying and bitter. Do you agree with this assessment? Describe your own reaction upon reading the paragraphs beginning, "So I was predictably stunned and devastated when, on our 40th wedding anniversary, my husband presented me with a divorce."

UNDERSTANDING MOM

Deborah Tannen

Professional women often confront a generational gap when discussing their life choices with their mothers, who grew up assuming that the highest calling of a woman was to marry, raise children, and run a household. In the following piece, Deborah Tannen stands her ground as she justifies her choice to divorce her husband and return to school; at the same time, she makes a generous and touching effort to understand the worlds of gender and marriage from her mother's perspective.

Deborah Tannen is a linguist who teaches at George Washington University in Washington, D.C. She has published numerous articles and books on interpersonal communication, social interaction, and public discourse. Her book *You Just Don't Understand: Women and Men in Conversation* (1990) remained on the *New York Times* Best Sellers list for four years. She has written nine other books, including *That's Not What I Meant! How Conversational Style Makes or Breaks Relationships* (1986) and *You're Wearing That?: Mothers and Daughters in Conversation* (2006).

This article first appeared as an op-ed in the *Los Angeles Times* on Mother's Day 2007 (May 13).

"My mother never saw me," several women have told me.

I think they meant that their mothers didn't perceive—or didn't value—the qualities these women most valued in themselves. But I wonder how many of us really saw our mothers.

My mother wanted for me the gifts of an ordinary life—a husband, children, a comfortable home. What I wanted was anything but. As a teenager, I identified with the heroine of "The Fantasticks," who whispered, "Please God, don't let me be ordinary."

Growing up in the 1960s, I disdained makeup even as my mother insisted, "Put on a little lipstick when you go out with me." My passion for books was so consuming that I frequently read while walking home from school—so engrossed that I didn't see my mother standing on the porch, worrying that I'd trip and fall on the sidewalk. And when I divorced at 29, my mother was not pleased that I decided to enroll in graduate school and work toward a doctorate instead of working toward finding a replacement husband.

All that time, I was convinced that it was unfair of my mother to scorn my values. It didn't occur to me that it was unfair of me to scorn hers.

Soon after I received my doctorate and joined the faculty at Georgetown University, my mother visited me. I was eager to prove to her that my life was good even though I hadn't remarried. I showed her my office with my name on the door and my publications on the shelf, hoping that she'd be proud of my success. And she was. But then she asked, "Do you think you would have accomplished all this if you'd stayed married?"

"I'm sure I wouldn't have," I replied. "If I'd stayed married, I wouldn't have gone back to school to get a PhD."

My mother thought for a moment, then said, "Well, if you'd stayed married, you wouldn't have had to."

I have told this story often, knowing my listeners would groan or gasp at how my mother hurtfully denigrated my professional success, caring only about my marital state. More recently, however, I tell this story for a different purpose: to understand her point of view.

10   My mother was born in Russia in 1911 and came to the United States before she turned 12. She left high school without graduating because she had to go to work to help support her family. What on Earth was she to make of a woman getting a doctorate and becoming a university professor—and of this unimaginable fate befalling her own daughter?

Surely every mother is proud of a daughter who soars. But from the perspective of the earthbound onlooker, a soaring daughter is receding in the sky, heading toward a universe her mother cannot know. Along with pride must come the pain of separation and of loss—plus the jolt of seeing the child she reared behaving as if she were an entirely different species.

Faced with the trappings of my professional life, my mother was probably trying to figure out how it all had happened. In her world, marriage ensured a woman's financial stability. An unmarried woman had to achieve that goal by going to work. "If you had stayed married, you wouldn't have had to" reflects this view.

Thinking of my mother's perspective reminds me of a remark a woman once made to me. "The shock of my life," she said, "was that my daughter didn't turn out exactly like me."

Though my mother would not have put that insight into words, I'll bet it describes what she was grappling with: trying to make sense of a life so different from any she could have imagined for herself.

15   We want our mothers to see us and love us for who we are, but we are often disappointed in them for falling short of who we think they should be. Mother's Day is a good time to try to see our mothers and love them for who they are: creations of their lives and their worlds, which doubtless are different from our own.

● Discussion and Writing Suggestions

1. Tannen's mother represents a generation of wives who believed that the goal of a young woman should be "a husband, children, a comfortable home." To what extent do you believe that hers is one of the last generations in this country to hold such a belief? In the future, will all—or most—women believe that their daughters should aspire to professional careers or to lives of work? Do you envision a significant percentage of women continuing to hold that a mother's primary job is to stay at home and take care of the children?

2. Consider the decisions women that you know have made regarding work and family. Approximately what proportion of these women has the economic means to opt out of the workforce to stay at home and raise children? Of those who can afford to choose whether to continue to work or to stay at home, how many chose full-time motherhood? Why? What support do these women receive personally and culturally for choosing as they did?

3. Tannen writes poignantly about the different perspectives of her mother and herself. In a paragraph or two, recount an anecdote between you and your mother (or father) that similarly demonstrates a difference in perspectives. To what extent can you, like Tannen, empathize with your parent's point of view, one based on a different set of cultural or generational values—a different "world"?

THE MYTH OF CO-PARENTING: HOW IT WAS SUPPOSED TO BE. HOW IT WAS.

Hope Edelman

In the following two essays, two professional writers—a woman and a man—offer personal perspectives on their own marriages. You are already familiar with some of the issues they will discuss. What is distinctive about these selections is their tone: The writing is by turns raw, wounded, angry, and defensive and offers an unflinchingly honest, if brutal, assessment of each writer's marriage. These essays strikingly reveal the miscommunication and resentment that can afflict even mature, thoughtful, dedicated couples. In the first, Hope Edelman describes the disillusionment and anger she felt when, after the birth of their child, her husband immersed himself in his career, leaving her to run their household alone.

Hope Edelman has written three nonfiction books, including *Motherless Daughters* (1995). Her essays and articles have appeared in the *New York Times*, the *Chicago Tribune*, the *San Francisco Chronicle*, and *Seventeen* magazine. She lives with her husband and two children in Los Angeles. This essay was written for the anthology *The Bitch in the House* (2002).

Throughout much of 1999 and 2000, my husband spent quite a lot of time at work. By "quite a lot" I mean the kind of time Fermilab scientists spent trying to split the atom, which is to say, every waking moment. The unofficial count one week came in at ninety-two hours, which didn't include cell phone calls answered on grocery checkout lines or middle-of-the-night brainstorms that had to be e-mailed before dawn. Often I would wake at 3:00 A.M. and find him editing a business plan down in the living room, drinking herbal tea in front of his laptop's ethereal glow. If he had been a lawyer tallying billable hours, he would have made some firm stinking rich.

He was launching an Internet company back then, and these were the kind of hours most people in his industry were putting in. Phrases like "window of opportunity" and "ensuring our long-term security" were bandied about our house a lot, usually during the kind of exasperating late-night conversations that began with "The red-eye to New York? *Again?*" and included "I mean, it's not like you're trying to find a cure for cancer," somewhere within. I was working nearly full-time myself, though it soon became clear this would have to end. Our daughter was a year and a half old, and the phrase "functionally orphaned" was also getting thrown around our house a lot, usually by me.

So as my husband's work hours exponentially increased, I started cutting back on mine. First a drop from thirty-five per week to twenty-five, and then a dwindle down to about eighteen. At first I didn't really mind. With the exception of six weeks postpartum, this was the first time since high school that I had a good excuse not to work like a maniac, and I was grateful for the break. Still, there was something more than vaguely unsettling about feeling that my choice hadn't been much of an actual choice. When one parent works ninety-two hours a week, the other one, by necessity, has to start picking up the slack. Otherwise, some fairly important things—like keeping the refrigerator stocked, or filing income taxes, or finding a reliable baby-sitter, not to mention giving a child some semblance of security and consistency around this place, for God's sake—won't get done. A lot of slack was starting to pile up around our house. And because I was the only parent spending any real time there, the primary de-slacker was me.

How did I feel about this? I don't mind saying. I was extremely pissed off.

5   Like virtually every woman friend I have, I entered marriage with the belief that co-parenting was an attainable goal. In truth, it was more of a vague assumption, a kind of imagined parity I had superimposed on the idea of marriage without ever really thinking it through. *If I'm going to contribute half of the income, then he'll contribute half of the housework and child care.* Like that. If you'd asked me to elaborate, I would have said something impassioned and emphatic, using terms like "shared responsibility" and "equal division of labor." The watered-down version of feminism I identified with espoused those catchphrases, and in lieu of a more sophisticated blueprint for domestic life, I co-opted the talk as my own. But really, I didn't know what I was talking about beyond the fact that I didn't want to be the dominant parent in the house.

When I was growing up in suburban New York, my mother seemed to do everything. *Everything.* Carpooling, haircuts, vet appointments, ice cream cakes, dinners in the Crock-Pot, book-report dioramas—the whole roll call for a housewife of the 1960s and 1970s. My father, from my child's point of view, did three things. He came home from work in time for dinner. He sat at the kitchen table once a month and paid the bills. And, on weekend trips, he drove the car. Certainly he did much more than that, including earn all of our family's income, but my mother's omnipresence

in our household meant that anyone else felt, well, incidental in comparison. The morning after she died, of breast cancer at forty-two, my younger
siblings and I sat at the kitchen table with our father as dawn filtered
through the yellow window shades. I looked at him sitting there, in a polo
shirt and baseball cap, suddenly so small beneath his collapsed shoulders.
I was barely seventeen. He was fifty-one. *Huh,* I thought. *Who are* you?

There were no chore charts taped to the refrigerator, no family pow-
wows, no enthusiastic TV nannies suddenly materializing outside our
front door. My father taught himself to use a microwave and I started driving my siblings for their haircuts and that, as they say, was that.

My cousin Lorraine, a devout Baha'i, once told me it doesn't matter
how many orgasms a potential husband gives you; what really matters is
the kind of father he'll be. At first I thought she said this because Baha'is
disavow premarital sex, but the more men I dated, the more I realized
Lorraine was right. Loyalty and devotion are undoubtedly better traits to
have in a spouse than those fleeting moments of passion, though I can't
deny the importance of the latter. When I met John, it was like winning the
boyfriend jackpot. He was beautiful and sexy, and devoted and smart, *so*
smart, and he had the kindest green eyes. The first time I saw those eyes,
when I was negotiating an office sublease from him in New York, he
smiled right at me and it happened, just the way you dream about when
you're twelve: I knew this was someone I would love. *And* he wanted children, which immediately separated him from a cool three-quarters of the
men I'd dated before. I was thirty-two when we started dating, and just
becoming acutely aware that I didn't have unlimited time to wait.

What happened next happened fast. Within two years, John and I were
parents and homeowners in a canyon outside Los Angeles. By then he was
deep into the process of starting his own company, which left us with
barely an hour to spend together at the end of each day. And even though
I so badly wanted him to succeed, to get the acclaim a smart, hardworking,
honest person deserves—and even though I was grateful that his hard,
honest work earned enough to support us both—well, let me put it bluntly.
Back there when I was single and imagining the perfect partnership? This
wasn't what I had in mind.

When John became so scarce around our house, I had to compensate
by being utterly present in every way: as a kisser of boo-boos; a dispenser
of discipline; an employer of baby-sitters; an assembler of child furniture; a
scary-monster slayer, mortgage refinancer, reseeder of dying backyards.
And that's before I even opened my office door for the day. Balancing act?
I was the whole damn circus, all three rings.

It began to make me spitting mad, the way the daily duties of parenting
and home ownership started to rest entirely on me. It wasn't even the additional work I minded as much as the total responsibility for every decision
made. The frustration I felt after researching and visiting six preschools
during my so-called work hours, trying to do a thorough job for both of us,
and then having John offhandedly say, "Just pick the one you like best." Or

the irritation I felt when, after three weeks of weighing the options, I finally made the choice, and then he raised his eyebrows at the cost. *I didn't sign up for this!* I began shouting at my sister over the phone.

How does it happen, I wondered both then and now, that even today, in this post–second wave, post-superwoman, dual-income society we're supposed to live in, the mother nearly always becomes the primary parent, even when she, too, works full-time—the one who meets most or all of the children's and the household's minute-by-minute needs? We start out with such grand intentions for sharing the job, yet ultimately how many fathers handle the dental appointments, shop for school clothes, or shuttle pets to and from the vet? Nine times out of ten, it's still the mother who plans and emcees the birthday parties, the mother who cuts the meeting short when the school nurse calls. Women have known about this Second Shift for years, the way the workday so often starts up again for women when they walk through the door at the end of the *other* workday—a time mandated perhaps by the baby-sitter's deadline, but also by their own guilt, sense of responsibility, tendency to prioritize their husband's job first, or a combination of all three. Still, I—like many other enlightened, equality-oriented women having babies in this era—had naïvely thought that a pro-feminist partner, plus my own sheer will power, would prevent this from happening to me. I hadn't bargained for how deeply the gender roles of "nurturer" and "provider" are ingrained in us all, or—no matter how much I love being a mother to my daughter—how much I would grow to resent them.

When it became clear that my husband and I were not achieving the kind of co-parenting I'd so badly wanted us to achieve, I felt duped and infuriated and frustrated and, beneath it all, terribly, impossibly sad. Sad for myself, and sad for my daughter, who—just like me as a child—had so little one-on-one time with her father. No matter how sincerely John and I tried to buck convention, no matter how often I was the one who sat down at the kitchen table to pay the bills, there we were: he absorbed in his own world of work, me consumed by mine at home. My parents all over again.

The intensity of John's workplace was, originally, supposed to last for six months, then for another six months, then for only about three months more. But there was always some obstacle on the horizon: first-round funding, second-round funding, hirings, firings, had to train a sales force, had to meet a new goal. And meetings, all those meetings. Seven in the morning, nine at night. How were all those other dot-com wives managing?

15   There was no time together for anything other than the most pragmatic exchanges. When he walked through the door at 10:00 P.M., I'd lunge at him with paint chips to approve, or insurance forms to sign, or leaks to examine before I called the plumber first thing in the morning. Fourteen hours of conversation compressed into twenty highly utilitarian minutes before we fell, exhausted, into bed. A healthy domestic situation, it was not.

I was angry with the kind of anger that had nothing to do with rationality. A lot of the time, I was mad at Gloria Steinem for having raised women's expectations when I was just a toddler—but at least she lived by her principles, marrying late and never trying to raise kids; so then I got mad at Betty Friedan for having started it all with *The Feminine Mystique*, and when that wasn't satisfying enough, I got mad at all the women in my feminist criticism class in graduate school, the ones who'd sat there and so smugly claimed it was impossible for a strong-willed woman to ever have an equal partnership with a man. Because it was starting to look as if they'd been right.

But mostly I was mad at John, because he'd never actually sat down with me to say, "This is what starting a dot-com company will involve," or even, "I'd like to do this—what do you think?"—the way I imagine I would have with him before taking on such a demanding project (which, of course, we'd then have realized together was not feasible unless he quit his job or cut back dramatically, which—of course—was out of the question). Legitimate or not, I felt that at least partly because he was "the husband" and his earning power currently eclipsed mine, his career took precedence, and I had to pick up the household slack, to the detriment of my own waning career—or in addition to it. Before our marriage, I had never expected that. I don't remember the conversation where I asked him to support me financially in exchange for me doing everything else. In fact, I'd never wanted that and still decidedly didn't. I was not only happy to put in my portion of the income (though it would inevitably be less than usual during any year I birthed and breast-fed an infant), I expected to and *wanted* to contribute as much as I could: Part of who I was—what defined me and constituted a main source of my happiness and vitality—was my longtime writing and teaching career. I didn't want to give it up, but I also didn't want hired professionals running my household and raising my child. It felt like an impossible catch-22.

Face-to-face, John and I didn't give ultimatums. At first, we didn't even argue much out loud. Instead we engaged in a kind of low-level quibbling where the stakes were comfortably low. Little digs that didn't mean much in isolation but eventually started to add up. Like bickering about whose fault it was we never took vacations. (He said mine, I said his.) And whether we should buy our daughter a swing set. (I said yes, he said not now.) And about who forgot to roll the trash cans to the bottom of the driveway, again. (Usually him.)

I'd been through therapy. I knew the spiel. How you were supposed to say, "When you're gone all the time, it makes me feel angry and resentful and lonely," instead of, "How much longer do you realistically think I'm going to put up with this crap?" I tried that first approach, and there was something to it, I admit. John listened respectfully. He asked what he could do to improve. Then it was his turn. He told me how he'd begun to feel like a punching bag in our home. How my moods ruled our household, how sometimes he felt like wilting when he heard that sharp edge in my voice. Then he said he was sorry and I said I was sorry, and he said he'd try to be home more and I said I'd try to lighten up. And this would work, for a while. Until the night John would say he'd be home at eight to put Maya to bed but would forget to call about the last-minute staff meeting that started at six, and when he'd walk through the door at ten I'd be too pissed off to even say hello. Instead, I'd snap, "How much longer do you realistically think I'm going to put up with this crap?" And the night would devolve from there.

20   Neither of us was "wrong." Neither was completely right. The culpability was shared. Both of us were stuck together on that crazy carousel, where the more time John spent away from home, the more pissed off I got, and the more pissed off I got, the less he wanted to be around.

One day I said fuck it, and I took John's credit card and bought a swing set. Not one of those fancy redwood kinds that look like a piece of the Alamo, but a sturdy wood one nonetheless with a tree house at the top of the slide, and I paid for delivery and assembly, too. On the way home I stopped at one of those places that sell the fancy redwood kind and ordered a playground-quality bucket swing for another seventy bucks.

Fuck it.

There were other purchases I'd made like this, without John's involvement—the silk bedroom curtains, the Kate Spade wallet I didn't really need—each one thrilling me with a momentary, devilish glee. But the swing set: the swing set was my gutsiest act of rebellion thus far. Still, when it was fully installed on our side lawn, the cloth roof of the tree house gently flapping in the breeze, I felt oddly unfulfilled. Because, after all, what had I really achieved? My daughter had a swing set, but I was still standing on the grass by myself, furiously poking at gopher holes with my foot, thinking about whether I'd have time on Thursday to reseed the lawn alone. When what I really wanted was for my husband to say, "Honey, let me help you with that reseeding, and then we'll all three go out for dinner together." I just wanted him to come home, to share with me—and Maya—all the joys and frustrations and responsibilities of domestic life.

On bad days, when the baby-sitter canceled or another short-notice business trip had just been announced, he would plead with me to hire a full-time nanny—we'd cut corners elsewhere, we'd go into savings, whatever it took, he said. I didn't want to hear it. "I don't need a nanny, I need a husband!" I shouted. Didn't he understand? My plan hadn't been to hire someone to raise our child. My plan had been to do it together: two responsible parents with two fulfilling jobs, in an egalitarian marriage with a well-adjusted kid who was equally bonded to us both.

25   In writing class I tell my students there are just two basic human motivators: desire and fear. Every decision we make, every action we take, springs from this divided well. Some characters are ruled by desire. Others are ruled by fear. So what was my story during the year and a half that John spent so much time at work? He claimed that I was fear-driven, that I was threatened by the loss of control, which may in fact have been true.

When I try to dissect my behavior then, reaching beneath all the months of anger and complaints, I do find fear: the fear that I'd never find a way to balance work and family life without constantly compromising one, the other, or both. But mostly what I find is desire. For my daughter to have a close relationship with her father, for my husband to have more time to spend with me, for me to find a way to have some control over my time, even with a husband and a child factored into the mix. And then there was the big one: for my husband to fulfill the promise I felt he made to me on our wedding day, which was to be my partner at home and in life. Somewhere along the way, we'd stopped feeling like a team, and I wanted that fellowship back.

I wish, if only to inject a flashy turning point into this story right about now, that I could say some climactic event occurred from which we emerged dazed yet transformed, or that one of us delivered an ultimatum the other couldn't ignore and our commitment to each other was then renewed. But in reality, the way we resolved all this was gradual, and—in retrospect—surprisingly simple. John got the company stabilized and, as he'd promised, finally started working fewer hours. And I, knowing he would be home that much more, slowly started adding hours to my workday. With the additional income, we hired a live-in nanny, who took over much of the housework as well. And then, a few months after Francis arrived, Maya started preschool two mornings a week. Those became blessed writing hours for me, time when I was fully released of the guilt of paying others to watch my child. Between 9:00 A.M. and 12:30 P.M. Maya was exactly where she was supposed to be and, within that time frame, so was I.

With Francis came an additional benefit: a baby-sitter on Friday nights. For the first time since Maya's birth, John and I had a set night each week to devote to each other, and as we split combination sushi plates and did side-by-side chatarangas in a 6:00 P.M. yoga class, we began to slowly build upon the foundation we'd laid with our marriage—and, thankfully, even in the darkest months, we'd always trusted hadn't disappeared. Yes, there were still some Friday nights when I watched TV alone because John was flying back from New York, and other Fridays when I had to sit late in front of the computer to meet a deadline. And there were some weekend days when John still had to take meetings, though they became fewer and fewer over time.

It has taken real effort for me to release the dream of completely equal co-parenting, or at least to accept that we may not be the family to make it real. We're still quite a distance from that goal, and even further when you factor in the amount of household support we now have. Does John do 50 percent of the remaining child care? No. But neither do I contribute 50 percent of the income, as I once did. Ours is still an imbalanced relationship in some ways, but imbalance I've learned to live with—especially after the extreme inequity we once had.

What really matters now—more than everything being absolutely equal, more than either my husband or me "striking it rich"—is that John is home before Maya's bedtime almost every night now to join the pileup on her bed, and that we took our first real family vacation last December. This is the essence of what I longed for during those bleak, angry months of my daughter's first two years. It was a desire almost embarrassing in its simplicity, yet one so strong that, in one of the greatest paradoxes of my marriage, it might have torn my husband and me apart: the desire to love and be loved, with reciprocity and conviction, with fairness and respect; the desire to capture that elusive animal we all grow up believing marriage is, and never stop wanting it to be.

● Discussion and Writing Questions

1. Reread paragraph 5, which begins, "Like virtually every woman friend I have." To what extent does this paragraph describe your own expectations regarding coparenting with your (eventual) spouse? To what extent has reading about an experience such as Edelman's caused you to adjust these expectations? Explain.

2. In a brief paragraph, describe the parenting roles played by your own parents when you were growing up. How much of the parenting did your mother perform? Your father? What were your feelings about this parenting arrangement then, and what are your feelings now? How likely is it that your parents' example will affect your own expectations of your husband or wife, when you are married and attempting to divide household responsibilities between yourself and your spouse?

3. Edelman writes that even though she wanted her husband to succeed and was glad for the money he was making, she couldn't escape the feeling that the life she was living "wasn't what [she] had in mind" when she had been single and "imagining the perfect partnership." In a brief paragraph, describe your own "perfect partnership" with a spouse. Be sure to take into account the "reality check" that essays such as Edelman's (and Shulman's) provide—that is, it's probably unrealistic to imagine a high-earning spouse who is also able to perform at least half of the housework and child-raising duties.

4. Edelman writes, "I hadn't bargained for how deeply the gender roles of 'nurturer' and 'provider' are ingrained in us all." To what extent do you agree that the kinds of division-of-household-labor problems Edelman describes stem from ingrained gender roles? In responding, draw upon your own experiences and observations.

5. Edelman writes: "Neither of us was 'wrong.' Neither was completely right." Do you agree? Explain your response.

6. Edelman explains that her problem was eventually solved when, among other things, she and her husband hired a nanny. However, elsewhere in the essay Edelman describes her resistance to the idea of hiring professional help. Describe your reaction to her (presumed) compromise. To what extent do you feel it was a betrayal of her ideals? To what extent do you feel it was the right thing to do in her situation?

7. *For men only:* Write a response to Edelman's essay, as if you were her husband.

MY PROBLEM WITH HER ANGER

Eric Bartels

In the previous selection, Hope Edelman describes how her husband's absence made her feel "angry and resentful and lonely." In the following essay, Eric Bartels writes about what it is like to be on the receiving end of such spousal anger. Eric Bartels is a feature writer for the *Portland Tribune* in Portland, Oregon, where he lives with his wife and two children. This is a revised version of the essay by this title that appeared in *The Bastard on the Couch: 27 Men Try Really Hard to Explain Their Feelings About Love, Loss, Fatherhood, and Freedom* (2004), an anthology edited by Daniel Jones.

My wife and kids were sleeping when I finished the dishes the other night, shook the water off my hands and smudged them dry with one of the grimy towels hanging on the door to the oven. I gave the kitchen floor a quick sweep, clearing it of all but the gossamer tufts of cat hair that always jet away from the broom as if under power.

I turned to shut the lights, but then I noticed the two metal grills I had left to soak in the basin. They're the detachable, (cast iron type) (stove-top kind) that we occasionally use to affect a kind of indoor, open-flame cooking experience. Submerging them in water for awhile makes it easier to remove the carbonized juices and bits of flesh that get welded on during use. It's a good, sensible way to save labor.

The problem was that they'd been in the sink for several days now. And then it occurred to me: What I was staring at was the dark heart of the divide between men and women.

It's unlikely I was any less harried or less tired the previous few nights as I went about my kitchen duties, a responsibility that has fallen to me more or less exclusively of late. No, my energy level is fairly constant—that is to say depleted—at that particular point of just about any day. I could, and probably should have finished the grill-cleaning project sooner. Just as I should make the bed every morning instead of occasionally. Just as I should always throw my underwear into the hamper before showering, rather than leaving them on top of it, or on the floor next to it.

These are the things men do that quietly annoy the living shit out of a woman. Until she becomes a mother. Then they inspire a level of fury unlike anything she has ever experienced. And that fury won't be kept secret. On the receiving end, the husband will be left to wonder why the punishment is so wildly out of line with the crime. This is the kind of vitriol that should be reserved for lying politicians, corporate greed and hitters who don't take a pitch when their team trails in the late innings—not a dedicated marriage partner with garden-variety human foibles.

Yet here we are, my wife and me. We're both good people. We have lots of friends. We make a decent living at relatively satisfying professional jobs: She, half-time at a small advertising firm; I, as a newspaper writer. And we're dedicated, attentive parents to a six-year old daughter and a two-year old son.

We don't use profanity in front of the children, unless we're arguing angrily. We don't talk to each other disrespectfully, except when arguing angrily. And we don't say bad things about each other to the kids, unless, of course, we just finished arguing angrily.

I know my wife's life is hard. She spends more time with the kids than I do and is almost completely responsible for running them around to day care and school. I contribute regularly and earnestly to the shopping, cooking and cleaning, but a fair amount of it still falls to her. And her job, although part-time for the last six years, presents her with Hell's own revolving door of guilt over neglecting her work for kids and vice versa.

I work hard to take pressure off her and have given up some freedoms myself since our first child was born: time with friends, regular pickup basketball games, beer. And I honestly don't mind living without these things. What gets me, though, is how little credit I get for the effort. My wife gets tired. She gets frustrated. She gets angry. And she seems to want to take it out on me.

10   Then logic starts moving backward in an ugly zigzag pattern. If, in her mind, my shortcomings provide the justification for her anger, then the perception of my behavior must be groomed like the playing field of a game I can't seem to win. The things I do that don't conform to my new loser image—and to think this woman once thought I was cooler than sliced bread—don't even show up on the scoreboard. Until, finally, nothing I do is right.

My efforts to organize the contents of the armoire one day—a project she had suggested—led to a screaming fight. The clutter I was planning to move to the basement would just create more junk down there, she said. But we hardly use the basement, I thought, and besides, why couldn't we just make another, separate project of sorting out the basement later? Doesn't it solve the more pressing armoire problem in the meantime? Isn't that logical?

Evidently not.

One night she stomped into the kitchen as I was cleaning up after a dinner that I may well have cooked and served and announced in angry tones that she needed more help getting the kids ready for bed than I had been providing, as if she had just found me drinking beer and playing video games. Isn't that something we could discuss rationally, I asked her, when we're not both right in the middle of our respective (unpleasant) (demanding) nightly routines?

It didn't occur to her, I guess.

And a few nights later, after bathing the kids in succession, putting them in their pajamas and feeding them their vitamins, I was rocking our son to sleep when I heard my wife approach. I think she had been downstairs doing laundry. She walks into the bathroom and scornfully asks no one in particular "Why is there still water in the bathtub?"

I missed it.

I make a nice dinner after a long day at work, broiled pork chops with steamed zuccini, perhaps, and she asks why I made rice instead of pasta. At the grocery store, I try to buy food that's somewhere between not entirely toxic and prohibitively expensive, but I often disappoint her. I wash clothes the wrong way, not separating them properly by color. I spend too much time rinsing off dishes before loading them into the dishwasher.

If this is my castle, it is under siege. From within.

At times, the negativity threatens to grind my spirit into dust. I make it through an arduous week, gleeful to have it behind me, only to come home to the sound of her loudly and impatiently scolding our son for standing on a chair or turning on the TV or dumping his cheese puffs on the floor, exactly the stuff two-year old boys are supposed to do. Okay, children need to learn "no," and my wife does a lot of the teaching, but I'm certain there's a gentler way to pronounce the word.

I try to make this point calmly, and when that doesn't work, I make it more forcefully. Then we fight, until the (shame and) futility of that leaves me feeling deflated and distant, in a place where passion of any kind has slipped into a coma. And then it's time to start all over.

At times I watch my wife's mercury rise steadily, predictably to that point where she lashes out, almost as if she wanted to get there. I tell her, in the quietest, most reasonable tone I can manage, to please relax. Choose: "(You, Your Daughter, Your Son) did/did not do (this, that, the other)," she replies, her ire mounting. But, I think to myself, I didn't ask her what she's angry about, I asked her to stay calm. Aren't those different things?

I think it's fairly well established by now that marriage is a challenge, a creaky, old institution that may not have fully adapted itself to modern life, one that now fails in this country more often than not. Put children in the picture and you have an exponentially higher degree of difficulty.

Motherhood asks the modern woman, who has grown up seeing professional success as hers for the taking, to add the loss of a linear career path to an already considerable burden: child rearing, body issues, a shifting self-image and a husband who fell off his white horse long, long ago. I suppose this would make anyone angry.

Perhaps for women of recent generations, anger has replaced the quiet desperation of the past. That seems like a healthy development to me. But that doesn't mean there aren't several good reasons why, having seen the frustrated, angry, resentful place that the demands of modern motherhood will almost certainly take them, women shouldn't take the next logical, evolutionary step.

25   It seems to me that a woman should now focus only secondarily on what the world, and more specifically, her partner can do for her during the challenging early years of child rearing. She must now truly empower herself by turning to the more important issue: Controlling the monstrous effects that motherhood can have on her own emotional landscape.

In other words, buck up.

For better or worse, men don't experience life the way women do. Absent the degree of intuition and empathy that seem an integral (natural) part of a woman's nurturing instinct, men grow up in a simpler milieu in which challenges are to be quickly surmounted, without a great deal of fanfare. Something breaks, you fix it and move on. (But don't throw it out, it could come in handy at some point.)

It's not a mindset that lends itself to a great deal of introspection and deep thought. That's not to say that women can't fix things or that men are shallow-minded. These (just seem like) are philosophical tendencies propelled by disparate biological imperatives. The result in men is an inclination not to worry about things before they happen. This imbues them with a confidence that, however vexing a problem might seem, it can and will be resolved.

I don't think most women share this confidence. A friend of mine says that everything in a woman's world starts with fear. Everything becomes tied in some way to fears of disapproval and abandonment and loss of control and God knows what else. To make matters worse, a man's more measured response to (in) certain situations is likely to suggest to his wife that he is not sufficiently engaged. Indifferent. Oblivious.

30   Am I the only guy who feels like he forever stands accused of not understanding the pressures my wife is under? That I can't possibly fathom her frustrations? After all, what would a man know about controlling his impulses?

What would he know? I like that one. Remember, we're talking about men here, the people with the built-in testosterone factory. The ones whose favorite childhood entertainments run to breaking windows, starting fires and dismembering small animals. The ones who instantly want to know if their first car will do 100 mph. The ones who attend beery high school parties with the goal of getting laid, but who'll settle for a good fistfight. Women should be eager to learn what most men know about managing anger.

For many years, I made a living as a bartender. I was good at it and loved the challenge of having to nimbly beat back the surging, immediate gallery of tasks that a big crowd and a busy night present. But it's a job where things go wrong pretty much constantly and I would occasionally lose my cool, kicking a cooler door closed or angrily sending an empty bottle smashing into a bin with an ear-splitting explosion. I imagined I was just blowing off a little steam.

I didn't know what I was really doing until I was a patron at someone else's bar one night. I watched a bartender momentarily capture everyone's attention with a loud fit of pique and realized quickly that witnesses saw the whole thing as landing somewhere between laughable and pathetic. We didn't care what was bothering him. We were having drinks and a good time. Too bad he wasn't enjoying the evening himself.

Was the guy under a lot of pressure? Yes. Was he being vexed by all manner of impediments to his ability to do his job? Almost certainly. Did anybody care? No.

I did a lot less kicking doors and throwing things after that.

Of course I care about my wife's happiness. Whether we're bothered by the same things or react to challenges the same way is irrelevant. She is my partner and I love her. We have important things to do together. The life we've built depends heavily on her ability to find contentment.

But she's not the only one in the family who has tough days. I have my own stuff to deal with and so do our kids, young as they are. When my wife decides it's okay to look darkly at her self or the day she's having, she's giving herself permission to ignore what's going on in other's lives. However little she regards the obligations and pressures of my existence, the fact is that I have some less than radiant days myself.

Women could try to accept that it is theoretically possible for a man to be tired, feel stress and even need a bit of emotional support himself. The children can certainly provide a lift, but they are also notoriously inconsistent about refraining from imperfect, untimely behaviors: talking in loud, excited voices, soiling themselves and moving at high speed in close proximity to valued objects and unforgiving hardwood furniture.

An overworked wife is certainly within her rights, as ever, to express her concerns and wishes at these moments. But that is not the same as a bilious, ill-timed attack that suggests her husband, through arrogance and selfishness, knows absolutely nothing of the realities of her world. In fact, he probably has a pretty good idea. He's probably even willing to meet any reasonable request to help. He'd just like it if someone would ask him nicely.

I'm amazed at how willing my wife is to push my buttons sometimes. And it's not like she's unfamiliar with the instrument panel. She evidently hasn't noticed that I occasionally ignite like dry kindling.

I should probably admit about now that I'm not always a model of decorum. I'm a personable, intelligent guy, but I'm not one of those wise, super-evolved aliens with the massive cranium from science fiction. I've said unkind things to people. I've thrown elbows on the basketball court. Gripped by paroxysmic anger, I've sent any number of small appliances to the promised land. And I do like to win. But this is about not fighting.

Anyone who's ever watched a young child's face crumple in fear and bewilderment as parents unleash their anger, in any direction, knows instantly what the stakes are. Parents do not need the toxic stew of anger coursing through them while in charge of small, impressionable children. And partners who are struggling to remember what particular disease of the brain led to their union won't be helped back to the right path by the rotating wheel of frustration, resentment and blame.

I fear that when anger is allowed to manifest itself regularly, it becomes less and less necessary to question its origins. No need to examine it, no need to work backward in the hope of identifying and defusing the triggers to the fast-replicating chain of events. And what is the hope of altering a behavior if you don't know where it came from and never see it coming?

It baffles me that someone of my wife's intelligence would shout at our son to stop yelling or demand in a voice twisted with exasperation that our daughter stop whining. Can't she see what she's doing? It's like hitting someone to curb his or her violent tendencies. Of course I understand her frustration. But to let the expression of that frustration take any form, however inappropriate or unproductive, is indefensible.

45   Anger can spread quickly and I don't want us to poison the house where our kids are growing up. I don't know for a fact that whiney, self-centered children are always the product of undisciplined, self-indulgent parents, but what reasonable person would want to take that chance? Isn't a bit of restraint a rather small price to pay?

Anger is not power. Managing anger is power. A good friend of many years, with whom I've had many passionate debates on all manner of issues, used to tell me how his father would sit impassively during their own lively exchanges. His father, a university department head, would never lose his temper, never so much as raise his voice. I think I dismissed it as humanly impossible. My friend said it drove him crazy. But he is now an eloquent, engaging orator who runs a weekly literary discussion group out of his home. Then again, he also has two young sons and is divorced.

The level of discipline my friend learned from his father doesn't generally reside where my wife grew up. Individually, my in-laws are charming, intelligent, accomplished people. But together, they struggle mightily to break old habits. You can get one or another of them to acknowledge the familiar cycle of intolerance, blame and recrimination that often cripples their dealings with each other, but no one seems to have the will to fix it. As if the patience it would require would be seen as weakness.

My wife is the black sheep of that family. She has a quick mind, both analytical and imaginative. She has no love for convention and looks easily through hypocrisy of all kinds. She also has big-time Type A tendencies, character traits that make her the choice for many of the organizational and administrative duties in our shared life like paying bills and scheduling the kids' activities.

But these proclivities also work against her. The chaotic, unpredictable reality of having two small children threatens and at times overwhelms her compulsion for order. She breaks down. Traveling, with the on-the-fly time-management it requires, makes her crazy. I watched her walk face-first into a glass door at the airport. Another time, near the baggage carousel, she distractedly pushed our son's stroller into another child. The child was seated at the time. A pointless quarrel over a trip to the Home Depot led to her backing out of the driveway and into a parked mail truck one morning.

My wife and I need to fix this anger thing. We knew, or should have known, what we were getting into. We signed the contract. Shook on it. Kissed, actually. But I think we missed some of the small print. We wanted kids and had a vague idea that it would involve some work. Well, I have a news flash: It can be really, really hard.

And that goes for guys, too. I don't recall being told about spending more money each year than I actually earn, with no exotic vacations, nice cars or fancy anything else to show for it. I wasn't informed that I would give up golf altogether, just as I was pushing my handicap down toward single digits. And I'm certain I was not warned that sex would become a rarer commodity than at any time in the thirty years since I learned to participate in it.

But I've gotten used to all that. I do what most men do. I take a deep breath and push ahead, fairly confident that if I can just soldier on, the things I've sacrificed and more will be my reward down the road.

I suppose the anger issues in our household loom as large as they do, in part, because of my fervor to confront (defeat) them. It's been a battle-field at times. My wife and I have been mean and fought dirty and we've hurt each other. We need to recognize that and make up our minds to change, no matter how much work it requires.

But hey, we're still here. Our children, who we love so dearly, are growing up and every day we can count on the reassuring rhythms of life: the sun rises in the morning, a weather system slips over the Oregon Cascades and blots it out, cats barf up hairballs on the carpet. I'm optimistic. I don't think we've done any permanent damage. I don't think it's anything we can't fix.

But that's just me.

Discussion and Writing Questions

1. Reflecting on his wife and other working mothers, Bartels concludes: "To truly empower herself, she will need to find a way to get beyond—on her own, with help, or however—the destructive impulses that the frustrations of modern motherhood can bring out in her." Your response?

2. Bartels suggests that women "of his generation" seem more comfortable expressing anger than women of previous generations did, and he attributes this, in part, to the fact that they have been in the workforce. To what extent do you find this explanation plausible? Explain your answer.

3. Bartels describes his failure to promptly clean the indoor grill, as well as a propensity for leaving dirty underwear on the floor, as typical "domestic

lapses" common to men. To what extent does this square with your own observations of male behavior? To what extent do you feel, as Bartels implies, that such behavior cannot be modified?

4. Write a critique of Bartels's argument that, for the sake of their marriage and family, his wife needs to move past her "destructive impulses." Pay particular attention to the persuasive strategies he employs to support his thesis. Now respond to his argument. With which of his points do you agree, and with which do you disagree? State your overall conclusion as to the validity of the piece. Follow the principles in Chapter 2.

5. With the goal of suggesting a possible solution to the challenges Bartels and his wife face, evaluate his marriage according to one or more of the principles you have read about in previous selections. If Bartels's grievances are to be assuaged, to what extent do he and his wife need to fundamentally reexamine their assumptions regarding, say, the household division of labor? How much of that change should be Bartels's? How much his wife's?

6. *For women only:* Write a response to Bartels, as if you were his wife.

WILL YOUR MARRIAGE LAST?

Aviva Patz

Every newly wedded couple expects—or at least hopes—that their marriage will endure the test of time. But in most parts of the world the statistics are not encouraging. As of 2002, the highest divorce rate was found in Sweden, where 55 percent of new marriages ended in divorce; Guatemala had the lowest rate: 0.13 percent. The divorce rate in the United States is on the high end of the scale: 46 percent.

Is it possible to predict, in the early stages of a marriage, whether it will likely succeed or fail? In the following selection, Aviva Patz, executive editor of *Psychology Today*, reports on a study designed to answer that intriguing question. Ted Huston, a professor of human ecology and psychology at the University of Texas at Austin, designed and conducted the PAIR Project (Processes of Adaptation in Intimate Relationships), which followed the experiences of 168 couples from their wedding day through the next thirteen years. The results should surprise you and may overturn some of your assumptions about what makes for a successful marriage.

This article first appeared in the *Los Angeles Times* on March 15, 2000, and, in slightly different form, in *Psychology Today* on April 23 of that year. The present selection is drawn from both versions of the article.

What if I told you that there is a man in America who can predict, from the outset, whether your marriage will last? He doesn't need to hear you arguing; he doesn't need to know what you argue about. He doesn't even care whether you argue at all.

I was dubious, too, but I was curious enough to attend a lecture on the subject at the most recent American Psychological Association convention in Boston. Ted Huston, a professor of human ecology and psychology at the University of Texas at Austin, was showcasing the results of a long-term study of married couples that pierces the heart of social-psychological science: the ability to forecast whether a husband and wife, two years after taking their vows, will stay together and whether they will be happy.

My press pass notwithstanding, I went to the seminar for reasons of my own. Fresh out of college I had gotten married—and burned. Some part of me was still reeling from three years of waking up angry every morning, not wanting to go home after work, feeling lonely even as my then-husband sat beside me. I went because I have recently remarried and just celebrated my one-year anniversary. Needless to say, I'd like to make this one work. So I scribbled furiously in my notebook, drinking in the graphs and charts—for psychology, for husbands and wives everywhere, but mostly for myself.

Huston, a pioneer in the psychology of relationships, launched the Processes of Adaptation in Intimate Relationships (the "PAIR Project") in 1981, in which he followed 168 couples—drawn from marriage license records in four counties in a rural and working-class area of Pennsylvania—from their wedding day through thirteen years of marriage.

Examining a Marriage's Early Stages

Through multiple interviews, Huston looked at the way partners related to one another during courtship, as newlyweds and through the early years of marriage. Were they "gaga"? Comfortable? Unsure? He measured their positive and negative feelings for each other and observed how those feelings changed over time. Are newlyweds who hug and kiss more likely than other couples to have a happy marriage, he wondered, or are they particularly susceptible to divorce if their romance dissipates? Are newlyweds who bicker destined to part ways?

Since one in two marriages ends in divorce in this country, there ought to be tons of research explaining why. But the existing literature provides only pieces of the larger puzzle.

Past research has led social scientists to believe that newlyweds begin their life together in romantic bliss and can then be brought down by their inability to navigate the issues that inevitably crop up during the marriage. When Benjamin Karny and Thomas Bradbury did a comprehensive review of the literature in 1995, they confirmed studies such as those of John Gottman and Neil Jacobson, maintaining that the best predictors of divorce are interactive difficulties, such as frequent expressions of antagonism, lack of respect for each other's ideas and similar interpersonal issues.

But most of this research was done on couples who had been married a number of years, with many of them already well on their way to divorce. It came as no surprise, then, that researchers thought their hostility toward one another predicted the further demise of the relationship.

Huston's study was unique in that it looked at couples much earlier, when they were courting and during the initial years of marriage, thus providing the first complete picture of the earliest stages of distress. Its four main findings were quite surprising.

10   First, contrary to popular belief, Huston found that many newlyweds are far from blissfully in love. Second, couples whose marriages begin in romantic bliss are particularly divorce-prone because such intensity is too hard to maintain. Believe it or not, marriages that start out with less "Hollywood romance" usually have more promising futures.

Accordingly, and this is the third major finding, spouses in lasting but lackluster marriages are not prone to divorce, as one might suspect; their marriages are less fulfilling to begin with, so there is no erosion of a Western-style romantic ideal. Lastly, and perhaps most important, it is the loss of love and affection, not the emergence of interpersonal issues, that sends couples journeying toward divorce.

By the end of Huston's study in 1994, the couples looked a lot like the rest of America, falling into four groups. They were either married and happy; married and unhappy; divorced early, within seven years; or divorced later, after seven years—and each category showed a distinct pattern.

Satisfied Spouses Were Happy Newlyweds

Those who remained happily married were very "in love" and affectionate as newlyweds. They showed less ambivalence, expressed negative feelings less often and viewed their mate more positively than other couples. Most important, these feelings remained stable over time. By contrast, although many couples who divorced later were very affectionate as newlyweds, they gradually became less loving, more negative and more critical of their spouse.

Indeed, Huston found that how well spouses got along as newlyweds affected their future, but the major distinguishing factor between those who divorced and those who remained married was the amount of change in the relationship over its first two years.

15   "The first two years are key—that's when the risk of divorce is particularly high," he says. "And the changes that take place during this time tell us a lot about where the marriage is headed."

What surprised Huston most was the nature of the changes that led to divorce: The experiences of the 56 participating couples who divorced showed that loss of initial levels of love and affection, rather than conflict, was the most salient predictor of distress and divorce. This loss sends that relationship into a downward spiral, leading to increased bickering and fighting, and to the collapse of the union.

"This ought to change the way we think about the early roots of what goes wrong in marriage," Huston said. "The dominant approach has been to work with couples to resolve conflict, but it should focus on preserving the positive feelings. That's a very important take-home lesson."

Feelings May Determine a Union's Fate

"Huston's research fills an important gap in the literature by suggesting that there is more to a successful relationship than simply managing conflict," said Harry Reis, of the University of Rochester, a leading social psychologist.

"My own research speaks to 'loss of intimacy,' in the sense that when people first become close they feel a tremendous sense of validation from each other, like their partner is the only other person on earth who sees things as they do. That feeling sometimes fades, and when it does, it can take a heavy toll on the marriage."

Social science has a name for that fading dynamic—"disillusionment": Lovers initially put their best foot forward, ignoring each other's—and the relationship's—shortcomings. But after they tie the knot, hidden aspects of their personalities emerge, and idealized images give way to more realistic ones. This can lead to disappointment, loss of love and, ultimately, distress and divorce.

When Marriage Fails

The story of Peter and Suzie, participants in the PAIR Project, shows classic disillusionment. When they met, Suzie was 24, a new waitress at the golf course where Peter, then 26, played. He was "awed" by her beauty. After a month, the two considered themselves an exclusive couple. Peter said Suzie "wasn't an airhead; she seemed kind of smart, and she's pretty." Suzie said Peter "cared a lot about me as a person, and was willing to overlook things."

By the time they strolled down the aisle on Valentine's Day in 1981, Peter and Suzie had dated only nine months, experiencing many ups and downs along the way.

Huston says couples are most vulnerable to disillusionment when their courtship is brief. In a whirlwind romance, it's easy to paint an unrealistically rosy picture of the relationship, one that cannot be sustained.

Sure enough, reality soon set in for Peter and Suzie. Within two years, Suzie was less satisfied with almost every aspect of their marriage. She expressed less affection for Peter and felt her love decline continuously. She considered him to have "contrary" traits, such as jealousy and possessiveness, and resented his propensity to find fault with her.

Peter, for his part, was disappointed that his wife did not become the flawless parent and homemaker he had envisioned.

Another danger sign for relationships is a courtship filled with drama and driven by external circumstances. For this pair, events related to Peter's jealousy propelled the relationship forward. He was the force behind their destroying letters and pictures from former lovers. It was a phone call between Suzie and an old flame that prompted him to bring up the idea of marriage in the first place. And it was a fit of jealousy—over Suzie's claiming to go shopping and then coming home suspiciously late—that convinced Peter he was ready to marry.

Theirs was a recipe for disaster: A short courtship, driven largely by Peter's jealousy, enabled the pair to ignore flaws in the relationship and in each other, setting them up for disappointment. That disappointment eroded their love and affection, which soured their perception of each other's personalities, creating feelings of ambivalence.

Ten years after saying "I do," the disaffected lovers were in the midst of divorce. When Suzie filed the papers, she cited as the primary reason a gradual loss of love.

The parallels between Peter and Suzie's failed marriage and my own are striking: My courtship with my first husband was short, also about nine months. Like Peter, I had shallow criteria: This guy was cool; he had long hair, wore a leather jacket, played guitar and adored the same obscure band that I did.

30   When it came time to build a life together, however, we were clearly mismatched. I wanted a traditional family with children; he would have been happy living on a hippie commune. In college, when we wanted to move in together, we thought our parents would be more approving if we got engaged first. So we did, even though we weren't completely sold on the idea of marriage.

The road to divorce was paved early, by the end of the first year: I had said I wanted us to spend more time together; he accused me of trying to keep him from his hobbies, and told me, in so many words, to "get a life." Well I did, and two years later, he wasn't in it.

When Marriage Succeeds

While the disillusionment model best describes those who divorce, Huston found that another model suits those who stay married, whether or not they are happy: The "enduring dynamics model," in which partners establish patterns of behavior early and maintain them over time, highlights stability in the relationship—the feature that distinguishes those who remain together from those who eventually split up.

The major difference between the unhappily married couples and their happy counterparts is simply a lower level of satisfaction across the board. Yet, oddly enough, this relative unhappiness by itself does not doom the marriage. "We have a whole group of people who are stable in unhappy marriages and not necessarily dissatisfied," Huston said. "It's just a different model of marriage. It's not that they're happy about their marriage; it's just that the discontent doesn't spill over and soil the rest of their lives."

And while all married couples eventually lose a bit of that honeymoon euphoria, Huston notes, those who remain married don't consider this a crushing blow, but rather a natural transition from "romantic relationship" to "working partnership." And when conflict does arise, they diffuse it with various constructive coping mechanisms.

35   Nancy and John, participants in Huston's study, are a shining example of happy, healthy balance. They met in February 1978 and were immediately attracted to each other. John said Nancy was "fun to be with" and he

"could take her anywhere." Nancy said John always complimented her and liked to do things she enjoyed, things "other guys wouldn't do."

During their courtship, they spent a lot of time together, going to dances at their high school and hanging out with friends. They became comfortable with each other and began to openly disclose their opinions and feelings, realizing they had a lot in common and enjoyed each other's company.

John paid many surprise visits to Nancy and bought her a number of gifts. Toward the end of the summer, John gave Nancy a charm necklace with a "genuine diamond." She recalls his saying: "This isn't your ring, honey, but you're going to get one." And she did. The two married on Jan. 17, 1981, nearly three years after they began dating.

The prognosis for this relationship is good. Nancy and John have a solid foundation of love and affection, built on honesty and intimacy. A three-year courtship enabled them to paint realistic portraits of one another.

In 1994, when they were last interviewed, Nancy and John were highly satisfied with their marriage. They were very compatible, disagreeing only about politics. Both felt they strongly benefited from the marriage and said they had no desire to leave.

When the seminar ends, I can't get to a pay phone fast enough. After two rings, the phone is answered. He's there, of course. Dependable. Predictable. That's one of the things that first set my husband apart. At the close of one date, he'd lock in the next. "Can I see you tomorrow for lunch?"

"Will you have dinner with me next week?"

Unlike the fantasy-quality of my first marriage, I felt a deep sense of comfort and companionship with him, and did not harbor outrageous expectations. We exchanged vows 3 1/2 years later, in August, 1998.

There at the convention center, I try to tell my husband about Huston's study, about the critical first few years, about "enduring dynamics," it all comes out in a jumble.

"You're saying we have a good marriage, that we're not going to get divorced?" he asks.

"Yes," I say breathlessly, relieved of the burden of explanation.

"Well I'm glad to hear that," he says, "but I wasn't really worried."

Sometimes I wonder: Knowing what I know now, could I have saved my first marriage? Probably not. Huston's research suggests that the harbingers of disaster were present even before my wedding day.

And he blames our culture. Unlike many other world cultures, he says Western society makes marriage the key adult relationship, which puts pressure on people to marry. "People feel they have to find a way to get there and one way is to force it, even if it only works for the time being," he says.

Our culture is also to blame, Huston says, for perpetuating the myth of storybook romance, which is more likely to doom a marriage than strengthen it. He has few kind words for Hollywood, which brings us unrealistic passion.

50   So if your new romance starts to resemble a movie script, try to remember: The audience never sees what happens after the credits roll.
Are you headed for bliss or a bust-up?

● Review Questions

1. What was the purpose of the PAIR project? Who were its subjects, and what procedures did investigators use? What were the chief conclusions?

2. What is the critical period in a marriage that tends to determine whether the marriage will endure or will end in divorce?

3. How do the findings of Huston's study suggest a need to shift focus in marital counseling?

4. What is the "enduring dynamics" model of marriage?

● Discussion and Writing Suggestions

1. Do the results of Ted Huston's study surprise you? To what extent did his findings contradict your expectations of what causes marriages to succeed or fail? In what ways do some of the marriages with which you are familiar support or rebut the conclusions of the study?

2. Huston's study was based on a study of 168 couples from "a rural and working-class area of Pennsylvania." Based on your own observations and knowledge, do you have any reason to believe that the results of the study would have been significantly different had the study been conducted with a different demographic—say, using professional couples from Chicago or from the suburbs of New York City? Explain.

3. Does the story of Suzie and Peter seem a familiar one? Describe one or two couples you know (changing the names and disguising their relationship to you) who fit the pattern indicated by Suzie and Peter. To what extent do Huston's findings allow you to better understand the factors at work in the marriage(s) you describe?

4. For generations, novelists and filmmakers have entertained and enthralled us with stories that end with the wedding, or the prospect of a wedding, between a happy couple. But as Patz observes, "[t]he audience never sees what happens after the credits roll." Drawing upon the results of Huston's study, imagine the life of a well-known fictional couple that follows their wedding day. Categorize the state of their marriage using Huston's template: "married and happy; married and unhappy; divorced early, within seven years; or divorced later, after seven years." Trace the developments of this marital state to factors that may have been apparent in the

premarital relationship. An example: Do you detect anything in the personal qualities or background of Romeo or Juliet that might have spelled
trouble for the marriage, had these characters actually lived to marry?

5. According to Patz, Huston blames our culture for creating conditions
that work against marital success. Apart from Hollywood, which aspects
of contemporary culture do you believe tend to pressure people to marry
before they may be ready or foster unrealistic expectations about life after
the wedding? Provide specific examples from your own knowledge or
observation.

SYNTHESIS ACTIVITIES

1. Write an explanatory synthesis focused on the development of the
"love match" model of marriage. Why did it emerge? When? How
does it differ from previous models? Explain the effect of the rise of
the "love match" model on the institution of marriage as a whole.
Focus particularly on the effect this model has had on people's
expectations of marriage and on who should get married. For your
sources, draw upon Coontz, Sullivan, Edelman, Bartels, and Patz.
An option: As part of an extended conclusion that might be as long
as a third of the final paper, explore the role you expect (hope?) love
to play in your own marriage. So that your conclusion remains a
part of the overall synthesis, let your exploration emerge from your
awareness of the historical determinants of the love match. You
now know that there have been other models for marriage—the
"economic" match, for instance, the "institutional" match, or the
"compatibility" match. As you contemplate your own (prospective)
marriage, to what extent will you insist on a love match?

2. Explain the working mother versus stay-at-home mother debate.
Focus in particular on the struggles women face as they try to
balance the concerns of work versus family. You may also wish to
touch upon the issue of housework, as the two issues sometimes
overlap. Because this is an *explanatory* synthesis, make sure that
your explanation of the varying viewpoints remains objective.
Draw primarily upon the selections by Hekker, Tannen, and
Edelman (as well as Bartels, if you find it relevant).

3. Argue that one parent should—or should not—stop working (at
least for a time) when children are born. In formulating your argument, be sure to acknowledge the various arguments on all sides of
the issue. Then assert which course of action, overall, would best
benefit American families. Draw upon as many of the articles in
this chapter as will support your case.

4. Devise a blueprint for contemporary wives and husbands to avoid (or at least effectively address) common marital conflicts. First explain elements of your blueprint and then argue for its viability. For example, first explain how best to take care of the children when both parents must work or prefer to work. Then argue that your plan is reasonable. You could do the same for devising a fair division of household labor. In developing this combination explanatory/argument synthesis, consult such sources as Coontz, Edelman, and Bartels.

5. To what extent is it a good idea for young people to delay getting married until their late twenties or beyond? In supporting your argument for earlier or later marriage, draw upon such sources as Edelman and Bartels.

6. Compare and contrast Terry Martin Hekker's first essay, on the satisfactions of being a stay-at-home mother, with the selection by Edelman. How does each of these women feel about her married and family lives? As points of comparison and contrast, consider their attitudes toward housework, their children, their husbands, and their desire for self-fulfillment. In writing your conclusion, consider what factors might have been responsible for these women's differing views on these matters.

7. Analyze a marital relationship—real or fictional—using one or more of the principles in articles from the chapter. (If you have read any Jane Austen novels or Leo Tolstoy's *Anna Karenina* or Gustave Flaubert's *Madame Bovary*, you may wish to use the marriages of characters in those books.) Focus on how the principle you have chosen allows one to better understand the relationship in question. Follow the general format for writing analyses discussed in Chapter 4.

8. Compare and contrast Andrew Sullivan's and William J. Bennett's arguments on gay marriage. In particular, focus on the assumptions regarding the nature of marriage that each brings to his argument. (You may want to consider how Sullivan's argument follows from a principle found in the selection by Coontz.)

9. Discuss whether or not, as Eric Bartels writes, "marriage is a creaky, old institution that may not have fully adapted itself to modern life." In supporting your argument, draw upon Coontz, Hekker, Edelman, Bartels, and any of the other selections you think relevant. Follow the "Guidelines for Writing Syntheses," pp. 60–61 in Chapter 3.

10. Conduct an analysis of a bridal or newlywed magazine, movie, or television show, guided by a principle you select from one or more selections in this chapter. Use this analytical principle to understand

more clearly how popular culture, as expressed in the magazine, movie, or television show you have selected, helps to form, reinforce, or (perhaps) undermine our expectations of marriage. Follow the "Guidelines for Writing Analyses," p. 124.

11. Offer—and explain—the one piece of advice that you would give to someone who is about to get married. In supporting your argument that this is the single most important advice that anybody who is getting married should follow, draw from among the following selections: Coontz, Hekker, Edelman, Bartels, and Patz.

RESEARCH ACTIVITIES

1. Do an Internet search, using Google, Bing, or another search engine, for reaction to the Terry Martin Hekker 2006 essay "Paradise Lost (Domestic Division)." Locate mentions of the piece on blogs (try sites dealing with the "Mommy Wars," working mothers, or stay-at-home mothers), in letters to the editor of the *New York Times,* and in op-ed pieces; then, synthesize some of the responses that Hekker's essay inspired.

2. Find and report on additional articles dealing with the "Mommy Wars"—the dispute over whether mothers should stay at home to take care of the children or whether they should pursue careers, leaving their children with other caregivers. To what extent has the controversy evolved over the past few years? To what extent does a critical consensus appear to be forming—perhaps by feminists, perhaps by traditionalists—over what young mothers should do? Write a synthesis explaining your findings and, perhaps, arguing your own position.

3. What is the state of gay marriage in the United States today? How many states, for example, allow gay marriage? Prohibit gay marriage? How many recognize civil unions? What has been the position of the federal government over the past fifteen years? What kinds of state and federal legislation have been passed (or debated) in recent years, and what kinds of decisions have been made by state and federal courts in response? What do recent polls about the subject reveal? Based on your findings, do you believe that the social and political climate for gay marriage is improving or deteriorating?

4. Research arranged marriages—either in an ethnic subculture in the United States or in a foreign country. On the whole, how happy do people report being in these marriages? Provide statistical and/or anecdotal evidence concerning this rate of satisfaction. Compare this

rate with that of people in nonarranged marriages, preferably in that same culture—or, if that information is not available, compare it with the rate of marital satisfaction in our country, as reported by sources such as the National Marriage Project (http://marriage .rutgers.edu/). If you know people who have been in an arranged marriage, ask for their views on the subject.

5. The prenuptial agreement has become a common feature of marriages where at least one partner has significant assets. Research and write an overview of prenuptial contracts (including, if possible, some of the more notorious lawsuits they have engendered). Search, in particular, for pieces that express an opinion regarding their use (op-ed pieces, magazine articles, letters to the editor). You may also wish to conduct an informal poll among your friends as to whether they approve of their use; whether they might insist, before their own marriage, on a prenuptial contract; etc. Report on your findings.

6. Investigate the effect that no-fault divorce laws have had on marriage in this country. Write a synthesis summarizing the circumstances under which the states passed such laws, the effect of these laws on the national divorce rate, and a brief overview of the controversy over the laws and their effect on the institution of marriage.

7. President John Adams and First Lady Abigail Adams had one of the more famous marriages in the history of the presidency. Abigail Adams's letters to her husband, in which she counseled him on matters public and private and in which she was an early advocate for women's issues, are still widely read, and in part form the lyrics for the Broadway musical *1776*. Research John and Abigail Adams's marriage. In which ways was it typical of its time and place? In which ways was it atypical—i.e., in which ways did it seem more like a modern marriage?

8. The 1950s are often considered the "Golden Age" of marriage. When conservative commentators evoke the "good old days" of marriage, it is almost always the 1950s model they have in mind—a father with a good job, a mother who stays home and raises the children, a house in the suburbs, and an extended family that is usually located in another town or even state. Such marriages were the basis of popular contemporary 1950s sitcoms like *Father Knows Best* and *Ozzie and Harriet*, and they were also satirized in the 1998 film *Pleasantville*.

   Research the realities of marriage in the 1950s. (Stephanie Coontz has written extensively on this subject.) To what extent is the stereotype accurate? Was there a "dark side" to marriage in the 1950s? Consider the political, economic, and cultural climate of the 1950s. What effect did these factors have on marriages of the day?

9. Research the issue of day care in this country. Locate studies that have shown positive or negative consequences to putting kids in day care. Draw also upon op-ed pieces, articles, sections in books, or personal opinions you have discovered (for example, on blogs concerning motherhood, working mothers, or stay-at-home mothers), and write a synthesis reporting on your findings.

10. Sociologist Andrew Cherlin has noted how weddings, once events controlled by kinship groups or parents, are now increasingly controlled by the couples themselves. One result is that the wedding has become a status symbol—"an important symbol of the partners' personal achievements and a stage in their self-development." Research the wedding industry in this country, which generates over $60 billion annually. On what is all this money being spent? What kinds of services are most popular among clients—and why? Where are people getting married? Examine a bridal magazine. What do you think the industry is *really* selling? Try to find quotations from wedding industry professionals on this topic.

11. Leslie Bennetts writes: "Compared with other Western nations, the family-related policies of the United States are a disgrace." Research some of the policies relating to families—ranging "from flexible work schedules to affordable quality child care"—in one or more other Western countries, such as Canada, the United Kingdom, France, or Sweden.

Chapter 8

To Sleep

Every night nearly every person on the planet undergoes an astounding metamorphosis. As the sun sets, a delicate timing device at the base of our brain sends a chemical signal throughout our body, and the gradual slide toward sleep begins. Our body becomes inert, and our lidded eyes roll slowly from side to side. Later, the eyes begin the rapid eye movements that accompany dreams, and our mind enters a highly active state where vivid dreams trace our deepest emotions. Throughout the night we traverse a broad landscape of dreaming and nondreaming realms, wholly unaware of the world outside. Hours later, as the sun rises, we are transported back to our bodies and to waking consciousness.

And we remember almost nothing.

So begins *The Promise of Sleep* by researcher and sleep pioneer William Dement, who for fifty years has investigated what happens each night after we close our eyes. Later in this chapter you will hear more from Dement, but for the moment, let his sense of wonder spark your own interest in sleep, a behavior that will occupy one-third of your life.

Not until 1929 did Johannes Berger use a new device called the electroencephalogram (EEG) to confirm that, far from shutting down while asleep, our brains remain highly active. With the insight that sleep is not merely the absence of wakefulness, and the subsequent discovery that each night's sleep unfolds in five classifiable stages, sleep research accelerated in the twentieth century. Yet for thousands of years sleep (and its frustrating absence) has sparked the inquiries of physicians, scientists, and philosophers. As early as 1300 BCE, the Egyptians used opium as a medication to treat insomnia. Nearly a thousand years later, Aristotle framed his inquiry into sleep with questions that occupy us still:

> With regard to sleep and waking, we must consider what they are: whether they are peculiar to soul or to body, or

common to both; and if common, to what part of soul or body they appertain: further, from what cause it arises that they are attributes of animals, and whether all animals share in them both....

On Sleep and Sleeplessness

Allowing for the fact that modern sleep researchers do not investigate the "soul," per se, they nevertheless retain a high level of interest in the nature of consciousness and what happens to it when we sleep. The ancients thought of sleep as a daily, metaphorical death. If sleep is not a death, then what precisely *is* it? Does sleep repair the body? Does it consolidate the day's learning? Is it a strategy for keeping the sleeper safe? Does it aid in development and maintenance of the central nervous system? Researchers have investigated each of these questions but have found no definitive answers. Theoretical explanations of sleep aside, at the clinical level specialists cannot yet remedy all eighty-four known sleep disorders, which rob sufferers of needed rest and keep them, according to the famous insomniac poet and critic Samuel Taylor Coleridge, in "anguish and in agony." The investigations, therefore, continue.

Up to forty million Americans suffer from sleep disruptions that for some trigger serious health risks, including cardiovascular disease, obesity, and depression. Sleep loss leads to measurable cognitive and physical deficits comparable to those observed in people impaired by alcohol. The sleep that we *don't* get each day adds up to a cumulative debt that we must "repay" in order to function at full capacity, say sleep specialists. Failure to sleep enough (eight hours is the norm, though individual requirements vary) leads to quantifiable costs:

- Americans spend $15 billion per year in direct health care costs related to problems with sleeping.

- The U.S. economy loses $50 billion per year in diminished productivity due to problems with sleeping.

- The National Highway Traffic and Safety Administration estimates that sleep-deprived drivers cause 100,000 accidents each year, resulting in 1,500 fatalities and 71,000 injuries.

The literature of sleep research is vast. Investigators study the sleep of insects, fish, amphibians, birds, and mammals (including humans) with the tools of biology, neurology, chemistry, psychology, and a host of other disciplines. This chapter brings the study of sleep to a focus very close to home for readers of this book: the sleep of adolescents, one of the many subspecialties of sleep medicine. You may know that the sleep of infants and toddlers merits special attention from specialists since, when children don't sleep well, few others in the home do, either. And you may be aware that the sleep of older people, which can grow troubled due to both physiological and psychological changes, has been the subject of intense study. An equally active area among researchers is the sleep of ten- to nineteen-year-olds, who require one hour more of sleep each night (due to rapidly maturing bodies) than do adults or children who no longer nap—and this at a time in life when the scheduling demands of school and work tend to decrease the amount of sleep available to adolescents.

If you find yourself at the threshold of late adolescence and early adulthood, or are otherwise connected to an adolescent who is a sibling or friend, you will discover much of interest in this chapter on the "strange state" of sleep. We begin with an overview of the subject, "A Third of Life" by Paul Martin, in which you will learn (among other things) that "[s]leep is observed in animals of every sort, including insects, molluscs, fish, amphibians, birds, and mammals." "Improving Sleep," edited by Lawrence Epstein, MD, reviews the fundamentals of sleep medicine, including REM (rapid eye movement) and non-REM sleep. We move next to a news release on the troubled state of adolescent sleep, based on a poll conducted by the National Sleep Foundation. William C. Dement and Christopher Vaughan follow with "Sleep Debt and the Mortgaged Mind," an inquiry into what happens to a body deprived of sleep.

So that you can assess the current state of your own sleep, we offer the Pittsburgh Sleep Quality Index, a self-scoring assessment used in many sleep studies. Use the PSQI to rate your sleep along seven dimensions and determine your overall sleep score. In "How Sleep Debt Hurts College Students," June J. Pilcher and Amy S. Walters deprive students of a night's sleep and test their cognitive functioning the next day. (The news is not good for those who pull "all-nighters.")

The National Institutes of Health distributes $200 million a year for sleep research, with some of that money reserved for new curricula that alert science students to the importance of good sleep hygiene. In effect, this chapter offers such a curriculum. In reading the selections that follow, not only will you gain an opportunity to practice the skills of summary, synthesis, critique, and analysis; you will also gain information that can help you feel and function better in your daily life.

A THIRD OF LIFE

Paul Martin

In our chapter opening, Paul Martin, who holds a PhD in behavioral biology from Cambridge University, provides an overview of sleep and its place in both human and animal evolution. Martin introduces the concept of sleep debt and its consequences—a principal focus of this chapter—and then reviews the behavioral characteristics of sleep. The present selection is taken from the first chapter of Martin's *Counting Sheep: The Science and Pleasures of Sleep and Dreams* (2002).

> Almost all other animals are observed to partake of sleep, aquatic, winged, and terrestrial creatures alike. For every kind of fish and the soft-shelled species have been seen sleeping, as has every other creature that has eyes.
>
> Aristotle (384–322 B.C.), *On Sleep and Waking*

Sleep is a universal human characteristic, like eating and drinking. Absolutely everybody does it. Sleep occupies about one third of each human life, and up to two thirds of a baby's time. (According to Groucho Marx, the proportion rises to three thirds if you live in Peoria.) It is a common bond that ties us all together. We have no choice: the longer we go without sleep, the stronger our desire for it grows. Tiredness, like hunger and thirst, will eventually force us to do the right thing whether we want to or not.

The dreams that accompany sleep are equally ubiquitous features of human life, even if many of us retain little memory of them after we awake. Dreaming is a classless activity that unites monarchs and paupers, a thought that Charles Dickens mused upon in one of his essays:

> Here, for example, is her Majesty Queen Victoria in her palace, this present blessed night, and here is Winking Charley, a sturdy vagrant, in one of her Majesty's jails...It is probable that we have all three committed murders and hidden bodies. It is pretty certain that we have all desperately wanted to cry out, and have had no voice; that we have all gone to the play and not been able to get in; that we have all dreamed much more of our youth than of our later lives.

Sleep is not a specifically human trait, of course. On the contrary, it is a universal characteristic of complex living organisms, as Aristotle deduced more than 23 centuries ago. Sleep is observed in animals of every sort, including insects, molluscs, fish, amphibians, birds and mammals. Within the animal world, sleep does vary enormously in quantity, quality and timing, accounting for anything up to 80 per cent of some animals' lifespans. But they all do it, one way or another. Some species, especially predators, spend more of their lives asleep than they do awake, a fact that TV documentaries and natural-history books seldom mention.

How do we know that an animal is sleeping? It is hard enough sometimes to be sure that a human is asleep, let alone a fish or a fly. The ultimate indicator of whether an animal or person is asleep is the distinctive pattern of electrical activity in its brain. During deep sleep the billions of individual nerve cells in the brain synchronise their electrical activity to some extent, generating characteristic waves of tiny voltage changes that can be detected by electrodes placed on the scalp. We shall be exploring the nature and internal structure of sleep later. The easiest way to recognise sleep, however, is from overt behaviour.

Sleep has several rather obvious distinguishing characteristics. A sleeping person or animal will generally remain in the same place for a prolonged period, perhaps several hours. There will be a certain amount of twitching, shifting of posture and fidgeting. Young animals will suckle while they sleep and ruminants will carry on chewing the cud. But sleepers normally do not get up and change their location. (When they do, we recognise it as a curious phenomenon and call it sleepwalking.)

Sleeping organisms also adopt a characteristic posture. Sloths and bats, for example, sleep hanging upside down from a branch. The Mediterranean flour moth sleeps with its antennae swivelled backwards and the tips tucked under its wings. If you are careful, you can gently lift the sleeping moth's wing without disturbing it—a trick that will definitely not work when it is awake. A lizard will settle on a branch during the hours before sunset, curl up its tail, close its eyelids, retract its eyeballs and remain in that distinctly sleep-like posture all night unless it is disturbed. A partridge, like many birds, will rest its weight on one leg while it sleeps. It is said that some gourmets can tell *which* leg, from its taste.

Monkeys and apes, including humans, usually sleep lying down. Indeed, we are built in such a way that we find it difficult to sleep properly unless we are lying down. People can and sometimes do sleep after a fashion while sitting, notably in aeroplanes, business meetings and school classrooms. If you are really exhausted, you might even manage to snatch some sleep standing up. But sleep taken while standing or sitting upright is generally fitful, shallow and unrefreshing. The non-horizontal sleeper may repeatedly nod off, but as soon as they descend beyond the shallowest stages of sleep their muscles relax, they begin to sway and their brain wakes them up again. That is why we 'nod off'. If you travel frequently on trains or buses, you might have had the dubious pleasure of sitting next to a weary commuter who has nodded off all over your shoulder. Recordings of brain-wave patterns show that people sleeping in an upright sitting position achieve only the initial stages of light sleep, not the sustained, deep sleep we require to wake up feeling truly refreshed. The reason is simple. Our muscles relax when we are fully asleep and we would fall over if we were not already lying down. Our brains therefore do not permit us to enter sustained, deep sleep unless we are in a physically stable, horizontal (or near-horizontal) posture.

10   Despite the virtual impossibility of sleeping deeply while sitting upright, we are sometimes forced to try. In *Down and Out in Paris and London,* George Orwell describes a particularly unwelcoming form of overnight accommodation that was known to the homeless of prewar London as the Twopenny Hangover. At the Twopenny Hangover the night's residents would sit in a row along a bench. In front of them was a rope, and the would-be sleepers would lean on this rope as though leaning over a fence. In that posture they were supposed to sleep. At five o'clock the next morning an official, wittily known as the valet, would cut the rope so that the residents could begin another day of wandering the streets.

Nowadays, tourist-class airline passengers travelling long distances can enjoy an experience similar to the Twopenny Hangover, albeit at vastly greater expense. George Orwell's autobiographical account of grinding poverty in the late 1920s is also a sharp reminder that lack of money is often accompanied by lack of decent sleep. Rough sleepers rarely get a good night's sleep.

Sleep has several other distinctive characteristics besides immobility and posture. In many species, including humans, individuals return to the same place each night (or each day, if they are nocturnal) in order to sleep. More generally, all members of a given species will tend to choose the same sorts of sleeping places. The distinctive feature of those places is often their security. Birds usually sleep on inaccessible branches or ledges. Many small mammals sleep in underground burrows where they are safer from predators. Fishes lie on the bottom, or wedge themselves into a crevice or against the underside of a rock. We humans prefer to sleep in relatively private and secure places. Given the choice, we rarely opt to sleep on busy streets or in crowded restaurants.

One obvious feature of sleep is a marked reduction in responsiveness to sights, sounds and other sensory stimuli. To provoke a response from a sleeping organism, stimuli have to be more intense or more relevant to the individual. For example, the reef fish known as the slippery dick sleeps during the hours of darkness, partly buried in the sand. While it is in this state, the sleeping slippery dick can be gently lifted to the surface by hand without it waking up and swimming off.

A sort of perceptual wall is erected during sleep, insulating the mind from the outside world. You would still be able to sleep if you had no eyelids, because your sleeping brain would not register what your eyes could see. This sensory isolation is highly selective, however. You can sleep through relatively loud noises from traffic or a radio, but a quiet mention of your name can rouse you immediately. Your brain is not simply blocked off during sleep. Moreover, this reduced responsiveness is rapidly reversible— a characteristic that distinguishes sleep from states such as unconsciousness, coma, anaesthesia and hibernation. A suitable stimulus, particularly one signifying immediate danger, can snap a sleeping person into staring-eyed alertness in an instant.

Another diagnostic feature of sleep is its regular cycle of waxing and waning. Living organisms sleep and wake according to a regular 24-hour cycle, or circadian rhythm. All members of a given species tend to sleep during the same part of the 24-hour cycle, when their environment is least favourable for other activities such as looking for food. For most species this means sleeping during the hours of darkness, but some species do the reverse. Many small mammals, which would be more vulnerable to predators during daylight, sleep by day and forage at night. Aside from a few nocturnal specialists such as owls, birds cannot easily fly in the dark, and most reptiles find it hard to maintain a sufficiently high body temperature to be active during the cool of night. Most birds and reptiles therefore sleep at night. Predators tend to sleep when their prey are asleep and hunt when their prey are up and about.

Sleep, then, is characterised by a special sleeping place and posture, prolonged immobility, a selective and rapidly reversible reduction in responsiveness to stimuli, and a 24-hour cycle. According to these and other criteria, all mammals, birds, fish, amphibians, reptiles and insects that have been inspected have been found to sleep.

Review Questions

1. What are the distinguishing characteristics of sleep, and which species have been observed to sleep?

2. Why is it difficult for humans to sleep properly without lying down?

Discussion and Writing Suggestions

1. Before reading Martin's article, to what extent did you consider sleep a "behavior"? How did you think of it, if not as a behavior? Explain.

2. What accounts for the relatively scant attention sleep has received in popular culture?

3. What single observation about sleep stands out for you from this article? Explain your fascination.

*IMPROVING SLEEP**

Lawrence Epstein, MD, Editor

Of the hundreds of introductions to the physiology of sleep, this selection appearing in a *Harvard Special Health Report* edited by Lawrence Epstein, MD, is among the clearest for audiences without a formal background in medicine. We excerpt the opening sections of the larger report.

Some nights, sleep comes easily, and you sail through the night in a satisfying slumber. Waking up after a night of good sleep feels wonderful—you're refreshed, energized, and ready to take on the world. Other nights, sleep comes slowly or not until the wee hours. Or you may fall asleep, only to awaken throughout the night.

If you have trouble sleeping, you're not alone. Almost everyone occasionally suffers from short-term insomnia. According to the National Institutes of Health, about 60 million Americans a year have insomnia frequently or for extended periods of time. About half of all people over 65 have frequent sleeping problems, and an estimated 40 million Americans have a chronic sleep disorder such as sleep apnea, restless legs syndrome, or narcolepsy. We pay a high price for all the sleep deprivation caused by sleep problems. For example:

- Insufficient sleep is directly linked to poor health, with new research suggesting it increases the risk of diabetes, heart disease, obesity, and even premature death. Even a few nights of bad sleep can be detrimental.

- The combination of sleep deprivation and driving can have deadly consequences. A 2006 review by the Institute of Medicine of the National Academy of Sciences found that almost 20% of all serious car accidents and 57% of fatal accidents are associated with driver sleepiness.

- Sleep deprivation played a role in catastrophes such as the Exxon Valdez oil spill off the coast of Alaska, the space shuttle Challenger explosion, and the nuclear accident at Three Mile Island.

Sleep problems affect virtually every aspect of day-to-day living, including mood, mental alertness, work performance, and energy level. Yet few Americans seek treatment for their sleep problems. If you aren't getting your share of sleep, you needn't fumble about in a fog of fatigue. This report describes the complex nature of sleep, the latest in sleep research, the factors that can disturb sleep, and, most importantly, what you can do to get the sleep you need for optimal health, safety, and well-being.

Sleep Mechanics

For centuries, scientists scrutinized minute aspects of human activity, but showed little interest in the time that people spent in sleep. Sleep seemed inaccessible to medical probing and was perceived as an unvarying period of inactivity—a subject best suited to poets and dream interpreters who could conjure meaning out of the void. All that changed in the 1930s, when scientists learned to place sensitive electrodes on the scalp and record the signals produced by electrical activity in the brain. These brain waves can be seen on an electroencephalogram, or EEG (see Figure 8.1), which today is captured on a computer screen. Since then, researchers gradually came to appreciate that sleep is a highly complex activity. Using electrodes to monitor sleepers' eye movements, muscle tone, and brain wave patterns, they identified several discrete stages of sleep. And today, researchers continue to learn how certain stages of sleep help to maintain health, growth, and functioning.

Scientists divide sleep into two major types: rapid eye movement (REM) sleep or dreaming sleep, and non-REM or quiet sleep. Surprisingly, they are as different from one another as sleeping is from waking.

Quiet Sleep   Sleep specialists have called non-REM or quiet sleep "an idling brain in a movable body." During this phase, thinking and most physiological activities slow down, but movement can still occur, and a person often shifts position while sinking into progressively deeper stages of sleep.

To an extent, the convention of describing people "dropping" into sleep actually parallels changes in brain wave patterns at the onset of non-REM sleep. When you are awake, billions of brain cells receive and analyze sensory information, coordinate behavior, and maintain bodily functions by sending electrical impulses to one another. If you're fully awake, the EEG will record a messy, irregular scribble of activity. Once your eyes are closed and your nerve cells no longer receive visual input, brain waves settle into a

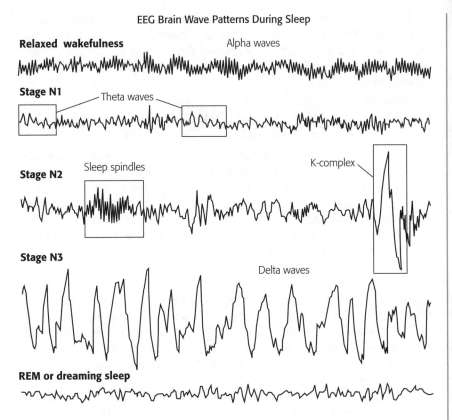

EEG Brain Wave Patterns During Sleep

Relaxed wakefulness   Alpha waves

Stage N1   — Theta waves —

Stage N2   Sleep spindles   K-complex

Stage N3   Delta waves

REM or dreaming sleep

Figure 8.1   These brain waves, taken by electroencephalogram, are used by sleep experts to identify the stages of sleep. Close your eyes and your brain waves will look like the first band, "relaxed wakefulness." Theta waves indicate Stage N1 sleep. (The "N" designates non-REM sleep.) Stage N2 sleep shows brief bursts of activity as sleep spindles and K-complex waves. Deep sleep is represented by large, slow delta waves (Stage N3).

steady and rhythmic pattern of about 10 cycles per second. This is the alpha-wave pattern, characteristic of calm, relaxed wakefulness.

The transition to quiet sleep is a quick one that might be likened to flipping a switch—that is, you are either awake (switch on) or asleep (switch off), according to recent research. Some brain centers and pathways stimulate the entire brain to wakefulness; others promote falling asleep. One chemical, hypocretin, seems to play an important role in regulating when the flip between states occurs and keeping you in the new state. Interestingly, people with narcolepsy often lack hypocretin, and they consequently flip back and forth between sleep and wakefulness frequently.

Three Stages of Quiet Sleep   Unless something disturbs the process, you will soon proceed smoothly through the three stages of quiet sleep.

STAGE N1.   In making the transition from wakefulness into light sleep, you spend about five minutes in Stage N1 sleep. On the EEG, the predominant brain waves slow to four to seven cycles per second, a pattern called theta waves. Body temperature begins to drop, muscles relax, and eyes often move slowly from side to side. People in Stage N1 sleep lose awareness of their surroundings, but they are easily jarred awake. However, not everyone experiences Stage N1 sleep in the same way: If awakened, one person might recall being drowsy, while another might describe having been asleep.

STAGE N2.   This first stage of true sleep lasts 10 to 25 minutes. Your eyes are still, and your heart rate and breathing are slower than when awake. Your brain's electrical activity is irregular. Large, slow waves intermingle with brief bursts of activity called sleep spindles, when brain waves speed up for roughly half a second or longer. About every two minutes, EEG tracings show a pattern called a K-complex, which scientists think represents a sort of built-in vigilance system that keeps you poised to awaken if necessary. K-complexes can also be provoked by certain sounds or other external or internal stimuli. Whisper someone's name during Stage N2 sleep, and a K-complex will appear on the EEG. You spend about half the night in Stage N2 sleep, which leaves you moderately refreshed.

STAGE N3.   Eventually, large slow brain waves called delta waves become a major feature on the EEG. This is Stage N3, known as deep sleep or slow-wave sleep. During this stage, breathing becomes more regular. Blood pressure falls, and pulse rate slows to about 20% to 30% below the waking rate. The brain becomes less responsive to external stimuli, making it difficult to wake the sleeper.

Slow-wave sleep seems to be a time for your body to renew and repair itself. Blood flow is directed less toward your brain, which cools measurably. At the beginning of this stage, the pituitary gland releases a pulse of growth hormone that stimulates tissue growth and muscle repair. Researchers have also detected increased blood levels of substances that activate your immune system, raising the possibility that slow-wave sleep helps the body defend itself against infection.

Normally, young people spend about 20% of their sleep time in stretches of slow-wave sleep lasting up to half an hour, but slow-wave sleep is nearly absent in most people over age 65. Someone whose slow-wave sleep is restricted will wake up feeling unrefreshed, no matter how long he or she has been in bed. When a sleep-deprived person gets some sleep, he or she will pass quickly through the lighter sleep stages into the deeper stages and spend a greater proportion of sleep time there, suggesting that slow-wave sleep fills an essential need.

Dreaming (REM) Sleep   Dreaming occurs during REM sleep, which has been described as an "active brain in a paralyzed body." Your brain races, thinking and dreaming, as your eyes dart back and forth rapidly behind closed lids. Your body temperature rises. Your blood pressure increases, and your heart rate and breathing speed up to daytime levels. The sympathetic nervous system, which creates the fight-or-flight response, is twice as active as when you're awake. Despite all this activity, your body hardly moves, except for intermittent twitches; muscles not needed for breathing or eye movement are quiet.

Just as slow-wave sleep restores your body, scientists believe that REM or dreaming sleep restores your mind, perhaps in part by helping clear out irrelevant information. Recent studies of students' ability to solve a complex puzzle involving abstract shapes suggest the brain processes information overnight; students who got a good night's sleep after seeing the puzzle fared much better than those asked to solve the puzzle immediately. Earlier studies found that REM sleep facilitates learning and memory. People tested to measure how well they had learned a new task improved their scores after a night's sleep. If they were roused from REM sleep, the improvements were lost. On the other hand, if they were awakened an equal number of times from slow-wave sleep, the improvements in the scores were unaffected. These findings may help explain why students who stay up all night cramming for an examination generally retain less information than classmates who get some sleep.

About three to five times a night, or about every 90 minutes, a sleeper enters REM sleep. The first such episode usually lasts only for a few minutes, but REM time increases progressively over the course of the night. The final period of REM sleep may last a half-hour. Altogether, REM sleep makes up about 25% of total sleep in young adults. If someone who has been deprived of REM sleep is left undisturbed for a night, he or she enters this stage earlier and spends a higher proportion of sleep time in it—a phenomenon called REM rebound.

Sleep Architecture   During the night, a normal sleeper moves between different sleep stages in a fairly predictable pattern, alternating between REM and non-REM sleep. When these stages are charted on a diagram, called a hypnogram (see Figure 8.2), the different levels resemble a drawing of a city skyline. Sleep experts call this pattern sleep architecture.

In a young adult, normal sleep architecture usually consists of four or five alternating non-REM and REM periods. Most deep sleep occurs in the first half of the night. As the night progresses, periods of REM sleep get longer and alternate with Stage N2 sleep. Later in life, the sleep skyline will change, with less Stage N3 sleep, more Stage N1 sleep, and more awakenings.

20 *Your Internal Clock*   Scientists have discovered that certain brain structures and chemicals produce the states of sleeping and waking.

A pacemaker-like mechanism in the brain regulates the circadian rhythm of sleeping and waking. ("Circadian" means "about a day.") This internal clock, which gradually becomes established during the first months of life, controls the daily ups and downs of biological patterns, including body temperature, blood pressure, and the release of hormones.

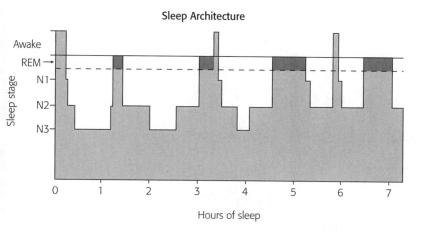

Figure 8.2   When experts chart sleep stages on a hypnogram, the different levels resemble a drawing of a city skyline. This pattern is known as sleep architecture. The hypnogram above shows a typical night's sleep of a healthy young adult.

The circadian rhythm makes people's desire for sleep strongest between midnight and dawn, and to a lesser extent in midafternoon. In one study, researchers instructed a group of people to try to stay awake for 24 hours. Not surprisingly, many slipped into naps despite their best efforts not to. When the investigators plotted the times when the unplanned naps occurred, they found peaks between 2 a.m. and 4 a.m. and between 2 p.m. and 3 p.m.

Most Americans sleep during the night as dictated by their circadian rhythms, although many nap in the afternoon on the weekends. In societies where taking a siesta is the norm, people can respond to their bodies' daily dips in alertness with a one- to two-hour afternoon nap during the workday and a correspondingly shorter sleep at night.

Mechanisms of Your "Sleep Clock"   In the 1970s, studies in rats identified the suprachiasmatic nucleus as the location of the internal clock. This cluster of cells is part of the hypothalamus, the brain center that regulates appetite and other biological states (see Figure 8.3). When this tiny area was damaged, the sleep/wake rhythm disappeared and the rats no longer slept on a normal schedule. Although the clock is largely self-regulating, its location allows it to respond to several types of external cues to keep it set at 24 hours. Scientists call these cues "zeitgebers," a German word meaning "time givers."

LIGHT.   Light striking your eyes is the most influential zeitgeber. When researchers invited volunteers into the laboratory and exposed them to light at intervals that were at odds with the outside world, the participants unconsciously reset their biological clocks to match the new light input. The circadian rhythm disturbances and sleep problems that affect up to 90% of blind people demonstrate the importance of light to sleep/wake patterns.

The Sleep Wake Control Center

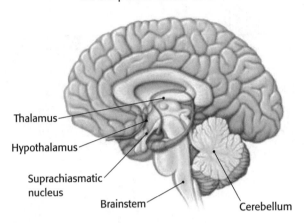

Thalamus

Hypothalamus

Suprachiasmatic
nucleus

Brainstem

Cerebellum

Figure 8.3 The pacemaker-like mechanism in your brain that regulates the circadian rhythm of sleeping and waking is thought to be located in the suprachiasmatic nucleus. This cluster of cells is part of the hypothalamus, the brain center that regulates appetite, body temperature, and other biological states.

TIME. As a person reads clocks, follows work and train schedules, and demands that the body remain alert for certain tasks and social events, there is cognitive pressure to stay on schedule.

MELATONIN. Cells in the suprachiasmatic nucleus contain receptors for melatonin, a hormone produced in a predictable daily rhythm by the pineal gland, which is located deep in the brain between the two hemispheres. Levels of melatonin begin climbing after dark and ebb after dawn. The hormone induces drowsiness in some people, and scientists believe its daily light-sensitive cycles help keep the sleep/wake cycle on track.

Your Clock's Hour Hand As the circadian rhythm counts off the days, another part of the brain acts like the hour hand on a watch. This timekeeper resides in a nugget of nerve cells within the brain stem, the area that controls breathing, blood pressure, and heartbeat. Fluctuating activity in the nerve cells and the chemical messengers they produce seem to coordinate the timing of wakefulness, arousal, and the 90-minute changeover between REM and non-REM sleep.

Several neurotransmitters (brain chemicals that neurons release to communicate with adjacent cells) play a role in arousal. Their actions help explain why medications that mimic or counteract their effects can influence sleep. Adenosine and gamma-aminobutyric acid (GABA) are believed to promote sleep. Acetylcholine regulates REM sleep. Norepinephrine, epinephrine, dopamine, and the recently discovered hypocretin stimulate wakefulness. Individuals vary greatly in their natural levels of neurotransmitters and in their sensitivity to these chemicals.

Review Questions

1. What are the costs of disturbed sleep?

2. Explain why sleep is an active, not a passive, state. In your answer, refer to REM and non-REM sleep.

3. Studies suggest that "students who stay up all night cramming for an examination generally retain less information than classmates who get some sleep." Why?

4. To what does the term "sleep architecture" refer? What pattern does a normal sleeper's sleep architecture follow?

5. What is "circadian rhythm"? For what is it responsible, and what part of the body controls it?

Discussion and Writing Suggestions

1. Study Figure 8.2, "Sleep Architecture." In a paragraph, describe the hypnogram's presentation of "a typical night's sleep of a healthy young adult." Describe transitions through stages of sleep, and REM and non-REM sleep. In a second paragraph, discuss your reactions upon learning of the complex architecture of sleep.

2. Have you ever suffered through a period of disrupted sleep? Describe the experience in two paragraphs—the first written in the first person (the "I" perspective), the second written in the third person (the "he" or "she" perspective). Compare paragraphs. Which do you prefer? Why?

AMERICA'S SLEEP-DEPRIVED TEENS NODDING OFF AT SCHOOL, BEHIND THE WHEEL

National Sleep Foundation

The National Sleep Foundation (NSF), according to its Web site, "is an independent nonprofit organization dedicated to improving public health and safety by achieving understanding of sleep and sleep disorders, and by supporting sleep-related education, research, and advocacy." (See http://www.sleepfoundation.org/.) The NSF periodically issues news releases on studies its member physicians conduct. The following release, dated March 28, 2006, helped focus national attention on the dangers of adolescent sleep debt.

Many of the nation's adolescents are falling asleep in class, arriving late to school, feeling down and driving drowsy because of a lack of sleep that gets worse as they get older, according to a new poll released today by the National Sleep Foundation (NSF).

In a national survey on the sleep patterns of U.S. adolescents (ages 11–17), NSF's 2006 *Sleep in America* poll finds that only 20% of adolescents get the recommended nine hours of sleep on school nights, and nearly one-half (45%) sleep less than eight hours on school nights.

What's more, the poll finds that parents are mostly in the dark about their adolescents' sleep. While most students know they're not getting the sleep they need, 90% of parents polled believe that their adolescent is getting enough sleep at least a few nights during the school week.

The poll indicates that the consequences of insufficient sleep affect nearly every aspect of teenage life. Among the most important findings:

- At least once a week, more than one-quarter (28%) of high school students fall asleep in school, 22% fall asleep doing homework, and 14% arrive late or miss school because they oversleep.

- Adolescents who get insufficient amounts of sleep are more likely than their peers to get lower grades, while 80% of adolescents who get an optimal amount of sleep say they're achieving As and Bs in school.

- More than one-half (51%) of adolescent drivers have driven drowsy during the past year. In fact, 15% of drivers in 10th to 12th grades drive drowsy at least once a week.

- Among those adolescents who report being unhappy, tense and nervous, 73% feel they don't get enough sleep at night and 59% are excessively sleepy during the day.

- More than one-quarter (28%) of adolescents say they're too tired to exercise.

5   The poll also finds that the amount of sleep declines as adolescents get older. The survey classifies nine or more hours a night as an optimal amount of sleep in line with sleep experts' recommendations for this age group, with less than eight hours classified as insufficient. Sixth-graders report they sleep an average of 8.4 hours on school nights, while 12th-graders sleep just 6.9 hours—1.5 hours less than their younger peers and two hours less than recommended. In fact, by the time adolescents become high school seniors, they're missing out on nearly 12 hours (11.7) of needed sleep each week.

"This poll identifies a serious reduction in adolescents' sleep as students transition from middle school to high school. This is particularly troubling as adolescence is a critical period of development and growth—academically, emotionally and physically," says Richard L. Gelula, NSF's chief executive officer. "At a time of heightened concerns about the quality of this next generation's health and education, our nation is ignoring a basic necessity for success in these areas: adequate sleep. We call on parents, educators and teenagers themselves to take an active role in making sleep a priority."

Awareness Gap Between Parents and Teens About Sleep

While nine out of ten parents state their adolescent is getting enough sleep at least a few nights during the school week, more than one-half (56%) of adolescents say they get less sleep than they think they need to feel their best. And, 51% say they feel too tired or sleepy during the day.

Also at issue is the quality of sleep once an adolescent goes to bed. Only 41% of adolescents say they get a good night's sleep every night or most nights. One in 10 teens reports that he/she rarely or never gets a good night's sleep.

Overall, 7% of parents think their adolescent may have a sleep problem, whereas 16% of adolescents think they have or may have one. Many adolescents (31%) who think they have a sleep problem have not told anyone about it.

Everyday Pressures + Nature = Less Sleep

As children reach adolescence, their circadian rhythms—or internal clocks—tend to shift, causing teens to naturally feel more alert later at night and wake up later in the morning. A trick of nature, this "phase delay" can make it difficult for them to fall asleep before 11:00 p.m.; more than one-half (54%) of high school seniors go to bed at 11:00 p.m. or later on school nights. However, the survey finds that on a typical school day, adolescents wake up around 6:30 a.m. in order to go to school, leaving many without the sleep they need.

"In the competition between the natural tendency to stay up late and early school start times, a teen's sleep is what loses out," notes Jodi A. Mindell, PhD, co-chair of the poll task force and an NSF vice chair. "Sending students to school without enough sleep is like sending them to school without breakfast. Sleep serves not only a restorative function for adolescents' bodies and brains, but it is also a key time when they process what they've learned during the day." Dr. Mindell is the director of the Graduate Program in Psychology at Saint Joseph's University and associate director of the Sleep Center at The Children's Hospital of Philadelphia.

It is also important for teens, like all people, to maintain a consistent sleep schedule across the entire week. Poll respondents overwhelmingly go to bed and get up later and sleep longer on non-school nights. However, teens rarely make up for the sleep that they lose during the school week. Overall, adolescents get an average of 8.9 hours of sleep on a non-school night, about equal to the optimal amount recommended per night. Again, the poll finds this amount trends downward as adolescents get older.

Survey results also show that sleepy adolescents are more likely to rely on naps, which sleep experts point out should not be a substitute for, but rather complement, a good night's sleep. About one-third (31%) of adolescents take naps regularly, and these nappers are more likely than non-nappers to say they feel cranky or irritable, too tired during the day, and fall asleep in school—all signs of insufficient sleep. And, their naps average 1.2 hours, well beyond the 45-minute maximum recommended by sleep experts so that naps do not interfere with nighttime sleep.

"Irregular sleep patterns that include long naps and sleeping in on the weekend negatively impact adolescents' biological clocks and sleep quality—which in turn affects their abilities and mood," says Mary Carskadon, PhD, who chairs the 2006 poll task force. "This rollercoaster system should be minimized. When students' schedules are more consistent and provide for plenty of sleep, they are better prepared to take on their busy days." Dr. Carskadon is the director of the E.P. Bradley Hospital Sleep and Chronobiology Research Lab at Brown University.

15   In terms of overall demographics, there are more similarities than differences among adolescents' responses to sleep-related questions. Boys and girls have similar sleep patterns. In terms of racial/ethnic comparisons, African-American adolescents report getting 7.2 hours of sleep on school nights, as compared to 7.6 hours reported by Hispanic adolescents, 7.4 hours by other minorities and 7.7 hours by White adolescents.

Other Factors Affecting Adolescent Sleep

Caffeine plays a prominent role in the life of today's adolescent. Three-quarters of those polled drink at least one caffeinated beverage every day, and nearly one-third (31%) consume two or more such drinks each day. Adolescents who drink two or more caffeinated beverages daily are more likely to get an insufficient amount of sleep on school nights and think they have a sleep problem.

Technology may also be encroaching on a good night's sleep. The poll finds that adolescents aren't heeding expert advice to engage in relaxing activities in the hour before bedtime or to keep the bedroom free from sleep distractions:

- Watching television is the most popular activity (76%) for adolescents in the hour before bedtime, while surfing the internet/instant-messaging (44%) and talking on the phone (40%) are close behind.

- Boys are more likely than girls to play electronic video games (40% vs. 12%) and/or exercise (37% vs. 27%) in the hour prior to bedtime; girls are more likely than boys to talk on the phone (51% vs. 29%) and/or do homework/ study (70% vs. 60%) in that time.

- Nearly all adolescents (97%) have at least one electronic item—such as a television, computer, phone or music device—in their bedroom. On average, 6th-graders have more than two of these items in their bedroom, while 12th-graders have about four.

- Adolescents with four or more such items in their bedrooms are much more likely than their peers to get an insufficient amount of sleep at night and almost twice as likely to fall asleep in school and while doing homework.

TIPS FOR TEENS

1. Sleep is food for the brain. Lack of sleep can make you look tired and feel depressed, irritable or angry. Even mild sleepiness can hurt your performance—from taking school exams to playing sports or video games. Learn how much sleep you need to function at your best—most adolescents need between 8.5 and 9.25 hours of sleep each night—and strive to get it every night. You should awaken refreshed, not tired.

2. Keep consistency in mind: establish a regular bedtime and wake-time schedule, and maintain this schedule during weekends and school (or work) vacations. Don't stray from your schedule frequently, and never do so for two or more consecutive nights. If you must go off schedule, avoid delaying your bedtime by more than one hour. Awaken the next day within two hours of your regular schedule, and, if you are sleepy during the day, take an early afternoon nap.

3. Get into bright light as soon as possible in the morning, but avoid it in the evening. The light helps to signal to the brain when it should wake up and when it should prepare to sleep.

4. Understand your circadian rhythms. Then you can try to maximize your schedule throughout the day according to your internal clock. For example, to compensate for your "slump (sleepy) times," participate in stimulating activities or classes that are interactive. Try to avoid lecture classes and potentially unsafe activities, including driving.

5. After lunch (or after noon), stay away from caffeinated coffee and colas as well as nicotine, which are all stimulants. Also avoid alcohol, which disrupts sleep.

6. Relax before going to bed. Avoid heavy reading, studying and computer games within one hour of going to bed. Don't fall asleep with the television on—flickering light and stimulating content can inhibit restful sleep.

"Many teens have a technological playground in their bedrooms that offers a variety of ways to stay stimulated and delay sleep. Ramping down from the day's activities with a warm bath and a good book are much better ways to transition to bedtime," notes Dr. Carskadon. "The brain learns when it's time to sleep from the lessons it receives. Teens need to give the brain better signals about when nighttime starts... turning off the lights—computer screens and TV, too—is the very best signal."

- **Be a bed head, not a dead head.** Understand the dangers of insufficient sleep—and avoid them! Encourage your friends to do the same. Ask others how much sleep they've had lately before you let them drive you somewhere. Remember: friends don't let friends drive drowsy.
- **Brag about your bedtime.** Tell your friends how good you feel after getting more than 8 hours of sleep!
- **Do you study with a buddy?** If you're getting together after school, tell your pal you need to catch a nap first, or take a nap break if needed. (Taking a nap in the evening may make it harder for you to sleep at night, however.)
- **Steer clear of raves and say no to all-nighters.** Staying up late can cause chaos in your sleep patterns and your ability to be alert the next day...and beyond. Remember, the best thing you can do to prepare for a test is to get plenty of sleep. All-nighters or late-night study sessions might seem to give you more time to cram for your exam, but they are also likely to drain your brainpower.

How Parents Can Help Teens Get More Sleep

Dr. Mindell notes that "the poll data suggest that parents may be missing red flags that their teenager is not getting the sleep that he or she desperately needs. Simply asking teens if they get enough sleep to feel their best is a good way for parents to begin a valuable conversation about sleep's importance."

20   Some warning signs that your child may not be getting the sleep he/she needs:

- Do you have to wake your child for school? And, is it difficult to do so?
- Has a teacher mentioned that your child is sleepy or tired during the day?
- Do you find your child falling asleep while doing homework?
- Is your child sleeping two hours later or more on weekends than on school nights?
- Is your child's behavior different on days that he/she gets a good night's sleep vs. days that he/she doesn't?
- Does he/she rely on a caffeinated drink in the morning to wake up? And/or drink two or more caffeinated drinks a day?
- Does he/she routinely nap for more than 45 minutes?

Parents can play a key role in helping their adolescents develop and maintain healthy sleep habits. In general, it is important for parents and adolescents to talk about sleep—including the natural phase delay—and learn more about good sleep habits in order to manage teens' busy schedules. What's more, teens often mirror their parents' habits, so adults are encouraged to be good role models by getting a full night's sleep themselves.

And, there are ways to make it easier for an adolescent to get more sleep and a better night's sleep:

- Set a consistent bedtime and waketime (even on weekends) that allows for the recommended nine or more hours of sleep every night.

- Have a relaxing bedtime routine, such as reading for fun or taking a warm bath or shower.

- Keep the bedroom comfortable, dark, cool and quiet.

- Get into bright light as soon as possible in the morning, but avoid it in the evening.

- Create a sleep-friendly environment by removing TVs and other distractions from the bedroom and setting limits on usage before bedtime.

- Avoid caffeine after lunchtime.

NSF released the poll findings as part of its 9th annual National Sleep Awareness Week® campaign, held March 27–April 2, 2006. For more sleep tips for parents and adolescents, as well as the Summary of Findings for the 2006 *Sleep in America* poll, visit NSF's website at www.sleepfoundation.org.

Methodology The 2006 *Sleep in America* poll was conducted for the National Sleep Foundation by WB&A Market Research. Telephone interviews were conducted between September 19 and November 29, 2005, with a targeted random sample of 1,602 caregivers and, separately, their adolescent children ages 11–17 in grades 6–12. Using the targeted random sample, quotas were established by grade and race/ethnicity, with minority respondents being oversampled to reflect equal proportions of respondents by grade, as well as the actual distribution of race/ethnicity based on the U.S. census. The poll's margin of error is plus or minus 2.4%; the response rate for the survey was 27%.

Review Questions

1. What is the recommended amount of sleep for a teenager? What percentage of American teenagers get this much sleep? How knowledgeable are their parents about their sleep?

2. How much sleep debt do high school seniors typically accumulate in a week? Cite some of the consequences of getting insufficient sleep as a teenager, according to the poll results.

3. Why is a lack of sleep in the teenage years particularly harmful, according to experts?

4. What is a "phase delay," and how does it contribute to an adolescent's sleep debt?

5. What percentage of adolescents take regular naps? Optimally, how should naps be used? What is the recommended amount of daytime napping? What is the danger of especially long naps?

6. What is "rollercoaster" sleep, and why is it not healthy?

7. How do consumer electronics affect adolescent sleep?

● Discussion and Writing Suggestions

1. According to the survey results, once a week roughly one-quarter of high school students fall asleep in class, 22 percent fall asleep doing homework, and 14 percent are late to or miss school because of insufficient sleep. Are/were you one of these students? Do you know these students? Why are America's teenagers not getting sufficient sleep, in your view?

2. How does the amount and quality of your sleep compare with that of teenagers who responded to the National Sleep Foundation survey?

3. To what extent do you believe that consumer electronics in your bedroom (or dorm room) affect the quality of your sleep? How do you respond to the finding that, with four or more such items, you are more likely to suffer a sleep deficit? Can you explain the correlation?

4. At the end of this article, the NSF offers several recommendations for helping adolescents get more sleep. How realistic do you find these recommendations? Cite some factors in the lives of active adolescents that make it problematic to get the recommended nine hours of sleep each night.

SLEEP DEBT AND THE MORTGAGED MIND

William C. Dement and Christopher Vaughan

William Dement, MD, PhD, is one of the founders of modern sleep medicine, universally acknowledged as a pioneer. A professor and researcher at Stanford University, Dement has authored numerous articles, books, and book chapters on sleep. His particular interest has been the topic of sleep "debt," the focus of the following selection, which appeared originally as a chapter in *The Promise of Sleep* (1999), cowritten with Christopher Vaughan.

The night of March 24, 1989, was cold and calm, the air crystalline, as the giant *Exxon Valdez* oil tanker pulled out of Valdez, Alaska, into the tranquil waters of Prince William Sound. In these clearest of possible conditions the ship made a planned turn out of the shipping channel and didn't turn back in time. The huge tanker ran aground, spilling millions of gallons of crude oil into the sound. The cost of the cleanup effort was over $2 billion. The ultimate cost of continuing environmental damage is incalculable. Furthermore, when the civil trial was finally over in the summer of 1995, the Exxon Corporation was assessed an additional $5 billion in punitive damages. Everyone I query in my travels vividly recalls the accident, and most have the impression that it had something to do with the master's alcohol consumption. No one is aware of the true cause of the tragedy. In its final report, the National Transportation Safety Board (NTSB) found that sleep deprivation and sleep debt were direct causes of the accident. This stunning result got a brief mention in the back pages of the newspapers.

Out of the vast ocean of knowledge about sleep, there are a few facts that are so important that I will try to burn them into your brain forever. None is more important than the topic of sleep debt. If we can learn to understand sleep indebtedness and manage it, we can improve everyday life as well as avoid many injuries, horribly diminished lives, and premature deaths.

The *Exxon Valdez* disaster offers a good example of how sleep debt can create a tragedy and how the true villain—sleep indebtedness—remains concealed. I am sure that I was just as shocked as anyone when I learned about America's worst oil spill. The TV coverage of the dead birds and seals filled me with outrage over the environmental devastation. One of my friends went to Alaska and participated in the cleanup. He brought back photos and a big jar of crude oil. If you haven't been exposed to crude oil, keep away from it. It isn't the purified stuff that goes into your car. It's awful. It stinks to high heaven. You want to vomit.

I was among the millions who were following the news, but I had no idea that it would have a special meaning for me a year later. The National Commission on Sleep Disorders Research finally mandated by Congress was convened for the first time in March 1990, and 20 commissioners were assembled in Washington, D.C. After the first meeting I decided to visit a friend, Dr. John Lauber, who had been confirmed by the Senate as one of five members of the National Transportation Safety Board. He told me that the board would very likely identify sleep deprivation as the "direct cause" of the grounding of the *Exxon Valdez*.

I had worked with John a few years earlier on a study of the layover sleep of pilots on intercontinental airlines. He was head of human factors research at NASA-Ames and at the beginning of the layover study knew little about "sleep debt." At the end of the study, he was one of the few real experts in the world. Two months after the visit with John he sent me the NTSB's final report.

The report noted that on the March night when the *Exxon Valdez* steamed out of Valdez there were ice floes across part of the shipping lane, forcing the ship to turn to avoid them. The captain determined that this maneuver could be done safely if the ship was steered back to the main channel when it was abeam of a well-known landmark, Busby Island. With this plan established, he turned over command to the third mate and left the bridge. Although news reports linked much of what happened next to the captain's alcohol consumption, the captain was off the bridge well before the accident. The direct cause of America's worst oil spill was the behavior of the third mate, who had slept only 6 hours in the previous 48 and was severely sleep deprived.

As the *Exxon Valdez* passed Busby Island, the third mate ordered the helm to starboard, but he didn't notice that the autopilot was still on and the ship did not turn. Instead it plowed farther out of the channel. Twice lookouts warned the third mate about the position of lights marking the reef, but he didn't change or check his previous orders. His brain was not interpreting the danger in what they said. Finally he noticed that he was far outside the channel, turned off the autopilot, and tried hard to get the great ship pointed back to safety—too late.

For several years I would ask every audience that I addressed if there was anyone in the audience who had not heard the words *"Exxon Valdez."* A hand was never raised. Then I would say, "Who knows what caused the grounding?" Many hands would be raised, and the answer would always be "alcohol." Thus I could never exploit the potential impact of this catastrophe in getting knowledge about sleep into the mainstream, because of the media emphasis on the captain's drinking. When the report finally came out, there was no real interest. Even at the trial, in the summer of 1995, the true cause of the accident received little attention. What everyone ought to be talking about is how to deal with sleep deprivation and how to avoid it in the transportation industry and throughout all components of society, saying over and over again "Look what it caused." But instead, the poor captain has been hounded for nearly a decade.

An even more dramatic tragedy was the explosion of the space shuttle *Challenger.* After a year-long investigation, the Rogers Commission declared that in the absence of adequate data on O-ring function at low temperatures the decision to launch the rocket was an error. Those of us who saw this catastrophic event on television over and over and over know the ghastly consequences of that error. But not well known at all is the fact that the Human Factors Subcommittee attributed the error to the severe sleep deprivation of the NASA managers. This conclusion was only included in the committee's final report, which only noted that top managers in such situations are generally the ones who sacrifice the most sleep.

10   Was this the most costly case of sleepiness in history? The parents of any teenager who has died while asleep at the wheel might not agree. Even the most careful drivers are at risk, because we simply do not tell people—not even young people in the driver-training courses required in many states—how to recognize signs of dangerous sleepiness.

Of course, even children are at risk. For example in the past several years I have received many reports of school bus accidents where the driver fell asleep. Unfortunately, it may take another *Exxon Valdez* or *Challenger* before the sleep community can mobilize public opinion to do something about this issue. Thus, I find myself in the bizarre circumstance of simultaneously fearing and at the same time hoping for another highly visible disaster.

Just last year I stepped up to the podium to make the danger absolutely clear to my Stanford students. Drowsiness, that feeling when the eyelids are trying to close and we cannot seem to keep them open, is the last step before we fall asleep, not the first. If at this moment we let sleep come, it will arrive instantly. When driving a car, or in any hazardous situation, the first wave of drowsiness should be a dramatic warning. Get out of harm's way instantly! My message to the students is "Drowsiness is red alert!" I delivered and explained this message over and over in my 1997 undergraduate course "Sleep and Dreams," and the students got it. I am confident few will ever drive while drowsy.

Everyone can recall a jolt of heart-stopping panic in the face of peril—when we realize a cab seems about to jump the curb we're standing on, or when we lose track of a child in a crowd. The response is instantaneous. We act. We should have a similar response the instant we feel drowsy at the wheel.

Ignorance About Sleepiness

...I now think of the continuum of sleepiness and alertness as the state upon which all human behavior is acted out. Today we can claim with confidence that where we are on this continuum, from the high peak of optimal alertness to the deep trough of extreme drowsiness, is the single most important determinant of how well we perform. Accordingly, the total absence of this subject from psychology textbooks or any other educational materials is incomprehensible. Although the scientific knowledge has been available for more than two decades, students are still not acquiring crucial knowledge about sleepiness, sleep debt, and sleep deprivation in any of our educational institutions....

The feeling of being tired and needing sleep is a basic drive of nature, like hunger. If you don't eat enough, you are driven to eat. If you go long enough without food, you can think of nothing else. Once you get food, you eat until you feel full and then you stop. Thus, the subjective responses of hunger and satiation ensure that you fulfill your overall daily requirement for calories. In essentially the same way, your sleep drive keeps an exact tally of accumulated waking hours. Like bricks in a backpack, accumulated sleep drive is a burden that weighs down on you. Every hour that you are awake adds another brick to the backpack: The brain's sleep load increases until you go to sleep, when the load starts to lighten.

In a very real sense all wakefulness is sleep deprivation. As soon as you wake up, the meter starts ticking, calculating how many hours of sleep you will need to pay off that night. Or, to continue the load metaphor, it tallies how many bricks you will have to shed to get back to zero. Generally people need to sleep one hour for every two hours awake, which means that most need around eight hours of sleep a night. Of course, some people need more and some need less, and a few people seem to need a great deal more or less. From the work we have done, we must conclude that each person has his or her own specific daily sleep requirement. The brain tries to hit this mark, and the further you are from getting the number of hours of sleep you need, the harder your brain tries to force you to get that sleep.

• • •

Sleep Debt: Nature's Loan Shark

...The brain keeps an exact accounting of how much sleep it is owed. In our first study, we restricted the sleep of 10 volunteers to exactly 5 hours each night for 7 nights and observed that the tendency to fall asleep increased progressively each successive day. For the first time in the history of sleep research, we discovered that the effect of each successive night of partial sleep loss carried over, and the effect appeared to accumulate in a precisely additive fashion. In other words, the strength of the tendency to fall asleep was progressively greater during each successive day with exactly the same amount of sleep each night. For some time Mary [Carskadon] and I referred to this as an increased sleep tendency, and it was clear that the increase did not dissipate without additional rest. How people recover from various levels of sleep deprivation after getting sleep has not been well studied. However, current evidence suggests that the accumulated lost sleep must be paid back at some time, perhaps even hour for hour.

We use the term "sleep debt" because accumulated lost sleep is like a monetary debt: It must be paid back. Regardless of how rapidly it can be paid back, the important thing is that the size of the sleep debt and its dangerous effects are definitely directly related to the amount of lost sleep. My guess is that after a period of substantial sleep loss, we can pay back a little and feel a lot better, although the remaining sleep debt is still large. The danger of an unintended sleep episode is still there. Until proven otherwise, it is reasonable and certainly safer to assume that accumulated lost sleep must be paid back hour for hour. Therefore, if you miss 3 hours one night, you must sleep 11 hours the next night (3 plus your normal 8) in order to feel alert throughout the day.

Your sleep debt may have accumulated in small increments over many days. For example, during a five-day work week where you needed 8 hours each night and instead got 6, you would build up a sleep debt of 10 hours (5 times 2). From this perspective, sleeping in until noon on Saturday is not enough to pay back the 10 lost hours plus your nightly requirement of 8; you would have to sleep until about 5:00 P.M. to balance the sleep ledger. Of course, most people won't sleep that long, and in fact it is difficult to do because of the alerting process of the biological clock. ... More likely, you will sleep in an extra hour or two and get up feeling better. But the debt is still there, demanding to be paid. Later that day you'll start feeling the effects of the sleep debt again. And if you borrow more sleep time over subsequent nights, you won't just stay sleepy, you'll get even sleepier. As your debt grows, your energy, mood, and cognition will be undermined.

There is another important way that sleep deprivation can occur and sleep debt can accumulate....[S]everal sleep disorders are characterized by very severe and impairing daytime sleepiness. In such patients we typically see hundreds of brief interruptions of sleep in a single night. In spite of this, careful tabulation of the intervening short periods of sleep can add up to what ought to be a satisfactory amount of total sleep.

Several groups of sleep researchers have carried out studies on normal volunteers which have clarified this situation. In these studies, subjects were awakened every minute or so throughout entire nights, and the next day's alertness was evaluated using the [Multiple Sleep Latency Test, which measures sleepiness, the speed with which subjects fall asleep]. The nocturnal awakenings were brief, 5 to 10 seconds, and subjects usually returned to sleep immediately. Although there were usually several hundred interruptions, the cumulative total sleep can add up to normal amounts. Nevertheless, daytime sleepiness is markedly increased, as if there had been no sleep at all, or very little.

Interrupting sleep every minute or so all night long is a heroic experimental manipulation. I am happy to report that the results of these particular experiments have been very consistent. Accordingly, we may conclude that the restorative value of sleep is severely curtailed if sleep periods are not allowed to continue for at least several minutes. If 10 to 15 minutes of sleep are allowed to occur before an interruption, this effect is greatly lessened. These studies have led to the concept that there are minimal units of restorative sleep. In other words, it is as if the bank that keeps track of sleep debt doesn't accept small deposits.

In one of our first studies we evaluated the clinical usefulness of the MSLT by comparing narcoleptics and normal sleepers. The results were fabulous. The MSLT sharply distinguished patients and normals. However, the MSLT scores of a few normal volunteers were in the pathologically sleepy range (1 to 5 minutes). This latter group tended to be college students. For a while we thought that these younger "normals" were in the early stages of the narcoleptic sleep disorder, not yet manifesting the other symptoms. But it was hard to imagine why Stanford University would attract so many budding narcoleptics. We tested a few more students, allowing a baseline normal amount of sleep (8 hours a day) and carefully measuring their sleep tendency day to day with the MSLT. Nearly all of the students appeared to be pathologically sleepy! I should not have been so surprised, because I have been watching students fall asleep in class ever since I was a college student myself.

The obvious explanation finally occurred to Mary and me: The students needed more sleep. To prove this we did studies where we extended their nightly hours in bed to 10, and over several days, the MSLT score steadily improved. Now that we know about sleep debt, we can only imagine how many thousands of observations on human behavior have been made over the decades on chronically sleep-deprived subjects whom researchers thought were "normal." Since people are so severely affected by a large sleep debt, its presence can potentially alter the results of almost all research measures, from I.Q. tests to observations of drug side effects. The baseline studies of all human research, regardless of their nature, now must include measures of daytime sleep tendency, so that the variable degree of chronic sleep loss does not contaminate every study.

25   Despite the fact that "sleep debt" has entered common parlance (some researchers also call it "sleep load" or "sleep tendency"), many people don't fully understand the concept. Again and again I hear people complain that they sleep a full night, even an extra hour or so, and still feel just as sleepy or even sleepier than before. "Well," they think, "I must be sleepy because I am sleeping too much." The fact is that you don't work off a large sleep debt, which is what most of us have, by getting one good night's sleep.

• • •

Driving Under the Influence of Sleep Debt

People *must* learn to pay attention to their own sleep debt and how it is affecting them. Not doing so, and misunderstanding the rules of sleep debt and arousal, can be extremely dangerous. A friend of mine, also a Stanford professor, once participated in a bicycle race that lasted several days and included a number of laps around Lake Tahoe. He got very little sleep at night during the period of the race, but then he slept about nine hours a night for the two nights he stayed at the lake after the race. He woke up on Sunday morning feeling rested, ready to pack up and drive home. But as he was coming down the winding mountain road he began to yawn and his eyelids felt heavy. He told me that he was a little surprised because he thought he had gotten plenty of sleep. If someone had been with him, he probably would have traded places, but it did not occur to him to pull over and take a nap. As he drove on, it became harder and harder to keep his eyes open, and he began to be concerned. At that moment he saw a sign for a restaurant only several miles farther down the road. "Good," he thought, "I'll be able to get some coffee." Right after that he fell asleep, just for a moment, and awoke with a terrible start to find that he had drifted into the oncoming lane. He jerked the wheel to the right, but the road curved to the left, and the car went over a 30-foot ledge. The next thing he knew he was upside down, suspended by his seat belt, the car impaled on a jagged rock that had sliced through the roof and into the empty passenger seat next to him. He sustained serious cuts and bruises, and his right arm was completely paralyzed, but miraculously he was alive.

When he told me the story later, he still didn't understand how he could have been so sleepy. "But Bill, I got two full nights of sleep before

I left Tahoe." Not knowing about sleep debt, he could not know that a few hours of extra sleep does not alleviate the sleep debt accumulated over the preceding nights or weeks. He was driving alone without the stimulation of conversation, along a route he knew fairly well. In short, there was little to act as a dike against the sea of sleep debt that he had built up. Ironically, his awareness of how terribly drowsy he was feeling may have forestalled sleep in the minutes before the crash. When he saw the sign for the restaurant up ahead and knew that he would soon get coffee, he relaxed and let that worry go. A few moments later he was hurtling off the mountain road. If the idea that drowsiness is supremely dangerous had been burned into his brain, he would have stopped driving no matter how difficult or inconvenient.

Fatal Fatigue: Alcohol and Sleep Debt

...[O]lder children never feel sleepy during the day. They were the only group we studied in the Stanford Summer Sleep Camp who never fell asleep in the 20 minutes allotted for the individual sleep latency tests. And of course, children are usually not sleep deprived. Putting all our results together, we can state with confidence that if you feel sleepy or drowsy in the daytime, then you must have a sizable sleep debt. Sleep debt is the physical side of the coin, and the feelings of sleepiness or drowsiness are the psychological side. As an analogy, dehydration is the physical side of the coin and the feeling of being thirsty is the psychological side. To carry the analogy a little further, if we have thoroughly quenched our thirst, we cannot immediately feel thirsty. But if we are becoming dehydrated, the desire to drink may be diminished if we are involved in something very interesting or demanding. At some point, of course, thirst becomes overwhelming. Likewise, we cannot feel sleepy in the daytime if we do not have a sleep debt, but we may not feel sleepy if we are doing something that excites us. If we have a very strong tendency to fall asleep and we reduce the stimuli that are keeping us awake, we will very soon begin to feel sleepy and will inevitably fall asleep, intentionally or otherwise.

But all those interested in traffic safety and all those who wish to have a long life as well must take note. When a crash is attributed to alcohol, the real culprit, or at least a coconspirator, is often sleep deprivation. In studies that are second to none in importance, the powerful interaction between sleep and alcohol was revealed by the outstanding sleep research team at Henry Ford Hospital Sleep Disorders Center. A group of volunteers slept 10 hours a night for one week, 8 hours a night during a separate week, and on a third schedule simulated a social weekend by getting 5 hours of sleep for 2 nights. In the morning after completing each schedule, all of the volunteers were given either a low dose of alcohol or a placebo. Then their degree of impaired alertness was evaluated utilizing the MSLT and performance tests. When the subjects were given the low dose of alcohol after the

8-hour schedule, they became slightly more sleepy than when given placebo. After the schedule of 2 nights with little sleep, the exact same dose of alcohol the next morning made them severely sleepy, barely able to stay awake. However, the exact same dose of alcohol after 10 hours of sleep every night for a week had no discernible effect. In other words, alcohol may not be a potent sedative by itself, but it becomes very sedating when paired with sleep debt. It is tempting to speculate that all sedatives, particularly sleeping pills, interact with sleep debt. This area deserves much more research....

30   The implications of this are far-reaching. People are well aware of the dangers of drinking and driving, but they don't know that a large sleep debt and even a small amount of alcohol can create a "fatal fatigue." People can be just fine driving after a single drink one day (when they have little sleep debt), yet be a hazard to themselves and others if they have that same drink on a day in which they have a large sleep debt. A fact little known by the public at large is that in nearly every accident linked to alcohol consumption, sleep debt almost certainly plays a major role.

In one state traffic agency, researchers are trying very hard to understand traffic accidents designated as alcohol related even though the alcohol in the tissue is far below any level thought to be impairing.

•   •   •

[E]xperiments demonstrate that individuals thought to be completely normal can be carrying a sizable sleep debt, which impairs their mood, energy, and performance. If you haven't already done so, I think it's worthwhile to ask yourself how your sleep debt is affecting you. How often do you think about taking a quick snooze? How often do you rub your eyes and yawn during the day? How often do you feel like you really need some coffee? Each of these is a warning of a sleep debt that you ignore at your peril. I can't overemphasize the dangers of unintended sleep episodes or severe drowsiness. I hope this information can save your life.

I know that people often are driven to stay up late and get up early, that the demands of modern life push us to stay up past our biological bedtime. But I also know it's not too onerous to avoid accumulating sleep debt....Studies suggest the likelihood that people can avoid dangerously high sleep debt by adding a relatively small amount of sleep to their normal sleep schedule. People who have lowered their sleep debt usually report that they gain a new sense of well-being. That may just mean not watching the news at night, or putting off some other nonessential pleasure, like the bedtime crossword puzzle. I bet most people would give up many late-night diversions if they could feel truly awake throughout the day—fresh and full of hope, senses wide open, the mind receptive to people and ideas.

Review Questions

1. What was the actual, though little reported, cause of the *Exxon Valdez* disaster?

2. Dement asserts that "Drowsiness is red alert!" What does he mean?

3. What is the "continuum of sleepiness and alertness"? What is its significance?

4. How is sleeping like eating and drinking?

5. What is sleep debt? How is it "carried over"? How is the amount of sleep debt correlated with the dangers posed by sleep debt?

6. Why may a person feel sleepy even after getting a full night's sleep?

7. In what way is sleep debt often a "co-conspirator" in alcohol-related crashes?

Discussion and Writing Suggestions

1. Consider your own sleep habits. Given what you've read in this article, are you currently sleep deprived? Have you ever been? Have you ever noticed in your daily performance of a task the kinds of impairments due to sleep debt that Dement discusses?

2. In the title and throughout the article, Dement uses a metaphor from the banking industry—mortgage—to discuss sleep debt. (This term is sometimes useful to politicians and social commentators—who speak of "mortgaging" our future.) Cite several instances of the use of this metaphor and comment on its effectiveness. To what extent does the metaphor help to convey Dement's central message? In your answer, discuss how a mind can be "mortgaged."

3. Have you ever experienced the sensation of driving drowsy—which Dement says should be a "red alert" to stop your car and rest? In a paragraph, describe the scene: the sensation of drowsiness, the conversation you have with yourself to stay awake, the efforts to fight off sleep (e.g., turning on the radio, opening a window, slapping your face)—and then the nodding head and the startled waking.

4. Do you respond to Dement's raising a "red alert" (paragraph 12) about driving and drowsiness any differently than you would if a parent raised the same alert? Why?

THE PITTSBURGH SLEEP QUALITY INDEX

Daniel Buysse

In light of William Dement's cautions on the dangers of sleep debt, we offer a tool to assess the quality of your own sleep: the Pittsburgh Sleep Quality Index, or PSQI. Because the test can be self-scored, you can get a numerical indicator of the quality of your own sleep. Daniel J. Buysse, MD, is medical director of the Sleep Evaluation Center in the department of psychiatry at the University of Pittsburgh. A past president of the American Academy of Sleep Medicine, Buysse developed the PSQI with Charles F. Reynolds, III, MD; Timothy H. Monk, PhD; Susan R. Berman; and David J. Kupfer, MD. The authors first presented the PSQI in *Psychiatry Research* (May 1989) as a tool "specifically designed to measure sleep quality in clinical populations." Today, the PSQI is a widely used instrument in sleep research.

Pittsburgh Sleep Quality Index (PSQI)

Name _____ ID # _____ Date _____ Age _____

Instructions:

The following questions relate to your usual sleep habits during the past month *only*. Your answers should indicate the most accurate reply for the *majority* of days and nights in the past month.
Please answer all questions.

1. During the past month, when have you usually gone to bed at night?
   USUAL BED TIME _____
2. During the past month, how long (in minutes) has it usually taken you to fall asleep each night?
   NUMBER OF MINUTES _____
3. During the past month, when have you usually gotten up in the morning?
   USUAL GETTING UP TIME _____
4. During the past month, how many hours of *actual sleep* did you get at night? (This may be different than the number of hours you spend in bed.)
   HOURS OF SLEEP PER NIGHT _____

For each of the remaining questions, check the one best response. Please answer *all* questions.

5. During the past month, how often have you had trouble sleeping because you . . .
   (a) Cannot get to sleep within 30 minutes

Not during the past month _____	Less than once a week _____	Once or twice a week _____	Three or more times a week _____

   (b) Wake up in the middle of the night or early morning

Not during the past month _____	Less than once a week _____	Once or twice a week _____	Three or more times a week _____

   (c) Have to get up to use the bathroom

Not during the past month _____	Less than once a week _____	Once or twice a week _____	Three or more times a week _____

   (d) Cannot breathe comfortably

Not during the past month _____	Less than once a week _____	Once or twice a week _____	Three or more times a week _____

   (e) Cough or snore loudly

Not during the past month _____	Less than once a week _____	Once or twice a week _____	Three or more times a week _____

(f) Feel too cold

| Not during the past month _____ | Less than once a week _____ | Once or twice a week _____ | Three or more times a week _____ |

(g) Feel too hot

| Not during the past month _____ | Less than once a week _____ | Once or twice a week _____ | Three or more times a week _____ |

(h) Had bad dreams

| Not during the past month _____ | Less than once a week _____ | Once or twice a week _____ | Three or more times a week _____ |

(i) Have pain

| Not during the past month _____ | Less than once a week _____ | Once or twice a week _____ | Three or more times a week _____ |

(j) Other reason(s), please describe _____

_____

How often during the past month have you had trouble sleeping because of this?

| Not during the past month _____ | Less than once a week _____ | Once or twice a week _____ | Three or more times a week _____ |

6. During the past month, how would you rate your sleep quality overall?

Very good _____
Fairly good _____
Fairly bad _____
Very bad _____

7. During the past month, how often have you taken medicine (prescribed or "over the counter") to help you sleep?

| Not during the past month _____ | Less than once a week _____ | Once or twice a week _____ | Three or more times a week _____ |

8. During the past month, how often have you had trouble staying awake while driving, eating meals, or engaging in social activity?

| Not during the past month _____ | Less than once a week _____ | Once or twice a week _____ | Three or more times a week _____ |

9. During the past month, how much of a problem has it been for you to keep up enough enthusiasm to get things done?

No problem at all _____
Only a very slight problem _____
Somewhat of a problem _____
A very big problem _____

10. Do you have a bed partner or roommate?

No bed partner or roommate _____
Partner/roommate in other room _____
Partner in same room, but not same bed _____
Partner in same bed _____

If you have a roommate or bed partner, ask him/her how often in the past month you have had . . .

(a) Loud snoring

| Not during the past month _____ | Less than once a week _____ | Once or twice a week _____ | Three or more times a week _____ |

(b) Long pauses between breaths while asleep

| Not during the past month _____ | Less than once a week _____ | Once or twice a week _____ | Three or more times a week _____ |

(c) Legs twitching or jerking while you sleep

| Not during the past month _____ | Less than once a week _____ | Once or twice a week _____ | Three or more times a week _____ |

(d) Episodes of disorientation or confusion during sleep

| Not during the past month _____ | Less than once a week _____ | Once or twice a week _____ | Three or more times a week _____ |

(e) Other restlessness while you sleep; please describe _____

_____

| Not during the past month _____ | Less than once a week _____ | Once or twice a week _____ | Three or more times a week _____ |

Scoring Instructions for the Pittsburgh Sleep Quality Index

The Pittsburgh Sleep Quality Index (PSQI) contains 19 self-rated questions and 5 questions rated by the bed partner or roommate (if one is available). Only self-rated questions are included in the scoring. The 19 self-rated items are combined to form seven "component" scores, each of which has a range of 0–3 points. In all cases, a score of "0" indicates no difficulty, while a score of "3" indicates severe difficulty. The seven component scores are then added to yield one "global" score, with a range of 0–21 points, "0" indicating no difficulty and "21" indicating severe difficulties in all areas.

Scoring proceeds as follows:

Component 1: Subjective sleep quality

Examine question #6, and assign scores as follows:

Response	Component 1 score
"Very good"	0
"Fairly good"	1
"Fairly bad"	2
"Very bad"	3

Component 1 score: _____

Component 2: Sleep latency [amount of time needed to fall asleep]

1. Examine question #2, and assign scores as follows:

Response	Score
≤ 15 minutes	0
16–30 minutes	1
31–60 minutes	2
> 60 minutes	3

Question #2 score: _____

2. Examine question #5a, and assign scores as follows:

Response	Score
Not during the past month	0
Less than once a week	1
Once or twice a week	2
Three or more times a week	3

Question #5a score: _____

3. Add #2 score and #5a score

Sum of #2 and #5a: _____

4. Assign component 2 score as follows:

Sum of #2 and #5a	Component 2 score
0	0
1–2	1
3–4	2
5–6	3

Component 2 score: _____

Component 3: Sleep duration

Examine question #4, and assign scores as follows:

Response	Component 3 score
≥ 7 hours	0
≥ 6 < 7 hours	1
≥ 5 < 6 hours	2
< 5 hours	3

Component 3 score: _____

Component 4: Habitual sleep efficiency

(1) Write the number of hours slept (question #4) here: _____
(2) Calculate the number of hours spent in bed:

Getting up time (question #3): _____
− Bedtime (question #1):   _____

Number of hours spent in bed: _____

(3) Calculate habitual sleep efficiency as follows:

(Number of hours slept/Number of hours spent in bed) × 100 = Habitual sleep efficiency (%)
(_____/_____) × 100 = _____%

(4) Assign component 4 score as follows:

Habitual sleep efficiency %	Component 4 score
>85%	0
75–84%	1
65–74%	2
<65%	3

Component 4 score: _____

Component 5: Sleep disturbances

(1) Examine questions #5b–5j, and assign scores for *each* question as follows:

Response	Score
Not during the past month	0
Less than once a week	1
Once or twice a week	2
Three or more times a week	3

#5b score _____
c score _____
d score _____
e score _____
f score _____
g score _____
h score _____
i score _____
j score _____

(2) Add the scores for questions #5b–5j:

Sum of #5b–5j: _____

(3) Assign component 5 score as follows:

Sum of #5b–5j	Component 5 score
0	0
1–9	1
10–18	2
19–27	3

Component 5 score: _____

Component 6: Use of sleeping medication

Examine question #7 and assign scores as follows:

Response	Component 6 score
Not during the past month	0
Less than once a week	1
Once or twice a week	2
Three or more times a week	3

Component 6 score: _____

Component 7: Daytime dysfunction

(1) Examine question #8, and assign scores as follows:

Response	Score
Never	0
Once or twice	1
Once or twice each week	2
Three or more times each week	3

Question #8 score: _____

(2) Examine question #9, and assign scores as follows:

Response	Score
No problem at all	0
Only a very slight problem	1
Somewhat of a problem	2
A very big problem	3

Question #9 score: _____

(3) Add the scores for question #8 and #9:

Sum of #8 and #9: _____

(4) Assign component 7 score as follows:

Sum of #8 and #9	Component 7 score
0	0
1–2	1
3–4	2
5–6	3

Component 7 score: _____

Global PSQI Score

Add the seven component scores together:

Global PSQI Score: ____

●   Discussion and Writing Suggestions

1. Complete the Pittsburgh Sleep Quality Index and compute your score, which will fall in a scale from 0 to 21 points. The higher your score, the greater your sleep difficulties. Where do you fall in the range?

2. Examine your seven "component" scores, which you will have calculated in computing your overall score. ("Sleep Latency" refers to the ease with which you fall asleep. The other six components are self-explanatory.) Which component(s) does the PSQI indicate are your strongest? Your weakest? Based on your subjective assessment of your own sleep, is the scoring accurate?

3. Did you need a formal test to determine how well you are sleeping? Were you aware that the quality of your sleep could be assessed along seven dimensions?

4. How useful do you find a numerical sleep score, as compared with an impressionistic assessment, such as "I sleep well" or "I'm a poor sleeper"? Why might sleep researchers develop an instrument that yields numerical scores?

5. If you are interested in seeing how an instrument such as the PSQI is created and clinically tested for accuracy, see the article that introduced it to the world in *Psychiatry Research* (Volume 28, No. 2, May 1989). You should be able to locate the article in your school library's electronic database—or via electronic interlibrary loan.

6. If your PSQI score suggests that you have difficulties sleeping, do you see any need to take action—especially in light of the preceding selection by William Dement? What action(s) (if any) might be appropriate?

How Sleep Debt Hurts College Students

June J. Pilcher and Amy S. Walters

The "all-nighter" is a rite of passage among many college students, who—pressed by competing schedules (and, let's be honest, the desire to have fun)—sometimes ignore the need to sleep, for 24 hours or more, in order to study for an exam or meet a paper deadline. Propped up by caffeinated beverages the next day, the student may even boast: "It was hard, but I got it done. I aced that exam." Perhaps not. Sleep researchers June Pilcher, who holds a PhD in biopsychology and teaches at Clemson University, and Amy Walters, MA, of Bradley University (when this article was published), report on an experiment that deprived students of a night's sleep and tested their cognitive functioning the next day. Both the results of these tests and the students' estimates of their performance may surprise (and deflate) you. This selection first appeared in the *Journal of American College Health* (November 1997).

A note on the specialized language of statistics: You should be able to understand this article whether or not you are familiar with the terms *standard deviation, mean,* or *probability* (e.g., p < .05). Like all researchers who collect numerical information, Pilcher and Walters run their data through statistical analyses to determine if their results are significant. For a useful guide to definitions of statistical terms, see the online "Statistics Glossary," by Valerie J. Easton and John H. McColl, http://www.stats.gla.ac.uk/steps/glossary/ index.html. Consult their "Alphabetical index of all entries."

ABSTRACT. The effects of sleep deprivation on cognitive performance and on psychological variables related to cognitive performance were studied in 44 college students. Participants completed the Watson-Glaser Critical Thinking Appraisal after either 24 hours of sleep deprivation or approximately 8 hours of sleep. After completing the cognitive task, the participants completed 2 questionnaires, one assessing self-reported effort, concentration, and estimated performance, the other assessing off-task cognitions. As expected, sleep-deprived participants performed significantly worse than the nondeprived participants on the cognitive task. However, the sleep-deprived participants rated their concentration and effort higher than the nondeprived participants did. In addition, the sleep-deprived participants rated their estimated performance significantly higher than the nondeprived participants did. The findings indicate that college students are not aware of the extent to which sleep deprivation negatively affects their ability to complete cognitive tasks.

Voluntary sleep deprivation is a common occurrence for many college students, who often partially deprive themselves of sleep during the week and compensate by increasing their sleep time over the weekend.(n1) This pattern of sleep deprivation and rebound becomes more pronounced around examination periods, sometimes resulting in 24 to 48 hours of total sleep deprivation. By depriving themselves of sleep, college students are not only increasing their feelings of sleepiness during the day, thus decreasing their ability to pay attention in class, but are also negatively affecting their ability to perform on exams.

It is well established that sleep deprivation of 24 hours or more leads to noticeable decrements in performance levels.(n2, n3) The psychological variables behind these decrements, however, are less clear. One theory states that decreases in performance are attributable to a decrease in the ability of the sleep-deprived person to focus the attention and effort necessary to complete the task successfully.(n4, n5) Similarly, a number of early sleep-deprivation studies concluded that the detrimental effects of sleep loss on performance result from periods of inattention called lapses.(n6-n8) Moreover, one early study specifically concluded that sleep loss leads to a decrease in attention to external stimuli.(n9) None of the earlier studies, however, attempted to assess self-reported variables that reflect changes in psychological events or thoughts that may be associated with the observed decrements in performance.

The effect of sleep deprivation on psychological variables associated with performance, such as self-reported estimates of attention, effort, and performance, have not been thoroughly investigated. Few studies have examined perceived effort and performance,(n11-n15) and the results from those studies have often been contradictory. For example, some researchers have suggested that sleep deprivation may affect the willingness of the individual to put forth the effort to perform well on a task more than the actual ability of the individual to perform.(n11, n12)

By contrast, other researchers have concluded that participants may recognize their decreased performance levels following sleep deprivation and attempt to overcome this decrease by increasing their effort.(n15) However, other studies have shown that a perceived increase in effort does not appear to overcome the detrimental effects of sleep deprivation. In one study,(n13) the participants were given a reward for better performance, which resulted in an increase in perceived effort but no change in actual performance. In addition, studies have shown that increasing amounts of sleep loss do not have a detrimental effect on participants' self-reported motivation levels.(n14, n15) As these results show, the relationships between sleep deprivation and psychological variables associated with performance are not clearly understood.

5   Another method of examining psychological variables that may be associated with the decrease in performance following sleep deprivation is assessment of off-task cognitions. Off-task cognitions are thoughts that are not directed to the completion of the task at hand but that intrude upon concentration. These cognitions can include negative evaluations of one's performance on the task, such as "I don't know how to do this," or completely unrelated thoughts, such as "I wonder what I should have for lunch today." Only one study to date has investigated the effect of sleep deprivation on off-task cognitions,(n10) but the participants in that study were specifically selected for their high baseline levels of off-task cognitions. Conclusions, therefore, could not be drawn about the effect of sleep deprivation on off-task cognitions independent of baseline levels.

Sleep-deprived participants' current mood state may provide additional information about the ability of the individual to perform following sleep deprivation. One of the best documented effects of sleep deprivation and one that would be expected to decrease complex task-solving ability is an increase in self-reported sleepiness and fatigue.(n14, n16, n17)

Other specific mood states could also influence successful task completion. For example, if sleep deprivation has a consistent negative effect on tension or anxiety, sleep-deprived participants would be expected to have more difficulty than nondeprived participants in maintaining the necessary attention and effort to complete a complex cognitive task. Although several studies have reported that sleep deprivation decreases positive mood states and increases negative mood states,(n13, n14, n18, n19) relatively few studies have examined the effect of sleep deprivation on specific mood states.

Another important consideration is the effect of sleep deprivation on an individual's ability to accurately assess psychological variables, such as concentration, effort, and estimated performance. Research findings have shown that the accuracy of self-reports varies, depending upon experimental characteristics surrounding the task. For example, Johnson and colleagues(n20) found that participants' self-reports of the amount of effort they put into a task corresponded better with performance on a difficult task than on a very easy task. The researchers also found that the amount of reported effort, but not necessarily actual performance, could be increased by giving an external incentive.

In addition, Beyer(n21) noted that self-evaluations of performance on longer tasks are more accurate than self-evaluations of performance on shorter tasks. Self-report estimates of performance have also been shown to be altered by feedback on the accuracy of actual performance as the person completes the task.(n22) These findings indicate that self-report data on psychological variables can be manipulated by a variety of experimental conditions. One experimental condition that has not been thoroughly investigated is sleep deprivation.

10 In sum, our current study addressed three specific issues. First, does sleep loss lead to changes in self-reported levels of psychological variables related to actual performance? As measures of psychological variables, we examined self-reported levels of concentration, effort, and estimated performance and self-reported off-task cognitions while the participant completed a complex cognitive task. Because sleep deprivation increases feelings of sleepiness and fatigue, we expected the sleep-deprived individuals to report lower levels of concentration, effort, and estimated performance and higher levels of off-task cognitions if they were capable of accurately assessing these psychological variables.

The second aim of our study was to determine whether sleep deprivation significantly alters mood states that may be related to performance. As specific measures of mood, we assessed feelings of tension, depression, anger, vigor, fatigue, and confusion. On the basis of a previous study that used the same mood measures,(n23) we expected sleep-deprived participants to report increased fatigue, confusion, and tension and decreased vigor.

The final purpose of our current study was to determine whether sleep deprivation alters people's ability to make an accurate assessment of their concentration, effort, and estimated performance. To investigate this aspect of sleep deprivation, we compared self-reported assessments with actual performance levels.

Method

Participants We solicited study participants from five psychology classes, two 100-level courses, one 200-level course, and two 400-level courses. Of the original 65 volunteers, 44 (26 women and 18 men) completed the study.

The mean age of the respondents, who were given extra credit points as an incentive to participate, was 20.5 years (SD = 4.37).*

Materials   We used the Watson-Glaser Critical Thinking Appraisal (WG; The Psychological Corporation, San Antonio, TX) to measure cognitive performance. We chose the WG because it would be cognitively challenging and similar to normal testing conditions for college students in that it is a linguistic task that requires mental but no physical effort. The WG contains three portions: inference, recognition of assumptions, and deduction. To increase the similarity of the task to normal testing conditions for college students, we administered the test with a 40-minute time limit.

We used self-report scales to measure mood, off-task cognitions, effort, concentration, and estimated performance. To assess current mood, we used the Profile of Mood States (POMS; Educational and Industrial Testing Service, San Diego, CA). The POMS scale provides a list of 65 words describing current mood states (see Table 8.1). The student participants rated each word based on their current mood.

Table 8.1 Examples of Self-Report Scale Used in Study of Sleep Deprivation

Test/question	Response/scale
Profile of Mood Status	
1. Friendly	Not at all (0) to extremely (4)
2. Tense	Not at all (0) to extremely (4)
3. Angry	Not at all (0) to extremely (4)
Cognitive Interference Questionnaire	
1. I thought about how poorly I was doing.	Never (1) to very often (5)
2. I thought about what the experimenter would think of me.	Never (1) to very often (5)
3. I thought about other activities (eg, assignments, work).	Never (1) to very often (5)
Psychological Variables Questionnaire	
1. How well were you able to concentrate on the task?	Not at all (1) to extremely (well) (7)
2. How well do you think you performed on this task?	Poorly (1) to extremely well (7)
3. How much effort did this task take?	Very little (1) to very much (7)

Note. These are examples of the types of questions to which participants were asked to respond.

---

*Standard deviation (SD) is a measure of how data in a set varies. A low SD means that the data is clustered tightly around the average of that data set; a high SD means the data is spread more broadly around that value.

We assessed the number of off-task cognitions while the participant completed the WG task, using the Cognitive Interference Questionnaire (CIQ).(n24) The CIQ provides a list of types of thoughts. The participants respond by stating how often they experienced those thoughts while completing the WG task. We developed a short psychological variables questionnaire, using Likert-type scales (1 to 7), to measure self-reported estimates of effort, concentration, and estimated performance. In the written instructions for the questionnaire, participants were told to respond to the questions in relation to the WG task. A complete copy of the psychological variables questionnaire is available from the author on request. Higher numbers on each of the self-report variables represent a greater frequency of that variable. For example, higher numbers on the estimated performance scale indicate a higher level of estimated performance.

Procedures   The experiment began at 10 PM on a Friday night and concluded at 11 AM the next morning. Approximately 8 participants were tested each Friday night. All participants were requested in advance not to drink alcoholic beverages or take nonprescription drugs from 10 PM on Thursday night until the conclusion of the experiment. In addition, we asked all participants to get out of bed between 7 AM and 9 AM on Friday morning and not to nap during the day.

The experiment commenced with all participants reporting to the sleep laboratory at 10 PM on Friday night. At that time, the students were randomly assigned in a block fashion to either a sleep-deprived (n = 23) or a nondeprived group (n = 21), were given the final set of instructions for the experiment, and signed consent forms. In an effort to create realistic sleep loss and nonsleep loss conditions for college students, we chose to limit the length of sleep deprivation to 24 hours for the sleep-deprived group and to allow the nondeprived group to sleep in their own beds under normal sleeping conditions for approximately 8 hours.

After the meeting at the sleep laboratory on the Friday night of the experiment, the members of the nondeprived group were told to go home and sleep approximately 8 hours. They were instructed to go to bed between 11 PM and 1 AM and to get out of bed between 7 AM and 9 AM on Saturday morning. The nondeprived participants were called at 9 AM on Saturday morning to ensure that they were awake, and they were encouraged to eat breakfast before reporting to the testing site at 10 AM.

20   The sleep-deprived group remained awake under the supervision of two research assistants in the sleep laboratory. Participants interacted with each other and with the research assistants, watched movies, played video and board games, or worked on personal projects during the night. They were allowed to bring food to eat during the night, but were asked to limit caffeinated beverages and sugary snacks to two of each. Sleep-deprived participants were escorted to a restaurant for breakfast at about 8 AM on Saturday morning. After breakfast, they were escorted to the testing area at 10:00 AM.

Testing took place at the university library in an isolated room of study cubicles, with one person per cubicle. To assess their compliance with instructions, we asked the participants to complete a short questionnaire that included questions on sleep times and items consumed since Thursday night. All participants then completed the POMS scale, followed by the WG. After finishing the WG, all of the participants completed the questionnaire assessing self-reported effort, concentration, and estimated performance in relation to the WG. The last 18 participants in each of the groups also filled out the CIQ. The entire testing period took less than 1 hour.

Data Analyses The data from the POMS, WG, and CIQ were initially scored according to the directions given for each measure. We calculated six POMS scores (tension-anxiety, depression-dejection, anger-hostility, vigor, fatigue, and confusion-bewilderment), one WG score representing the performance percentile of the individual in relation to other college students, and three CIQ scores (off-task cognitions relevant to task, off-task cognitions irrelevant to task, and general mind wandering). We derived self-reported effort, concentration, and estimated performance from the questions on the psychological variables questionnaire. We averaged self-reported sleep data for the sleep-deprived and the nondeprived groups separately, by group, for Thursday and Friday nights.

All statistical analyses were completed on SAS (SAS Institute, Cary, NC). To assess whether sleep deprivation had an effect on actual performance and self-reported estimates of psychological variables and mood states, we performed multiple analysis of variance (MANOVA), by sleep condition, on all variables.

Results

All of the student participants reported that they slept approximately 8 hours on Thursday night. The sleep-deprived participants reported sleeping an average of 7.91 hours (SD = 1.26), whereas nondeprived participants reported sleeping an average of 7.79 hours (SD = 0.69). The wake-up times on Friday morning were very similar for both groups. The deprived group reported a mean time of getting out of bed of 8:55 AM (SD = 1.22 hours), and the nondeprived group reported a mean time of getting out of bed time of 8:30 AM (SD = 1.10 hours).

On Friday night, nondeprived participants reported sleeping an average of 7.92 hours (SD = 0.51 hours) and a mean time of getting out of bed on Saturday morning of 8:40 AM (SD = 0.73 hours). Two participants, one in each sleep condition, reported taking a nap of less than 30 minutes on Friday. We analyzed the data both with and without the two napping participants included. Because the results from the two analyses were very similar, we report the results from all participants. None of the participants reported using alcohol or nonprescription drugs (except for acetaminophen) between 10 PM on Thursday and 10 AM on Saturday.

Table 8.2 Means and Standard Deviations of Sleep-and Nondeprived Participant Groups

	Sleep-deprived		Nondeprived	
Variables	M	SD	M	SD
Watson-Glaser	24.52	21.29	38.71	25.63[*]
Cognitive Interference Questionnaire				
Distracting task-relevant thoughts	2.36	0.62	2.22	0.53
Distracting task-irrelevant thoughts	1.59	0.70	1.58	0.58
General mind wandering	4.17	1.92	3.72	1.60
Estimated effort	4.03	1.00	3.41	0.70 [*]
Estimated concentration	4.30	1.66	3.28	1.31 [*]
Estimated performance	4.54	1.36	3.36	0.84 [***]
Profile of Mood States				
Tension/anxiety	14.22	7.30	11.19	8.05
Depression/dejection	11.96	12.08	9.86	10.22
Anger/hostility	11.65	9.00	8.00	7.46
Vigor	16.87	6.90	17.86	6.06
Fatigue	12.35	6.80	7.95	5.88 [*]
Confusion/bewilderment	10.65	5.22	5.95	4.10 [**]

Note. Significant differences between groups: [*] p < .05; [**] p < .01; [***] p < .001.

For means and standard deviations on the WG and the self-report tasks, see Table 8.2. As expected, the sleep-deprived participants performed significantly worse on the WG than the nondeprived participants did, $F_{(1,42)} = 4.02$, p < .05.

Although we expected that sleep-deprived participants would have more difficulty concentrating on the task and, thus, would show an increase in off-task cognitions, none of the CIQ scales was significantly increased in the sleep-deprived group. Furthermore, instead of the expected decrease in self-reported concentration, as measured by the psychological variables questionnaire, the sleep-deprived participants reported higher subjective levels of concentration while completing the task than the nondeprived participants did, $F_{(1,42)} = 5.03$, p < .05.*

The sleep-deprived participants also estimated that they expended significantly more effort to complete the task than did the nondeprived participants, $F_{(1,42)} = 5.49$, p < .05. Interestingly, although sleep-deprived participants actually performed worse on the WG than the nondeprived participants, the students deprived of sleep reported significantly higher levels of estimated performance than the nondeprived participants did, $F_{(1,42)} = 11.79$, p < .001.

*The p-value is a statistical measure used to evaluate data. A low p-value suggests a statistically significant result—*significant* meaning the result was not likely to have occurred by chance.

The sleep-deprived participants reported higher levels on five of the six POMS scales, but only the increases in the fatigue and confusion scales were significant: fatigue, $F_{(1,42)} = 5.21$, $p < .05$; confusion, $F_{(1,42)} = 10.88$, $p < .01$.

Discussion

As we expected, the results from our current study indicated that participants who were deprived of sleep for 24 hours performed significantly worse on a complex cognitive task than nondeprived participants. Although they actually performed worse, the sleep-deprived participants reported significantly higher levels of estimated performance, as well as more effort expended on the cognitive task, than the nondeprived participants did. In addition, sleep-deprived participants reported a significantly higher level of self-rated concentration than nondeprived participants did. We found no significant differences in levels of off-task cognitions between the sleep-deprived and nondeprived groups.

The apparent contradiction between the self-reported data on effort, concentration, and estimated performance and the actual performance level of sleep-deprived participants is somewhat surprising. It is unlikely that the disagreement between the self-reported variables and actual performance was a result of the type of task used. The Watson-Glaser task should have provided a suitable scenario for accurately assessing psychological variables because more difficult and longer tasks have been shown to result in more accurate self-estimates of both effort and performance.(n20, n21)

Several explanations for the disagreement between the self-report data and the actual performance levels are possible. Sleep-deprived participants may have expended more effort to complete the task, but the effort was not sufficient to overcome the performance decrements caused by being deprived of sleep. Furthermore, the increase in effort could have led the sleep-deprived participants to believe that they were performing better and concentrating more than they actually were.

An alternative explanation is that sleep deprivation may have negatively affected the degree to which participants recognized internal effort. In turn, this could have led the sleep-deprived participants to believe that they were expending more effort than they actually were, which may also have led to increases in estimated performance and self-rated concentration. Regardless of the mechanism behind the self-report data, the results indicated that our sleep-deprived participants did not realize the extent to which their own performances were affected by sleep loss, and they appeared to be making incorrect assumptions about their ability to concentrate and to provide the necessary effort to complete the task.

Interestingly, sleep deprivation did not result in the expected change in reporting off-task cognitions. Although a previous study(n10) found that participants who habitually reported distracting thoughts were more likely to do so when deprived of sleep, it appears that the effect of sleep deprivation on off-task cognitions depends on whether the sleep-deprived person regularly experiences high levels of off-task cognitions. Therefore, reporting off-task cognitions does not appear to be specifically affected by sleep deprivation, independent of baseline levels.

35   A second major finding of this research is that sleep deprivation differentially affected mood states in these college students. The current findings indicate that sleep deprivation significantly affected only the fatigue and confusion subscales on the POMS. The reported increase in fatigue and confusion could have contributed to the significant decrease in actual performance that we observed in the sleep-deprived student participants. It is interesting to note that none of the remaining POMS subscales changed significantly in the sleep-deprived participants, indicating that some mood changes commonly ascribed to sleep deprivation, such as anger, irritability, and anxiety, were not necessarily products of 24 hours of sleep loss.

The current findings on mood states are very similar to those reported by Dinges and colleagues.(n23) Sleep-deprived participants in both studies reported significantly more fatigue and confusion than nondeprived participants. Dinges and colleagues reported significantly more tension and significantly less vigor in sleep-deprived participants.

Similarly, we noted a trend for more tension and less vigor in the sleep-deprived participants in our study. The most likely reason for the small differences between the two studies is that Dinges and colleagues collected mood data every 2 hours for a 64-hour sleep-deprivation period, whereas we collected mood data only once—immediately before the students' completion of the cognitive task. Furthermore, neither study reported a significant increase in angry or depressed feelings following sleep deprivation, indicating that sleep deprivation does not necessarily increase reports of anger and depression, as is commonly believed.

In sum, our findings suggest that college students are not aware of the extent to which sleep deprivation impairs their ability to complete cognitive tasks successfully because they consistently overrate their concentration and effort, as well as their estimated performance. In addition, the current data suggest that 24 hours of sleep deprivation significantly affects only fatigue and confusion and does not have a more general effect on positive or negative mood states. The practical implication of these findings is that many college students are unknowingly sabotaging their own performance by choosing to deprive themselves of sleep [while] they complete complex cognitive tasks.

References

(n1.) Hawkins J, Shaw P. Self-reported sleep quality in college students: A repeated measures approach. Sleep. 1992;15(6):545–549.

(n2.) Dinges DE. The nature of sleepiness: Causes, contexts, and consequences. In: Eating, Sleeping, and Sex. Stunkard A, Baum A, eds. Hillsdale, NJ: Erlbaum; 1988.

(n3.) Pilcher JJ, Huffcutt AI. Effects of sleep deprivation on performance: A meta-analysis. Sleep. 1996;19(4):318–326.

(n4.) Johnson LC. Sleep deprivation and performance. In: Webb WW, ed. Biological Rhythms, Sleep, and Performance. New York: Wiley; 1982.

(n5.) Meddis R. Cognitive dysfunction following loss of sleep. In: Burton E, ed. The Pathology and Psychology of Cognition. London: Methuen; 1982.

(n6.) Williams HL, Lubin A. Speeded addition and sleep loss. J EXP Psychol. 1967;73:313–317.

(n7.) Elkin AL, Murray DJ. The effects of sleep loss on short-term recognition memory. Can J Psychol. 1974;28:192–198.

(n8.) Polzella DJ. Effects of sleep-deprivation on short-term memory and recognition. J Exp Psychol. 1975;104:194–200.

(n9.) Hockey GRJ. Changes in attention allocation in a multicomponent task under loss of sleep. Br J Psychol. 1970;61(4):473–480.

(n10.) Mikulincer M, Babkoff H, Caspy T, Weiss H. The impact of cognitive interference on performance during prolonged sleep loss. Psychol Res. 1990;52:80–86.

(n11.) Kjellberg A. Sleep deprivation and some aspects of performance. Waking Sleeping. 1977;1:139–154.

(n12.) Horne JA. Why We Sleep. New York: Oxford University Press; 1988.

(n13.) Horne JA, Pettitt AN. High incentive effects on vigilance performance during 72 hours of total sleep deprivation. Acta Psychologica. 1985;58:123–139.

(n14.) Mikulincer M, Babkoff H, Caspy T, Sing H. The effects of 72 hours of sleep loss on psychological variables. Br J Psychol. 1989;80:145–162.

(n15.) Dinges DF, Kribbs NB, Steinberg KN, Powell JW. Do we lose the willingness to perform during sleep deprivation? Sleep Res. 1992;21:318.

(n16.) Angus RG, Heslegrave RJ. Effects of sleep loss on sustained cognitive performance during a command and control simulation. Behav Res Methods Instruments Computers. 1985;17:55–67.

(n17.) Linde L, Bergstrom M. The effect of one night without sleep on problem-solving and immediate recall. Psychol Res. 1992;54:127–136.

(n18.) Brendel DH, Reynolds CF III, Jennings JR, et al. Sleep stage physiology, mood, and vigilance responses to total sleep deprivation in healthy 80-year-olds and 20-year-olds. Psychophysiology. 1990;27:677–686.

(n19.) Leung L, Becker CE. Sleep deprivation and house staff performance: Update. J Occup Med. 1992;34:1153–1160.

(n20.) Johnson NE, Saccuzzo DP, Larson GE. Self-reported effort versus actual performance in information processing paradigms. J Gen Psychol. 1995;122(2):195–210.

(n21.) Beyer S. Gender differences in the accuracy of self-evaluations of performance. J Pers Soc Psychol. 1990;59(5):960–970.

(n22.) Critchfield TS. Bias in self-evaluation: Signal probability effects. J Exp Anal Behav. 1994;62:235–250.

(n23.) Dinges DF, Gillen KA, Powell JW, et al. Mood reports during total and partial sleep deprivation: Is anger inevitable? Sleep Res. 1995;24:441.

(n24.) Sarason IG, Sarason B, Keefe D, Hayes B, Shearin EN. Cognitive interference: Situational determinants and traitlike characteristics. J Pers Soc Psychol. 1986;51:215–226.

Discussion and Writing Suggestions

1. Have you ever stayed awake all night to complete schoolwork? How many college students of your acquaintance (or, perhaps, you yourself) believe that it is possible to "pull an all-nighter" without degrading your performance the next day? Does the study by Pilcher and Walters change your opinion? Explain your response.

2. The authors conclude that "college students are not aware of the extent to which sleep deprivation impairs their ability to complete cognitive tasks successfully because they consistently overrate their concentration and effort, as well as their estimated performance.... [M]any college students are unknowingly sabotaging their own performance by choosing to deprive themselves of sleep [while] they complete complex cognitive tasks." To what extent do these conclusions describe you?

3. In paragraphs 32–33, the authors present several explanations to account for the discrepancy between students' "self-report data and [their] actual performance levels" on the cognitive task in the experiment. Which of these explanations seems most plausible? Why?

4. How convincing do you find the results of this study? Can you refute them? Do you find yourself *wanting* to refute them? To the extent that you are convinced, what are the odds you will stop staying awake all night to study for exams or to write papers?

5. Carefully review paragraphs 1–12 to understand how the authors justify the need to conduct their present research. Summarize how they go about making this justification. Focus on how they make their argument, not on the content of their argument.

6. Why does the experimental method lend itself to studying questions related to sleep deprivation and self-reports of concentration, effort, etc.?

7. Would you volunteer for an experiment similar to the one Pilcher and Walters conducted? Why or why not?

Synthesis Activities

1. Explain the fundamentals of sleep for an audience (perhaps someone like yourself before reading this chapter) who regards sleep as a passive state characterized by the absence of wakefulness. Make clear that sleep is ubiquitous (fruit flies, fish, cats, alligators, and humans all sleep); is an active, not a passive behavior; has an "architecture" that changes over one's life; can be especially troubling for adolescents; and can be delayed or otherwise disrupted in ways that cause sleep debt and associated problems. Refer to the

Harvard Special Health Report ("Improving Sleep") and to the selections by the National Sleep Foundation, Dement and Vaughan, and Pilcher and Walters.

2. Use one or more of the selections in this chapter to analyze the quality of your sleep in a typical week. As part of your analysis, be sure to take (and score) the Pittsburgh Sleep Quality Index. Recall that the purpose of any analysis is to increase understanding of a little-understood phenomenon—in this case, *your* sleep patterns. What principle(s) or definition(s) will you use from the chapter readings to guide your analysis? Follow the general format for writing analyses on p. 124.

3. The selection by Pilcher and Walters first appeared in journal intended for professionals interested in sleep. Using standards of good writing established by your composition instructor and text-books, evaluate the presentation of this selection. In your critique, focus on the authors' success at communicating a key idea. What are your standards for evaluation: a writer's ability to organize at the global, section, or paragraph level? Sentence style? Word choice? Conciseness? Tone? How many criteria will you use in making your overall assessment? Follow the general format for writing critiques on p. 43.

4. In an explanatory synthesis, discuss phase-delayed sleep: whom it affects; its biological, behavioral, and social causes; its related problems; and its remedies (to the extent they exist). Refer to chapter selections as needed, but be sure to reference Dement and Vaughan. Follow the general format for writing syntheses on pp. 60–61.

5. Discuss why cramming for an examination (staying awake all night to study or to write a paper) can be a mistake. Your discussion should include an account of sleep debt and its consequences. Refer to chapter selections as needed, but be sure to reference Dement and Vaughan and also Pilcher and Walters. Follow the general format for writing syntheses on pp. 60–61.

6. Draw upon the selections in this chapter to create an advertising campaign aimed at promoting good sleep hygiene among college students. The campaign might take the form of a brochure, a poster, a series of e-mails, or a Web site. In your campaign, explain the importance of sleep, particularly for adolescents. Create a separate Works Cited page for the sources you reference in your campaign.

7. Argue for or against the proposition that the health office at your college should set up an educational program to promote good sleep hygiene among students. In developing your argument, refer to the scientific evidence on adolescent sleep needs and sleep debt and its consequences. Among the selections you refer to should be

those by the National Sleep Foundation, Dement and Vaughan, and Pilcher and Walters.

8. Argue for or against the proposition that the start time of the high school you attended should be later than it currently is. In your argument, consider the scientific evidence relating to problems associated with phase-delayed sleep. Consider also the complications of coordinating schedules among the various stakeholders in any change of start time: for instance, among students, teachers, parents, coaches, and staff. In your paper, refer to the selections by the National Sleep Foundation and Dement and Vaughan.

9. Explain your reactions to the reading selections in this chapter. What you have learned about sleep will inevitably find its way into this paper. But keep the focus on your *reactions* to learning about one or more of the following: sleep debt and cramming for exams; sleep debt and the dangers of drowsiness while driving; the problems caused when adolescent sleep patterns collide with the scheduling demands of the business and scholastic worlds. Let your interest in the topic dictate the specific focus of your explanation.

RESEARCH ACTIVITIES

1. Sleep specialists do not agree on the purpose of sleep. Investigate theories of why we—as well as other creatures—sleep. The oldest theories—based largely on speculation—date to the times of Aristotle and earlier. In recent decades, biologists and physicians have proposed theories based on current scientific research.

2. Discuss references to sleep in one or more artistic works. Macbeth's and Lady Macbeth's troubled sleep following their murder of King Duncan comes to mind. You might consider, as well, cinematic works like the Al Pacino film *Insomnia* (2002), directed by Christopher Nolan, or the unusual dreamlike visions of Richard Linklater in films like *Waking Life* (2001) and *A Scanner Darkly* (2006).

3. Research and write an overview of sleep disorders (there are eighty-four, divided into four general classifications). If you find yourself especially intrigued by one disorder—for instance, sleep apnea, restless leg syndrome, or night terrors—focus your research on that.

4. Investigate sleep specialists' use of the polysomnograph to monitor body functions as patients sleep in a laboratory. What does the polysomnograph measure? How is the patient monitored? How is the polysomnograph read and interpreted? What role does it play in the diagnosis and treatment of sleep disorders?

5. Several authors in this chapter discuss circadian rhythm. Conduct more research into the "internal clock" that determines for us (and other creatures) patterns of wakefulness and sleep. What is this clock? Where is it located? When, in response to what, and how did it evolve?

6. Investigate NASA's interest in the sleep problems of astronauts, a select group whose accelerated daily exposure to patterns of light and dark plays havoc with their sleep. What, precisely, are the problems? What solutions is NASA devising? (You might also want to investigate the sleep challenges that NASA anticipates for long-distance missions to Mars and beyond.)

7. Investigate sleep researchers' inquiries into sleep deprivation. Begin with a close reading of Pilcher and Walters in this chapter. Consult their reference list, and see especially the pioneering work of William Dement, whose scholarship is also represented in this chapter.

8. Investigate the history or promotion of sleeping aids—medicinal (for instance, opiates, melatonin, and the new prescription drugs), behavioral (what's "counting sheep" all about?), and mechanical (white noise machines, etc.). If one particular area of this research captures your attention (for example, the business aspects of sleeping aids, or the social consequences), pursue that area, rather than preparing a broad overview.

9. The inventor of psychoanalysis, Sigmund Freud, initially made his reputation with his startling theories about the interpretation of dreams. (In Freud's theories, people and objects occurring in dreams were frequently symbolic.) Investigate one or more current theories on the content of the dreams that occur during REM sleep, as discussed, for example, in the *Harvard Health Letter (Improving Sleep)*. How does the content of dreams correlate with the dreamer's life?

10. Several authors in this chapter discuss the sometimes catastrophic consequences (such as the *Exxon Valdez* disaster) of sleep deprivation. In some cases, insufficient sleep time is built into the job—for example, the duty schedules of some airline flight crews, long-distance truck drivers, or medical interns. Select one such job area, and discuss the particular problems caused by enforced (or voluntary) sleep deprivation. Or discuss recent attempts to address such long-standing problems with policies designed to ensure that people get sufficient sleep so as not to pose a danger to themselves or others.

Chapter 9

New and Improved: Six Decades of Advertising

Possibly the most memorable ad campaign of the twentieth century (dating from the late 1920s) takes the form of a comic strip. A bully kicks sand into the face of a skinny man relaxing on the beach with his girlfriend. Humiliated, the skinny man vows to get even. "Don't bother, little boy!" huffs the scornful girlfriend, who promptly dumps him. At home, the skinny man kicks a chair in frustration, declares that he's sick of being a scarecrow, and says that if Charles Atlas (once a "97-lb. weakling" himself) can give him a "real body," he'll send for his FREE book. In the next frame, the once-skinny man, now transformed into a hunk, thanks to Atlas's "Dynamic Tension" fitness program, admires himself in front of the mirror: "Boy, it didn't take Atlas long to do this for me. Look, how those muscles bulge!...That big stiff won't dare insult me now!" Back on the beach, the bully is decked by the once-skinny man, as his adoring girlfriend looks on: "Oh Mac! You are a real man after all!"

Crude? Undoubtedly. But variations of this ad, which made Atlas a multimillionaire, ran for decades (his company is still in business). Like other successful ads, it draws its power from skillful appeals to almost primitive urges—in this particular case, the urge to gain dominance over a rival for the attention of the opposite sex. Of course, effective ads don't always work on such a primal level. Another famous ad of the 1920s appeals to our need to gain respect from others for higher accomplishments than punching out opponents. Headlined "They Laughed When I Sat Down at the Piano—But When I Started to Play...!" the text offers a first-person account of a man who sits down to play the piano at a party. As he does so, the guests make good-natured fun of him. But once he began to play, "a tense silence fell on the guests. The laughter died on their lips as if by magic.

I played through the first bars of Liszt's immortal 'Liebenstraum.' I heard gasps of amazement. My friends sat breathless—spellbound." For sixteen additional paragraphs, the writer goes on to detail the effect of his playing upon the guests and to explain how "You, too, can now *teach yourself* to be an accomplished musician—right at home," by purchasing the program of the U.S. School of Music. Again, the reader is encouraged to send for the free booklet. And by the way, "Forget the old-fashioned idea that you need 'special talent'" to play an instrument.

The ubiquity of advertising is a fact of modern life. In fact, advertising can be traced as far back as ancient Roman times when pictures were inscribed on walls to promote gladiatorial contests. In those days, however, the illiteracy of most of the population and the fact that goods were made by hand and could not be mass produced limited the need for more widespread advertising. One of the first American advertisers was Benjamin Franklin, who pioneered the use of large headlines and made strategic use of white space. But advertising as the mass phenomenon we know is a product of the twentieth century, when the United States became an industrial nation—and particularly of the post–World War II period, when a prosperous economy created our modern consumer society, marked by the middle-class acquisition of goods, the symbols of status, success, style, and social acceptance. Today, we are surrounded not only by a familiar array of billboards, print ads, and broadcast ads, but also by the Internet, which has given us "spam," the generic name for an entire category of digital pitches for debt reduction, low mortgage rates, and enhanced body parts—compared to which the average Buick ad in a glossy magazine reads like great literature.

Advertisements are more than just appeals to buy; they are windows into our psyches and our culture. They reveal our values, our (not-so-hidden) desires, our yearnings for a different lifestyle. For example, the Marlboro man, that quintessence of taciturn cowboy masculinity, at home only in the wide open spaces of Marlboro Country, is a mid-twentieth-century American tribute to (what is perceived as) nineteenth-century American values, popularized in hundreds of westerns. According to James Twitchell, a professor of English and advertising at the University of Florida, "He is what we have for royalty, distilled manhood....The Marlboro Man needs to tell you nothing. He carries no scepter, no gun. He never even speaks. Doesn't need to." He is also the product of a bolt of advertising inspiration: Previously, Marlboro had been marketed—unsuccessfully—as a woman's cigarette. Another example of how ads reveal culture is the memorable campaign for the Volkswagen Beetle in the 1960s. That campaign spoke to the counterculture mentality of the day: Instead of appealing to the traditional automobile customer's desire for luxury, beauty, size, power, and comfort, Volkswagen emphasized how small, funny looking, and bare bones—but economical and sensible—their cars were. On the other hand, snob appeal—at an affordable price, of course—has generally been a winning strategy. In the 1980s and 1990s, Grey Poupon mustard ran a successful campaign of TV commercials featuring one Rolls-Royce pulling up alongside another. A voice from one vehicle asks,

"Pardon me; do you have any Grey Poupon?" "But of course!" replies a voice in the other car, and a hand with a jar of mustard reaches out from the window of the second car to pass to the unseen occupant of the first car. This campaign is a perfect illustration of what University of California at Davis history professor Roland Marchand calls the appeal of the democracy of goods: "the wonders of modern mass production and distribution enable…everyone to enjoy society's most desirable pleasures, conveniences, or benefits."

So pervasive and influential has advertising become that it has created a significant backlash among social critics. Among the most familiar charges against advertising: It fosters materialism, it psychologically manipulates people to buy things they don't need, it perpetuates gender and racial stereotypes (particularly in its illustrations), it is deceptive, it is offensive, it debases the language, and it is omnipresent—we cannot escape it. Although arguing the truth or falsity of these assertions makes for lively debate, our focus in this chapter is not on the ethics of advertising but rather on how it works. What makes for successful advertising? How do advertisers—and by advertisers we mean not only manufacturers but also the agencies they hire to produce their advertisements—pull our psychological levers to influence us to buy (or think favorably of) their products? What are the textual and graphic components of an effective advertisement—of an effective advertising campaign? How—if at all—has advertising evolved over the past several decades? (You may be interested in seeking out the documentary film *Art and Copy* [2009], about some of the great ad campaigns created during this period.)

Advertising has seen significant changes in the six decades since the end of World War II. It is unlikely that the comic strip Charles Atlas ad or the verbose "They Laughed When I Sat Down at the Piano" ad would succeed today. Both seem extremely dated. More representative of today's advertising style is the successful milk campaign; each ad features a celebrity such as Bernie Mac or Lauren Bacall with a milk mustache, a headline that says simply "got milk?", and a few short words of text supposedly spoken by the pictured celebrity. But the changes in advertising during the six decades covered in this chapter are more of style than of substance. On the whole, the similarities between an ad produced in the 1950s and one produced today are more significant than the differences. Of course, hair and clothing styles change with the times, message length recedes, and both text and graphics assume a lesser degree of apple-pie social consensus on values. But on the whole, the same psychological appeals, the same principles of headline and graphic design that worked 60 years ago, continue to work today. We choose one automobile over another, for instance, less because our vehicle of choice gets us from point A to point B than because we invest it—or the advertiser does—with rich psychological and cultural values. In 1957 the French anthropologist and philosopher Roland Barthes wrote (in a review of a French automobile, the Citroën DS), "I think that cars today are almost the exact equivalent of the great Gothic cathedrals: I mean the supreme creation of an era, conceived with passion by unknown artists, and consumed in image if not in usage by a whole population which appropriates them as a purely magical object." Barthes might have had a good career as an advertising copywriter.

How advertising works, then, is the subject of the present chapter. By applying a variety of theoretical and practical perspectives to a gallery of six decades of advertisements (and on other ads of your own choosing), you'll be able to practice your analytical skills on one of the more fascinating areas of American mass culture. Following the introductory selection on the chief psychological appeals of advertising, you will find the main objects of your analyses: (1) a portfolio of *print advertisements* that originally appeared in such magazines as *Time, Newsweek, U.S. News and World Report,* and *Sunset*; and (2) a portfolio of memorable *TV commercials*, available for viewing on the YouTube Web site. For ease of comparison and contrast, most of the print ads can be classified into a relatively few categories: cigarettes, alcohol, automobiles, food, and "miscellaneous." We have selected both the print ads and the TV commercials for their inherent interest, as well as for the variety of tools employed to communicate their message about what sets their product or service apart from the competition—what some advertisers call their *USP*, or unique selling proposition.

The chapter's opening selection provides analytical tools, particular perspectives from which to view individual advertisements. In "Advertising's Fifteen Basic Appeals," Jib Fowles offers a psychological perspective. Fowles identifies and discusses the most common needs to which advertisers attempt to appeal—among these the need for sex, affiliation with other people, dominance, and autonomy.

Charles O'Neill, an independent marketing consultant, has written, "Perhaps, by learning how advertising works, we can become better equipped to sort out content from hype, product values from emotions, and salesmanship from propaganda." We hope that the selections in this chapter will equip you to do just that, as well as to develop a greater understanding of one of the most pervasive components of American mass culture.

ADVERTISING'S FIFTEEN BASIC APPEALS

Jib Fowles

Our first selection provides what you will likely find the single most useful analytical tool for studying advertisements. Drawing upon studies of numerous ads and upon interviews with subjects conducted by Harvard psychologist Henry A. Murray, Fowles developed a set of fifteen basic appeals he believes to be at the heart of American advertising. These appeals, according to Fowles and to Murray, are directed primarily to the "lower brain," to those "unfulfilled urges and motives swirling in the bottom half of [our] minds," rather than to the part of the brain that processes our more rational thoughts and impulses. As you read Fowles's article and his descriptions of the individual appeals, other examples from contemporary print and broadcast ads may occur to you. You may find it useful to jot down these examples for later incorporation into your responses to the discussion and synthesis questions that follow.

Jib Fowles has written numerous articles and books on the popular media, including *Mass Advertising as Social Forecast: A Method for Futures Research* (1976), *Why Viewers Watch: A Reappraisal of Television's Effects* (1992), *Advertising and Popular Culture* (1996), and *The Case for Television Violence* (1999). This selection first appeared in *Etc.* 39:3 (1982) and was reprinted in *Advertising and Popular Culture.*

Emotional Appeals

The nature of effective advertisements was recognized full well by the late media philosopher Marshall McLuhan. In his *Understanding Media,* the first sentence of the section on advertising reads, "The continuous pressure is to create ads more and more in the image of audience motives and desires."

By giving form to people's deep-lying desires, and picturing states of being that individuals privately yearn for, advertisers have the best chance of arresting attention and affecting communication. And that is the immediate goal of advertising: to tug at our psychological shirtsleeves and slow us down long enough for a word or two about whatever is being sold. We glance at a picture of a solitary rancher at work, and "Marlboro" slips into our minds.

Advertisers (I'm using the term as a shorthand for both the products' manufacturers, who bring the ambition and money to the process, and the advertising agencies, who supply the know-how) are ever more compelled to invoke consumers' drives and longings; this is the "continuous pressure" McLuhan refers to. Over the past century, the American marketplace has grown increasingly congested as more and more products have entered into the frenzied competition after the public's dollars. The economies of other nations are quieter than ours since the volume of goods being hawked does not so greatly exceed demand. In some economies, consumer wares are scarce enough that no advertising at all is necessary. But in the United States, we go to the other extreme. In order to stay in business, an advertiser must strive to cut through the considerable commercial hub-bub by any means available—including the emotional appeals that some observers have held to be abhorrent and underhanded.

The use of subconscious appeals is a comment not only on conditions among sellers. As time has gone by, buyers have become stoutly resistant to advertisements. We live in a blizzard of these messages and have learned to turn up our collars and ward off most of them. A study done a few years ago at Harvard University's Graduate School of Business Administration ventured that the average American is exposed to some 500 ads daily from television, newspapers, magazines, radio, billboards, direct mail, and so on. If for no other reason than to preserve one's sanity, a filter must be developed in every mind to lower the number of ads a person is actually aware of—a number this particular study estimated at about seventy-five ads per day. (Of these, only twelve typically produced a reaction—nine positive and three negative, on the average.) To be among the few messages that do manage to gain access to minds, advertisers must be strategic, perhaps even a little underhanded at times.

There are assumptions about personality underlying advertisers' efforts to communicate via emotional appeals, and while these assumptions have stood the test of time, they still deserve to be aired. Human beings, it is presumed, walk around with a variety of unfulfilled urges and motives swirling in the bottom half of their minds. Lusts, ambitions, tendernesses, vulnerabilities—they are constantly bubbling up, seeking resolution. These mental forces energize people, but they are too crude and irregular to be given excessive play in the real world. They must be capped with the competent, sensible behavior that permits individuals to get along well in society. However, this upper layer of mental activity, shot through with caution and rationality, is not receptive to advertising's pitches. Advertisers want to circumvent this shell of consciousness if they can, and latch on to one of the lurching, subconscious drives.

In effect, advertisers over the years have blindly felt their way around the underside of the American psyche, and by trial and error have discovered the softest points of entree, the places where their messages have the greatest likelihood of getting by consumers' defenses. As McLuhan says elsewhere, "Gouging away at the surface of public sales resistance, the ad men are constantly breaking through into the *Alice in Wonderland* territory behind the looking glass, which is the world of subrational impulses and appetites."

An advertisement communicates by making use of a specially selected image (of a supine female, say, or a curly-haired child, or a celebrity) which is designed to stimulate "subrational impulses and desires" even when they are at ebb, even if they are unacknowledged by their possessor. Some few ads have their emotional appeal in the text, but for the greater number by far the appeal is contained in the artwork. This makes sense, since visual communication better suits more primal levels of the brain. If the viewer of an advertisement actually has the importuned motive, and if the appeal is sufficiently well fashioned to call it up, then the person can be hooked. The product in the ad may then appear to take on the semblance of gratification for the summoned motive. Many ads seem to be saying, "If you have this need, then this product will help satisfy it." It is a primitive equation, but not an ineffective one for selling.

Thus, most advertisements appearing in national media can be understood as having two orders of content. The first is the appeal to deep-running drives in the minds of consumers. The second is information regarding the good[s] or service being sold: its name, its manufacturer, its picture, its packaging, its objective attributes, its functions. For example, the reader of a brassiere advertisement sees a partially undraped but blandly unperturbed woman standing in an otherwise commonplace public setting, and may experience certain sensations; the reader also sees the name "Maidenform," a particular brassiere style, and, in tiny print, words about the material, colors, price. Or, the viewer of a television commercial sees a demonstration with four small boxes labeled 650, 650, 650, and 800; something in the viewer's mind catches hold of this, as trivial as thoughtful consideration might reveal it to be. The viewer is also exposed to the name "Anacin," its bottle, and its purpose.

Sometimes there is an apparently logical link between an ad's emotional appeal and its product information. It does not violate common sense that Cadillac automobiles be photographed at country clubs, or that Japan Air Lines be associated with Orientalia. But there is no real need for the linkage to have a bit of reason behind it. Is there anything inherent to the connection between Salem cigarettes and mountains, Coke and a smile, Miller Beer and comradeship? The link being forged in minds between product and appeal is a pre-logical one.

10   People involved in the advertising industry do not necessarily talk in the terms being used here. They are stationed at the sending end of this communications channel, and may think they are up to any number of things—Unique Selling Propositions, explosive copywriting, the optimal use of demographics or psychographics, ideal media buys, high recall ratings, or whatever. But when attention shifts to the receiving end of the channel, and focuses on the instant of reception, then commentary becomes much more elemental: an advertising message contains something primary and primitive, an emotional appeal, that in effect is the thin end of the wedge, trying to find its way into a mind. Should this occur, the product information comes along behind.

When enough advertisements are examined in this light, it becomes clear that the emotional appeals fall into several distinguishable categories, and that every ad is a variation on one of a limited number of basic appeals. While there may be several ways of classifying these appeals, one particular list of fifteen has proven to be especially valuable.

Advertisements can appeal to:

1. The need for sex
2. The need for affiliation
3. The need to nurture
4. The need for guidance
5. The need to aggress
6. The need to achieve
7. The need to dominate
8. The need for prominence
9. The need for attention
10. The need for autonomy
11. The need to escape
12. The need to feel safe
13. The need for aesthetic sensations
14. The need to satisfy curiosity
15. Physiological needs: food, drink, sleep, etc.

Murray's List

Where does this list of advertising's fifteen basic appeals come from? Several years ago, I was involved in a research project which was to have as one segment an objective analysis of the changing appeals made in post-World War II American advertising. A sample of magazine ads would have their appeals coded into the categories of psychological needs they seemed aimed at. For this content analysis to happen, a complete roster of human motives would have to be found.

The first thing that came to mind was Abraham Maslow's famous four-part hierarchy of needs. But the briefest look at the range of appeals made in advertising was enough to reveal that they are more varied, and more profane, than Maslow had cared to account for. The search led on to the work of psychologist Henry A. Murray, who together with his colleagues at the Harvard Psychological Clinic has constructed a full taxonomy of needs. As described in *Explorations in Personality*, Murray's team had conducted a lengthy series of in-depth interviews with a number of subjects in order to derive from scratch what they felt to be the essential variables of personality. Forty-four variables were distinguished by the Harvard group, of which twenty were motives. The need for achievement ("to overcome obstacles and obtain a high standard") was one, for instance; the need to defer was another; the need to aggress was a third; and so forth.

Murray's list had served as the groundwork for a number of subsequent projects. Perhaps the best-known of these was David C. McClelland's extensive study of the need for achievement, reported in his *The Achieving Society*. In the process of demonstrating that a people's high need for achievement is predictive of later economic growth, McClelland coded achievement imagery and references out of a nation's folklore, songs, legends, and children's tales.

Following McClelland, I too wanted to cull the motivational appeals from a culture's imaginative product—in this case, advertising. To develop categories expressly for this purpose, I took Murray's twenty motives and added to them others he had mentioned in passing in *Explorations in Personality* but not included on the final list. The extended list was tried out on a sample of advertisements, and motives which never seemed to be invoked were dropped. I ended up with eighteen of Murrays' motives, into which 770 print ads were coded. The resulting distribution is included in the 1976 book *Mass Advertising as Social Forecast*.

Since that time, the list of appeals has undergone refinements as a result of using it to analyze television commercials. A few more adjustments stemmed from the efforts of students in my advertising classes to decode appeals; tens of term papers surveying thousands of advertisements have caused some inconsistencies in the list to be hammered out. Fundamentally, though, the list remains the creation of Henry Murray. In developing a comprehensive, parsimonious inventory of human motives, he pinpointed the subsurface mental forces that are the least quiescent and most susceptible to advertising's entreaties.

Fifteen Appeals

1. Need for Sex. Let's start with sex, because this is the appeal which seems to pop up first whenever the topic of advertising is raised. Whole books have been written about this one alone, to find a large audience of mildly titillated readers. Lately, due to campaigns to sell blue jeans, concern with sex in ads has redoubled.

The fascinating thing is not how much sex there is in advertising, but how little. Contrary to impressions, unambiguous sex is rare in these messages. Some of this surprising observation may be a matter of definition: the Jordache ads with the lithe, blouse-less female astride a similarly clad male is clearly an appeal to the audience's sexual drives, but the same cannot be said about Brooke Shields* in the Calvin Klein commercials. Directed at young women and their credit-card carrying mothers, the image of Miss Shields instead invokes the need to be looked at. Buy Calvins and you'll be the center of much attention, just as Brooke is, the ads imply; they do not primarily inveigle their target audience's need for sexual intercourse.

In the content analysis reported in *Mass Advertising as Social Forecast* only two percent of ads were found to pander to this motive. Even *Playboy* ads shy away from sexual appeals: a recent issue contained eighty-three full-page ads, and just four of them (or less than five percent) could be said to have sex on their minds.

20   The reason this appeal is so little used is that it is too blaring and tends to obliterate the product information. Nudity in advertising has the effect of reducing brand recall. The people who do remember the product may do so because they have been made indignant by the ad; this is not the response most advertisers seek.

To the extent that sexual imagery is used, it conventionally works better on men than women; typically a female figure is offered up to the male reader. A Black Velvet liquor advertisement displays an attractive woman wearing a tight black outfit, recumbent under the legend, "Feel the Velvet." The figure does not have to be horizontal, however, for the appeal to be present as National Airlines revealed in its "Fly me" campaign. Indeed, there does not even have to be a female in the ad; "Flick my Bic"† was sufficient to convey the idea to many.

As a rule, though, advertisers have found sex to be a tricky appeal, to be used sparingly. Less controversial and equally fetching are the appeals to our need for affectionate human contact.

2. Need for Affiliation. American mythology upholds autonomous individuals, and social statistics suggest that people are ever more going it alone in their lives, yet the high frequency of affiliative appeals in ads

---

*Brooke Shields (b. 1965) is a model (at age 3 she was the Ivory Snow baby), as well as a stage (*Grease*), TV, and film actress; her most well-known films are *Pretty Baby* (1978) and *Blue Lagoon* (1980).

†"Flick my Bic" became a famous and successful slogan in advertisements for Bic cigarette lighters during the late 1970s and 1980s. Fowles hints at the not-too-subtle sexual implications of the line.

belies this. Or maybe it does not: maybe all the images of companionship are compensation for what Americans privately lack. In any case, the need to associate with others is widely invoked in advertising and is probably the most prevalent appeal. All sorts of goods and services are sold by linking them to our unfulfilled desires to be in good company.

According to Henry Murray, the need for affiliation consists of desires "to draw near and enjoyably cooperate or reciprocate with another; to please and win affection of another; to adhere and remain loyal to a friend." The manifestations of this motive can be segmented into several different types of affiliation, beginning with romance.

Courtship may be swifter nowadays, but the desire for pair-bonding is far from satiated. Ads reaching for this need commonly depict a youngish male and female engrossed in each other. The head of the male is usually higher than the female's, even at this late date; she may be sitting or leaning while he is standing. They are not touching in the Smirnoff vodka ads, but obviously there is an intimacy, sometimes frolicsome, between them. The couple does touch for Martell Cognac when "The moment was Martell." For Wind Song perfume they have touched, and "Your Wind Song stays on his mind."

Depending on the audience, the pair does not absolutely have to be young—just together. He gives her a DeBeers diamond, and there is a tear in her laugh lines. She takes Geritol* and preserves herself for him. And numbers of consumers, wanting affection too, follow suit.

Warm family feelings are fanned in ads when another generation is added to the pair. Hallmark Cards brings grandparents into the picture, and Johnson and Johnson Baby Powder has Dad, Mom, and baby, all fresh from the bath, encircled in arms and emblazoned with "Share the Feeling." A talc has been fused to familial love.

Friendship is yet another form of affiliation pursued by advertisers. Two women confide and drink Maxwell House coffee together; two men walk through the woods smoking Salem cigarettes. Miller Beer promises that afternoon "Miller Time" will be staffed with three or four good buddies. Drink Dr. Pepper, as Mickey Rooney is coaxed to do, and join in with all the other Peppers. Coca-Cola does not even need to portray the friendliness; it has reduced this appeal to "a Coke and a smile."

The warmth can be toned down and disguised, but it is the same affiliative need that is being fished for. The blonde has a direct gaze and her friends are firm businessmen in appearance, but with a glass of Old Bushmill you can sit down and fit right in. Or, for something more upbeat, sing along with the Pontiac choirboys.

The original Geritol (a combination of the words "geriatric" and "tolerance") was an iron tonic and vitamin supplement marketed to people over 40 between 1950 and 1979 with the slogan, "Do you have iron poor, tired blood?" Though today Geritol is the label on a group of health-related products, the name became famous—and, to some extent, funny—as a means of restoring energy and youthful vigor to middle-age and elderly people.

30   As well as presenting positive images, advertisers can play to the need for affiliation in negative ways, by invoking the fear of rejection. If we don't use Scope, we'll have the "Ugh! Morning Breath" that causes the male and female models to avert their faces. Unless we apply Ultra Brite or Close-Up to our teeth, it's good-bye romance. Our family will be cursed with "House-a-tosis" if we don't take care. Without Dr. Scholl's antiperspirant foot spray, the bowling team will keel over. There go all the guests when the supply of Dorito's nacho cheese chips is exhausted. Still more rejection if our shirts have ring-around-the-collar, if our car needs to be Midasized. But make a few purchases, and we are back in the bosom of human contact.

As self-directed as Americans pretend to be, in the last analysis we remain social animals, hungering for the positive, endorsing feelings that only those around us can supply. Advertisers respond, urging us to "Reach out and touch someone," in the hopes our monthly [phone] bills will rise.

3. Need to Nurture.   Akin to affiliative needs is the need to take care of small, defenseless creatures—children and pets, largely. Reciprocity is of less consequence here, though; it is the giving that counts. Murray uses synonyms like "to feed, help, support, console, protect, comfort, nurse, heal." A strong need it is, woven deep into our genetic fabric, for if it did not exist we could not successfully raise up our replacements. When advertisers put forth the image of something diminutive and furry, something that elicits the word "cute" or "precious," then they are trying to trigger this motive. We listen to the childish voice singing the Oscar Mayer wiener song, and our next hot-dog purchase is prescribed. Aren't those darling kittens something, and how did this Meow Mix get into our shopping cart?

This pitch is often directed at women, as Mother Nature's chief nurturers. "Make me some Kraft macaroni and cheese, please," says the elfin preschooler just in from the snowstorm, and mothers' hearts go out, and Kraft's sales go up. "We're cold, wet, and hungry," whine the husband and kids, and the little woman gets the Manwiches ready. A facsimile of this need can be hit without children or pets: the husband is ill and sleepless in the television commercial, and the wife grudgingly fetches the NyQuil.

But it is not women alone who can be touched by this appeal. The father nurses his son Eddie through adolescence while the John Deere lawn tractor survives the years. Another father counts pennies with his young son as the subject of New York Life Insurance comes up. And all over America are businessmen who don't know why they dial Qantas Airlines* when they have to take a trans-Pacific trip; the koala bear knows.

35   **4. Need for Guidance.**   The opposite of the need to nurture is the need to be nurtured: to be protected, shielded, guided. We may be loath to admit it, but the child lingers on inside every adult—and a good thing it does, or we would not be instructable in our advancing years. Who wants a nation of nothing but flinty personalities?

---

*Qantas Airlines is an Australian airline whose ads during the 1980s and 1990s featured a cuddly koala bear standing in for both the airline and the exotic delights of Australia.

Parent-like figures can successfully call up this need. Robert Young[*] recommends Sanka coffee, and since we have experienced him for twenty-five years as television father and doctor, we take his word for it. Florence Henderson[†] as the expert mom knows a lot about the advantages of Wesson oil.

The parent-ness of the spokesperson need not be so salient; sometimes pure authoritativeness is better. When Orson Welles[‡] scowls and intones, "Paul Masson will sell no wine before its time," we may not know exactly what he means, but we still take direction from him. There is little maternal about Brenda Vaccaro[§] when she speaks up for Tampax, but there is a certainty to her that many accept.

A celebrity is not a necessity in making a pitch to the need for guidance, since a fantasy figure can serve just as well. People accede to the Green Giant, or Betty Crocker, or Mr. Goodwrench.[**] Some advertisers can get by with no figure at all: "When E. F. Hutton[§§] talks, people listen."

Often it is tradition or custom that advertisers point to and consumers take guidance from. Bits and pieces of American history are used to sell whiskeys like Old Crow, Southern Comfort, Jack Daniel's. We conform to traditional male/female roles and age-old social norms when we purchase Barclay cigarettes, which informs us "The pleasure is back."

The product itself, if it has been around for a long time, can constitute a tradition. All those old labels in the ad for Morton salt convince us that we should continue to buy it. Kool-Aid says "You loved it as a kid. You trust it as a mother," hoping to get yet more consumers to go along.

Even when the product has no history at all, our need to conform to tradition and to be guided are strong enough that they can be invoked through

---

[*]Robert Young (1907–1988) acted in movies—including Alfred Hitchcock's *Secret Agent* (1936) and *Crossfire* (1947)—and TV (starring in the long-running 1950s series *Father Knows Best* and the 1960s series *Marcus Welby, M.D.*). A classic father figure, in his later career he appeared in ads for Sanka coffee.

[†]Florence Henderson (b. 1934), acted on Broadway and TV (primarily, in musical and comedy roles). Her most famous TV show was *The Brady Bunch* (1968–1974), where she played a mother of three daughters who married a man with three sons.

[‡]Orson Welles (1915–1985) was a major American filmmaker and actor whose films include *Citizen Kane* (1941—generally considered the greatest American film of all time), *The Magnificent Ambersons* (1942), *The Lady from Shanghai* (1947), *Macbeth* (1948), and *Touch of Evil* (1958). Toward the end of his life—to the dismay of many who revered him—the magisterial but financially depleted Welles became a spokesman for Paul Masson wines.

[§]Brenda Vaccaro (b. 1939) is a stage, TV, and film actress; her films include *Midnight Cowboy* (1969), *Airport '77* (1977), *Supergirl* (1984), and *The Mirror Has Two Faces* (1996).

[**]Mr. Goodwrench (and the slogan "Looking for Mr. Goodwrench"), personified as an engaging and highly capable auto mechanic, is a product of the General Motors marketing department.

[§§]E. F. Hutton (named after its founder, Edward Francis Hutton) was a major brokerage firm that was brought down in the 1980s by corporate misconduct. Its most famous TV ad portrayed, typically, two well-dressed businesspeople in conversation in a crowded dining room or club room. The first man says to the other, "My broker says...." The second man listens politely and responds, "Well, my broker is E. F. Hutton, and *he* says...," and everyone else in the room strains to overhear the conversation. The tag line: "When E. F. Hutton talks, people listen."

bogus nostalgia and older actors. Country-Time lemonade sells because consumers want to believe it has a past they can defer to.

So far the needs and the ways they can be invoked which have been looked at are largely warm and affiliative; they stand in contrast to the next set of needs, which are much more egoistic and assertive.

5. Need to Aggress. The pressures of the real world create strong retaliatory feelings in every functioning human being. Since these impulses can come forth as bursts of anger and violence, their display is normally tabooed. Existing as harbored energy, aggressive drives present a large, tempting target for advertisers. It is not a target to be aimed at thoughtlessly, though, for few manufacturers want their products associated with destructive motives. There is always the danger that, as in the case of sex, if the appeal is too blatant, public opinion will turn against what is being sold.

Jack-in-the-Box sought to abruptly alter its marketing by going after older customers and forgetting the younger ones. Their television commercials had a seventy-ish lady command, "Waste him," and the Jack-in-the-Box clown exploded before our eyes. So did public reaction until the commercials were toned down. Print ads for Club cocktails carried the faces of octogenarians under the headline, "Hit me with a Club"; response was contrary enough to bring the campaign to a stop.

45   Better disguised aggressive appeals are less likely to backfire: Triumph cigarettes has models making a lewd gesture with their uplifted cigarettes, but the individuals are often laughing and usually in close company of others. When Exxon said, "There's a Tiger in your tank," the implausibility of it concealed the invocation of aggressive feelings.

Depicted arguments are a common way for advertisers to tap the audience's needs to aggress. Don Rickles* and Lynda Carter[†] trade gibes, and consumers take sides as the name of Seven-Up is stitched on minds. The Parkay [margarine] tub has a difference of opinion with the user; who can forget it, or who (or what) got the last word in?

6. Need to Achieve. This is the drive that energizes people, causing them to strive in their lives and careers. According to Murray, the need for achievement is signalled by the desires "to accomplish something difficult. To overcome obstacles and attain a high standard. To excel one's self. To rival and surpass others." A prominent American trait, it is one that advertisers like to hook on to because it identifies their product with winning and success.

The Cutty Sark ad does not disclose that Ted Turner failed at his latest attempt at yachting's America Cup; here he is represented as a champion on the water as well as off in his television enterprises. If we drink this

---

*Don Rickles (b. 1926) is a night-club comedian (who has also appeared in TV and films) famous for his caustic wit and for humorously insulting people in the audience.
[†]Lynda Carter (b. 1951) is an actress whose most famous role was the heroine of the 1976 TV series *Wonder Woman*.

whiskey, we will be victorious alongside Turner. We can also succeed with O. J. Simpson* by renting Hertz cars, or with Reggie Jackson† by bringing home some Panasonic equipment. Cathy Rigby‡ and Stayfree maxipads will put people out front.

Sports heroes are the most convenient means to snare consumers' needs to achieve, but they are not the only one. Role models can be established, ones which invite emulation, as with the profiles put forth by Dewar's scotch. Successful, tweedy individuals relate they have "graduated to the flavor of Myer's rum." Or the advertiser can establish a prize: two neighbors play one-on-one basketball for a Michelob beer in a television commercial, while in a print ad a bottle of Johnnie Walker Black Label has been gilded like a trophy.

Any product that advertises itself in superlatives—the best, the first, the finest—is trying to make contact with our needs to succeed. For many consumers, sales and bargains belong in this category of appeals, too; the person who manages to buy something at fifty percent off is seizing an opportunity and coming out ahead of others.

7. Need to Dominate. This fundamental need is the craving to be powerful—perhaps omnipotent, as in the Xerox ad where Brother Dominic exhibits heavenly powers and creates miraculous copies. Most of us will settle for being just a regular potentate, though. We drink Budweiser because it is the King of Beers, and here comes the powerful Clydesdales to prove it. A taste of Wolfschmidt vodka and "The spirit of the Czar lives on."

The need to dominate and control one's environment is often thought of as being masculine, but as close students of human nature, advertisers know it is not so circumscribed. Women's aspirations for control are suggested in the campaign theme, "I like my men in English Leather, or nothing at all." The females in the Chanel No. 19 ads are "outspoken" and wrestle their men around.

Male and female, what we long for is clout; what we get in its place is Mastercard.

---

* O. J. Simpson (b. 1957) is a famous football player–turned film actor (*The Naked Gun*) and defendant in a notorious murder trial in the 1990s. In a highly controversial decision, Simpson was acquitted of killing his ex-wife Nicole Simpson and her friend Ron Goldman, but in a subsequent civil trial he was found liable for the two deaths. Before the trial, Simpson was well known for his TV commercials for Hertz rental cars, featuring him sprinting through airports to get to the gate to demonstrate what you *wouldn't* have to do if you rented a car through Hertz.

† Reggie Jackson (b. 1946), a member of the Baseball Hall of Fame, played as an outfielder between 1967 and 1987. Known as "Mr. October" for his dramatic game-winning at-bats during post-season play, he had more strikeouts (2,597) than any other player. He was the first baseball player to have a candy bar (the "Reggie Bar") named after him, and toward the end of his career was a pitchman for Panasonic televisions.

‡ Cathy Rigby, an Olympian, was the first American gymnast to win a medal (in 1970) at the World Championships. She went on to star in a Broadway revival of the musical *Peter Pan* (surpassing Mary Martin for the greatest number of performances). Subsequently, she became a sportscaster for ABC Sports.

8. Need for Prominence.   Here comes the need to be admired and respected, to enjoy prestige and high social status. These times, it appears, are not so egalitarian after all. Many ads picture the trappings of high position; the Oldsmobile stands before a manorial doorway, the Volvo is parked beside a steeplechase. A book-lined study is the setting for Dewar's 12, and Lenox China is displayed in a dining room chock full of antiques.

55   Beefeater gin represents itself as "The Crown Jewel of England" and uses no illustrations of jewels or things British, for the words are sufficient indicators of distinction. Buy that gin and you will rise up the prestige hierarchy, or achieve the same effect on yourself with Seagram's 7 Crown, which ambiguously describes itself as "classy."

Being respected does not have to entail the usual accoutrements of wealth: "Do you know who I am?" the commercials ask, and we learn that the prominent person is not so prominent without his American Express card.

9. Need for Attention.   The previous need involved being *looked up to,* while this is the need to be *looked at.* The desire to exhibit ourselves in such a way as to make others look at us is a primitive, insuppressible instinct. The clothing and cosmetic industries exist just to serve this need, and this is the way they pitch their wares. Some of this effort is aimed at males, as the ads for Hathaway shirts and Jockey underclothes. But the greater bulk of such appeals is targeted singlemindedly at women.

To come back to Brooke Shields: this is where she fits into American marketing. If I buy Calvin Klein jeans, consumers infer, I'll be the object of fascination. The desire for exhibition has been most strikingly played to in a print campaign of many years' duration, that of Maidenform lingerie. The woman exposes herself, and sales surge. "Gentlemen prefer Hanes" the ads dissemble, and women who want eyes upon them know what they should do. Peggy Fleming* flutters her legs for L'eggs, encouraging females who want to be the star in their own lives to purchase this product.

The same appeal works for cosmetics and lotions. For years, the little girl with the exposed backside sold gobs of Coppertone, but now the company has picked up the pace a little: as a female, you are supposed to "Flash 'em a Coppertone tan." Food can be sold the same way, especially to the diet-conscious; Angie Dickinson poses for California avocados and says, "Would this body lie to you?" Our eyes are too fixed on her for us to think to ask if she got that way by eating mounds of guacomole.

60   **10. Need for Autonomy.**   There are several ways to sell credit card services, as has been noted: Mastercard appeals to the need to dominate, and American Express to the need for prominence. When Visa claims, "You can have it the way you want it," yet another primary motive is being beckoned forward—the need to endorse the self. The focus here is upon the independence and integrity of the individual; this need is the antithesis

---

*Peggy Fleming (b. 1948), an Olympic figure skater and Gold Medal winner (1968), later became a TV sports commentator and a representative for UNICEF (the United Nations Children's Emergency Fund).

of the need for guidance and is unlike any of the social needs. "If running with the herd isn't your style, try ours," says Rotan-Mosle, and many Americans feel they have finally found the right brokerage firm.

The photo is of a red-coated Mountie on his horse, posed on a snow-covered ledge; the copy reads, "Windsor—One Canadian stands alone." This epitome of the solitary and proud individual may work best with male customers, as may Winston's man in the red cap. But one-figure advertisements also strike the strong need for autonomy among American women. As Shelly Hack* strides for Charlie perfume, females respond to her obvious pride and flair; she is her own person. The Virginia Slims tale is of people who have come a long way from subservience to independence. Cachet perfume feels it does not need a solo figure to work this appeal, and uses three different faces in its ads; it insists, though, "It's different on every woman who wears it."

Like many psychological needs, this one can also be appealed to in a negative fashion, by invoking the loss of independence or self-regard. Guilt and regrets can be stimulated: "Gee, I could have had a V-8." Next time, get one and be good to yourself.

11. Need to Escape. An appeal to the need for autonomy often co-occurs with one for the need to escape, since the desire to duck out of our social obligations, to seek rest or adventure, frequently takes the form of one-person flight. The dashing image of a pilot, in fact, is a standard way of quickening this need to get away from it all.

Freedom is the pitch here, the freedom that every individual yearns for whenever life becomes too oppressive. Many advertisers like appealing to the need for escape because the sensation of pleasure often accompanies escape, and what nicer emotional nimbus could there be for a product? "You deserve a break today," says McDonald's, and Stouffer's frozen foods chime in, "Set yourself free."

For decades men have imaginatively bonded themselves to the Marlboro cowboy who dwells untarnished and unencumbered in Marlboro Country some distance from modern life; smokers' aching needs for autonomy and escape are personified by that cowpoke. Many women can identify with the lady ambling through the woods behind the words, "Benson and Hedges and mornings and me."

But escape does not have to be solitary. Other Benson and Hedges ads, part of the same campaign, contain two strolling figures. In Salem cigarette advertisements, it can be several people who escape together into the mountaintops. A commercial for Levi's pictured a cloudbank above a city through which ran a whole chain of young people.

There are varieties of escape, some wistful like the Boeing "Someday" campaign of dream vacations, some kinetic like the play and parties in soft drink ads. But in every instance, the consumer exposed to the advertisement is invited to momentarily depart his everyday life for a more carefree experience, preferably with the product in hand.

---

*Shelly Hack (b. 1952) portrayed Tiffany Welles in the 1970s TV show *Charlie's Angels*.

12. Need to Feel Safe. Nobody in their right mind wants to be intimidated, menaced, battered, poisoned. We naturally want to do whatever it takes to stave off threats to our well-being, and to our families'. It is the instinct of self-preservation that makes us responsive to the ad of the St. Bernard with the keg of Chivas Regal. We pay attention to the stern talk of Karl Malden* and the plight of the vacationing couples who have lost all their funds in the American Express travelers cheques commercials. We want the omnipresent stag from Hartford Insurance to watch over us too.

In the interest of keeping failure and calamity from our lives, we like to see the durability of products demonstrated. Can we ever forget that Timex takes a licking and keeps on ticking? When the American Tourister suitcase bounces all over the highway and the egg inside doesn't break, the need to feel safe has been adroitly plucked.

70 We take precautions to diminish future threats. We buy Volkswagen Rabbits for the extraordinary mileage, and MONY insurance policies to avoid the tragedies depicted in their black-and-white ads of widows and orphans.

We are careful about our health. We consume Mazola margarine because it has "corn goodness" backed by the natural food traditions of the American Indians. In the medicine cabinet is Alka-Seltzer, the "home remedy"; having it, we are snug in our little cottage.

We want to be safe and secure; buy these products, advertisers are saying, and you'll be safer than you are without them.

13. Need for Aesthetic Sensations. There is an undeniable aesthetic component to virtually every ad run in the national media: the photography or filming or drawing is near-perfect, the type style is well chosen, the layout could scarcely be improved upon. Advertisers know there is little chance of good communication occurring if an ad is not visually pleasing. Consumers may not be aware of the extent of their own sensitivity to artwork, but it is undeniably large.

Sometimes the aesthetic element is expanded and made into an ad's primary appeal. Charles Jordan shoes may or may not appear in the accompanying avant-grade photographs; Kohler plumbing fixtures catch attention through the high style of their desert settings. Beneath the slightly out of focus photograph, languid and sensuous in tone, General Electric feels called upon to explain, "This is an ad for the hair dryer."

75 This appeal is not limited to female consumers: J&B scotch says "It whispers" and shows a bucolic scene of lake and castle.

14. Need to Satisfy Curiosity. It may seem odd to list a need for information among basic motives, but this need can be as primal and compelling as

---

*Karl Malden (1912–2009), with his familiar craggy face and outsized nose, was a stage and later a film actor. He was the original Mitch in the Broadway production of Tennessee Williams's *Streetcar Named Desire*, a role he reprised in the 1951 movie version. His films include *On the Waterfront* (1954), *Cheyenne Autumn* (1964), and *Patton* (1970), and he starred in the 1972 TV series *Streets of San Francisco*. Malden became famous to a later generation of viewers as a pitchman for the American Express card, with the slogan, "Don't leave home without it!"

any of the others. Human beings are curious by nature, interested in the world around them, and intrigued by tidbits of knowledge and new developments. Trivia, percentages, observations counter to conventional wisdom—these items all help sell products. Any advertisement in a question-and-answer format is strumming this need.

A dog groomer has a question about long distance rates, and Bell Telephone has a chart with all the figures. An ad for Porsche 911 is replete with diagrams and schematics, numbers and arrows. Lo and behold, Anacin pills have 150 more milligrams than its competitors; should we wonder if this is better or worse for us?

15. Physiological Needs. To the extent that sex is solely a biological need, we are now coming around full circle, back toward the start of the list. In this final category are clustered appeals to sleeping, eating, drinking. The art of photographing food and drink is so advanced, sometimes these temptations are wondrously caught in the camera's lens: the crab meat in the Red Lobster restaurant ads can start us salivating, the Quarterpounder can almost be smelled, the liquor in the glass glows invitingly. Imbibe, these ads scream.

Styles

Some common ingredients of advertisements were not singled out for separate mention in the list of fifteen because they are not appeals in and of themselves. They are stylistic features, influencing the way a basic appeal is presented. The use of humor is one, and the use of celebrities is another. A third is time imagery, past and future, which goes to several purposes.

For all of its employment in advertising, humor can be treacherous, because it can get out of hand and smother the product information. Supposedly, this is what Alka-Seltzer discovered with its comic commercials of the late sixties; "I can't believe I ate the whole thing," the sad-faced husband lamented, and the audience cackled so much it forgot the antacid. Or, did not take it seriously.

But used carefully, humor can punctuate some of the softer appeals and soften some of the harsher ones. When Emma says to the Fruit-of-the-Loom fruits, "Hi, cuties. Whatcha doing in my laundry basket?" we smile as our curiosity is assuaged along with hers. Bill Cosby gets consumers tickled about the children in his Jell-O commercials, and strokes the need to nurture.

An insurance company wants to invoke the need to feel safe, but does not want to leave readers with an unpleasant aftertaste; cartoonist Rowland Wilson creates an avalanche about to crush a gentleman who is saying to another, "My insurance company? New England Life, of course. Why?" The same tactic of humor undercutting threat is used in the cartoon commercials for Safeco when the Pink Panther wanders from one disaster to another. Often humor masks aggression: comedian Bob Hope in the outfit of a boxer promises to knock out the knock-knocks with Texaco; Rodney Dangerfield, who "can't get no respect," invites aggression as the comic relief in Miller Lite commercials.

Roughly fifteen percent of all advertisements incorporate a celebrity, almost always from the fields of entertainment or sports. The approach can also prove troublesome for advertisers, for celebrities are human beings too, and fully capable of the most remarkable behavior. If anything distasteful about them emerges, it is likely to reflect on the product. The advertisers making use of Anita Bryant* and Billy Jean King† suffered several anxious moments. An untimely death can also react poorly on a product. But advertisers are willing to take risks because celebrities can be such a good link between producers and consumers, performing the social role of introducer.

There are several psychological needs these middlemen can play upon. Let's take the product class of cameras and see how different celebrities can hit different needs. The need for guidance can be invoked by Michael Landon, who plays such a wonderful dad on "Little House on the Prairie"; when he says to buy Kodak equipment, many people listen. James Garner for Polaroid cameras is put in a similar authoritative role, so defined by a mocking spouse. The need to achieve is summoned up by Tracy Austin and other tennis stars for Canon AE-1; the advertiser first makes sure we see these athletes playing to win. When Cheryl Tiegs‡ speaks up for Olympus cameras, it is the need for attention that is being targeted.

85   The past and future, being outside our grasp, are exploited by advertisers as locales for the projection of needs. History can offer up heroes (and call up the need to achieve) or traditions (need for guidance) as well as art objects (need for aesthetic sensations). Nostalgia is a kindly version of personal history and is deployed by advertisers to rouse needs for affiliation and for guidance; the need to escape can come in here, too. The same need to escape is sometimes the point of futuristic appeals but picturing the avant-garde can also be a way to get at the need to achieve.

Analyzing Advertisements

When analyzing ads yourself for their emotional appeals, it takes a bit of practice to learn to ignore the product information (as well as one's own experience and feelings about the product). But that skill comes soon enough, as does the ability to quickly sort out from all the non-product aspects of an ad the chief element which is the most striking, the most

---

*Anita Bryant (b. 1940), a singer and entertainer (and, as Miss Oklahoma, runner-up in the 1958 Miss America competition), became controversial during the late 1970s with her campaigns against homosexuality and AIDS. At the time, she was making ads and TV commercials for Florida orange juice but was dropped by the sponsor after boycotts by activists.

†Billy Jean King (b. 1943) was a championship tennis player in the late 1960s and 1970s. In 1973 she was named *Sports Illustrated*'s "Sportsperson of the Year," the first woman to win this honor. She won four U.S. championships and six Wimbledon's single championships. In 1973, in a much publicized "Battle of the Sexes" match, King won all three sets against the 55-year-old Bobby Riggs (once ranked as the best tennis player in the world), who had claimed that "any half-decent male player could defeat even the best female players."

‡Cheryl Tiegs (b. 1947) is a supermodel perhaps best known for her affiliation with the *Sports Illustrated Annual Swimsuit Issue*. A 1978 poster of Tiegs in a pink swimsuit became a cultural icon. Recently, she has entered the business world with an accessory and wig line for Revlon.

likely to snag attention first and penetrate brains farthest. The key to the appeal, this element usually presents itself centrally and forwardly to the reader or viewer.

Another clue: the viewing angle which the audience has on the ad's subjects is informative. If the subjects are photographed or filmed from below and thus are looking down at you much as the Green Giant does, then the need to be guided is a good candidate for the ad's emotional appeal. If, on the other hand, the subjects are shot from above and appear deferential, as is often the case with children or female models, then other needs are being appealed to.

To figure out an ad's emotional appeal, it is wise to know (or have a good hunch about) who the targeted consumers are; this can often be inferred from the magazine or television show it appears in. This piece of information is a great help in determining the appeal and in deciding between two different interpretations. For example, if an ad features a partially undressed female, this would typically signal one appeal for readers of *Penthouse* (need for sex) and another for readers of *Cosmopolitan* (need for attention).

It would be convenient if every ad made just one appeal, were aimed at just one need. Unfortunately, things are often not that simple. A cigarette ad with a couple at the edge of a polo field is trying to hit both the need for affiliation and the need for prominence; depending on the attitude of the male, dominance could also be an ingredient in this. An ad for Chimere perfume incorporates two photos: in the top one the lady is being commanding at a business luncheon (need to dominate), but in the lower one she is being bussed (need for affiliation). Better ads, however, seem to avoid being too diffused; in the study of post-World War II advertising described earlier, appeals grew more focused as the decades passed. As a rule of thumb, [only twenty percent of ads have one primary appeal,] about sixty percent have two conspicuous appeals; the last twenty percent have three or more. Rather than looking for the greatest number of appeals, decoding ads is most productive when the loudest one or two appeals are discerned, since those are the appeals with the best chance of grabbing people's attention.

Finally, analyzing ads does not have to be a solo activity and probably should not be. The greater number of people there are involved, the better chance there is of transcending individual biases and discerning the essential emotional lure built into an advertisement.

Do They or Don't They?

Do the emotional appeals made in advertisements add up to the sinister manipulation of consumers?

It is clear that these ads work. Attention is caught, communication occurs between producers and consumers, and sales result. It turns out to be difficult to detail the exact relationship between a specific ad and a specific purchase, or even between a campaign and subsequent sales figures, because advertising is only one of a host of influences upon consumption. Yet no one is fooled by this lack of perfect proof; everyone knows that advertising sells. If this were not the case, then tight-fisted American businesses would not spend a total of fifty billion dollars annually on these messages.

But before anyone despairs that advertisers have our number to the extent that they can marshal us at will and march us like automatons to the check-out counters, we should recall the resiliency and obduracy of the American consumer. Advertisers may have uncovered the softest spots in minds, but that does not mean they have found truly gaping apertures. There is no evidence that advertising can get people to do things contrary to their self-interests. Despite all the finesse of advertisements, and all the subtle emotional tugs, the public resists the vast majority of the petitions. According to the marketing division of the A. C. Nielsen Company, a whopping seventy-five percent of all new products die within a year in the marketplace, the victims of consumer disinterest which no amount of advertising could overcome. The appeals in advertising may be the most captivating there are to be had, but they are not enough to entrap the wily consumer.

The key to understanding the discrepancy between, on the one hand, the fact that advertising truly works, and, on the other, the fact that it hardly works, is to take into account the enormous numbers of people exposed to an ad. Modern-day communications permit an ad to be displayed to millions upon millions of individuals; if the smallest fraction of that audience can be moved to buy the product, then the ad has been successful. When one percent of the people exposed to a television advertising campaign reach for their wallets, that could be one million sales, which may be enough to keep the product in production and the advertisements coming.

95   In arriving at an evenhanded judgment about advertisements and their emotional appeals, it is good to keep in mind that many of the purchases which might be credited to these ads are experienced as genuinely gratifying to the consumer. We sincerely like the goods or service we have bought, and we may even like some of the emotional drapery that an ad suggests comes with it. It has sometimes been noted that the most avid students of advertisements are the people who have just bought the product; they want to steep themselves in the associated imagery. This may be the reason that Americans, when polled, are not negative about advertising and do not disclose any sense of being misused. The volume of advertising may be an irritant, but the product information as well as the imaginative material in ads are partial compensation.

A productive understanding is that advertising messages involve costs and benefits at both ends of the communications channel. For those few ads which do make contact, the consumer surrenders a moment of time, has the lower brain curried, and receives notice of a product; the advertiser has given up money and has increased the chance of sales. In this sort of communications activity, neither party can be said to be the loser.

Review Questions

1. Why is advertising more common in highly industrialized countries like the United States than in countries with "quieter" economies?

2. How are advertisers' attempts to communicate their messages, and to break through customer resistance, keyed to their conception of human psychology, according to Fowles?

3. What are the "two orders of content" of most advertisements, according to Fowles?

4. How is Fowles indebted to Henry Murray?

5. Why must appeals to our need for sex and our need to aggress be handled carefully, according to Fowles?

6. How does the use of humor or the use of celebrities fit into Fowles's scheme?

Discussion and Writing Suggestions

1. In paragraph 4, Fowles cites a study indicating that only a fraction of the advertisements bombarding consumers every day are even noticed, much less acted upon. How do the results of this study square with your own experience? About how many of the commercial messages that you view and hear every day do you actually pay attention to? What kinds of messages draw your attention? What elicits positive reactions? Negative reactions? What kinds of appeals are most successful in making you want to actually purchase the advertised product?

2. What do you think of Fowles's analysis of "advertising's fifteen basic appeals"? Does this classification seem an accurate and useful way of accounting for how most advertising works upon us? Would you drop any of his categories or perhaps incorporate one set into another set? Has Fowles neglected to consider other appeals that you believe to be equally important? If so, can you think of one or more advertisements that employ such appeals omitted by Fowles?

3. Categorize several of the print ads in the ad portfolio later in the chapter (pp. 382–406) using Fowles's schema. Explain how the headlines, body text, and graphics support your categorization choices.

4. Fowles asserts that "[c]ontrary to impressions, unambiguous sex is rare in [advertising] messages." This article first appeared in 1982. Does Fowles's statement still seem true today? To what extent do you believe that advertisers in recent years have increased their reliance on overt sexual appeals? Cite examples.

5. Fowles believes that "the need to associate with others [affiliation] . . . is probably the most prevalent appeal" in advertising. To what extent

do you agree with this statement? Locate or cite print or broadcast ads that rely on the need for affiliation. How do the graphics and text of these ads work on what Fowles calls "the deep running drives" of our psyches or "the lower brain"?

6. Locate ads that rely upon the converse appeals to nurture and to guidance. Explain how the graphics and text in these ads work upon our human motivations. If possible, further categorize the appeal: for example, are we provided with guidance from a parent figure, some other authority figure, or from the force of tradition?

7. Conduct (perhaps with one or more classmates) your own analysis of a set of contemporary advertisements. Select a single issue of a particular magazine, such as *Time* or the *New Yorker*. Review all of the full-page ads, classifying each according to Fowles's categories. An ad may make more than one appeal (as Fowles points out in paragraph 89), but generally one will be primary. What do your findings show? Which appeals are the most frequent? The least frequent? Which are most effective? Why? You may find it interesting to compare the appeals of advertising in different magazines aimed at different audiences—for example, a general-interest magazine, such as *Newsweek*, compared with a more specialized magazine, such as the *New Republic, People, Glamour,* or *Guns and Ammo*. To what extent do the types of appeals shift with the gender or interests of the target audience?

A PORTFOLIO OF PRINT ADVERTISEMENTS

The following portfolio offers for your consideration and analysis a selection of 22 full-page advertisements that appeared in American and British magazines between 1945 (shortly after the end of World War II) and 2003. In terms of products represented, the ads fall into several categories—cigarettes, alcohol (beer and liquor), automobiles, food and drink, household cleaners, lotions, and perfumes. The portfolio also includes a few miscellaneous ads for such diverse products as exercise equipment, telephones, and airlines. These ads originally appeared in such magazines as *Time, Newsweek, U.S. News and World Report, Sports Illustrated, Ladies Home Journal, Ebony,* and *Ms.* A number of the ads were researched in the Advertising Archive, an online (and subscription) collection maintained by The Picture Desk.

The advertisements in this portfolio are not representative of all ads that appeared during the last sixty years. We made our selection largely on the basis of how interesting, striking, provocative, and unusual these particular ads appeared to us. Admittedly, the selection process was biased. That said, the ads in this portfolio offer rich possibilities for analysis. With practice, and by applying principles for analysis that you will find in Fowles, you will be able to "read" into these ads numerous messages about cultural attitudes toward gender relations, romance, smoking, and automobiles. The ads will prompt you to consider why we buy products that we may not need or why we prefer one product over another when the two products are essentially identical. Each advertisement is a window into the culture. Through careful analysis, you will gain insights not only into the era in which the ads were produced but also into shifting cultural attitudes over the last sixty years.

Following the portfolio, we provide two or three specific questions for each ad (pp. 407–411), questions designed to stimulate your thinking about the particular ways that the graphics and text are intended to work. As you review the ads, however, you may want to think about more general questions about advertisements raised by the readings in this chapter, including those raised by Fowles:

1. Who appears to be the target audience for the ad? If this ad was produced more than two decades ago, does its same target audience exist today? If so, how would this audience likely react today to the ad?

2. What is the primary appeal made by the ad, in terms of Fowles's categories? What, if any, are the secondary appeals?

3. What assumptions do the ad's sponsors make about such matters as (1) commonly accepted roles of women and men; (2) the relationship between the sexes; (3) the priorities of men and women?

4. What is the chief attention-getting device in the ad?

5. How does the headline and body text communicate the ad's essential appeals?

6. How do the ad's graphics communicate the ad's essential appeals?

7. How do the expressions, clothing, and postures of the models, as well as the physical objects in the illustration, help communicate the ad's message?

8. How do the graphic qualities of balance, proportion, movement, unity, clarity and simplicity, and emphasis help communicate the ad's message?

Consider, also, the following evaluative questions[1]:

- Is it a good ad? Why?
- What do you like most about it? Why?
- What do you dislike the most? Why?
- Do you think it "works"? Why or why not?
- How could the ad be improved?
- Could the sender have conveyed the same message using other strategies, other persuasive means? If so, explain.
- Even if you don't believe that this particular ad works or persuades you, is there anything in the ad that still affects you or persuades you indirectly?
- Does the ad have effects on you perhaps not intended by its creators?

---

[1]Lars Thoger Christensen, "How to Analyze an Advertisement." University of Southern Denmark—Odense. Jan. 2004; <http://wms-soros.mngt.waikato.ac.nz/NR/rdonlyres/ebabz4jhzmg5fr5p45ypc53mdvuxva5wxhe7323onb4ylelbaq3se5xjrslfc4mi3qgk6dmsx5dqbp/Advertisinganalysis.doc>.

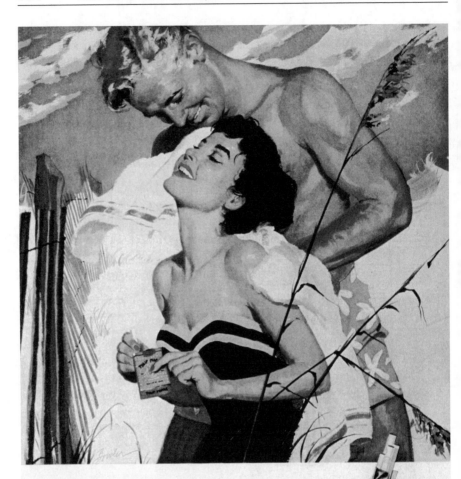

Gently Does It

Gentleness makes good friends in fun-making... and in a cigarette, where gentleness is one of the greatest requirements of modern taste. That's why today's Philip Morris, born gentle, refined to special gentleness in the making, makes so many friends among our young smokers. Enjoy the gentle pleasure, the fresh unfiltered flavor, of today's Philip Morris. In the convenient snap-open pack, regular or smart king-size.

Philip Morris

...gentle for modern taste

Philip Morris, 1950s

Marlboro, 1970s

Camel, 1979

America is returning to the genuine—in foods, fashions and tastes. Today's trend to Ballantine light Ale fits right into this modern picture. In all the world, no other beverage brewed has such extra excellence brewed into it. And "Brewer's Gold" is one big reason for Ballantine Ale's deep, rich, genuine flavor.

They all ask for ale **Ballantine** LIGHT **Ale !**

Ballantine Ale, 1950s

BACARDI. rum is so "mixable"...
It's a one-brand bar.

Big, bold highballs, sassy Daiquiris, cool tonics and colas—Bacardi rum is enjoyable always and *all* ways. Extra Special: our man Fernando is pouring very rare Bacardi Añejo rum (Ahn-YAY-ho), one of the fine rums from Bacardi. So incredibly smooth he enjoys it even in a snifter. Try it, too!

Bacardi Rum, 1960s

AT THE PULITZER FOUNTAIN, N.Y.C.

In Fine Whiskey...

FLEISCHMANN'S
is the BIG buy!

The First Taste will tell you why!

Established 1870

BLENDED WHISKEY • 86 AND 90 PROOF • 65% GRAIN NEUTRAL SPIRITS
THE FLEISCHMANN DISTILLING CORPORATION, NEW YORK CITY

Fleischmann's Whiskey, 1964

"I'll have a Hennessy Very Superior Old Pale Reserve Cognac, thank you."

The Taste of Success

Every drop of Hennessy V.S.O.P. Reserve is Grande Fine Champagne Cognac.
It's made solely from grapes grown in La Grande Champagne—the small district in
the Cognac region which is the source of the very greatest Cognac.
What's more, Hennessy is selected from the largest reserves of aged Cognacs in existence.
Enjoy a taste of success today...

Hennessy V.S.O.P. Reserve Cognac

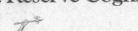

Hennessy V.S.O.P. Grande Fine Champagne Cognac, 80 Proof. ©Schieffelin & Co., N.Y.

Hennessy Cognac, 1968

Now comes Miller time.
Time to head for the best-tasting beer
you can find. Miller High Life.
America's quality beer since 1855.

© 1979 Miller Brewing Co., Milwaukee, Wis.

Miller Beer, 1979

Of all the De Soto cars ever built, 7 out of 10 are still running

8 out of 10 owners say, "De Soto is the most satisfactory car I ever owned"*

*FROM A MAIL SURVEY AMONG THOUSANDS OF OWNERS
OF 1941 AND 1942 DE SOTO CARS

DE SOTO DIVISION OF CHRYSLER CORPORATION

De Soto, 1947

"Ford's out Front from a Woman's Angle"

1. **"I don't know** synthetic enamel from a box of my children's paints... but if synthetic enamel is what it takes to make that beautiful, shiny Ford finish, I'm all for it!

2. **"My husband says the brakes** are self-centering and hydraulic—whatever that means! All I know is they're so easy that I can taxi the children all day without tiring out!

3. **"Peter, he's my teen-age son,** tells me that 'Ford is the only car in its price class with a choice of a 100-horsepower V-8 engine or a brilliant new Six.' He says no matter which engine people pick, they're out front with Ford!

6. **"Now here's another thing** women like and that's a blissfully comfortable ride—one that isn't bumpity-bump even on some of our completely forgotten roads."

Listen to the Ford Show starring Dinah Shore on Columbia Network Stations Wednesday Evenings.

4. **"The interior** of our Ford is strictly *my* department! It's tailored with the dreamiest broadcloth. Such a perfect fit! Mary Jane says women help design Ford interiors. There's certainly a woman's touch there!

5. **"Do you like** lovely silver, beautifully simple and chaste looking? That's what I always think of when I touch those smart Ford door handles and window openers.

There's a *Ford* in your future

Ford, 1947

Worth Its Price

If a motorist wanted to make the move to Cadillac solely for the car's prestige—he would most certainly be justified in doing so. For the Cadillac car has never stood so high in public esteem as it does today—and the rewards which grow out of this unprecedented acceptance comprise the rarest and greatest satisfactions in all motordom.

There is, for instance, *the inescapable feeling of pride* that comes with ownership of so distinguished and beloved a possession . . . the wonderful *sense of well-being* that comes from having reached a point of achievement where you can enjoy one of the world's most sought-after manufactured products . . . and the *marvelous feeling of confidence and self-esteem* that is found

CADILLAC   MOTOR   CAR   DIVISION

Cadillac, 1954

in PRESTIGE !

in the respect and admiration universally accorded the owner of a Cadillac car. Those who presently enjoy these unique Cadillac virtues will tell you that they are, in themselves, worth the car's whole purchase price.

Of course, most motorists would hesitate to take such a step purely for their personal edification. But in Cadillac's case, this wonderful prestige is actually a "bonus", so to speak—an extra dividend that comes with every Cadillac car, in addition to its breath-taking styling, its magnificent performance, its superlative luxury and its remarkable economy.

Have you seen and driven the 1954 Cadillac? If you haven't, then you've a truly wonderful adventure awaiting you—and one that you should postpone no longer.

GENERAL   MOTORS   CORPORATION

Corvette Sting Ray Sport Coupe with eight standard safety features, including outside rearview mirror. Use it always before passing.

The day she flew the coupe

What manner of woman is this, you ask, who stands in the midst of a mountain stream eating a peach?

Actually she's a normal everyday girl except that she and her husband own the Corvette Coupe in the background. (He's at work right now, wondering where he misplaced his car keys.)

The temptation, you see, was over-powering. They'd had the car a whole week now, and not once had he offered to let her drive. His excuse was that this, uh, was a big hairy sports car. Too much for a woman to handle: the trigger-quick steering, the independent rear suspension, the disc brakes—plus the 4-speed transmission and that 425-hp engine they had ordered—egad! He would teach her to drive it some weekend. So he said.

That's why she hid the keys, forcing him to seek public transportation. Sure of his departure, she went to the garage, started the Corvette, and was off for the hills, soon upshifting and downshifting as smoothly as he. His car. Hard to drive. What propaganda!

'66 CORVETTE BY CHEVROLET
Chevrolet Division of General Motors, Detroit, Michigan

Corvette, 1966

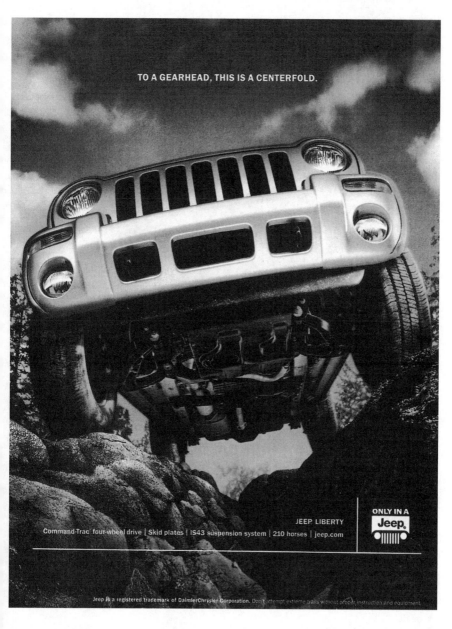

Jeep vehicle, 2003

Coca-Cola, 1945

What's for dinner, Duchess?

Prediction: The new wives of 1947 are going to have more fun in the kitchen.

Previous cooking experience is desirable, perhaps, but not essential. There are so many new easy-to-use foods, so many new ways to prepare foods, so many interesting ways to serve foods, cooking will be a novel and exciting adventure.

Further prediction: Cheese dishes will be featured more often on their menus. They'll know that cheese gives tastiness and variety to meals. And cheese, like milk (nature's most nearly perfect food), is rich in protein, calcium, phosphorus, in vitamins A and G.

Yes, we have a personal interest in cheese. For Kraft, pioneer in cheese, is a unit of National Dairy. And what we've said about housewives using more cheese is entirely true.

It's also true that they're learning more about the whys and wherefores of food each year — just as the scientists in our laboratories are learning more about better ways to process, improve and supply it.

These men are backed by the resources of a great organization. They explore every field of dairy products, discover new ones. And the health of America benefits constantly by this National Dairy research.

Dedicated to the wider use and better understanding of dairy products as human food . . . as a base for the development of new products and materials . . . as a source of health and enduring progress on the farms and in the towns and cities of America.

NATIONAL DAIRY
PRODUCTS CORPORATION
AND AFFILIATED COMPANIES

National Dairy Products Corporation, 1947

MAY: # Heavens, Ann —
wish I could clean up quick as that!

ANN: You could, hon! Just use a cleanser that doesn't leave dirt-catching scratches.

MAY: Goodness! What in the world do scratches have to do with it?

ANN: A lot, silly! Those tiny scratches you get from gritty cleansers hold onto dirt and double your cleaning time.

MAY: Well, you old smartie! I'd never thought of *that* before.

ANN: I hadn't thought of it either—till I discovered Bon Ami! See how fine-textured and white it is. It just *slides* dirt off—and when you rinse it away, it doesn't leave any of that horrid grit in the tub.

MAY: Say no more, darling! From now on there's going to be a new cleaning team in our house —me and Bon Ami!

Bon Ami

THE SPEEDY CLEANSER *that "hasn't scratched yet!"*

EASY ON YOUR HANDS, Bon Ami *Powder* is the ideal cleanser for kitchen sinks, as well as bathtubs. Also try Bon Ami *Cake* for cleaner windows, mirrors and windshields.

Bon Ami, 1947

Mrs. Dorian Mehle of Morrisville, Pa., is all three: a housewife, a mother, and a very lovely lady.

"I wash 22,000 dishes a year... but I'm proud of my pretty hands!"

You and Dorian Mehle have something in common. Every year, you wash a stack of dishes a quarter-mile high!

Detergents make your job so much easier. They cut right into grease and grime. They get you through dishwashing in much less time, but while they dissolve grease, they also take away the natural oils and youthful softness of your hands!

Although Dorian hasn't given up detergents her hands are as soft, as smooth, as young-looking as a teenager's. Her secret is no secret at all. It's the world's best-known beauty routine. It's pure, white Jergens Lotion, after every chore.

When you smooth on Jergens Lotion, this liquid formula doesn't just "coat" your hands. It penetrates right away, to help *replace* that softening moisture your skin needs.

Jergens Lotion has two ingredients doctors recommend for softening. Women must be recommending it, too, for more women use it than any other hand care in the world. Dorian's husband is the best testimonial to Jergens Lotion care. Even after years of married life, he still loves to hold her pretty hands!

Use Jergens Lotion like a prescription: three times a day, after every meal!

Now—lotion dispenser FREE of extra cost with $1.00 size. Supply limited.

Use JERGENS LOTION—avoid detergent hands

Jergens Lotion, 1954

Madam! Suppose you traded jobs with your husband?

You can just bet the first thing he'd ask for would be a telephone in the kitchen.

You wouldn't catch him dashing to another room every time the telephone rang, or he had to make a call.

He doesn't have to do it in his office in town. It would be mighty helpful if you didn't have to do it in your "office" at home.

That's in the kitchen where you do so much of your work. And it's right there that an additional telephone comes in so handy for so many things.

Along with a lot of convenience is that nice feeling of pride in having the best of everything—especially if it is one of those attractive new telephones in color.

P.S. *Additional telephones in kitchen, bedroom and other convenient places around the house cost little. The service charge is just pennies a day.*

Bell Telephone System

Bell Telephone, 1956

The phone company wants more installers like Alana MacFarlane.

Alana MacFarlane is a 20-year-old from San Rafael, California. She's one of our first women telephone installers. She won't be the last.

We also have several hundred male telephone operators. And a policy that there are no all-male or all-female jobs at the phone company.

We want the men and women of the telephone company to do what they want to do, and do best.

For example, Alana likes working outdoors. "I don't go for office routine," she said. "But as an installer, I get plenty of variety and a chance to move around."

Some people like to work with their hands, or, like Alana, get a kick out of working 20 feet up in the air.

Others like to drive trucks. Some we're helping to develop into good managers.

Today, when openings exist, local Bell Companies are offering applicants and present employees some jobs they may never have thought about before. We want to help all advance to the best of their abilities.

AT&T and your local Bell Company are equal opportunity employers.

Bell Telephone, 1974

Think of her as your mother.

She only wants what's best for you.
A cool drink. A good dinner. A soft pillow and a warm blanket.
This is not just maternal instinct. It's the result of the longest
Stewardess training in the industry.
Training in service, not just a beauty course.
Service, after all, is what makes professional travelers prefer American.
And makes new travelers want to keep on flying with us.
So we see that every passenger gets the same professional treatment.
That's the American Way.

Fly the American Way
American Airlines.

American Airlines, 1968

Charlie, 1988

Soloflex, 1985

Discussion and Writing Suggestions

TOBACCO

Philip Morris, 1950s (p. 384)

1. How do the placement, posture, and dress of the models in the ad help create its essential psychological appeal? Why do you suppose (in relation to the selling of cigarettes) the models' eyes are closed?

2. Discuss some of the messages communicated both by the graphic and the text of this ad. Focus in particular on the quality of "gentleness" emphasized in the ad.

Marlboro, 1970s (p. 385)

1. The Marlboro Man has become one of the most famous—and successful— icons of American advertising. What elements of the Marlboro Man (and his setting, Marlboro Country) do you notice, and what role do these elements play in the appeal being made by this ad?

2. This ad appeared during the 1970s. (The popularity of the Marlboro Man extended into the 1980s, however.) To what extent do you think it would have the same appeal today?

3. Comment on the elements of graphic design (balance, proportion, movement, unity, clarity and simplicity, emphasis) that help make this ad effective. Focus particularly on the element of movement.

Camel, 1979 (p. 386)

1. What do the relative positions and postures of the man and the woman in the ad indicate about the ad's basic appeal?

2. What roles do the props—particularly, the motorcycle and the models' outfits—and the setting play in helping to sell the product?

3. How do the design elements in the ad emphasize the product?

4. Compare the graphic elements of this ad to those of the Fleischmann's Whiskey ad (p. 389).

BEER AND LIQUOR

Ballantine Ale, 1950s (p. 387)

1. This illustration, reminiscent of some of Norman Rockwell's paintings, is typical of many beer and ale ads in the 1950s, which depict a group of well-dressed young adults enjoying their brew at a social event. Comment on the distinctive graphic elements in this ad and speculate as to why these elements are seldom employed in contemporary advertisements for beer and ale. Why, in other words, does this ad seem old-fashioned?

2. Contrast the appeal and graphics of this ad with the ad for Miller later in this portfolio.

3. Identify the adjectives in the body text and attempt to correlate them to the graphic in helping to construct the message of the ad.

Bacardi Rum, 1960s (p. 388)

1. What meaning is conveyed by the placement, posture, and expressions of the four models in this ad? How do you think this meaning is intended to help sell the product? (Does the picture remind you of a particular movie hero?)

2. Comment on the significance of the props in the photo.

3. How does the text ("Big, bold highballs, sassy Daiquiris, cool tonics...") help reinforce the meaning created by the picture?

Fleischmann's Whiskey, 1964 (p. 389)

1. Comment on (1) the significance of the extra-large bottle of whiskey; (2) the stances of the two models in the ad; (3) the way the headline contributes to the ad's meaning.

2. Compare and contrast the graphic in this ad with that of the 1979 Camel ad earlier in this portfolio (the man on the motorcycle).

Hennessy Cognac, 1968 (p. 390)

1. What is the primary appeal of this ad? How do the woman, the horse, and the headline work to create and reinforce this appeal?

Miller Beer, 1979 (p. 391)

1. To what extent does this 1979 ad embody marketing techniques for beer that are still employed today?

2. Comment on the posture and expressions of the three models depicted in the ad. How do these elements help create the ad's essential appeal?

3. Compare and contrast this ad with the 1950s Ballantine Ale ad earlier in this portfolio (p. 387).

AUTOMOBILES

De Soto, 1947 (p. 392)

1. How does the scene portrayed in the illustration help create the basic appeal of this ad? Focus on as many significant individual elements of the illustration as you can.

2. To what extent does the caption (in the illustration) and the headline support the message communicated by the graphic?

3. Explain why both this ad and the following ad for Ford are products of their particular times.

Ford, 1947 (p. 393)

I. Cite and discuss those textual elements in the ad that reflect a traditional conception of the American woman.

2. How do the visual elements of the ad reinforce the assumptions about traditional gender roles reflected in the ad?

Cadillac, 1954 (pp. 394–395)

I. What is the particular marketing strategy behind this ad? Based on the ad's text, compose a memo from the head of marketing to the chief copywriter proposing this particular ad and focusing on the strategy. The memo doesn't have to be cynical or to insult the prospective Cadillac buyers; it should just be straightforward and direct.

2. How do the ad's graphics reinforce the message in the text?

Corvette, 1966 (p. 396)

I. How do the graphic elements reinforce the message developed in the text of this ad?

2. Comment on the dress and the posture of the model, as these relate to the ad's essential appeal. What's the significance of the woman eating a peach in a mountain stream?

3. The body text in this ad tells a story. What kind of husband-wife dynamic is implied by this story? To what extent do you find similarities between the implied gender roles in this ad and those in the 1947 Ford ad ("Ford's out Front from a Woman's Angle," p. 393)? To what extent do you find differences, ones that may be attributable to the twenty years between the two ads?

Jeep vehicle, 2003 (p. 397)

I. Explain the meaning of the ad's headline.

2. Discuss the graphic, in terms of the ad's headline. Consider the significance of the viewing angle.

FOOD, CLEANSERS, BEAUTY PRODUCTS, AND OTHER

Coca-Cola, 1945 (p. 398)

I. This ad appeared shortly after the conclusion of World War II. How do the text and the graphics of the ad take advantage of the international mood at the time? Comment on the appearance and arrangement of the men portrayed in the ad.

2. Compare the strategy of this Coca-Cola ad (text and graphics) with that of the 1950s Ballantine ad (p. 387).

National Dairy Products Corporation, 1947 (p. 399)

1. How does the couple pictured in the ad illustrate gender expectations of the period? Comment on the dress, postures, and expressions of the models.

2. What, exactly, is this ad *selling?* (It is presented more as a newsmagazine article than as a conventional advertisement.) How is the appeal tied to contemporary developments by "scientists" and their "research," particularly as these relate to "the new wives of 1947"?

3. What does the text of this ad imply about the situation of young married couples in postwar households?

Bon Ami, 1947 (p. 400)

1. How do the text and graphics of this ad illustrate a bygone cultural attitude toward gender roles? Notice, in particular, the dress, postures, and expressions of the women pictured, as well as the style of the illustration. Focus also on the wording of the text.

2. In terms of Jib Fowles's categories, what kind of appeal is being made by the Bon Ami ad?

Jergens Lotion, 1954 (p. 401)

1. Compare and contrast the appeals and the strategies of this Jergens Lotion ad and the Bon Ami ad preceding it. Are the ads intended to appeal to the same target audiences? To what extent are the psychological appeals of the two ads similar? Compare the illustrations of the two ads. How do they differ in basic strategy?

2. The model in the Jergens Lotion ad is immaculately dressed and groomed, and she is sitting among stacks of fine china (as opposed to everyday dishware). What do you think is the marketing strategy behind these graphic choices?

Bell Telephone, 1956 (p. 402)

1. Discuss the attitude toward gender roles implicit in the 1956 Bell ad. How do the graphics, the headline, and the body text reinforce this attitude? What is the significance of the quotation marks around "office" in the final sentence of the third paragraph?

2. Notice that the woman at the desk seems a lot more comfortable and at ease than the man holding the crying baby and the dishes. What does this fact tell us about the attitudes toward gender roles of those who created this ad?

Bell Telephone, 1974 (p. 403)

1. Compare and contrast the 1956 Bell ad with the 1974 Bell ad, in terms of their attitudes toward gender roles. How do the text and graphics reinforce the essential differences?

2. The 1956 Bell ad pictures a woman at a desk (a white-collar job); the 1974 ad pictures a woman working at a telephone pole (a blue-collar job). Would the 1974 ad have the same impact if "Alana MacFarlane" had, like her 1956 counterpart, been pictured at a desk?

3. Like the 1954 Cadillac ad (pp. 394–395), the 1974 Bell ad seems more of a public service announcement than a conventional advertisement. Compare and contrast these ads in terms of their messages to readers.

American Airlines, 1968 (p. 404)

1. Discuss the mixed messages (in terms of appeal) being transmitted by the American Airlines ad. To what extent do you think the apparently conflicting appeals make for an effective ad?

2. Comment on the dress, pose, and expression of the model in the ad, which appeared in *Ebony* magazine. How do these create a different impact than would an illustration, say, of a flight attendant serving a drink or giving a pillow to an airline passenger?

Charlie, 1988 (p. 405)

1. Notice the woman's outfit, as well as her briefcase, in the Charlie ad. How is the appearance of this woman as significant as the appearance of the woman in the Hennessy Cognac ad (p. 390) for the ad's basic message?

2. The Charlie ad and the 1974 Bell ad (p. 403) are as different as can be imagined from the Jergens ad. Yet, the Bell and the Charlie ads make quite different appeals. Explain. Consider, for example, how a woman— or a man—of the late 1940s might respond to the Bell ad, on the one hand, and the Charlie ad, on the other.

Soloflex, 1985 (p. 406)

1. How does the illustration in this ad reinforce the basic appeal of the headline?

2. Ads are frequently criticized for the incongruity between illustration and product being advertised—for example, a scantily clad woman posed provocatively in front of a pickup truck. To what extent does the Soloflex ad present an appropriate fit between graphic and product advertised?

A PORTFOLIO OF TV COMMERCIALS

The world's first television commercial was a ten-second Bulova watch ad broadcast in 1941. But it wasn't until the 1950s, when TV became a mass medium, that the commercial became a ubiquitous feature of popular culture. Before viewers had the technology to fast-forward through commercials, many probably regarded TV ads as annoying, occasionally informative or entertaining, but generally unnecessary accompaniments to their television experience. But of course, the commercial is not simply an extraneous byproduct of TV programming. It is television's very reason for existence. Before the age of public TV and of cable and satellite providers, television programs were financed entirely by the companies that created the commercials and that paid networks and local stations to broadcast them. Viewed from a marketing angle, the only purpose of commercial television is to provide a medium for advertising. The news, comedy, drama, game, and variety shows offered by TV are simply ways of luring viewers to watch the commercials.

Still, the unceasing deluge of commercials of every type means that advertisers have to figure out ways of making their messages stand out by being unusually creative, funny, surprising, or otherwise noteworthy. The standard jingles, primitive animation, catch-phrases ("Winston tastes good like a cigarette should"), and problem-solution mini-dramas of TV commercials work for a while but are quickly forgotten in the onslaught of new messages. It becomes the job of advertising agencies (of the type represented in *Mad Men*) that create both print and TV ads to make their clients' products stand out by ever more ingenious and striking ways of delivering their messages. To do this, these agencies rely not just on information about the product and clever audiovisual techniques; they attempt to respond to what they believe consumers crave, deep down. TV commercials, no less than print ads, rely on psychological appeals of the type discussed by Jib Fowles in his "Fifteen Basic Appeals."

The following portfolio includes some of the most noteworthy and successful TV commercials of the past sixty years. Many (though not all) of these commercials are featured in Bernice Kanner's *The 100 Best TV Commercials...and Why They Worked* (1999), where you will find additional description and commentary. To access the commercials, go to YouTube (YouTube.com), and enter the search terms provided under the commercial's title into the search box. In some cases, additional information is presented, in brackets, to help you navigate to the commercial. In cases where multiple versions of the same commercial are available, you may have to experiment to determine which one offers the best video and audio quality. In a few cases, uploaded commercials have been truncated, so you should generally select the longest version. In some cases, the indicated commercials may have been removed from the YouTube Web site. No matter; thousands more remain available for your observation and consideration.

As with the print ads, we provide two or three sets of specific questions for each TV commercial. These questions are intended to stimulate your thinking and writing process about the particular ways that the audio and visuals are intended to work. As you review these commercials, however, you might be thinking of more general questions about advertisements, including those raised by Fowles. Here are some of those general questions:

1. Who appears to be the target audience for this TV commercial? If it was produced more than two decades ago, how would this target audience likely react today to the ad?
2. What is the primary appeal made by the ad, in terms of Fowles's categories? What, if any, are the secondary appeals?
3. What is the chief attention-getting technique in the commercial?
4. How does the commercial make use of such tools as humor, surprise, fantasy, wonder, human interest, or social concern to achieve its goals?
5. What is the relationship between the visuals and the audio track? How do audio and video work together—or in contrast—to achieve the sponsor's purpose?

6. How do the commercial's visual techniques work to convey the message? Consider camera movement (or the lack of camera movement); the style and pace of editing (the juxtaposition of individual shots); and visual composition (the framing of the people and/or objects within the shot).

7. How do the expressions, the clothing, the postures of the person or people, and the physical objects in the shots help communicate the ad's message?

8. How do the words used by the actor(s) or by the voice-over narrator work to communicate the message of the commercial?

Consider, also, the following evaluative questions[1]:

- Is it a good ad? Why?
- What do you like most about it? Why?
- What do you dislike the most? Why?
- Do you think it "works"? Why or why not?
- How could the ad be improved?
- Could the sender have conveyed the same message using other strategies, other persuasive means? If so, explain.
- Even if you don't believe that this particular ad works or persuades you, is there anything in the ad that still affects you or persuades you indirectly?
- Does the ad have effects on you perhaps not intended by its creators?

● Discussion and Writing Suggestions

Note: Because Web content frequently changes without warning, not all of the listed videos may be available when you attempt to access them. It is possible that errant searches may lead to other videos with objectionable content. Such videos, as well as user-submitted comments under the specified videos below, do not reflect the views of the authors or of Pearson Publishing.

COMMERCIALS OF THE 1960s

Volkswagen: Snowplow

YouTube Search Terms: vw snow plow commercial [select black and white version]

I. In the 1960s, Volkswagen became famous in the United States not only for its funny-looking cars—so different in style from Detroit's massive passenger vehicles—but also for its "soft-sell" approach to print ads and TV commercials. How does that soft-sell approach work in this

---

[1]Lars Thoger Christensen, "How to Analyze an Advertisement." University of Southern Denmark—Odense. Jan. 2004. <http://wms-soros.mngt.waikato.ac.nz/NR/rdonlyres/ebabz4jhzmg5fr5p45ypc53mdvuxva5wxhe7323onb4ylelbaq3se5xjrslfc4mi3qgk6dmsx5dqbp/Advertisinganalysis.doc>.

ad? What is the sales strategy, as embodied in the relatively primitive visuals and the voice-over track? What exactly is being sold?

2. The closing shot of this commercial shows a snowplow driving past a Volkswagen. How does this image encapsulate the message of this ad? Write a sentence that expresses the message Volkswagen wants to communicate, without regard to the particular visuals of this ad.

Union Carbide: Chick

YouTube Search Terms: union carbide chick

1. Based on the opening image, what is the essential psychological appeal (see Jib Fowles) of this ad?

2. How does the visual (the commercial is unusual in consisting of a single, continuous shot) work *with* and work *against* the soundtrack voice-over? To what extent do you "hear" the narrator's voice—and his message—as you watch the image of the metal box in the beaker of boiling water? To what extent is there a danger that this commercial could backfire and create bad feeling about Union Carbide because of what is portrayed?

Alka Seltzer: Spicy Meatball

YouTube Search Terms: alka seltzer meatball

1. Some TV commercials employ a "fake-out" strategy, based partially on our knowledge of other commercials. How does this approach work in the Alka Seltzer ad? Do you think it is likely to succeed in persuading viewers to buy the product?

2. Like many successful TV commercials, this one relies on humor, grounded in human foibles and imperfections, and based on our experience that if things can go wrong, they generally will. How do the visuals and the audio track of the Alka Selzter ad employ this kind of humor as a sales strategy?

COMMERCIALS OF THE 1970s

Chanel No. 5: Share the Fantasy

YouTube Search Terms: chanel 5 fantasy

1. In many ways, this celebrated commercial—directed by filmmaker Ridley Scott (*Alien, Blade Runner, Thelma and Louise, Gladiator*)—is, stylistically, at the opposite pole from the gritty Volkswagen "Snowplow" commercial. Comment.

2. Chanel No. 5 is one of those products sold primarily on its "mystique." How do the visuals and the soundtrack of this commercial reinforce that mystique? "Read" the images and interpret them, in light of the product.

3. In terms of Fowles's categories, what are the central appeals of this ad?

Quaker Oats: Mikey

YouTube Search Terms: quaker oats mikey

1. Why don't the older kids want to try Life cereal? How does reluctance tie into Quaker Oats's larger marketing problem with the product? How does the commercial attempt to deal with this problem?

2. Many viewers came to hate this commercial because it was shown repeatedly and because it lasted so many years. Still, it endured because many other viewers found it endearing—and it did the job of publicizing the product. Do you think a commercial like this would work today? Explain.

Coca-Cola: Mean Joe Green

YouTube Search Terms: coca cola joe green

1. This commercial is a study in contrasts. Identify some of these contrasts (both visual and aural), and explain how they work as part of the sales strategy.

2. To what emotions does this commercial attempt to appeal? Did you find this appeal successful?

3. Like many commercials, this one is presented as a minidrama, complete with plot, character, setting, theme, and other elements found in longer dramas. Explain the way that the drama functions in this ad, particularly as it concerns the characterization of the two actors.

COMMERCIALS OF THE 1980s

Federal Express (FedEx): Fast-Paced World [with John Moschitta]

YouTube Search Terms: federal express fast talker

1. The actor in this commercial, John Moschitta, was for many years celebrated in the *Guinness Book of World Records* as the world's fastest talker (he was clocked at 586 words per minute). How does Moschitta's unique skill make him an ideal spokesperson for Federal Express?

2. There is always a danger that particularly striking ads may be counterproductive, in that they draw attention to their own cleverness or unusual stylistic qualities, rather than to the product being sold. Put yourself in the position of a Federal Express executive. To what extent might you be concerned that this commercial, clever as it is, would not succeed in making more people select Federal Express as their express delivery service? On the other hand, might any striking commercial for Federal Express be successful if it heightened public recognition of the brand?

Pepsi-Cola: Archaeology

YouTube Search Terms: pepsi cola archaeology

1. Summarize the main selling point of this commercial. How does this selling point relate to (1) the basic situation presented in the commercial and (2) Pepsi's slogan, as it appears at the end?

2. Pepsi-Cola and Coca-Cola have been engaged in fierce rivalry for more than a century. How does this commercial exploit that rivalry to humorous effect? How is each product visually represented in the ad?

3. As contrasted with the Volkswagen "Snowplow" ad or the Quaker Oats "Mikey" ad, this ad features lavish production values and is presented as if it were a science fiction film. How do the sets, costumes, props, and special effects help support the overall sales strategy of the ad?

Levi's: Launderette

YouTube Search Terms: levi's laundrette

1. What is the primary appeal of this British ad (in Jib Fowles's terms)? Do you think it is directed primarily to men or primarily to women? Explain.

2. How do the reactions of the various characters in this ad to the young man contribute to its overall effect? How does the young man's appearance figure into the overall effect?

3. What role does the musical track (Marvin Gaye's "I Heard It Through The Grapevine") play in this commercial?

COMMERCIALS OF THE 1990s

Jeep: Snow Covered

YouTube Search Terms: jeep snow covered

1. "This may have been the most arrogant commercial ever made," declared the creative director of the agency that produced it. In what way might this be so? Possible arrogance aside, is this an effective advertisement for Jeep? Explain.

2. How do the visuals support the message of the ad? What *is* that message?

3. Which appeals are most evident in this commercial?

Energizer: Darth Vader

YouTube Search Terms: energizer darth vader

1. The Energizer bunny was featured in numerous commercials of the 1990s, generally in settings where its sudden appearance was totally unexpected. How do the creators of this add draw upon the *Star Wars* mythology to support their sales pitch? In what way is the strategy of this ad similar to that of Alka Seltzer's "Spicy Meatball"?

2. In a sentence, summarize the message of this ad—without mentioning *Star Wars* or Darth Vader.

Got Milk? (California Milk Processor Board): Aaron Burr [Original Got Milk? Commercial]

YouTube Search Terms: got milk burr

1. The opening of this commercial is intended to convey a sense of culture and sophistication. How do the images and the soundtrack do this? Why is this "setup" necessary in terms of the ad's message? What is that message?

2. In the latter half of the commercial, how does the accelerated pace of the editing and camera work—and of the soundtrack—contribute to the ad's overall impact?

COMMERCIALS OF THE 2000s

The Gap: Pardon Our Dust

YouTube Search Terms: gap dust

1. This commercial was directed by filmmaker Spike Jonze (*Adaptation, Where the Wild Things Are*). Describe your reactions as you watched this ad. What did you think was happening as the mayhem within the store accelerated? What is the effect of the "Pardon Our Dust" title when it appears? What is the relationship of the prior visuals and the soundtrack (including the music of Grieg's "In the Hall of the Mountain King") to the last two titles?

2. In Jib Fowles's terms ("Fifteen Basic Appeals"), to what desires is this commercial intended to appeal?

3. According to the Web site "Top 10 Coolest Commercials by Movie Directors," Spike Jonze was asked by Gap executives to produce a commercial about the stores' new look. Bewildered by what Jonze delivered, the company ran the commercial in a few cities, then pulled it off the air after about a month. Did the company make the right decision (from a marketing standpoint)?

Honda: Physics

YouTube Search Terms: honda physics

1. Put yourself in the position of the ad agency copywriters for Honda *before* they conceived of this particular ad. What is your main selling point? Express, in a sentence, what you want to communicate to the public about Honda automobiles and engineering.

2. This commercial involves no computer graphics or digital tricks: everything that happens is real. All the components we see came from the disassembling of two Honda Accords. (The voice is that of *Lake Woebegon Days* author Garrison Keillor.) According to Honda, this single continuous shot required 606 takes—meaning that for the first 605 takes, something,

usually minor, went wrong, and the recording team had to install the setup again and again. There is always a danger (for the client) that memorable commercials like this will amaze and impress viewers but will also fail to implant brand identification in their minds. Do you think there may be such a problem with this commercial? To what extent are viewers who have seen it likely, days or weeks later, to identify it with Honda and to associate whatever message (if any) they draw from the commercial with the particular qualities of Honda automobiles?

Sony Bravia: Bunnies

YouTube Search Terms: sony bunnies

1. Some of the same visual techniques used in this ad (to portray an unstoppable swarm of creatures that speedily overrun an urban area) have also been used—to very different effect—in horror films. What mood is conveyed—and how—by the visual and soundtrack elements of this commercial?

2. To what consumer desires (refer to Jib Fowles's categories) is this commercial designed to appeal?

3. Discuss how some of the visual techniques and special effects of this ad contribute to its effectiveness in conveying the benefits of the Sony Bravia.

Dove: Onslaught

YouTube Search Terms: dove onslaught

1. What is the message of this ad? How does the cinematic style of the visuals reinforce that message? Focus, in particular, on the contrasting visual styles used for the child and (later in the ad) her classmates, on the one hand, and the rest of the images, on the other. Consider, for example, how long the first image remains on screen, compared to those that follow.

2. How many of Jib Fowles's fifteen basic appeals do you detect at work in this ad? How do these appeals work to convey the essential contrast of values underlying the ad?

Tide to Go: Interview

YouTube Search Terms: tide to go interview

1. What is the message of this ad? How do the simple visuals and the more complex soundtrack work together (and against one another) to support that idea? How does that idea relate to one or more of Fowles's fifteen basic appeals?

2. Like many contemporary TV ads, this one relies on humor. To what extent do you find humor used effectively here? What is the source of the humor? How do the two actors help create that humor? How is this humor rooted in common concerns and fears that we all share?

Planters Peanuts: Perfume

YouTube Search Terms: planters perfume

I. Many of the elements in this ad are also found in perfume commercials. How are these elements used here to comic effect? Compare the mood and the visual style of this ad to that of a real perfume ad, the Chanel No. 5 "Share the Fantasy" commercial. Of what other commercials does this one remind you? Why?

2. Like the Gap "Pardon Our Dust" commercial, the Planter's ad relies on the visual motif of comic mayhem. Do you think such visuals are an effective way of selling the product? Explain.

ADDITIONAL TV COMMERCIALS

Note: Unless otherwise indicated, all commercials listed were produced in the United States.

Democratic National Committee: "Daisy Girl" (1964)
    YouTube Search Terms: democratic daisy ad

American Tourister Luggage: Gorilla (1969)
    YouTube Search Terms: luggage gorilla

Chevrolet: "Baseball, Hot Dogs, Apple Pie" (1969)
    YouTube Search Terms: america baseball hotdogs

Keep America Beautiful: "Crying Indian" (1970)
    YouTube Search Terms: America crying indian

Coca Cola: "Hilltop" ("I'd Like to Buy the World a Coke") (1971)
    YouTube Search Terms: buy world coke 1971

Hovis: "Bike Ride" (UK, 1973) [shot by Ridley Scott]
    YouTube Search Terms: hovis bike

Xerox: "Monks" (1975)
    YouTube Search Terms: xerox monks

Hebrew National: "Higher Authority" (1975)
    YouTube Search Terms: hebrew national higher

Basf: "Dear John" (New Zealand, 1979)
    Search Terms: basf dear john

Lego: "Kipper" (UK, 1980)
    YouTube Search Terms: lego kipper

Apple: Macintosh (1984)
    YouTube Search Terms: apple macintosh

Sony Trinitron: "Lifespan" (UK, 1984)
    YouTube Search Terms: sony trinitron advert

American Express: "Stephen King" (1984)
    YouTube Search Terms: american express king

The Guardian: "Points of View" (UK, 1987)
YouTube Search Terms: guardian points of view

Volkswagen: "Changes" (UK, 1988)
YouTube Search Terms: vw changes

Energizer: "Bunny Introduction" (1989)
YouTube Search Terms: energizer bunny introduction 1989

Dunlop: "Tested for the Unexpected" (1993)
YouTube Search Terms: dunlop tested unexpected

Swedish Televerket: "Noxin" (Sweden, 1993)
YouTube Search Terms: Noxin

Little Caesar's Pizza: "Training Camp" (1994)
YouTube Search Terms: caesar's training camp

Campbell's Soup: Winter Commercial (1995)
YouTube Search Terms: campbell's soup winter

California Milk Processor Board: "Got Milk? Heaven" (1996)
YouTube Search Terms: got milk heaven

Ameriquest Mortgage: "Plane Ride" (2008)
YouTube Search Terms: ameriquest plane ride

Audi: "Oil Parade" (2009)
YouTube Search Terms: audi oil parade

Synthesis Activities

1. Select one *category* of advertisements (cigarettes, alcohol, etc.) represented in the ad portfolio. Compare and contrast the types of appeals underlying these ads, as discussed by Fowles. To what extent do you notice significant shifts of appeal from the 1940s to the present? Which types of appeal seem to you most effective with particular product categories? Is it more likely, for example, that people will buy cigarettes because they want to feel autonomous or because the cigarettes will make them more attractive to the opposite sex?

2. Select a series of ads in different product categories that all appear to rely on the same primary appeal—perhaps the appeal to sex or the appeal to affiliation. Compare and contrast the overall strategies of these ads. Draw upon Fowles to develop your ideas. To what extent do your analyses support arguments often made by social critics (and advertising people) that what people are really buying is the image, rather than the product?

3. Discuss how a selection of ads reveals shifting cultural attitudes over the past six decades toward (a) gender relations, (b) romance between men and women, (c) smoking, or (d) automobiles. In the

case of (a) or (b) above, the ads don't have to be for the same category of product. In terms of their underlying appeal, in terms of the implicit or explicit messages embodied both in the text and the graphics, how and to what extent do the ads reveal that attitudes of the target audiences have changed over the years?

4. Select a TV commercial or a TV ad campaign (for example, for Sprint phone service) and analyze the commercial(s) in terms of Fowles's categories, as well as the discussions of some of the authors in this chapter. To what extent do the principles discussed by these authors apply to broadcast, as well as to print ads? What are the special requirements of TV advertising?

5. Find a small group of ads that rely upon little or no body copy—just a graphic, perhaps a headline, and the product name. What common features underlie the marketing strategies of such ads? What kinds of appeals do they make? How do their graphic aspects compare? What makes the need for text superfluous?

6. As indicated in the introduction to this chapter, social critics have charged advertising with numerous offenses: "It fosters materialism, it psychologically manipulates people to buy things they don't need, it perpetuates gender and racial stereotypes (particularly in its illustrations), it is deceptive, it is offensive, it debases the language." To what extent do some of the advertisements presented in the ad portfolio (and perhaps others of your own choosing) demonstrate the truth of one or more of these charges? In developing your response, draw upon some of the ads in the portfolio (or elsewhere).

7. Read the textual content (headlines and body text) of several ads *without* paying attention (if possible) to the graphics. Compare the effectiveness of the headline and body text by themselves with the effectiveness of the ads, *including* the graphic elements. Focusing on a group of related ads (related by product category, by appeal, by decade, etc.), devise an explanation of how graphics work to effectively communicate the appeal and meaning of the products advertised.

8. Many ads employ humor—in the graphics, in the body copy, or both—to sell a product. Examine a group of advertisements that rely on humor to make their appeal and explain how they work. For example, do they play off an incongruity between one element of the ad and another (such as between the headline and the graphic), or between one element of the ad (or the basic message of the ad) and what we know or assume to be the case in the "real world"? Do they employ wordplay or irony? Do they picture people doing funny things (funny because inappropriate or unrealistic)? What appeal underlines the humor? Aggression? Sex? Nurturing?

Based on your examination and analyses, what appear to be some of the more effective ways of employing humor?

9. Think of a new product that you have just invented. This product, in your opinion, will revolutionize the world of (fill in the blank). Devise an advertisement to announce this product to the world. Consider (or reject) using a celebrity to help sell your product. Select the basic appeal of your product (see Fowles). Then, write the headline, subhead, and body copy for the product. Sketch out (or at least describe) the graphic that will accompany the text. Show your proposed ad to one or more of your classmates, get reactions, and then revise the ad, taking into account your market feedback.

10. Imagine that you own a small business—perhaps an independent coffee shop (not Starbucks, Peet's, or Coffee Bean), a video game company, or a pedicab service that conveys tourists around a chic beach town. Devise an ad that announces your services and extols its benefits. Apply the principles discussed by Fowles and other writers in this chapter.

11. Write a parody ad—one that would never ordinarily be written—applying the selling principles discussed by Fowles and other authors in this chapter. For example, imagine you are the manager of the Globe Theatre in Elizabethan England and want to sell season tickets to this season's plays, including a couple of new tragedies by your playwright-in-residence, Will Shakespeare. Or imagine that you are trying to sell Remington typewriters in the age of computers (no software glitches!). Or—as long as people are selling bottled water—you have found a way to package and sell air. Advertisers can reportedly sell anything with the right message. Give it your best shot.

12. Based on the reading you have done in this chapter, discuss the extent to which you believe advertisements create needs in consumers, reflect existing needs, or some combination of both. In developing your paper, draw on both particular advertisements and on the more theoretical overviews of advertising developed in the chapter.

13. Select one advertisement and conduct two analyses of it, using two different analytical principles: perhaps from Fowles's list of fifteen emotional appeals. Having conducted your analyses and developed your insights, compare and contrast the strengths and weaknesses of the analytical principles you've employed. Conclude more broadly with a discussion of how a single analytical principle can close down, as well as open up, understanding of an object under study.

14. As you have seen, advertisements change over time, both across product categories and within categories. And yet the advertisements

remain a constant, their presence built on the assumption that consumers can be swayed both overtly and covertly in making purchasing decisions. In a paper drawing on the selections in this chapter, develop a theory on why ads change over time. Is it because people's needs have changed and, therefore, new ads are required? (Do the older ads appeal to the same needs as newer ads?) In developing your discussion, you might track the changes over time in one product category.

Research Activities

1. Drawing upon contemporary magazines (or magazines from a given period), select a set of advertisements in a particular product category. Analyze these advertisements according to Fowles's categories, and assess their effectiveness in terms of the discussions of other authors in this chapter.

2. Select a particular product that has been selling for at least twenty-five years (e.g., Bayer aspirin, Tide detergent, IBM computers, Oldsmobile—as in "This is not your father's Oldsmobile") and trace the history of print advertising for this product over the years. To what extent has the advertising changed over the years? To what extent has the essential sales appeal remained the same? In addition to examining the ads themselves, you may want to research the company and its marketing practices. You will find two business databases particularly useful: ABI/INFORM and the academic version of LexisNexis.

3. One of the landmark campaigns in American advertising was Doyle, Dane, Bernbach's series of ads for the Volkswagen Beetle in the 1960s. In effect a rebellion against standard auto advertising, the VW ads' Unique Selling Proposition was that ugly is beautiful—an appeal that was overwhelmingly successful. Research the VW ad campaign for this period, setting it in the context of the agency's overall marketing strategy.

4. Among the great marketing debacles of recent decades was Coca-Cola's development in 1985 of a new formula for its soft drink that (at least temporarily) replaced the much-beloved old formula. Research this major development in soft drink history, focusing on the marketing of New Coke and the attempt of the Atlanta-based Coca-Coca company to deal with the public reception of its new product.

5. Advertising agencies are hired not only by manufacturers and by service industries; they are also hired by political candidates.

In fact, one of the common complaints about American politics is that candidates for public office are marketed just as if they were bars of soap. Select a particular presidential or gubernatorial election and research the print and broadcast advertising used by the rival candidates. You may want to examine the ads not only of the candidates of the major parties but also the candidates of the smaller parties, such as the Green and the Libertarian parties. How do the appeals and strategies used by product ads compare and contrast with those used in ads for political candidates?

6. Public service ads comprise another major category of advertising (in addition to product and service advertising and political advertising). Such ads have been used to recruit people to military service, to get citizens to buy war bonds, to contribute to charitable causes, to get people to support or oppose strikes, to persuade people to stop using (or not to start using) drugs, to prevent drunk driving, etc. Locate a group of public service ads, describe them, and assess their effectiveness. Draw upon Fowles in developing your conclusions.

7. Research advertising in American magazines and newspapers before World War II. Focus on a limited number of product lines— for example, soft drinks, soap and beauty products, health-related products. What kind of differences do you see between ads in the first part of the twentieth century and more recent or contemporary advertising for the same types of products? In general, how have the predominant types of appeal used to sell products in the past changed (if they have) with the times? How are the graphics of early ads different from preferred graphics today? How has the body copy changed? (Hint: You may want to be on the alert for ads that make primarily negative appeals—i.e., what may happen to you if you don't use the product advertised.)

Credits

CHAPTER 1

Page 8: Reprinted with permission from Alan Blinder, "Outsourcing: Bigger Than You Thought," *The American Prospect*, Volume 17, Number 11: October 22, 2006. www.prospect.org. The American Prospect, 1710 Rhode Island Avenue, NW, 12th Floor, Washington, DC 20036. All rights reserved.

CHAPTER 2

Page 31: "We Are Not Created Equal in Every Way" by Joan Ryan from *San Francisco Chronicle*, December 12, 2000. Copyright © 2000 by *San Francisco Chronicle*. Reproduced with permission of *San Francisco Chronicle* via Copyright Clearance Center, Inc.

CHAPTER 3

Page 56: Excerpts from "Private Gets 3 Years for Iraq Prison Abuse" by David S. Cloud, from *The New York Times*, September 28, 2005. © 2005 The New York Times. All rights reserved. Used by permission and protected by the Copyright Laws of the United States. The printing, copying, redistribution, or retransmission of the Material without express written permission is prohibited. **Page 57:** Excerpt from "Military Abuse," Globe Editorial, published in *The Boston Globe*, September 28, 2005. Copyright © 2005 Globe Newspaper Company, Inc. Reprinted with permission. **Page 66:** "Summary of Key Findings" from "Mass Shootings at Virginia Tech, April 17, 2007: Report of the Review Panel Presented to Governor Kaine, Commonwealth of Virginia, August 2007." Used with permission. **Page 68:** "Laws Limit Schools Even After Alarms," by Jeff Gammage and Stacey Burling, from *The Philadelphia Inquirer*, April 19, 2007. Used with permission of The Philadelphia Inquirer, copyright © 2007. All rights reserved. **Page 71:** Editorial reproduced with permission from the September 4, 2007, issue of *The Christian Science Monitor* (www.csmonitor.com). © 2007 The Christian Science Monitor. **Page 72:** "Colleges are Watching Troubled Students" by Jeffrey McMurray, from The Associated Press, March 28, 2008. Used with permission of The Associated Press, copyright © 2008. All rights reserved. **Page 73:** "Virginia Tech Massacre Has Altered Campus Mental Health Systems," from The Associated Press, April 14, 2008. Used with permission of The Associated Press, copyright © 2008. All rights reserved.

CHAPTER 4

Page 111: "The Satisfactions of Housewifery and Motherhood in an Age of 'Do-Your-Own-Thing'" by Terry Martin Hekker, originally published in *The New York Times*, Dec. 20, 1977. Reprinted by permission of the author. **Page 112:** "Modern Love: Paradise Lost (Domestic Division)," by Terry Martin Hekker, from *The New York Times*, January 1, 2006. Copyright © 2006 The New York Times. All rights reserved. Used by permission and protected by the Copyright Laws of the United States. The printing, copying, redistribution, or retransmission of the Material without express written permission is prohibited. **Page 113:** "Cookies or Heroin?" from THE PLUG-IN DRUG, REVISED AND UPDATED – 25TH ANNIVERSARY EDITION by Marie Winn, copyright © 1977, 1985, 2002 by Marie Winn Miller. Used by permission of Viking Penguin, a division of Penguin Group (USA) Inc.

CHAPTER 5

Page 136: From THE WORKING LIFE by Joanne B. Ciulla, copyright © 2000 by Joanne B. Ciulla. Used by permission of Crown Business, a division of Random House, Inc. **Page 137:** "History of the Organization of Work" by Melvin Kranzberg. Reprinted with permission from the Encyclopædia Britannica, © 2005 by Encyclopædia Britannica, Inc. **Page 138:** Excerpts from THE CULTURE OF PROFESSIONALISM: THE MIDDLE CLASS AND THE DEVELOPMENT OF HIGHER EDUCATION IN AMERICA by Burton Bledstein. Reprinted by permission of the author. **Page 135:** Excerpts from "What is Vocation?" are reprinted by permission of the Initiative on Faith and Practice at Guilford College. **Page 139:** Excerpted from Vitae, www.vitae.ac.uk. Copyright © 2009 Careers Research and Advisory Centre (CRAC). Reprinted by permission. **Page 143:** Excerpted from "Fixed, Footloose, or Fractured: Work, Identity, and the Spatial Division of Labor in the Twenty-first Century" by Ursula Huws, from *Monthly Review*, 57.10, March 2006. Copyright © 2006 by Monthly Review Press. Reprinted by permission of Monthly Review Foundation. **Page 150:** From THE CORROSION OF CHARACTER: THE PERSONAL CONSEQUENCES OF WORK IN THE NEW CAPITALISM by Richard Sennett. Copyright © 1998 by Richard Sennett. Used by permission of W.W. Norton & Company, Inc. **Page 160:** "The New Wired World of Work: A More Transparent Workplace Will Mean More White-collar Accountability and Less Tolerance for Hangers-on" by Tom Peters, reprinted from August 28, 2000 issue of *BusinessWeek* by special permission, copyright © 2000 by The McGraw-Hill Companies, Inc. **Page 163:** Richard W. Judy and Carol D'Amico, Excerpt from Executive Summary, pp. 1-7, WORKFORCE 2020: WORK AND WORKERS IN THE 21ST CENTURY (Hudson Institute, 1998). Reprinted by permission of Hudson Institute. **Page 169:** Excerpts from "The Untouchables" from THE WORLD IS FLAT: A BRIEF HISTORY OF THE TWENTY-FIRST CENTURY [Updated and Expanded] [Further Updated and Expanded] by Thomas L. Friedman. Copyright © 2005, 2006, 2007 by Thomas L. Friedman. Reprinted by permission of Farrar, Straus and Giroux, LLC. **Page 175:** "Into the Unknown" from *The Economist*. © The Economist Newspaper Limited, London (November 13, 2004). Reprinted by permission.

CHAPTER 6

Page 189: "205 Easy Ways to Save the Earth" from HOT, FLAT AND CROWDED: WHY WE NEED A GREEN REVOLUTION—AND HOW IT CAN RENEW AMERICA by Thomas L. Friedman. Copyright © 2008 by Thomas L. Friedman. Reprinted by permission of Farrar, Straus and Giroux, LLC. **Page 201:** Robert Bryce, from "Introduction: The Persistent Delusion" from GUSHER OF LIES: THE DANGEROUS DELUSIONS OF ENERGY INDEPENDENCE. Copyright © 2008 by Robert Bryce. Reprinted by permission of PublicAffairs, a member of the Perseus Books Group. **Page 208:** "Why the Gasoline Engine Isn't Going Away Any Time Soon" by Joseph B. White, from *The Wall Street Journal*, September 15, 2008. Reprinted with permission of *The Wall Street Journal*, Copyright © 2008 Dow Jones & Company, Inc. All Rights Reserved Worldwide. **Page 211:** Chart of "The Road Ahead" by Kelly McDaniel-Timon is reprinted by permission of *The Wall Street Journal*, Copyright © 2008 Dow Jones & Company, Inc. All Rights Reserved Worldwide. License number 2235411311781. **Page 215:** "The Case for and against Nuclear Power" by Michael Totty, from *The Wall Street Journal*, June 30, 2008. Reprinted with permission of *The Wall Street Journal*, Copyright © 2008 Dow Jones & Company, Inc. All Rights Reserved Worldwide. **Page 216:** Tennessee Valley Authority. **Page 224:** "The Island in the Wind" by Elizabeth Kolbert, originally published in *The New Yorker*, July 7, 2008. Reprinted by permission of the author. **Page 225:** "Catching the Wind" by Doug Stevens, *Los Angeles Times* illustration, copyright © 2009. Reprinted with permission. **Page 231:** "Wind Power Puffery" by H. Sterling Burnett, published in *The Washington Times*, Feb. 4, 2004. Reprinted by permission of the author. **Page 234:** "State Solar Power Plans Are as Big as All Outdoors" by Marla Dickerson, *Los Angeles Times*, December 3, 2008. Copyright © 2008 Los Angeles Times. Reprinted with permission. **Page 235:** "How Solar Energy Works," illustration by Maury Aaseng. Copyright © 2006 by Maury Aaseng. Originally published in ENERGY ALTERNATIVES, edited by Laura K. Egendorf (Thomson Gale, 2006). Reprinted by permission of Maury Aaseng. **Page 238:** Originally appeared as "Solar Projects Draw New Opposition" by Peter Maloney, in *The New York Times*, September 24, 2008. © 2008 The New York Times. All rights reserved. Used by permission and protected by the Copyright Laws of the United States. The printing, copying, redistribution, or retransmission of the Material without express written permission is prohibited.

CHAPTER 7

Page 252: "The Radical Idea of Marrying for Love," "From Yoke Mates to Soul Mates," from MARRIAGE, A HISTORY by Stephanie Coontz, copyright © 2005 by the S.J. Coontz Company. Used by permission of Viking Penguin, a division of Penguin Group (USA) Inc. **Page 266:** From

Index

428

QUICK INDEX: APA DOCUMENTATION BASICS

APA In-text Citations in Brief

When you quote or paraphrase a source, place a parenthetical citation in your sentence. Include the following information: author, publication year, and a passage locator (page or paragraph number).

Direct quotation—author and publication year *not* mentioned in sentence:

> A good deal of research suggests that punishing a child "promotes only momentary compliance" (Berk & Ellis, 2002, p. 383).

Paraphrase—author and year mentioned in the sentence:

> Berk and Ellis (2002) suggest that many researchers view punishing a child as a quick but temporary fix for problem behavior (p. 383).

Direct quotation, Internet source:

Provide the page number, paragraph number (using the abbreviation *para.*), or paragraph number within a section, as available:

> Others have noted a rise in "problems that mimic the dysfunctional behaviors seen on reality television" (Spivek, Jones, & Connelly, 2006, Introduction section, para. 3).

APA References List in Brief

At the end of the paper, on a separate page titled "References" (no italics or quotation marks), alphabetize sources, providing full bibliographic information for each. The most common entry types follow.

Article from a Journal

After author, date, and title information, provide the volume number of the journal and, when available, the issue number (in parentheses); provide the page range of the entire article. Conclude your entry with the DOI (digital object identifier)—the article's unique reference number. When a DOI is not available and you have located the article on the Web, provide a URL by concluding with *Retrieved from* and the home page of the journal. Provide a detailed URL only if the content is likely to change, as in references to a wiki or if the source would be difficult to locate from the home page of the journal. If you locate the article through an online database such as *LexisNexis*, do *not* list the database in your reference entry.

Article (with volume and issue number) located via print or database:

> Ivanenko, A., & Massie, C. (2006). Assessment and management of sleep disorders in children. *Psychiatric Times, 23*(11), 90–95.

Article (with DOI and volume number but no issue number) located via print or database:

> Jones, K. L. (1986). Fetal alcohol syndrome. *Pediatrics in Review, 8*, 122–126. doi:10.1542/10.1542/pir.8-4-122

Article located via Web:

> Ivanenko, A., & Massie, C. (2006). Assessment and management of sleep disorders in children. *Psychiatric Times, 23*(11), 90–95. Retrieved from http://www.psychiatrictimes.com

Article from a Magazine

Article (with volume and issue numbers) located via print or database:

> Landi, A. (2010, January). Is beauty in the brain of the beholder? *ARTnews, 109*(1), 19–21.

Article located via Web:

> Landi, A. (2010, January). Is beauty in the brain of the beholder? *ARTnews, 109*(1). Retrieved from http://www.artnews.com/

Unsigned article (with no volume, issue, or page numbers) located via Web:

> Money men ignoring climate change: Survey finds global financial decision makers ignoring climate risks and opportunities. (2010, January 7). *The Ecologist.* Retrieved from http://www.theecologist.org

Article from a Newspaper

Article located via print or database:

> Wakabayashi, D. (2010, January 7). Sony pins future on a 3-D revival. *The Wall Street Journal,* pp. A1, A14.

Article located via Web:

> Wakabayashi, D. (2010, January 7). Sony pins future on a 3-D revival. *The Wall Street Journal.* Retrieved from http://www.wsj.com

Book

Book located via print:

> Mansfield, R. S., & Busse, T. V. (1981). *The psychology of creativity and discovery: Scientists and their work.* Chicago, IL: Nelson-Hall.

Book located via Web:

Freud, S. (1920). *Dream psychology: Psychoanalysis for beginners* (M. D. Elder, Trans.). Retrieved from http://www.gutenberg.org

Freud, S. (2008). *Dream psychology: Psychoanalysis for beginners* (M. D. Elder, Trans.) [AZW Reader version]. Retrieved from http://www.amazon.com (Original work published 1920)

Selection from an edited book:

Halberstam, D. (2002). Who we are. In S. J. Gould (Ed.), *The best American essays 2002* (pp. 124–136). New York, NY: Houghton Mifflin.

Later edition

Samuelson, P., & Nordhaus, W. D. (2005). *Economics* (18th ed.). Boston, MA: McGraw-Hill/Irwin.

QUICK INDEX: MLA DOCUMENTATION BASICS

MLA In-text Citations in Brief

When referring to a source, use parentheses to enclose a page number reference to that source. Include the author's name if you do not mention it in your sentence:

> From the beginning, the AIDS test has been "mired in controversy" (Bayer 101).

Or, if you name the author in the sentence:

> According to Bayer, from the beginning, the AIDS test has been "mired in controversy" (101).

MLA Works Cited List in Brief

At the end of the paper, on a separate page titled "Works Cited," alphabetize each cited source by author's last name. Provide full bibliographic information, as shown. State how you accessed the source, via print, Web, or downloaded digital file. As appropriate, precede "Web" with database name (e.g., *LexisNexis*) or the title of a Web site and a publisher. Follow "Web" with your date of access. Note the use of punctuation and italics. Note, as well: *in MLA, the medium by which you access a source (print, Web, database, download) determines its Works Cited format.*

Magazine or Newspaper Article

Article accessed via magazine or newspaper

> Packer, George. "The Choice." *New Yorker* 28 Jan. 2008: 28–35. Print.
>
> Warner, Judith. "Goodbye to All This." *New York Times* 18 Dec. 2009: A27. Print.

Printed article accessed via downloaded digital file

> Packer, George. "The Choice." *New Yorker* 28 Jan. 2008: 28–35. AZW file.
>
> Warner, Judith. "Goodbye to All This." *New York Times* 18 Dec. 2009: A27. PDF file.

Printed article accessed via database

> Packer, George. "The Choice." *New Yorker* 28 Jan. 2008: 28–35. *Academic Search Premier*. Web. 12 Mar. 2010.
>
> Warner, Judith. "Goodbye to All This." *New York Times* 18 Dec. 2009: A27. *LexisNexis*. Web. 14 Jan. 2010.

(Version of) printed article accessed via Web is considered different from printed version

> Packer, George. "The Choice." *New Yorker.com.* CondéNet, 28 Jan. 2008. Web. 12 Mar. 2010.
>
> Warner, Judith. "Goodbye to All This." *New York Times.* New York Times, 18 Dec. 2009. Web. 14 Jan. 2010.

Scholarly Article

Scholarly article accessed via print

> Ivanenko, Anna, and Clifford Massie. "Assessment and Management of Sleep Disorders in Children." *Psychiatric Times* 23.11 (2006): 90–95. Print.

Printed scholarly article accessed via downloaded digital file

> Ivanenko, Anna, and Clifford Massie. "Assessment and Management of Sleep Disorders in Children." *Psychiatric Times* 23.11 (2006): 90–95. PDF file.

Printed scholarly article accessed via database

> Ivanenko, Anna, and Clifford Massie. "Assessment and Management of Sleep Disorders in Children." *Psychiatric Times* 23.11 (2006): 90–95. *AcademicOne File.* Web. 3 Nov. 2010.

Printed scholarly article accessed via Web

> Ivanenko, Anna, and Clifford Massie. "Assessment and Management of Sleep Disorders in Children." *Psychiatric Times.* United Business Media, 1 Oct. 2006. Web. 3 Nov. 2010.

Scholarly article from an e-journal: has no print equivalent

> Blackwood, Jothany. "Coaching Educational Leaders." *Academic Leadership: The Online Journal* 7.3 (2009): n. pag. Web. 2 Feb. 2010.

Book

Book accessed via print

> James, William. *The Varieties of Religious Experience: A Study in Human Nature; Being the Gifford Lectures on Natural Religion Delivered at Edinburgh in 1901–1902.* New York: Longmans, 1902. Print.

Printed book accessed via downloaded digital file

> James, William. *The Varieties of Religious Experience: A Study in Human Nature; Being the Gifford Lectures on Natural Religion Delivered at Edinburgh in 1901–1902.* New York: Longmans, 1902. MOBI file.

Printed book accessed via Web or database

James, William. *The Varieties of Religious Experience: A Study in Human Nature; Being the Gifford Lectures on Natural Religion Delivered at Edinburgh in 1901–1902*. New York: Longmans, 1902. *U. of Virginia Etext Center*. Web. 12 Jan. 2010.

James, William. *The Varieties of Religious Experience: A Study in Human Nature; Being the Gifford Lectures on Natural Religion Delivered at Edinburgh in 1901–1902*. New York: Longmans, 1902. *ACLS Humanities E-Book*. Web. 12 Mar. 2010.

Online book: has no print equivalent

Langer, Maria. *Mastering Microsoft Word*. *Designprovideo.com*. Nonlinear Educating, 2009. Web. 23 Jan. 2010.

Web-only Publication (content created for and published on the Web)

Home page

Boucher, Marc, ed. Home page. *The Space Elevator Reference*. *Spaceelevator.com*. SpaceRef Interactive, 2009. Web. 17 Dec. 2009.

Web-based article on a larger site

Landau, Elizabeth. "Stem Cell Therapies for Hearts Inching Closer to Wide Use." *CNN.com*. Cable News Network, 18 Dec. 2009. Web. 14 Jan. 2010.

White, Veronica. "Glan Lorenzo Bernini." *Heilbrunn Timeline of Art History*. Metropolitan Museum of Art, New York, 2009. Web. 18 Mar. 2010.

Blog

Lubber, Mindy. "The Climate Treaty Announcement." *Climate Experts' Forum—Copenhagen*. Financial Times, 19 Dec. 2009. Web. 22 Dec. 2009.

CHECKLIST FOR WRITING SUMMARIES

- **Read the passage carefully.** Determine its structure. Identify the author's purpose in writing.
- **Reread.** *Label* each section or stage of thought. *Highlight* key ideas and terms.
- **Write one-sentence summaries** of each stage of thought.
- **Write a thesis:** a one- or two-sentence summary of the entire passage.
- **Write the first draft** of your summary.
- **Check your summary** against the original passage.
- **Revise** your summary.

CHECKLIST FOR WRITING CRITIQUES

- **Introduce** both the passage being critiqued and the author.
- **Summarize** the author's main points, making sure to state the author's purpose for writing.
- **Evaluate** the validity of the presentation.
- **Respond** to the presentation: agree and/or disagree.
- **Conclude** with your overall assessment.